Principles of
Skill Acquisition

Contributors

Earl A. Alluisi   Marshall B. Jones
Edward A. Bilodeau   Harry Kay
Ina McD. Bilodeau   Clyde E. Noble
George E. Briggs   E. C. Poulton
Arthur L. Irion   Karl U. Smith
             Harvey Sussman

Principles of

Skill Acquisition

Edited by

E. A. BILODEAU

With the assistance of
INA McD. BILODEAU

ACADEMIC PRESS   New York and London

ACADEMIC PRESS, INC.
111 Fifth Avenue, New York, New York 10003

United Kingdom Edition published by
ACADEMIC PRESS, INC. (LONDON) LTD.
Berkeley Square House, London W.1

LIBRARY OF CONGRESS CATALOG CARD NUMBER: 68-8434

PRINTED IN THE UNITED STATES OF AMERICA

List of Contributors

Numbers in parentheses indicate the pages on which the authors' contributions begin.

Earl A. Alluisi (59), Department of Psychology, University of Louisville, Louisville, Kentucky

Edward A. Bilodeau* (171, 235), Department of Psychology, Tulane University, New Orleans, Louisiana

Ina McD. Bilodeau (255), Department of Psychology, Tulane University, New Orleans, Louisiana

George E. Briggs+ (205), Department of Psychology, Ohio State University, Columbus, Ohio

Arthur L. Irion** (1), Department of Psychology, Tulane University, New Orleans, Louisiana

Marshall B. Jones (141), Department of Behavioral Science, The Hershey Medical Center, Hershey, Pennsylvania

Harry Kay (33), Department of Psychology, University of Sheffield, Sheffield, England

Clyde E. Noble (319), Department of Psychology, The University of Georgia, Athens, Georgia

E. C. Poulton (287), Medical Research Council, Applied Psychology Research Unit, Cambridge, England

Karl U. Smith (103), Behavioral Cybernetics Laboratory, University of Wisconsin, Madison, Wisconsin

Harvey Sussman (103), Behavioral Cybernetics Laboratory, University of Wisconsin, Madison, Wisconsin

*Deceased.
+Present Address: Human Performance Center, Columbus, Ohio.
**Present Address: Department of Psychology, University of Missouri, St. Louis, Missouri.

Preface

Perceptual motor skill learning and performance are studied both within experimental psychology and in engineering, industrial, military, and athletic settings. Although this text includes references to uses of basic findings and to basic findings in applied settings, it is intended as a survey of acquisition of skill as a part of the experimental psychology of human behavior.

This is the first book-length presentation to junior and senior students of skill acquisition. A first survey has alternatives beyond the decision on basic-applied emphasis. With none of the gaps yet filled, many orientations—to task taxonomy, significant variables, systematic points of view—have reason; and, as both are needed, a first work might aim either for wide coverage or great depth on the most significant matters.

This text, however, has its origin in the 1966 publication of *Acquisition of Skill*, written for a professional and near-professional audience. The policy followed for that work was to invite a number of experts to prepare original chapters on their individual specialties. Depth of coverage was thus automatically assured. Breadth came from the diversity of specialties and the dimensions defining the specialties—individual authors stressed task, research area, variables, design, system, or a mixture. It meant a loose organization, but it worked; the same policy was followed for this book, which is, in part, a revision of *Acquisition of Skill*. Six contributors to the original version revised or rewrote their material as needed for the advanced undergraduate student; one with a new co-author wrote on his original topic; and four authors contributed new chapters.

Chapter 1 includes an introduction to the field and a historical review of the areas of research that have been emphasized. Chapter 2 offers a different kind of beginning—the development of skill in the early years of life—and outlines a developmental hierarchy of skill that is meaningful for the remainder of the work. Chapters 3 and 4 both combine one of the areas of research treated in the historical introduction with an approach that diverges from historical projection. Together, Chapters 1-4 provide a broad introduction to perceptual motor behavior. Chapters 5-9 are treatments in depth of current areas of research — individual differences, retention, transfer of training and feedback — that are also major topics in the historical review. Chapters 10, on tracking, and 11, on selective learning, survey a wide range of variables; they are, effectively, overviews of the variables in human behavior and at near-opposite ends in the taxonomy of perceptual motor tasks. Chapter 11, in addition, seriously treats its variables within a general theory of learning. (The chapter order is by no means limiting. Chapters 5-9, for example, might well be read first, while their historical background can be easily recalled, or Chapters 10 and 11 first rather than last, because they *are* comprehensive overviews of many variables and their effects.)

For the editor, the writer thanks the authors for their contributions and cooperation; each deserves a special acknowledgment for making it possible to complete this work.

INA McD. BILODEAU

Contents

Contents *xi*

7. **Transfer of Training**
GEORGE E. BRIGGS

I. Introduction 205
II. Functional Relationships in Transfer 208
III. Interpretation 230
References 232

8. **Supplementary Feedback and Instructions**
EDWARD A. BILODEAU

I. Introduction 235
II. Research: Contributions and Evaluation 237
III. Summary 249
References 251

9. **Information Feedback**
INA McD. BILODEAU

I. Introduction 255
II. Frequency 260
III. Scale Transformations 264
IV. Locus 275
V. Augmented IF 279
VI. Summary 282
References 282

10. **Tracking**
E. C. POULTON

I. Introduction 287
II. Characteristics of Tracking Tasks 289
III. The Track 290
IV. The Display 295
V. The Control 300
VI. The Control-System Dynamics 303
VII. Human Limitations 310
VIII. Summary 314
References 316

7. **Transfer of Training**
GEORGE E. BRIGGS

8. **Supplementary Feedback and Instructions**
EDWARD A. BILODEAU

9. **Information Feedback**
INA McD. BILODEAU

10. **Tracking**
E. C. POULTON

11. Outline of Human Selective Learning
CLYDE E. NOBLE

Principles of
Skill Acquisition

CHAPTER 1

Historical Introduction

ARTHUR L. IRION[1]
Tulane University

I. Introduction

The history of research in the area of motor skills extends from the very end of the last century to the present day. Although it is difficult to identify a first experiment, the best-known early investigations were those of Bryan and Harter (1897, 1899) on the learning of telegraphic language. These papers were preceded by an earlier study of Bryan's (1892) and a paper by Dresslar (1891–1892). However, there does not appear to have been a "founder" of this area of research in the sense that Pavlov founded the work in conditioned response learning or Ebbinghaus founded the field of verbal rote learning. Recently, Noble (1968) has nominated Woodworth as a candidate for foundership on the basis of his book, *Le Mouvement* (1903). However, neither this work nor Woodworth's earlier monograph (1899) on the accuracy of voluntary movement appears to have been referred to by a significant number of subsequent authors until Ammons (1958) pointed to the importance of Woodworth's contributions.

While it is undeniably true that here, as in other situations, want of identifiable ancestry can be an embarrassment, it is also true that the field of motor skills probably owes some of its vitality to just that deficiency. A founder tends to define the field of discourse, to set the methods of investigation, to identify the problems to be solved, and, all too often, to bequeath a legacy of sterility as well. Too frequently,

[1]Now at the University of Missouri at St. Louis.

the dead hand of the founder continues to rest on the helm of the ship, the weight of the tradition he has established serving to limit the scope and imaginativeness of the work of those who have followed. The field of motor skills does not suffer from a lack of variety or imaginativeness. Indeed, the approaches are so extremely various that there is some difficulty in defining just what the field of motor skills is. The diverse skeins of interest and activity in the skills area tend to overlap with the whole remaining field of experimental psychology to such an extent that an argument could be made in support of the proposition that the history of skills research *is* a miniature version of the total history of experimental psychology. The traditional experimental areas of learning, sensation, perception, cognition, work phenomena, physiological correlates of behavior, motivation, and psychometrics have all been represented in the research on skills.

While part of the difficulty of defining the area of skills may stem from the lack of a founding father, the lack of a serviceable basic concept is probably a more significant deficiency. Other areas of investigation have been more fortunate in this respect. The concept of the *idea*, developed so thoroughly by the associationists, proved to have great value for the workers in the field of rote learning. The concept that was the obvious analog to the idea and that should have been useful to the workers in the skills area, the Cartesian reflex, turned out to be not so very useful, after all, in the skills context. Quite evidently, the concept of the reflex has been much more valuable to the physiological psychologists and to the Pavlovians than it has been to the workers in the skills area. The difficulty is that while the idea and the reflex are excellent concepts for describing behaviors that naturally break into discrete units, they are not nearly as satisfactory for describing behaviors that are essentially continuous. It is true that some motor performances may be considered as a series of discrete events, and it is also true that the exigencies of the laboratory have forced workers to consider some other motor events in the conceptual framework of discrete events whether or not this could be accomplished with realism. While it cannot be denied that, because of the former circumstance and in spite of the latter one, considerable advances have been made in understanding skills in terms of a model for discrete events, it is also possible that the use of this kind of model may, in the long run, prove to be more harmful than beneficial.

In their excellent review, E. A. Bilodeau and Bilodeau (1961) offer a "deliberately naive" definition that differentiates the motor-skills field from other areas in terms of the relative importance of the hand, the tongue, and the eye. Although their definition turns out — particularly when one considers the restrictions they place upon it — to be considerably more deliberate than naive, a somewhat more precise definition of coordination has been offered by Fitts (1964), to wit: "By a skilled response I shall mean one in which receptor-effector-feed-back processes are highly organized, both spatially and temporally. The central problem for the study of skill learning is how such organizations or patterning comes about" (Fitts, 1964, p. 244).

The history of skills research can be broken into two rather obvious segments, and each of these, in turn, can be split into two smaller divisions. The major shift or break in the history appears to have occurred about 1945. The causes appear to be multiple. First, there was the publication of the very influential book, *Principles of Behavior*, by Hull (1943). Second, at the close of World War II there existed a considerable number of young experimental psychologists who had been exposed to skills problems in the research and aircrew selection programs of the Army Air Corps (in Great Britain a similar influence was exerted by the program sponsored by the RAF and directed by Sir Frederic Bartlett). Then, too, following the war there was a considerable amount of federal support for research in the area of skills. Finally, and most significantly, the immediate postwar period saw the introduction of new statistical techniques for handling skills data. One who gives more than a cursory glance at the pre-1945 skills literature is struck by the fact that the investigators seem to have been handcuffed by their inability to treat their data in meaningful ways. Occasionally quantitative data were presented in the form of means with their probable errors and/or with appended critical ratios for pairs of conditions. More often, the investigator presented his data in the form of learning curves. The great preoccupation that the early experimenters exhibited with respect to learning curves probably reflects, as much as anything else, the want of a technique for treating their data in any other meaningful way. The lack of analytical power also had another influence. Since the research worker was more or less limited to the drawing of one or more curves and letting the reader come to his own conclusions, the experimenter was virtually forced to confine his investigations to variables that produced large effects. Lacking the tools for analyzing even large differences, he did not dare to venture into the investigation of variables that produced more subtle effects.

If the major break in the character of skills research is accepted as having occurred, the further subdivision of each of the two resulting historical periods may be suggested. These subdivisions must be proposed in a more tentative fashion. However, it does appear that the pre-1945 period exhibits a change of emphasis that took place between 1925 and 1935. Before 1925, much of the work was exploratory in character—or, at least, it seems so when examined in retrospect.

After 1935 a greater degree of theoretical orientation can be observed. If a definite date is desired for the dividing point, perhaps the appearance of McGeoch's (1927) review of the skills literature could serve as a reference date. The post-1945 era also appears to be divisible into two segments. The first of these was marked by extremely high research productivity in the skills area while the more recent period is marked by a turning away from some of the traditional core problems (distribution of practice and reminiscence, for example) and by the exploration of new theoretical approaches to the study of skills. There has also been a modest decrease in research productivity during this fourth period. If a dividing event to separate the third from the fourth period is wanted, the closing down of the Air Force Personnel Training and Research Center in 1957 might be suggested.

We are left, then, with four periods: 1890–1927, 1927–1945, 1945–1957, and 1957 to the present time. The first period was a time of definition and exploration. The second was marked by an increase in the sophistication of experimental work, by the borrowing of techniques and concepts from other areas of psychology, and, particularly, by the emergence of several theoretical formulations that gave structure to the work of the period. The third period was marked by enormous productivity. Although the time occupied by the third period (12 years) is short, very nearly half of all of the published research in the field was produced during this time. It is more difficult to describe the characteristics of the fourth period since we are still in it. Certainly some changes of theoretical orientation are to be seen, but such changes are to be found throughout the history of research on skills and particularly during the two previous transition periods.

The contribution of each era to the total literature of the skills field can be estimated only approximately since the estimates must reflect a judgment as to what should be, and should not be, counted as skills research. For what it may be worth, such an estimate is offered. It would seem that the first era contributed about 7 % of the total published research; the second era contributed about 16 %; the third era about 47 %; and the fourth era (to the present) about 30 %.

II. Areas of Research[2]

A. Distribution of Practice Effects and the Reminiscence Phenomenon

One of the first skills areas to receive research attention was the problem of distribution of practice. Over the years, more studies have been conducted in this area (and the related field of reminiscence) than in any other specific skills area. Early work, such as that by Starch (1912) and Pyle (1913, 1914), was mainly concerned with determining whether or not the introduction of rest periods between practice sessions did, in fact, affect performance. In very general terms, the findings of the early research may be summarized as follows:

1. In most learning situations, but not in all of them, distributed practice is superior to massed practice when performance is plotted against amount of practice.

2. In general, long rests are superior to short rests.

3. As a rule, short practice sessions between rests yield better scores than do long practice sessions.

There are obvious practical limitations to the implementation of the last two findings. Much of the early work on the distribution effects is summarized in Ruch's (1928) review of the literature.

During the second era, work on distribution effects continued and was marked by the emergence of several theories and hypotheses that were advanced to replace the "fatigue" theory that had fallen from favor by the 1930's. Only two of these theories seem to have had much impact on the skills field. These were (1) the two hypotheses concerning age maturation and stimulation maturation advanced by Wheeler and Perkins (1932), and (2) the Snoddy hypothesis (1935).

Both of the Wheeler and Perkins hypotheses tend to identify the process of learning with the phenomenon of maturation and, in effect, to consider learning as a special form of stimulus-induced growth. The age-maturation hypothesis merely holds that the ability to benefit from practice depends upon the age-maturational level of the subject. Doré and Hilgard (1937) describe the stimulation-maturation hypothesis as follows: "At any given age-maturational level, the optimum rate of stimulation to secure improvement in a given function depends

---

[2]Detailed histories of several important areas of research are not offered in this chapter. In general, topics that are important for learning and the conditions of practice have been considered. Not covered is all of the work on the mechanics of movement, the discrimination of stimulus situations, quantitative set, the dynamogenic effects of muscular tension, the psychological refractory period, and applications of information theory. Some of this work has been reviewed by Adams (1961a, 1962, 1964), Attneave (1959), Courts (1942), Meyer (1953), Poulton (1957), Saufley and Bilodeau (1963), and Smith and Smith (1962). The reader is also referred to Melton (1964) and to E. A. Bilodeau (1966). It is a matter of particular regret that the excellent and comprehensive work of Fitts and his associates in the broadly defined field of human engineering cannot be covered here. The interested reader should consult the following works (which are barely representative of the enormous volume of material): Fitts (1951, 1958, 1964), Melton and Briggs (1960), and Bahrick, Fitts, and Briggs (1957).

upon the normal rate of stimulation-induced maturation in that function" (Doré & Hilgard, p. 246). An implication of this formulation is that, given a particular age-maturational level, stimulation (practice) will give rise to a rate of growth (improvement) that is related more closely to total elapsed time since the beginning of practice than to the total amount of practice given in that time. This last implication of the theory was specifically tested by Doré and Hilgard (1937) in a skills situation. Using the pursuit rotor, they distributed different amounts of practice through the same total amount of elapsed time. Their acquisition curves, when performance was plotted against trials in the conventional manner, showed the usual distribution benefit. When performance was plotted against elapsed time, however, the performance curves tended to coincide, thereby lending support to the theory. The results obtained by Hilgard and Smith (1942) also seemed to support the hypothesis, although later findings by Bell (1942) did not. McGeoch and Irion (1952) have attempted to reconcile these contradictory results by pointing out that, in view of what is known about the relative effects of practice and rest, it is possible to predict on purely empirical grounds that a range of practice-rest conditions exists for which the predictions of Wheeler and Perkins should be fulfilled.

The Snoddy hypothesis posits two opposed processes of mental growth: primary growth and secondary growth. Primary growth is supposed to occur early in practice and to be a joint function of amount of practice and amount of interpolated time. The cumulative mean of the scores during practice is held to be a measure of the amount of primary growth. This measure was attacked on logical grounds by Doré and Hilgard (1938) and on empirical grounds by Payne (1942). Secondary growth is supposed to be a function of the base established by primary growth. It tends, therefore, to occur later in practice. Secondary growth is held to dissipate spontaneously in time and, hence, to benefit from massed trials.

Snoddy's results (1935) and those of Humphreys (1937) appeared to agree with predictions that could be made from the theory as did the findings of Renshaw and Schwarzbek (1938). However, Bell's (1942) data offered small support to the theory and the results obtained by Doré and Hilgard (1938) were nearly devastating to it. Not only were their findings contrary to a clear prediction from the theory, but their replotting of earlier data seemed to change the interpretation of earlier findings in a radical manner. Still more significantly, Doré and Hilgard offered a two-factor theory of their own that anticipated later formulations by Hull and Ammons. Their two-factor theory was based on (1) learning and (2) work decrement.

The third period of our history was ushered in by Hull's (1943) introduction of the concepts of reactive inhibition (I_R) and conditioned inhibition $(_SI_R)$ and by Ammons' (1947a) theoretical analysis.[3] With the introduction of these theories, people began to stop thinking about distribution of practice as a variable that affects learning and began to think of distribution as a performance variable. As if to emphasize this point, two important studies by Kientzle (1946, 1949) were published at about this time. The results of these studies seemed to indicate that the effects of practice and the effects of rest resulted from the operation of distinct and separate processes.

The design of reminiscence experiments is continuous with the design of experiments on the distribution of practice (Buxton, 1942). With the advent of the third era, three studies of reminiscence in pursuit rotor learning appeared in quick succession: Ammons (1947b), Kimble and Horenstein (1948), and Irion (1949). All of the studies varied length of rest and, in addition, the experiments of Ammons and Irion varied amount of prerest practice. From the standpoint of Hullian theory, however, the most significant of the three experiments was the one by Kimble and Horenstein. They plotted their data for amount of reminiscence as a function of length of rest against Hull's function for the decay of I_R in time and obtained a tolerably good fit. A second experiment by Kimble (1949) used both a massed practice control group and a distributed practice control group and yielded results that seemed to show that reminiscence gains could be accounted for in terms of the joint operation of the Hullian variables of reactive inhibition and conditioned inhibition. However, results obtained by Adams and Reynolds (1954) in a subsequent experiment did not offer much support for the notion that $_SI_R$ operates in postrest performance to depress scores below the level of a distributed practice control group—at least in cases where the experimental groups shift (as Kimble's groups did not) to distributed trials following the rest. The conclusion that $_SI_R$ plays a negligible role in motor performance has been arrived at independently by Ammons and Willig (1956) and by Digman (1956, 1959). Analogous and corroborative studies using a manual cranking task have been conducted by E. A. Bilodeau (1952a, b, 1954b). The cranking situation has the virtue of keeping learning factors to a minimum, thereby allowing inhibitory factors to be revealed

---

[3]Ammons (1947a) advanced a theoretical analysis that was very similar to Hull's and that was specifically designed to apply to the motor-learning situation in human subjects. Perhaps unfortunately, the general enthusiasm generated by Hull's theory among that segment of psychologists who could become enthused by theories of the general Hullian type tended to carry over into the field of motor-skills research so that Hull's theory was destined to be much more influential in determining future research than was the more specific, and in some ways more satisfactory, theory of Ammons.

in relatively "pure" form. Again, there is little evidence that $_sI_R$ plays a significant role.

As of the end of the third era of our history, the weight of evidence suggested that (1) distribution of practice affects performance but not learning and (2) almost all of the distribution (or reminiscence) benefits can be accounted for in terms of the dissipation of a single inhibitory factor that accumulates during practice and dissipates during rest.[4] Once these conclusions had been reached there was a sharp decline in the amount of research conducted in this area—a decline which coincides with the end of the third era.

If it is conceded that distribution and reminiscence effects are results of the dissipation of a single kind of inhibition, it might then be profitable to inquire into the nature of that inhibitory process. A small amount of research, not all of it illuminating, has been performed in respect to this problem. One approach has had to do with the fact that reminiscence gains are found in bilateral transfer situations. In 1952, Irion and Gustafson (1952) and Kimble (1952) demonstrated that such effects could be obtained. Grice and Reynolds (1952) followed these studies with one that demonstrated that amount of bilateral reminiscence was a function of the length of the interpolated rest period, a variable known to be important in determining amount of unilateral reminiscence. The findings of Grice and Reynolds, in turn, were corroborated and extended by Rockway (1953) who varied length of rest and amount of first-hand (prerest) practice. Rockway found that performance with the second hand was an increasing function of length of rest and of amount of first-hand practice. The cogent suggestion was made by Grice and Reynolds (1952) that "the gains in bilateral transfer indicate the presence of temporary inhibitory factors either associated with generalized postural adjustment or of a perceptual or central character." Early attempts to isolate postural and/or perceptual factors yielded negative results. These studies dealt with the effects of

---

[4]This view, perhaps, rather oversimplifies matters. Ammons (1951a) and Jahnke (1958, 1961) have obtained data that are not readily accounted for under this view while the findings of Bourne and Archer (1956) and Archer (1958) have led to suggestions that the accumulation of inhibition may interfere with practice to such an extent that acquisition is degraded. A more ambitious countercurrent of theory should also be noted. H. J. Eysenck (1965) proposes a "three-factor" theory of reminiscence in which the two familiar factors of I_R and $_sI_R$ are combined with a consolidation factor. While some support is given to this view by results previously obtained by H. J. Eysenck and Maxwell (1961), H. J. Eysenck and Willett (1961), and by Rachman and Grassi (1965), some of this supporting evidence can be interpreted in other ways than as offering support to a consolidation theory. The notion of consolidation or perseveration was first introduced by Müller and Pilzecker (1900).

such variables as standing, standing and watching the rotors revolve, standing and watching other subjects practicing on the rotors, etc. However, Adams' (1955) study suggested a line of explanation. He used a rest-filling activity that might be called active or attentive observation. Such active observation (as opposed to ordinary rest or passive observation) had the effect of depressing the amount of reminiscence in the unilateral reminiscence situations, and Adams' findings have been extended to the bilateral reminiscence situation by Rosenquist (1965).

In the light of the present evidence, it would seem to be reasonable to conclude that the bilateral reminiscence effect is attributable to the dissipation of inhibition accumulated in connection with response systems that are common to right-handed and left-handed performance. This conclusion, of course, fails to shed additional light upon the nature of the inhibitory process.[5]

B. INDIVIDUAL DIFFERENCES

The thread of psychometrics runs through the entire history of skills research. From the beginning, skills situations have been seen as likely situations for the measurement of specific aptitudes or for predicting particular kinds of performances. The heaviest use of skills situations for such purposes occurred during World War II in connection with the various aircrew selection programs, but the general notion of psychomotor testing is much more ancient than this and Whipple's *Manual* (1910) contains descriptions of a number of simple psychomotor tests that were still being used for selection purposes during World War II.

In the context of this chapter, the most important aspect of the psychometric approach concerns the study of individual variations in performance, the use of test scores to determine the factors in skilled performances, and, especially, the study of the course of individual variations and factor structures under the conditions of practice.

Early work in the psychometric area tended to be concerned with the measurement of the dispersions of scores about mean performances and with the contributions to total variability of such factors as age and sex. For the most part, these studies were empirical in orientation and the specific findings of them need not be discussed here.

---

[5] One not very hopeful suggestion concerning this problem which has been offered by Köhler and Fishback (1950) and defended by Duncan (1956) would identify reactive inhibition with such perceptual "satiation" phenomena as figural aftereffects. According to this view, the important variable involved in the effects of work is not the work, itself, but the kinesthetic stimulation resulting from the work.

However, toward the end of the second era of our history, a stunning set of papers was produced by Woodrow (1938a, b, c, 1939a, b, 1940, 1946).

It was Woodrow who first exploited the interesting pattern of correlations, called the superdiagonal form, that has frequently been observed in learning situations following its discovery by Perl (1934). When successive trial scores are correlated, the correlations between the initial score and the successively following scores that are generated as practice progresses show a tendency to decrease so that the correlation between trial one and the nth trial will typically be the lowest of the set. At the same time, there is a tendency for the correlations between successive trials to increase in magnitude from the beginning of practice to the end so that the highest correlation is between trials n-1 and n.

In accounting for this effect, Woodrow (1938b, p. 277) noted:

> Now when the scores are accounted for in terms of uncorrelated abilities, it is obvious that if initial scores were altogether dependent on ability X and final scores altogether dependent on ability Y, the correlation between initial and final score would be zero; and further, that any considerable change in the degree to which the scores depended upon the two uncorrelated abilities would result in a correlation between initial and final score markedly below a perfect correlation. The greater the change in the ability pattern, when the abilities are uncorrelated, the lower should be the correlation between initial and final score.

Several of Woodrow's conclusions and observations have a remarkably contemporary aura about them. Writing in 1938, he noted that marked changes in factor loadings may occur as a result of practice (1938a, p. 227) and he concluded:

> If the goodness of the scores be regarded as determined by a set of cooperating but independently variable abilities, then practice may be regarded as a change in the conditions under which the various constituents of this set of abilities operate.

Woodrow also noted that gain scores usually correlate highly with final (postpractice) scores, but poorly with initial scores. In 1938 and again in 1946, he failed to uncover a general improvement factor (Woodrow, 1938a, 1946). Finally, Woodrow's conclusion (1938b, pp. 277–278) deserves to be quoted.

> In recent years, experimental psychologists, working largely with the white rat, have made notable progress in the explanation of learning. Applied to practice, however, the theories advanced are helpful mainly in understanding simply the fact that performance improves with practice, i.e., that the practice curves rise. Before any account of the phenomena of practice and learning can be complete, however, it must take account of two other important phenomena; namely, the change in individual differences and the falling-off with practice in the correlation between the first obtained and the last obtained scores.

World War II lent further impetus to the psychometric approach, both in terms of the collection of large amounts of data in aircrew selection situations and in the development of a considerable number of relatively sophisticated devices for testing psychomotor abilities (Melton, 1947a, b). Following the war, one of the first problems to be attacked was the relative power of tests to predict psychomotor performances early and late in practice. For example, Reynolds (1952) correlated a considerable number of test scores with performance on the Complex Coordinator at various stages of practice on the latter. He found that the predictive value of the tests decreased as practice on the Complex Coordinator increased. Reynolds suggested that, as practice increased, the abilities demanded in performance might shift to those that were more specific to the particular task at hand. This hypothesis was not given much support by the findings of Adams (1953, 1957) or by the results of Parker and Fleishman (1961) which showed that selected outside tests, presumably those that measure abilities relative to performance later in practice, were more predictive of final performances than were scores taken from the same task early in practice. However, in fairness to the specificity hypothesis of Reynolds, it should be noted that Fleishman and Hempel (1954, 1955) found that the loadings of some task-specific factors (in the Complex Coordinator and the Discrimination Reaction Time tests) increase with practice.

From such findings, it would seem to follow that practice can be regarded as being accompanied by a change in the pattern of abilities being employed in performance. Such an interpretation was made by Woodrow (1938b), Fleishman (1956), and by Fleishman and Hempel (1955). Jones (1959, 1960, 1962, 1966) presents strong arguments in favor of what he terms a simplicial hypothesis to account for the superdiagonal form of the correlation matrix and for the data relating to the prediction of scores at various levels of practice from outside test scores.

A series of studies (e.g., Woodrow, 1938b; Adams, 1957; Reynolds and Adams, 1954; Zeaman and Kaufman, 1955) relating to this general problem area should be mentioned in passing. These investigations concern the fate under practice of groups that have been fractionated according to initial scores. Following the logic imposed by the decreasing correlation between trial one scores and performance on subsequent trials, it might be assumed that the groups will converge as practice progresses. This result is sometimes, but not always, obtained in the laboratory. However, if x represents an individual's score early in practice and y represents his score late in practice (both x and y being stated in deviation form), then, according to a common form of the regression equation, $y = r\,(\sigma y/\sigma x)\,x$. If the value of r exhibits a systematic decrease, and if the ratio of $\sigma y/\sigma x$ remains constant, then y should, indeed, be less deviant than x and the scores should converge. Although in many skills situations there appears to be a tendency for variability to increase with practice (which would enhance the convergence effect), this need not always be true. In cases where variability increases with practice, the ratio of $\sigma y/\sigma x$ will become increasingly larger than 1.00 which will tend to compensate (or more than compensate) for the decreasing value of r, thereby producing curves that are parallel or divergent.

C. THE WHOLE-PART PROBLEM

An area of research that, in its original form, was more or less confined to the early period of our history, was the whole-part problem. This problem seems to have represented many things to many people, but the one thing it does not seem to have been is a unitary problem, in and of itself.

The whole-part problem overlaps with a considerable number of other problems. For example, it tends to merge with the problem of distribution of practice in that each of the parts may be considered to be a shorter unit of practice than is the practicing of the whole task. If the parts be practiced in alternation or succession, practice on each part is distributed by the length of time required for practice on the other part or parts. However, the fact that the parts must be practiced in some order also throws the whole-part problem into the category of transfer-of-training experiments including designs for the study of proactive and retroactive inhibition. If a task, X, is broken down into parts A and B (so that $A + B = X$), if A is practiced first, B is practiced second, and finally a test is made of $A + B$, negative transfer from A to B can be considered as proactive inhibition, and negative transfer from B to A (in $A + B$) can be considered as retroactive inhibition. Moreover, it should be noted that, although the early experiments on the whole-part problem were not designed to test for combination effects, these investigations can be considered in this way. If A and B are separate components of X and if there is a combining rule for predicting the value of X if values are known for A and B separately, the whole-part problem becomes a special case of the combination problem. Finally, it should be noted that the whole-part problem is a part of the problem that deals with length-difficulty relationships, and it is out of this context that the whole-part problem seems to have arisen. The length-difficulty relationship, itself, has been studied in conjunction with a number of other variables. The classic paper on the length-difficulty problem by Lyon (1914) also dealt with this relationship under conditions of massing and distribution and reported a strong interaction effect, the longer materials being disproportionately easier to learn under distributed than under massed practice conditions. In the case of the whole-part problem and its relation to research on the distribution of practice, there have been experiments in which both whole and part methods of practice were used with and without the addition of rests. For example, Crafts (1930) used a letter-substitution task and found that the whole method was about equal (or slightly inferior) to the part methods he employed when practice was massed, but that the whole method was distinctly and consistently superior under conditions of distributed practice.[6]

D. FEEDBACK

The problem of knowledge of results or feedback has a long and involved history, but the majority of the studies of feedback have been conducted during the third and fourth periods of our history.

Early work on knowledge of results flows more or less directly from Thorndike's (1911) statement of the Law of Effect. By the late 1930's, a considerable number of studies had been conducted which showed that knowledge of results was an effective variable, that little improvement occurred without it, that the introduction of it was followed by improvement, and that withdrawal of knowledge of results was followed by a deterioration of performance.

Most of the early studies of knowledge of results were concerned with the effects of either giving or not giving knowledge of results rather than with the effects that could be produced by varying the ways in which knowledge of results was given. Furthermore, the results of animal experimentation on reinforcement and the formulation of reinforcement theory by Hull (1943) exerted a strong influence on the way knowledge of results was considered in the motor learning situation. There was a considerable, and an unfortunate, tendency to accept the findings of animal research on problems of reinforcement as being directly translatable to human verbal and motor-learning situations.

A return to the study of knowledge of results in the context of hu-

---

[6]An interesting "solution" to the whole-part problem has recently been offered by Annett and Kay (1956). They point out that a series of recurring events is probably best learned by the whole method. If, however, the responses of the subject serve to alter the series of events, part practice will tend to reduce the variability or randomness of the series. They pose the paradox that "if the elements of a task are highly independent the task is best learned as a whole, but where the elements are highly interdependent they should be split up and the task learned in parts."

man learning was initiated by Brown (1949) who was working in the framework of Hullian theory, but whose analysis achieved a rapprochement between the views of Hull and the earlier conceptions of Thorndike.

A number of problems have been investigated in this area. These include (1) delay of knowledge of results, (2) the effects of filling the delay period in such experiments in various ways, (3) the frequency of knowledge of results, and (4) transformations of knowledge of results.[7]

In contrast to the findings concerning delay of reinforcement in animal studies, the general conclusion that can be reached concerning the effects of delay of feedback in the skills situation is that, within very wide limits, delay has little effect upon the learning of discrete tasks provided that the subject is not required to make other responses of the same class during the delay period. This conclusion is in general agreement with the classic finding of Lorge and Thorndike (1935). Intervals of delay of from 25 seconds (Noble & Alcock, 1958) through 1 week (Ryan & Bilodeau, 1962) to 4 weeks (E. A. Bilodeau, Sulzer, & Levy, 1962) have been used without obtaining impressive evidence for the degrading effects of delay (see also, E. A. Bilodeau & Bilodeau, 1958b). It should be emphasized that these conclusions do not apply to continuous tracking tasks where delay or lag in informative feedback can have seriously disruptive effects upon learning and performance (Conklin, 1957, 1959; Garvey, Sweeney, & Birmingham, 1958). In the population of discrete tasks, the experimental analog to the situation that applies in the case of continuous tasks is the situation in which knowledge of results is delayed for a specific number of stimulus-response sequences rather than for a particular length of (unfilled) time. In such situations, the subject is given knowledge of results for his performance on some specified, but not immediately preceding, trial. This is the situation that was used by Lorge and Thorndike (1935) and more recently by I. McD. Bilodeau (1956). Under these circumstances, delay is disruptive of performance and learning.

[7]General summaries of portions of the work in these areas will be found in Wolfle (1951), Ammons (1956), E. A. Bilodeau (1956), E. A. Bilodeau and Bilodeau (1961), I. McD. Bilodeau (1966), and Noble (1968). A related problem, not considered here, is the effect of distorted, diminished, or delayed feedback upon the performance of skillful acts that are relatively continuous and that have already been acquired. Aside from such anticipations as Aristotle's illusion, the first work in this area would appear to have been done by Stratton (1896, 1897). The work of Fairbanks (1955), Bahrick (1957), Chase, Harvey, Standfast, Rapin, and Sutton (1961a), and Chase, Rapin, Gilden, Sutton, and Guilfoyle (1961b) should be mentioned. The most extensive recent work on this problem has been undertaken by Smith and his associates (see Smith, 1961, 1962; Smith & Smith, 1962; Smith, Wargo, Jones, and Smith, 1963; Smith, Gould, and Wargo, 1964).

In a study of learning as a function of frequency of feedback, E. A. Bilodeau and Bilodeau (1958a) compared the learning of groups that received 100, 33, 25, and 10 % knowledge of results in a lever positioning task. Although, as the authors point out, there are numerous differences between the partial reinforcement situation as it has been studied in animal experiments and the "partial knowledge of results" procedures used in their experiment, their finding that "learning is independent of relative frequency and positively related to absolute frequency" of knowledge of results does not seem to mesh very well with the results of the animal experiments as these are usually interpreted. More recently, Taylor and Noble (1962) have obtained somewhat similar results using 100, 75, 50, and 25 % knowledge of results in the Selective Mathometer situation. They found that their 100 % group was best in acquisition (when performance is plotted against either number of trials or number of reinforcements). There was a suggestion that the 100 % group was slightly more susceptible to extinction, although this result was confined to the early extinction trials.

A considerable number of studies involve transformations of knowledge of results. The simplest of these transformations involves varying target size in tracking or pursuit situations (E. A. Bilodeau, 1956). Over a considerable range of target sizes, target size does not appear to affect learning. It should be pointed out that target size can be increased as well by transforming the subject's true score into a reported feedback that contains a good bit of latitude for response error as by increasing the physical size of the target button on a pursuit rotor. The reporting procedure has the advantage that the recorded score and the reported score are not both affected by the "size" of the target—a factor that seems to account for all of the performance differences of subjects using different physical sizes of targets. Using such verbal transformations, it can be shown that drastic reductions or increases in the error reported as feedback can have a deleterious effect upon performance, with reduction having more effect than increase (if the subject is *always* informed that he "hit the target," his performance fails to improve). For example, using the Manual Lever Test, E. A. Bilodeau (1954a) transformed true scores by making them 0, 2, 4, 8, or 16 units closer to the goal score than they actually were. In this situation, the 0 group was given its true score as feedback, and the 2, 4, 8, and 16 groups worked with successively broader targets. The results indicated that the groups with the narrower targets learned more rapidly than the groups with the broader targets. In a second study, E. A. Bilodeau (1955b) compared transformations that reduced error by various amounts to transformations that increased error by the same amounts.

Again, reduced error transformations resulted in poorer performance with the greater degrees of transformation. Transformations that reduced or increased error were approximately equal in their effects with small transformations, but with the larger transformations, reduced error resulted in a considerably poorer performance than increased error.[8]

Linear transformations of feedback have also been studied. E. A. Bilodeau (1953) found that transformations that increasingly minimize error do not affect final performance but do, increasingly, degrade the rate of approach to the common asymptote. Working with transformations that magnify error, Noble and Broussard (1955) have shown that feedback transformed to inflate reported error has the effect of making the subject "overshoot" the target. This is followed by a rapid reapproach to zero error, but with some evidence of "hunting." In this case, the variability of response early in practice is much larger for the transformation that inflates error than it is for the transformation that deflates error.

E. RETENTION

Studies of retention in the skills context gained momentum during the second period of our history. It had long been assumed that motor habits were better retained than verbal habits, but at the beginning of the second era this assumption was called into question by McGeoch and Melton (1929), who reviewed the literature on the subject and then compared the retention values of mazes and nonsense syllables, each task being presented at three levels of difficulty. Although their conclusion that retention differences were small was called into question by Freeman and Abernethy (1930, 1932), subsequent findings of McGeoch (1932) and by Waters and Poole (1933) tended to support the earlier findings of McGeoch and Melton. Waters and Poole went on to conclude that "the relative retention value of what have been conventionally called motor and verbal habits is a function of the relative degree of learning of the two habits compared." Leavitt and Schlosberg (1944) attempted to equate degree of learning in the pursuit-rotor situation and the rote-learning situation, and then to com-

---

[8]Such results can be expected only when the subject is given feedback that specifies degree and/or direction of error. If the subject is told only "hit" or "miss," it would be expected that a **U**-shaped function would be obtained when amount of learning is plotted against target width. With extremely small targets (of the invisible variety we are discussing), the subject would spend an inordinate amount of practice time locating them. With extremely broad targets, so much information is lost in the feedback that it ceases to be "informative" feedback.

pare retention of the two habits. In their experiment, the pursuit rotor habit was better retained than the verbal habit, although the difference was attributable, in part, to the fact that the motor habit exhibited a considerable amount of reminiscence, especially after the shorter retention intervals.

The problem of the relative retention value of verbal and motor habits was not to be raised again in precisely this form and, in retrospect, the issue may be argued from a number of viewpoints. The first of these would have it that such comparisons are meaningless because it is not possible to work with truly comparable situations and that the equation of such factors as degree of learning cannot be accomplished in a meaningful way. A second kind of argument would state that there is little difference between motor forgetting and verbal forgetting because verbal forgetting is really much smaller than it is traditionally supposed to be (cf. Underwood, 1957). A final point of view would concede that motor habits are remarkably resistant to forgetting and would then marshall arguments to explain this resistance. The most familiar arguments are (1) that motor habits are generally better learned than verbal habits and, hence, are less susceptible to forgetting; (2) that motor habits are less susceptible to interference effects than are verbal habits because the extraexperimental world offers fewer opportunities for the learning of competing habits in the case of motor habits than in the case of verbal habits; and (3) that the situations for measuring motor retention are biased to produce high memory scores while the situations for measuring verbal memory are biased to produce high amounts of interference and forgetting (cf. Irion, 1966).

During the third period, the problem of retention also received a considerable amount of attention. In the contemporary period, studies of retention have tended to turn away from tracking-type, time-on-target situations and the concepts these situations use, and have shifted more in the directions that have been taken by studies of retention in verbal-learning situations. The influence of the kind of theoretical work done by Underwood (1957) and Underwood and Postman (1960) is beginning to be felt.

A variety of studies of the retention of motor skills were conducted during the third era. For the early part of the period, these studies may be divided into two varieties; those concerned with retention, as such, and those concerned with the warming-up phenomenon.

A number of studies using the pursuit rotor were conducted. These employed retention intervals ranging from 1 week (Jahnke, 1958) through 4 weeks (Jahnke & Duncan, 1956) and 1 year (Bell, 1950; S. B. G. Eysenck, 1960), to 2 years (Koonce, Chambliss, & Irion, 1964). All

studies showed high degrees of retention and rapid recovery of retention losses (if any) in relearning. Both the Jahnke and Duncan study
and the one by Koonce *et al.* revealed that reminiscence effects might
be observed after relatively long retention intervals (4 weeks and 2
years, respectively). The S. B. G. Eysenck study was noteworthy for
the fact that a great deal of prerest practice (fifty 15-minute practice
sessions) was given which, together with the fact that the prerest practice was relatively distributed, probably precluded the obtaining of
reminiscence. In this study, an average retention loss of about 10% in
mean time-on-target score was found after a year of rest.

In other, generally more complicated, learning situations, a high
degree of retention has also been demonstrated, although habits involving discrete motor responses seem to be less well remembered
than habits involving continuous responses (Adams & Hufford, 1962).
Representative studies include those by E. I. Jones and Bilodeau
(1953), Battig, Nagel, Voss, and Brogden (1957), and R. B. Ammons,
Farr, Bloch, Neumann, Dey, Marion, and C. H. Ammons (1958).
Naylor and Briggs (1961) have reviewed the literature on long-term
retention of learned skills.

Very early in the history of experimental psychology, the warming-
up phenomenon had been noted in connection with work phenomena. As early as 1914, it had been linked to practice situations by
Thorndike (1914). In their study of the warming-up effect, Robinson
and Heron (1924) defined it in the following terms: "Warming-up is a
rise in efficiency which is steeper and more temporary than the rise
which can be seen in, let us say, successive daily performances" (p.
81). Interest in the warming-up phenomenon in relation to problems
of memory was restimulated during the third period by the emphasis
placed upon this concept by Ammons (1947a) and Irion (1948). Adams
(1961b) has reviewed the literature in this area.

Amount of warming-up as a function of the number of times the activity has been resumed can be studied in distribution-of-practice situations by comparing the postrest performance curves that follow successive periods of rest. If the results of Adams (1952) and Barch (1954)
are considered together, it seems probable that the amount of the
warming-up effect, as measured on such successive resumptions of
practice, at first increases and then decreases. Warming-up as a function of length of interpolated rest can be studied in reminiscence experiments that vary length of rest. The results of Jahnke and Duncan
(1956) and Koonce *et al.* (1964) suggest that, as length of rest increases,
the magnitude of the warming-up effect at first increases and then
decreases.

Attempts either to influence the level of initial performance or to reduce the amount of warm-up decrement present in postrest performance by introducing an independent warming-up activity have met with mixed success. Ammons (1951b) failed to obtain any indication of improved initial or postrest performance on the rotor as a result of using any one of several kinds of prepractice activities. Walker, DeSoto, and Shelly (1957) also report negative results. In this investigation, right-handed rotoring failed to serve as an effective warming-up activity for left-handed rotoring. On the other hand, Silver (1952) used the reversed alphabet task and found that postrest performance was facilitated by prerecall warming-up. He found that amount of facilitation increased and then decreased as a function of amount of massed warming-up activity, that the optimum amount of massed warming-up depended upon the amount of prerest practice, and that subjects could tolerate greater amounts of distributed warming-up than massed warming-up. These findings are generally more compatible with results obtained in verbal retention situations, but perhaps this greater compatibility results from the fact that the alphabet printing task more resembles verbal learning situations than it resembles the rotoring situation. Perhaps, and for reasons unknown, it is not possible to reinstate facilitative sets in learning situations that involve small amounts of response selectivity or high amounts of response unavailability, or both.

F. Transfer of Training

An area of research that emerged during the second period and was destined to grow in importance dealt with the problem of transfer of training. The early findings of Thorndike and Woodworth (1901) served as a basis for several early studies of transfer such as those by Pyle (1919), McGinnis (1929), and Crafts (1935). These studies, which were exploratory in character, yielded a finding that was to become discouragingly familiar to later investigators: that it is much easier to produce positive than negative transfer effects in motor-learning situations. During the second period, much of the work on transfer appears to have been influenced by the statement of the Skaggs-Robinson hypothesis (Robinson, 1927), by Bruce's (1933) formulation of the conditions of transfer, and by the growing literature on proactive and retroactive inhibition in the field of verbal learning (reviewed by Britt, 1935). These influences are revealed in the studies that attempted to produce interference effects (Buxton & Henry, 1939; Buxton & Grant, 1939; Buxton, 1940). Attempts to produce retroactive inhibition failed to yield absolute losses although "relative" retroactive inhibition was obtained. In retrospect, a study by Siipola and Israel (1933) appears to have particular value in that it showed amount of interference between two tasks to depend upon the relative amounts of training on each of them.

A somewhat different theoretical background is reflected in the two well-known studies by Hovland and Sears (1938; Sears & Hovland, 1941). These experiments were based on a model of conflict behavior, but they can be considered in the context of classic transfer theory. The studies are especially valuable in that, in addition to measuring "amount of interference," they analyzed the kinds of interference or conflict resolutions that were taking place. Hovland and Sears' conclusion that "the probability of blockage as a reaction to conflict increases with the approach of the strengths of the conflicting responses to equality" is in essential agreement with the earlier, and less analytic, finding of Siipola and Israel (1933).

The third period of research was ushered in by two important papers, Gagné, Foster, and Crowley (1948) on the measurement of transfer and Osgood's (1949) theoretical analysis. The third era was also marked by a massive attack on the transfer problem. In particular, the work of Lewis and his associates deserves to be mentioned. A very few, representative, studies from this series are cited. Lewis, McAllister, and Adams (1951) used a conventional retroactive inhibition design to study the effects of differing amounts of original training on proactive and retroactive inhibition in the Mashburn Apparatus situation. They found that original learning exerts both facilitating and interfering effects upon the learning of the reversed (interpolated) learning task, although the amounts of these effects did not appear to be closely related to the amount of original learning. Conspicuous amounts of retroactive inhibition were obtained during the early phases of relearning. A second study, McAllister and Lewis (1951) varied the amount of interpolated learning. Again, retroactive inhibition effects were obtained, amount of inhibition being related to the number of trials of interpolated learning. Somewhat similar findings were reported by Lewis, Smith, and McAllister (1952) for the Two-Hand Coordinator situation.

Despite these findings, and others like them, it would appear that the research in interference effects in skills situations has not been productive of very much interference. Except under very carefully controlled and arranged conditions, positive transfer appears to be much more likely to occur than negative transfer. Even when optimum conditions for the production of interference are arranged, the negative transfer effects seem to be somewhat weak, quite transitory, and very apt to shift to facilitation during relearning. Sometimes, as in Duncan's (1953) experiment, conditions that might have been expected to yield negative transfer (on the basis of the analogy with verbal-learning situations) have yielded positive transfer, instead. Massive and persistent negative transfer effects do not seem to be obtainable, probably for the reason that the subject is learning the same things in the tasks that are supposed to interfere with each other. A pair of correlational studies by Lewis, McAllister, and Bechtoldt (1953a,b) supports the notion that subjects may be learning the same structure of skills in both the original learning and interpolated learning practice sessions. Their findings are relevant to an observation made by Woodrow (1938b) to the effect that, if two practice situations have a common factor in their gain scores, practice in one should result in positive transfer to the other.

In short, interference and negative transfer effects are difficult to produce in skills situations. Those who favor an interference theory of forgetting can take some meager comfort from the fact that motor skills seem to be impervious to both interference *and* forgetting.

A second approach to the problem of transfer represents an extension of work on the old whole-part problem. At the beginning of the third period of our history, Gagné and his associates performed a series of studies concerned with transfer from training on components to performance on the whole task. They also studied the effects of verbal and other kinds of pretraining upon the whole task performance (Gagné & Foster, 1949a,b; Gagné, Baker, & Foster, 1950; Baker & Wylie, 1950). These investigations generally yielded positive transfer effects. Moreover, the Gagné, Baker, and Foster experiment suggests that, at least as far as pretraining in stimulus discrimination is concerned, pretraining on the more difficult of two useful discriminations produces the greatest amount of positive transfer. In a somewhat more advanced approach to the whole-part problem, rules concerning the combination of component activities in predicting performance on the whole activity have been sought. For example, following Ellson's (1947) demonstration of the practical independence of component performances on the Pedestal Sight Manipulation Test, E. A. Bilodeau and Bilodeau (1954) were able to predict total task means and variances for this test from the use of two components and, using the Stevens Pursuitmeter device, they were able to predict total task means and variances using three scores of component performance. In this study, and in the studies of E. A. Bilodeau (1955a, 1957b), the rule of multiplicative proportions was found to hold approximately true, with the implication that the assumption of independence of component performances is supportable. The first of these studies also indicated that component performances can be independently manipulated, and that total performance, following the multiplicative rule, can be modified accordingly. There results the general hypothesis that, in any complex motor task in which two (or more) component responses must be made simultaneously, total performance may be drastically improved by an increase in the proficiency of the subject on the poorer component, even though that increase may be at the expense of the better component.[9]

III. Conclusion

In most areas of psychology, investigation reveals that, in any given historical period, a few authors and a few laboratories tend to dominate the field. This phenomenon is very apparent in the realm of motor skills. As in most fields of research, when number of authors is plotted against number of papers per author, a **J**-curve is obtained which symbolizes the fact that most authors are extremely unproductive while an exceedingly few people are very productive. Nearly half of the contributors to the skills literature have been the co-author of one paper only. About one experimenter in a hundred has contributed as many as 20 papers to the literature, and an author who has written more than three papers is in the top 10 % on the scale of productivity. It may be that this distribution of productivity results from the fact that some research workers tend to scatter their efforts over a number of fields while others tend to concentrate in one area. However, since the same general curve seems to be obtained for contributors in other fields and, especially, since contributors to the *Journal of Experimen-*

---

[9]A somewhat different kind of combination rule has been proposed by E. A. Bilodeau (1957a) in connection with the prediction of performance in a two-handed tracking task from the performances on similar one-handed tasks. Here, prediction was made in terms of the one-handed scores weighted in terms of the contributions made by each hand to the total performance:

$$t_{R,L} = at_R + (1-a)t_L$$

where t_R and t_L are the times for traversal using the right and left hands (measured separately) and a and $(1-a)$ represent the input proportions of the right and left hands on the total task. Bilodeau suggests that, with highly practiced subjects, "the time for two-hand performance is equal to the larger term of the equation since prediction can be made on the data from a single hand. Such subjects are said to be coordinated because the time of the hand taking the shorter time is completely distributed over the time of the hand taking the longer time." This work has been extended by E. A. Bilodeau and Ryan (1961).

tal Psychology (regardless of field) are distributed in the same way, it would seem more likely that the **J**-curve reflects a basic fact concerning the productivity of experimental psychologists.

A few concluding remarks should be made concerning the systematic predilections of those who have worked in the field of motor skills. Through the years, this group has been remarkable for its homogeneity of systematic viewpoint and, since 1945, for the similarity of the ages and backgrounds of its members. Earlier workers in the skills field were mostly quantitatively minded functionalists. During more recent times, they have been behaviorists. This is not to say that a variety of theoretical viewpoints have not been represented. It is to say that there has been very little controversy concerning ultimate aims and purposes. The earlier work is remarkably free from the methods and strictures of structuralism. In later years, the intrusions of Gestalt theory have been so infrequent as to make each instance remarkable. There appears to be no example of psychoanalytically oriented research in the skills literature, and it is difficult even to conceive of the role an existentialist might play in the psychomotor laboratory. Homogeneity of viewpoint can, without doubt, be a curse as well as a blessing, and it is not within the province of this chapter to speculate about the kinds of work that might have been accomplished under different systematic leadership, but history must record that those who have worked in the skills field have been behaviorists.

References

Adams, J. A. Warm-up decrement in performance on the pursuit-rotor. *American Journal of Psychology*, 1952, **65**, 404–414.

Adams, J. A. The prediction of performance at advanced stages of training on a complex psychomotor task. *USAF Human Resources Research Center, Research Bulletin*, 1953, No. 53-49.

Adams, J. A. A source of decrement in psychomotor performance. *Journal of Experimental Psychology*, 1955, **49**, 390–394.

Adams, J. A. The relationship between certain measures of ability and the acquisition of a psychomotor criterion response. *Journal of General Psychology*, 1957, **56**, 121–134.

Adams, J. A. Human tracking behavior. *Psychological Bulletin*, 1961, **58**, 55–79. (a)

Adams, J. A. The second facet of forgetting: A review of warm-up decrement. *Psychological Bulletin*, 1961, **58**, 257–273. (b)

Adams, J. A. Test of the hypothesis of psychological refractory period. *Journal of Experimental Psychology*, 1962, **64**, 280–287.

Adams, J. A. Motor skills. *Annual Review of Psychology*, 1964, **15**, 181–202.

Adams, J. A., & Hufford, L. E. Contributions of a part-task trainer to the learning and relearning of a time-shared flight maneuver. *Human Factors*, 1962, **4**, 159–170.

Adams, J. A., & Reynolds, B. Effect of shift in distribution of practice conditions following interpolated rest. *Journal of Experimental Psychology*, 1954, **47**, 32–36.

Ammons, R. B. Acquisition of motor skill: I. Quantitative analysis and theoretical formulation. *Psychological Review*, 1947, **54**, 263–281. (a)

Ammons, R. B. Acquisition of motor skill: II. Rotary pursuit performance with continuous practice before and after a single rest. *Journal of Experimental Psychology*, 1947, **37**, 393–411. (b)

Ammons, R. B. Effect of distribution of practice on rotary pursuit "hits." *Journal of Experimental Psychology*, 1951,**41**, 17–22. (a)

Ammons, R. B. Effects of pre-practice activities on rotary pursuit performance. *Journal of Experimental Psychology*, 1951, **41**, 187–191.(b)

Ammons, R. B. Effects of knowledge of performance: A survey and tentative theoretical formulation. *Journal of General Psychology*, 1956, **54**, 279–299.

Ammons, R. B. "Le mouvement." In G. S. Seward & J. P. Seward (Eds.), *Current psychological issues: Essays in honor of Robert S. Woodworth*. New York: Holt, 1958. Pp. 146-183.

Ammons, R. B., Farr, R. G., Bloch, E., Neumann, E., Dey, M., Marion, R., & Ammons, C. H. Long-term retention of perceptual-motor skills. *Journal of Experimental Psychology*, 1958, **55**, 318–328.

Ammons, R. B., & Willig, L. Acquisition of motor skill: IV. Effects of repeated periods of massed practice. *Journal of Experimental Psychology*, 1956, **51**, 118–126.

Annett, J., & Kay, H. 'Skilled performance.' *Occupational Psychology*, 1956, **30**, 112-117.

Archer, E. J. Effect of distribution of practice on a component skill of rotary pursuit tracking. *Journal of Experimental Psychology*, 1958, **56**, 427–436.

Attneave, F. *Applications of information theory to psychology*. New York: Holt, 1959.

Bahrick, H. P. An analysis of stimulus variables influencing the proprioceptive control of movements. *Psychological Review*, 1957, **64**, 324–328.

Bahrick, H. P., Fitts, P. M., & Briggs, G. E. Learning curves — facts or artifacts? *Psychological Bulletin*, 1957, **54**, 256–268.

Baker, K. E., & Wylie, R. C. Transfer of verbal training to a motor task. *Journal of Experimental Psychology*, 1950, **40**, 632–638.

Barch, A. M. Warm-up in massed and distributed pursuit rotor performance. *Journal of Experimental Psychology*, 1954, **47**, 357–361.

Battig, W. F., Nagel, E. H., Voss, J. F., & Brogden, W. J. Transfer and retention of bidimensional compensatory tracking after extended practice. *American Journal of Psychology*, 1957, **70**, 75–80.

Bell, H. M. Rest pauses in motor learning as related to Snoddy's hypothesis of mental growth. *Psychological Monographs*, 1942, **54**, No. 1 (Whole No. 243).

Bell, H. M. Retention of pursuit rotor skill after one year. *Journal of Experimental Psychology*, 1950, **40**, 648–649.

Bilodeau, E. A. Decrements and recovery from decrements in a simple work task with variation in force requirements at different stages of practice. *Journal of Experimental Psychology*, 1952, **44**, 96–100. (a)

Bilodeau, E. A. Massing and spacing phenomena as functions of prolonged and extended practice. *Journal of Experimental Psychology*, 1952, **44**, 108–113. (b)

Bilodeau, E. A. Speed of acquiring a simple motor response as a function of the systematic transformation of knowledge of results. *American Journal of Psychology*, 1953, **66**, 409-420.

Bilodeau, E. A. Accuracy of response as a function of target width. *Journal of Experimental Psychology*, 1954,**47**, 201–207. (a)

Bilodeau, E. A. Rate recovery in a repetitive motor task as a function of successive rest periods. *Journal of Experimental Psychology*, 1954, **48**, 197–203. (b)

Bilodeau, E. A. Variations in knowledge of component performance and its effects upon part-part and part-whole relations. *Journal of Experimental Psychology*, 1955, **50**, 215–224.(a)

Bilodeau, E. A. Motor performance as affected by magnitude of error contained in knowledge of results. *Journal of Psychology*, 1955, **40**, 103–113. (b)

Bilodeau, E. A. Studies of target size and the control of psychomotor behavior through systematic transformation of knowledge of results. In G. Finch & F. Cameron (Eds.), *Symposium on Air Force human engineering, personnel and training research*. Publ. No. 445. Washington, D.C.: National Academy of Sciences–National Research Council, 1956. Pp. 17–24.

Bilodeau, E. A. The relationship between a relatively complex motor skill and its components. *American Journal of Psychology*, 1957, **70**, 49–55. (a)

Bilodeau, E. A. Patterns of internal consistency in multipart skilled performances. *American Journal of Psychology*, 1957, **70**, 550–559. (b)

Bilodeau, E. A. (Ed.) *Acquisition of skill*. New York: Academic Press, 1966.

Bilodeau, E. A., & Bilodeau, I. McD. The contribution of component activities to the total psychomotor task. *Journal of Experimental Psychology*, 1954, **47**, 37–46.

Bilodeau, E. A., & Bilodeau, I. McD. Variable frequency of knowledge of results and the learning of a simple skill. *Journal of Experimental Psychology*, 1958, **55**, 379–383. (a)

Bilodeau, E. A., & Bilodeau, I. McD. Variation of temporal intervals among critical events in five studies of knowledge of results. *Journal of Experimental Psychology*, 1958, **55**, 603–612. (b)

Bilodeau, E. A., & Bilodeau, I. McD. Motor-skills learning. *Annual Review of Psychology*, 1961, **12**, 243–280.

Bilodeau, E. A., & Ryan, F. J. Prediction of complex task proficiency by means of component responses. *Perceptual and Motor Skills*, 1961, **12**, 299–306.

Bilodeau, E. A., Sulzer, J. L., & Levy, C. M. Theory and data on the interrelationships of three factors of memory. *Psychological Monographs*, 1962, **76**, No. 20 (Whole No. 539).

Bilodeau, I. McD. Accuracy of a simple positioning response with variation in the number of trials by which knowledge of results is delayed. *American Journal of Psychology*, 1956, **69**, 434–437.

Bilodeau, I. McD. Information feedback. In E. A. Bilodeau (Ed.), *Acquisition of skill*. New York: Academic Press, 1966. Pp. 255–296.

Bourne, L. E., Jr., & Archer, E. J. Time continuously on target as a function of distribution of practice. *Journal of Experimental Psychology*, 1956, **51**, 25–33.

Britt, S. H. Retroactive inhibition: A review of the literature. *Psychological Bulletin*, 1935, **32**, 381–440.

Brown, J. S. A proposed program of research on psychological feedback (knowledge of results) in the performance of psychomotor tasks. In *Research Planning Conference on Perceptual and Motor Skills*. San Antonio, Texas: Human Resources Research Center, Lackland Air Force Base, 1949. (Conference Report 49-2.)

Bruce, R. W. Conditions of transfer of training. *Journal of Experimental Psychology*, 1933, **16**, 343–361.

Bryan, W. L. On the development of voluntary motor ability. *American Journal of Psychology*, 1892, **5**, 125–204.

Bryan, W. L., & Harter, N. Studies in the physiology and psychology of the telegraphic language. *Psychological Review*, 1897, **4**, 27–53.

Bryan, W. L., & Harter, N. Studies on the telegraphic language: The acquisition of a hierarchy of habits. *Psychological Review*, 1899, **6**, 345-375.

Buxton, C. E. Retroaction and gains in motor learning: III. Evaluation of results. *Journal of General Psychology*, 1940, **22**, 309-320.

Buxton, C. E. Reminiscence in the acquisition of skill. *Psychological Review*, 1942, **49**, 191-196.

Buxton, C. E., & Grant, D. A. Retroaction and gains in motor learning: II. Sex differences, and a further analysis of gains. *Journal of Experimental Psychology*, 1939, **25**, 198-208.

Buxton, C. E., & Henry, C. E. Retroaction and gains in motor learning: I. Similarity of interpolated task as a factor in gains. *Journal of Experimental Psychology*, 1939, **25**, 1-17.

Chase, R. A., Harvey, S., Standfast, S., Rapin, I., & Sutton, S. Studies on sensory feedback: I. Effect of delayed auditory feedback on speech and keytapping. *Quarterly Journal of Experimental Psychology*, 1961, **13**, 141-152. (a)

Chase, R. A., Rapin, I., Gilden, L., Sutton, S., & Guilfoyle, G. Studies on sensory feedback: II. Sensory feedback influences on keytapping motor tasks. *Quarterly Journal of Experimental Psychology*, 1961, **13**, 153-167. (b)

Conklin, J. E. Effect of control lag on performance in a tracking task. *Journal of Experimental Psychology*, 1957, **53**, 261-268.

Conklin, J. E. Linearity of the tracking performance function. *Perceptual and Motor Skills*, 1959, **9**, 387-391.

Courts, F. Relations between muscular tension and performance. *Psychological Bulletin*, 1942, **39**, 347-368.

Crafts, L. W. Whole and part methods with unrelated reactions. *American Journal of Psychology*, 1930, **42**, 591-601.

Crafts, L. W. Transfer as related to number of common elements. *Journal of General Psychology*, 1935, **13**, 147-158.

Digman, J. M. Performance under optimal practice conditions following three degrees of massing of early practice. *Journal of Experimental Psychology*, 1956, **52**, 189-193.

Digman, J. M. Growth of a motor skill as a function of distribution of practice. *Journal of Experimental Psychology*, 1959, **57**, 310-316.

Doré, L. R., & Hilgard, E. R. Spaced practice and the maturation hypothesis. *Journal of Psychology*, 1937, **4**, 245-259.

Doré, L. R., & Hilgard, E. R. Spaced practice as a test of Snoddy's two processes in mental growth. *Journal of Experimental Psychology*, 1938, **23**, 359-374.

Dresslar, F. B. Some influences which affect the rapidity of voluntary movements. *American Journal of Psychology*, 1891-1892, **4**, 514-527.

Duncan, C. P. Transfer in motor learning as a function of degree of first-task learning and inter-task similarity. *Journal of Experimental Psychology*, 1953, **45**, 1-11.

Duncan, C. P. On the similarity between reactive inhibition and neural satiation. *American Journal of Psychology*, 1956, **69**, 227-235.

Ellson, D. G. The independence of tracking in two and three dimensions with the G. E. Pedestal Sight. In G. Finch (Ed.), *Memorandum report*. TSEAA-694-2G. AAF Air Materiel Command, Engineering Division, 1947.

Eysenck, H. J. A three-factor theory of reminiscence. *British Journal of Psychology*, 1965, **56**, 163-181.

Eysenck, H. J., & Maxwell, A. E. Reminiscence as a function of drive. *British Journal of Psychology*, 1961, **52**, 43-52.

Eysenck, H. J., & Willett, R. A. The measurement of motivation through the use of objective indices. *Journal of Mental Science,* 1961, **107,** 961–968.

Eysenck. S. B. G. Retention of a well-developed motor skill after one year. *Journal of General Psychology,* 1960, **63,** 267–273.

Fairbanks, G. Selective vocal effects of delayed auditory feedback. *Journal of Speech and Hearing Disorders,* 1955, **20,** 333–345.

Fitts, P. M. Engineering psychology and equipment design. In S. S. Stevens (Ed.), *Handbook of experimental psychology.* New York: Wiley, 1951. Pp. 1287–1340.

Fitts, P. M. Engineering psychology. *Annual Review of Psychology,* 1958, **9,** 267–294.

Fitts, P. M. Perceptual-motor skill learning. In A. W. Melton (Ed.), *Categories of human learning.* New York: Academic Press, 1964. Pp. 243–285.

Fleishman, E. A. Predicting advanced levels of proficiency in psychomotor skills. In G. Finch & F. Cameron (Eds.), *Symposium on Air Force human engineering, personnel and training research.* Publ. No. 445. Washington, D.C.: National Academy of Sciences-National Research Council, 1956.

Fleishman, E. A., & Hempel, W. E., Jr. Changes in factor structure of a complex psychomotor test as a function of practice. *Psychometrika,* 1954, **19,** 239–252.

Fleishman, E. A., & Hempel, W. E., Jr. The relation between abilities and improvement with practice in a visual discrimination reaction task. *Journal of Experimental Psychology,* 1955, **49,** 301–312.

Freeman, F. N., & Abernethy, E. M. Comparative retention of typewriting and of substitution with analogous material. *Journal of Educational Psychology,* 1930, **21,** 639–647.

Freeman, F. N., & Abernethy, E. M. New evidence of the superior retention of typewriting to that of substitution. *Journal of Educational Psychology,* 1932, **23,** 331–334.

Gagné, R. M., Baker, K. E., & Foster, H. Transfer of discrimination training to a motor task. *Journal of Experimental Psychology,* 1950, **40,** 314–328.

Gagné, R. M., & Foster, H. Transfer of training from practice on components in a motor skill. *Journal of Experimental Psychology,* 1949, **39,** 47–68. (a)

Gagné, R. M., & Foster, H. Transfer to a motor skill from practice on a pictured representation. *Journal of Experimental Psychology,* 1949, **39,** 342–354. (b)

Gagné, R. M., Foster, H., & Crowley, M. E. The measurement of transfer of training. *Psychological Bulletin,* 1948, **45,** 97–130.

Garvey, W. D., Sweeney, J. S., & Birmingham, H. P. Differential effects of "display lags" and "control lags" on the performance of manual tracking systems. *Journal of Experimental Psychology,* 1958, **56,** 8–10.

Grice, G. R., & Reynolds, B. Effect of varying amounts of rest on conventional and bilateral transfer "reminiscence." *Journal of Experimental Psychology,* 1952, **44,** 247–252.

Hilgard, E. R., & Smith, M. B. Distributed practice in motor learning: Score changes within and between daily sessions. *Journal of Experimental Psychology,* 1942, **30,** 136–146.

Hovland, C. I., & Sears, R. R. Experiments on motor conflict: I. Types of conflict and their modes of resolution. *Journal of Experimental Psychology,* 1938, **23,** 477–493.

Hull, C. L. *Principles of behavior.* New York: Appleton-Century, 1943.

Humphreys, L. G. The factor of time in pursuit rotor learning. *Journal of Psychology,* 1937, **3,** 429–436.

Irion, A. L. The relation of 'set' to retention. *Psychological Review,* 1948, **55,** 336–341.

Irion, A. L. Reminiscence in pursuit-rotor learning as a function of length of rest and of amount of pre-rest practice. *Journal of Experimental Psychology*, 1949, **39**, 492–499.

Irion, A. L. A brief history of research on the acquisition of skill. In E. A. Bilodeau (Ed.), *Acquisition of skill*. New York: Academic Press, 1966. Pp. 1–46.

Irion, A. L., & Gustafson, L. M. "Reminiscence" in bilateral transfer. *Journal of Experimental Psychology*, 1952, **43**, 321–323.

Jahnke, J. C. Retention in motor learning as a function of amount of practice and rest. *Journal of Experimental Psychology*, 1958, **55**, 270–273.

Jahnke, J. C. Postrest motor learning performance as a function of degree of learning. *Journal of Experimental Psychology*, 1961, **62**, 605–611.

Jahnke, J. C., & Duncan, C. P. Reminiscence and forgetting in motor learning after extended rest intervals. *Journal of Experimental Psychology*, 1956, **52**, 273–282.

Jones, E. I., & Bilodeau, E. A. Retention and relearning of a complex perceptual-motor skill after 10 months of no practice. *USAF Human Resources Center Research Bulletin*, 1953, No. 53-17.

Jones, M. B. Simplex theory. *USN SAM Monograph*, 1959, No. 3.

Jones, M. B. Molar correlational analysis. *USN SAM Monograph*, 1960, No. 4.

Jones, M. B. Practice as a process of simplification. *Psychological Review*, 1962, **69**, 274–294.

Jones, M. B. Individual differences. In E. A. Bilodeau (Ed.), *Acquisition of skill*. New York: Academic Press, 1966. Pp. 109–146.

Kientzle, M. J. Properties of learning curves under varied distributions of practice. *Journal of Experimental Psychology*, 1946, **36**, 187–211.

Kientzle, M. J. Ability patterns under distributed practice. *Journal of Experimental Psychology*, 1949, **39**, 532–537.

Kimble, G. A. An experimental test of a two-factor theory of inhibition. *Journal of Experimental Psychology*, 1949, **39**, 15–23.

Kimble, G. A. Transfer of work inhibition in motor learning. *Journal of Experimental Psychology*, 1952, **43**, 391–392.

Kimble, G. A., & Horenstein, B. R. Reminiscence in motor learning as a function of length of interpolated rest. *Journal of Experimental Psychology*, 1948, **38**, 239–244.

Köhler, W., & Fishback, J. The destruction of the Müller-Lyer illusion in repeated trials: II. Satiation patterns and memory traces. *Journal of Experimental Psychology*, 1950, **40**, 398–410.

Koonce, J. M., Chambliss, D. J., & Irion, A. L. Supplementary report: Long-term reminiscence in the pursuit-rotor habit. *Journal of Experimental Psychology*, 1964, **67**, 498–500.

Leavitt, H. J., & Schlosberg, H. The retention of verbal and of motor skills. *Journal of Experimental Psychology*, 1944, **34**, 404–417.

Lewis, D., McAllister, D. E., & Adams, J. A. Facilitation and interference in performance on the Modified Mashburn Apparatus: I. The effects of varying the amount of original learning. *Journal of Experimental Psychology*, 1951, **41**, 247–260.

Lewis, D., McAllister, D. E., & Bechtoldt, H. P. Correlational analysis of the learning and relearning of four different tasks on the Modified Mashburn Apparatus. *Journal of Psychology*, 1953, **36**, 83–109. (a)

Lewis, D., McAllister, D. E., & Bechtoldt, H. P. Correlational study of performance during successive phases of practice on the standard and reversed tasks on the SAM Complex Coordinator. *Journal of Psychology*, 1953, **36**, 111–126. (b)

Lewis, D., Smith, P. N., & McAllister, D. E. Retroactive facilitation and interference in performance on the Modified Two-Hand Coordinator. *Journal of Experimental Psychology*, 1952, **44**, 44–50.

Lorge, I., & Thorndike, E. L. The influence of delay in the after-effect of a connection. *Journal of Experimental Psychology*, 1935, **18**, 186–194.

Lyon, D. O. The relation of length of material to time taken for learning and the optimum distribution of time. *Journal of Educational Psychology,* 1914, **5,** 1–9, 85–91, 155–163.

McAllister, D. E., & Lewis, D. Facilitation and interference in performance on the Modified Mashburn Apparatus: II. The effects of varying the amount of interpolated learning. *Journal of Experimental Psychology,* 1951, **41,** 356–363.

McGeoch, J. A. The acquisition of skill. *Psychological Bulletin,* 1927, **24,** 437–466.

McGeoch, J. A. The comparative retention values of a maze habit, of nonsense syllables, and of rational learning. *Journal of Experimental Psychology,* 1932, **15,** 662–680.

McGeoch, J. A., & Irion, A. L. *The psychology of human learning.* (2nd Ed.) New York: Longmans, Green, 1952.

McGeoch, J. A., & Melton, A. W. The comparative retention values of maze habits and of nonsense syllables. *Journal of Experimental Psychology,* 1929, **12,** 392–414.

McGinnis, E. The acquisition and interference of motor habits in young children. *Genetic Psychology Monographs,* 1929, **6,** 203–311.

Melton, A. W. (Ed.) *Apparatus tests.* Washington, D.C.: U. S. Govt. Printing Office, 1947. (AAF Aviation Psychology Program Research Report No. 4.) (a)

Melton, A. W. (Ed.) *Apparatus tests (supplement).* Washington, D.C.: U. S. Govt. Printing Office, 1947. (AAF Aviation Psychology Program Research Report No. 4, Supplement.) (b)

Melton, A. W. (Ed.) *Categories of human learning.* New York: Academic Press, 1964.

Melton, A. W., & Briggs, G. E. Engineering psychology. *Annual Review of Psychology,* 1960, **11,** 71–98.

Meyer, D. R. On the interaction of simultaneous responses. *Psychological Bulletin,* 1953, **50,** 204–220.

Müller, G. E., & Pilzecker, A. Experimentelle Beiträge zur Lehre vom Gedächtniss. *Zeitschrift für Psychologie,* 1900, vol. 1.

Naylor, J. C., & Briggs, G. E. Long-term retention of learned skills: A review of the literature. *USAF ASD Technical Report,* 1961, No. 61-390.

Noble, C. E. The learning of psychomotor skills. *Annual Review of Psychology,* 1968, **19,** (in press).

Noble, C. E., & Alcock, W. T. Human delayed-reward learning with different lengths of task. *Journal of Experimental Psychology,* 1958, **56,** 407–412.

Noble, C. E., & Broussard, I. G. Effects of complex transformations of feedback upon simple instrumental behavior. *Journal of Experimental Psychology,* 1955, **50,** 381–386.

Osgood, C. E. The similarity paradox in human learning: A resolution. *Psychological Review,* 1949, **56,** 132–143.

Parker, J. F., Jr., & Fleishman, E. A. Use of analytical information concerning task requirements to increase the effectiveness of skill training. *Journal of Applied Psychology,* 1961, **45,** 295–302.

Payne, B. Does the cumulative mean measure 'primary growth'? *Journal of Experimental Psychology,* 1942, **30,** 512–514.

Perl, R. E. An application of Thurstone's method of factor analysis to practice series. *Journal of General Psychology,* 1934, **11,** 209–212.

Poulton, E. C. On prediction in skilled movements. *Psychological Bulletin,* 1957, **54,** 467–478.

Pyle, W. H. Economical learning. *Journal of Educational Psychology,* 1913, **4,** 148–158.

Pyle, W. H. Concentrated versus distributed practice. *Journal of Educational Psychology,* 1914, **5,** 247–251.

Pyle, W. H. Transfer and interference in card-distributing. *Journal of Educational Psychology,* 1919, **10,** 107–110.

Rachman, S., & Grassi, J. Reminiscence, inhibition and consolidation. *British Journal of Psychology*, 1965, **56**, 157–162.

Renshaw, S., & Schwarzbek, W. C. The dependence of the form of the pursuit-meter learning function on the length of the inter-practice rests: I. Experimental. *Journal of General Psychology*, 1938, **18**, 3–16.

Reynolds, B. The effect of learning on the predictability of psychomotor performance. *Journal of Experimental Psychology*, 1952, **44**, 189–198.

Reynolds, B., & Adams, J. A. Psychomotor performance as a function of initial level of ability. *American Journal of Psychology*, 1954, **67**, 268–277.

Robinson, E. S. The 'similarity' factor in retroaction. *American Journal of Psychology*, 1927, **39**, 297–312.

Robinson, E. S., & Heron, W. T. The warming-up effect. *Journal of Experimental Psychology*, 1924, **7**, 81–97.

Rockway, M. R. Bilateral reminiscence in pursuit-rotor learning as a function of amount of first-hand practice and length of rest. *Journal of Experimental Psychology*, 1953, **46**, 337–344.

Rosenquist, H. S. The visual response component of rotary pursuit tracking. *Perceptual and Motor Skills*, 1965, **21**, 555–560.

Ruch, T. C. Factors influencing the relative economy of massed and distributed practice in learning. *Psychological Review*, 1928, **35**, 19–45.

Ryan, F. J., & Bilodeau, E. A. Countertraining of a simple skill with immediate and 1-week delays of informative feedback. *Journal of Experimental Psychology*, 1962, **63**, 19–22.

Saufley, W. H., Jr., & Bilodeau, I. McD. Protective self-pacing during learning. *Journal of Experimental Psychology*, 1963, **66**, 596–600.

Sears, R. R., & Hovland, C. I. Experiments on motor conflict: II. Determination of mode of resolution by comparative strengths of conflicting responses. *Journal of Experimental Psychology*, 1941, **28**, 280–286.

Siipola, E. M., & Israel, H. E. Habit-interference as dependent upon stage of training. *American Journal of Psychology*, 1933, **45**, 205–227.

Silver, R. J. Effect of amount and distribution of warming-up activity on retention in motor learning. *Journal of Experimental Psychology*, 1952, **44**, 88–95.

Smith, K. U. The geometry of human motion and its neural foundations: I. Perceptual and motor adaptation to displaced vision. *American Journal of Physical Medicine*, 1961, **40**, 71–87.

Smith, K. U. *Delayed sensory feedback and behavior*. Philadelphia: Saunders, 1962.

Smith, K. U. (with Gould, J., & Wargo, L.) Spatial organization of neurobehavioral systems. *American Journal of Physical Medicine*, 1964, **43**, 49–84.

Smith, K. U., & Smith, W. M. *Perception and motion*. Philadelphia: Saunders, 1962.

Smith, K. U., Wargo, L., Jones, R., & Smith, W. M. Delayed and space-displaced sensory feedback and learning. *Perceptual and Motor Skills*, 1963, **16**, 781–796.

Snoddy, G. S. *Evidence for two opposed processes in mental growth*. Lancaster, Penn.: Science Press, 1935.

Starch, D. Periods of work in learning. *Journal of Educational Psychology*, 1912, **3**, 209–213.

Stratton, G. M. Some preliminary experiments on vision without inversion of the retinal image. *Psychological Review*, 1896, **3**, 611–617.

Stratton, G. M. Vision without inversion of the retinal image. *Psychological Review*, 1897, **4**, 341–360.

Taylor, A., & Noble, C. E. Acquisition and extinction phenomena in human trial-and-error learning under different schedules of reinforcing feedback. *Perceptual and Motor Skills*, 1962, **15**, 31–44.

Thorndike, E. L. *Animal intelligence.* New York: Macmillan, 1911.
Thorndike, E. L. *Educational psychology.* New York: Teachers College, Columbia Univer., 1914.
Thorndike, E. L., & Woodworth, R. S. I. The influence of improvement in one mental function upon the efficiency of other functions. II. The estimation of magnitudes. III. Functions involving attention, observation and discrimination. *Psychological Review,* 1901, **8,** 247–261, 384–395, 553–564.
Underwood, B. J. Interference and forgetting. *Psychological Review,* 1957, **64,** 49–60.
Underwood, B. J., & Postman, L. Extraexperimental sources of interference in forgetting. *Psychological Review,* 1960, **67,** 73–95.
Walker, L. C., DeSoto, C. B., & Shelly, M. W. Rest and warm-up in bilateral transfer on a pursuit rotor task. *Journal of Experimental Psychology,* 1957, **53,** 394–398.
Waters, R. H., & Poole, G. B. The relative retention values of stylus and mental maze habits. *Journal of Experimental Psychology,* 1933, **16,** 429–434.
Wheeler, R. H., & Perkins, F. T. *Principles of mental development.* New York: Crowell, 1932.
Whipple, G. M. *Manual of mental and physical tests.* Baltimore: Warwick & York, 1910.
Wolfle, D. Training. In S. S. Stevens (Ed.), *Handbook of experimental psychology.* New York: Wiley, 1951. Pp. 1267–1286.
Woodrow, H. The relation between abilities and improvement with practice. *Journal of Educational Psychology,* 1938, **29,** 215–230. (a)
Woodrow, H. The effect of practice on groups of different initial ability. *Journal of Educational Psychology,* 1938, **29,** 268–278. (b)
Woodrow, H. The effect of practice on test intercorrelations. *Journal of Educational Psychology,* 1938, **29,** 561–572. (c)
Woodrow, H. Factors in improvement with practice. *Journal of Psychology,* 1939, **7,** 55–70. (a)
Woodrow, H. The relation of verbal ability to improvement with practice in verbal tests. *Journal of Educational Psychology,* 1939, **30,** 179–186. (b)
Woodrow, H. Interrelations of measures of learning. *Journal of Psychology,* 1940, **10,** 49–73.
Woodrow, H. The ability to learn. *Psychological Review,* 1946, **53,** 147–158.
Woodworth, R. S. The accuracy of voluntary movement. *Psychological Review,* 1899 (Monograph Suppl., Whole No. 13).
Woodworth, R. S. *Le mouvement.* Paris: Doin, 1903.
Zeaman, D., & Kaufman, H. Individual differences and theory in a motor learning task. *Psychological Monographs,* 1955, **69,** No. 6 (Whole No. 391).

CHAPTER 2

The Development of Motor Skills From Birth to Adolescence[1]

HARRY KAY
University of Sheffield

This chapter has three aims: (1) to present briefly an orientation to the study of psychomotor skills and to say why developmental studies have so much to contribute; (2) to examine what has been accomplished in the developmental field; and (3) to indicate future needs in this area.

I. Orientation to the Study of Skills

Homo sapiens has perhaps inevitably always given greatest weight to those studies of himself where he stores and utilizes information. Here was man's unique ability, his manipulation of symbols, his mastery over the limitations of his immediate temporal-spatial environment. By contrast he shares his motor abilities with other animal species who are often superior to him. The psychologists should not be surprised to find that the study of skills has been relegated to a secondary position where it has generally been considered within the

[1]The writer wishes to acknowledge the support of the Spastics Society, London, for work in the Department of Psychology at Sheffield. He is particularly indebted to his colleague, Mr. Kevin Connolly, for his invaluable help, and to Miss Susan Stuart-Harris.

framework of other psychological theories, notably learning theory (Irion, 1966).

For the writer, brought up in the Cambridge (England) orientation to the study of skills, the approach has always been different. Skills did not come in by the back door. They were an essential part of our psychological thinking (Bartlett, 1948). Many of the characteristics of skills hold over a wide range of human performance such as perceptual-motor tasks, gross bodily movements, fine manipulations, speech production, problem solving, and the like. These activities were examined as examples of how man processes information and the necessary problems which he faces because of the system that his senses, muscular, and central nervous system constitute. For example, the receptor and effector system is so organized that the serial ordering of events is one of its main features. This problem is much the same whether we consider it in terms of muscular control requiring temporal coordination as in a simple grasp response, or the obvious sequential ordering required in everyday speech. Where man is able to program a series of events which he is able to execute with the minimum reference to external criteria he achieves an astonishing degree of speed and coordination, as in skills such as piano playing, singing, or simultaneously running and throwing. The skilled performance exhibits on the one hand a more and more efficient execution of its specific motor responses and on the other a greater flexibility in meeting the contingencies that do occur. It is one of the features of a biological machine that when properly trained and practiced its performance is improved both on repetitive tasks and on variations upon them. The significance of this may lie in the argument that no two responses are exactly identical. Certainly, the skilled games player is adept at producing those responses which aim to be repetitive and also at varying them to meet new conditions. Equally, in the verbal field the well-practiced A, B, C is easily manipulated into its reversal C, B, A; that is much easier to reverse than some middle letters of the alphabet such as P, Q, R.

In contrast to the smooth and rapid execution of a serially organized task is the halting and intermittent responses that man makes when his performance is controlled by external signals of uncertain origin. We are familiar enough with the inevitable reaction-time delays as a response is initiated to a signal and this delay is increased where independent signals occur closely together (Welford, 1960). The "stop-go" nature of this type of performance brings out why it is necessary to anticipate signals if performance is to be smooth and rapid. A system with a built-in temporal delay of the order of a reaction time has to circumvent its limitations by learning the probability of signals and presetting its responses accordingly.

The marked restriction both in initiating responses to discrete external signals and in maintaining a complex, serially organized task is in the amount of information which the system can handle. Here again the characteristics of skills are those of auditory or visual perception or cognitive activities. Variables such as discriminability of signal (Crossman, 1955), compatibility between signal and response (Leonard, 1959), the amount of practice at a task (Mowbray & Rhoades, 1959) will further influence response time; but in the main motor performance in both the reaction-time type of task and the ongoing continuous skill is determined primarily by the uncertainty (information) of signals. Where the signals arise from an external source, as in reaction-time studies, their uncertainty can be specified and the rate at which the operator is transmitting information calculated directly. Where the signals arise from internal sources, as the operator monitors his performance, then the rate has to be inferred from such sources as the speed of movement or the accuracy of the responses (Fitts, 1954). The picture that emerges is the subtle way in which the organism learns to cope with an otherwise unmanageable flood of information. When a series of signals is known they may either be disregarded, or monitored at such a level that they require the minimum channel capacity, leaving the remainder of the system free to cope with the mainstream of information. The significance of this for our present subject will be appreciated if we consider that it would not be possible, for example, to sit on a chair and write a letter at one and the same time if full attention were being given to all the signals from the vestibular system in order to balance oneself on the chair—this a very young child has to do.

The present approach, then, argues that skills in their own right are far more likely to reveal some of the secrets of the adaptive mechanism of a biological system than many of the more frequently studied learning situations in other contexts, and that work in this field has already contributed in a fresh and insightful way to our understanding of many human activities. But there is one obvious weakness in the approach of the psychologist who is interested in the acquisition of skills. For practical reasons he has been concerned with adult performance where he has excellent examples of complex skills, sometimes being conducted under adverse conditions of fatigue or climate. Much of adult life is spent in carrying out such skills, often in an apparently confusing simultaneity. We walk and talk; we run and kick a ball; we watch and listen. These constantly practiced skills have come to require the minimum of attention. By the time the adult is asked to acquire a new skill he has built up such a complexity of subskills that any new act is inevitably attempted as a part of an existing routine. It is even difficult for an adult to make a random movement with his foot or hand, for when he does not think about it he carries out some easily predictable response such as a salute or hand signal. With an adult we rarely witness the learning of a new skill *ab initio*; rather we have the putting together of practiced sequences into a new totality. For example, if a man were asked to learn to thread a needle quickly much of the hand-eye coordination, the visual judgment of depth, the maintenance of a steady posture both of body and of limb have all been practiced throughout life. The acquisition of skill in adult life is the regrouping of constituent responses. This is not necessarily to be underrated—the same single notes still produce a different melody when their serial ordering is changed. Nevertheless the constituent parts of many adult skills are relatively large units and maintain their individual characteristics. We observe this in the style of games players which is remarkably consistent over a number of games.

If this general argument is as true as we think it is, then it would follow that one of the focal points where we should gain insight into skilled performance would be where the initial responses were being learned. The study of the deterioration of skills has certainly given the psychologist a deeper understanding of their nature and the argument for a study of their earliest acquisition seems, if anything, more soundly based. It has been left to the developmental psychologist to contribute to this field and his interests have necessarily differed from those of the human engineers and experimental psychologists. This chapter is a contribution toward bringing the two together in the belief that each has much to offer toward an understanding of how skills are acquired and maintained.

II. Developmental Studies

When we compare the motor performance of a 2-year-old child, who is able to walk quickly and with confidence, against the relative immobility of the neonate, the considerable progress that has taken place seems obvious enough. But appearance may be misleading so let us examine how this has come about and what exactly has been acquired. We will begin at what is taken to be the beginning—birth—even if it is only to find that this is misleading.

A. THE NEWBORN

The newborn is not so immobile as we might think. Life started before birth and development has taken place continuously *in utero*. For the baby, birth is that event in the course of his development where he changes the relative stability of the uterus to face the greater variability of the external environment. The motor activity of the neonate is a continuation of the movements of the fetus which are largely reflexes to tactile stimulation. But some of these are surprisingly complex and might appear to represent further advances in motor responses. For example, consider the primary or automatic walking of the neonate at a time when the cerebral hemispheres are not controlling it. If the trunk of a baby several months old is held by the examiner's hands so that the baby's feet touch the ground both legs will be immediately pulled up. But the neonate reacts differently. "Both legs are extended, and by simultaneous contraction of the flexors and extensors they become rigid supports more or less capable of carrying the body" (Peiper, 1963). The standing baby will flex one leg at the knee and if the trunk is kept slightly forward he will place one foot down in front of the other and then make the same movement with the other foot or leg. Thus, even at this surprisingly early stage we see regular and coordinated stepping movements with the position of one leg dictating the action of the other.

It is easy to draw the wrong conclusion from such a performance in the newborn. Some of the neonate's reflexes, such as the rhythmic sucking, the lowering and lifting of the jaw, and swallowing, are adaptive responses that are immediately necessary to ensure that it will receive nutrition. But primary walking is an anticipatory reflex that is spontaneously evoked by stimulation and which will in fact be gradually inhibited as the brain begins to control the spinal cord action. Even in cases where attempts have been made to continue primary walking by repeated practice this spontaneous activity has died out after a few months. On the other hand we have here a clear indication of an underlying mechanism responsible for such important rhythmic activity. The brain will eventually be the controlling center for such movements but a mechanism by which these responses are carried out is already functioning. This would seem to provide us with a significant example of how motor responses may be controlled from different hierarchical levels such as the spinal cord or the motor centers of the cortex. We need hardly stress that this is an important and recurring problem in skills as the complexity of performance increases.

Primary walking has been quoted because it is so essential to appreciate the complexity of the behavior patterning with which we are dealing. Text books on developmental psychology include tables of the developmental sequences in motor behavior from birth onward. These are instructive but they tend to give the impression that the newborn is devoid of motor responses. He has, indeed, much to learn, but, as Gesell says, the organization of behavior begins long before birth; it is indicated in his developmental diagrams (Fig. 1).

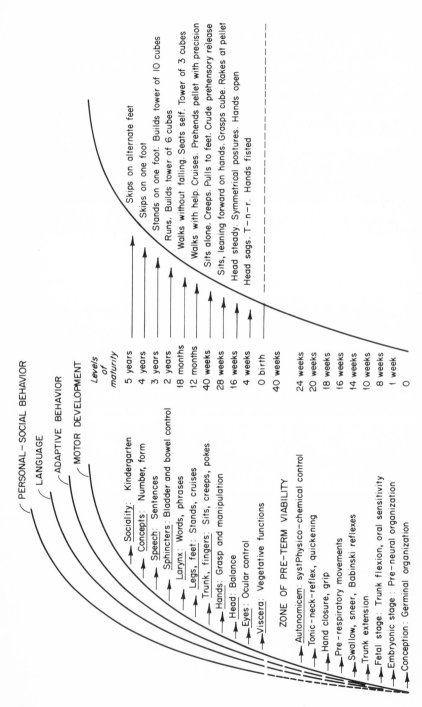

Fig. 1. The development of behavior in the four major fields and the sequence of motor behavior. (From Gesell & Amatruda, 1947.)

B. The Sequence of Development

The significance of the sequence of development in the first few years is that it is much the same for all children. The rate of development varies from child to child so that one may sit or walk before another, but a child who cannot sit will not stand nor walk. Here, then, is a clear indication of the interdependence of many basic motor skills. It is often a prerequisite that one act be accomplished before another if we find that the first is a constituent part of the second. Shirley (1931) proposed a classificatory system in which passive and then active postural control preceded various stages of locomotion. Bayley's (1935) monograph did not support Shirley's idea of prerequisite phases and more support has been given to such general proposals that coordinated development progresses from head to foot—the cephalo-caudal trend—and from those parts of the body closest to the torso to the more distal segments—the proximodistal trend.

C. Locomotion

What, in fact, do these trends imply? If we consider an example such as locomotion then the first stage toward walking is control of head movements. When a newborn is held in the prone position with the hand under the abdomen there is no head control and it is not until about 6 weeks before the head is held momentarily in the same plane as the rest of the body. By 12 weeks a baby in the prone position can take his weight on his forearms and lift his head to almost 90° to the couch. When, during this time, he is picked up and put in the sitting position his back is rounded at 4 weeks and only gradually is he able to control his posture, so that it is not until about 20 weeks that the back is straight and the position maintained. At this time, too, the head no longer wobbles as he sits. He progresses to sit without support around 36 weeks and can also stand at this age while holding on to furniture. Gradually, around 12 to 15 months he walks unaided, but he will be 2 years old before he runs.

Workers such as Ames (1937), Bayley (1965), Burnside (1927), McGraw (1932, 1941, 1943), and Illingworth (1966) have studied these developments in prone progression, erect posture, and final walking in great detail and have illustrated the various stages most helpfully as shown in Fig. 2 (see also Munn, 1965; Thompson, 1962). McGraw, in contrast to Shirley, sees the development as a gradual process in which the patterns of one stage merge into those of the next. For our purpose we do not need to insist upon the details of these stages, but when we consider their sequence rather than their actual times of occurrence, their contribution to an understanding of the skill of walk-

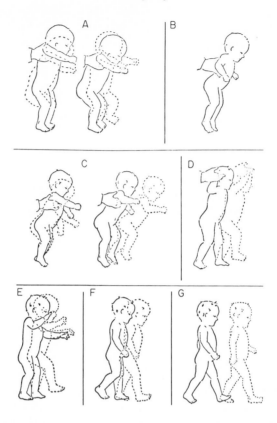

Fig. 2. Developmental phases in erect locomotion. A. Newborn posture with reflex stepping movements which become somewhat more prevalent during the first three weeks. B. Inhibition, or static phase. This is characterized especially by better head control, as well as suppression of reflex stepping reactions. C. Transition stage, noted for up-and-down movements of the body and stepping motions which are noticeably different from those of the newborn. D. Deliberate stepping while supported. E. Independent stepping. F. Heel-toe progression. G. More mature, well-integrated locomotion. (From McGraw, 1943.)

ing is apparent. Walking is not one skill; it is a complex of delicately coordinated motor activities involving posture, balance, and locomotion. The muscle groups concerned are those not only of the feet and legs but the arms, trunk, and neck. If at any one point too much attention is paid to the signals from one source then inevitably too little will be paid to those from some other and this may be disastrous to the skill. If we think of walking as a series of subskills, neatly coordinated, then in the case of the adult each subskill is sufficiently well practiced as to be preprogrammed and run off with the minimum of attention. It may be argued that this is necessary with all speed-stressed continuous skills where actions have been preset and then relegated to a hierarchical level where they no longer require constant monitoring. The performer is often unaware that he is controlling such actions, say, holding his head at a particular inclination or coordinating his arm movements, and it is only when signals arise which are totally unexpected that he attends to them. What seems to happen is that the normal pattern of signals, from both external and internal sources, is broken by a series of unpredicted signals which the performer has to monitor. Put another way, the uncertainty of the signals ensures that their high information rate will take the operator some time to process.

In the case of the baby no one of the subskills is sufficiently practiced to be left without some monitoring, and this is often the explanation of why a child attends to one part of a skill and unfortunately "forgets" the remainder. It is literally necessary for him to concentrate upon all the constituent parts of the total skill; certainly he has to attend far more than the adult who has practiced them throughout his life. Until a child has reached the stage where some actions can be preprogrammed he has to monitor signals as they arise and initiate responses to them, and, in many instances, there is not sufficient time to do this. Here, as so often with skills, the worse the player the harder the task.

The extent to which children have to attend to every part of a skill is brought out when they are asked to walk along boards of various widths. Halverson (1940) used boards of 8, 6, 4, and 2 cm with children aged 3, 4, 5, and 6 years. Only a few of the 3-year-old children walked the board with both feet; the others always had one foot on the floor and had to be excluded from the records. It was found that the speed of walking the individual boards increased with age while the number of errors decreased. The narrower the board the greater the difficulty of performance and the greater the variability of performance in terms of errors. This type of task can be nicely suited to the ability of the child and brings out the difficulty a younger child has in walking with his feet in alignment, and in keeping his balance.

D. MANIPULATIVE SKILLS

The human hand is the most unique of machines and not less because it is a "primitive survival, shockingly similar to the hand of the ancient tortoise . . . millions of years before the advent of man" (Gesell, 1954). The same human hand grips a shovel or a violin bow, a pick or a pen. Its manipulative range, its flexibility, and its finger dexterity are all outstanding. Man's muscles may be inferior to the ape's but the size and position of the thumb on his hand give him a clear advantage in making a precise thumb-forefinger opposition as required in picking up small objects (Thompson, 1962). These fine, precise manipulations are such an integral part of everyday life that we forget the painstaking way in which the skills were acquired.

E. REACH AND GRASP

Again the primitive reflex—here the grasp reflex—of the first two or three months disappears before the voluntary grasp begins. It is not until 12 weeks that the baby's hands are mostly open and 20 weeks before he grasps an object voluntarily. Halverson (1931, 1937a, b, c) has made detailed studies of how a baby's reaching and grasping skills develop. If the baby is in the sitting position he at first makes no contact with an object such as a cube when his arm and hand move toward it. There is a crude palming movement in which the three ulnar fingers predominate with the thumb almost inactive. White, Castle, and Held (1964) refer to this as "swiping behavior." At about 20 weeks the cube is touched, followed by a primitive closure of the hand on the cube. It is around 28 weeks that the cube is grasped in the palm and the baby will be a year old before he places the forefinger over the cube and grips it between thumb and forefinger. Now the baby is able to grasp a small object using the volar pads of the finger tip and the distal volar pad of the thumb. But he still approaches the cube with a wide open hand until he makes contact. His grasp is "of an enveloping rather than a manipulating nature though he has good thumb opposition."

Through the years of early childhood these everyday actions are practiced and improved. Reaching for an object gradually becomes more accurate as a sitting or standing posture can be maintained. The child begins to make postural adjustments to accommodate his own position to that of an object so that it can now be placed farther away from the hand. At 3 years he aligns his fingers to pick up an object without necessarily making any other contact with the supporting surface. The finger alignment is typical of anticipatory responses and, as might be expected, he grasps the object more readily and with extended fingers (see Crowell, 1967).

F. RELEASE

It is in keeping with the characteristics of development that one of the most difficult stages to master is the release of an object. In grasping, the extensors are inhibited; in releasing the flexors are inhibited and this latter response is acquired much later in children. During the first 6 months infants cannot voluntarily release an object. From 28 to 40 weeks they begin to do so against a restricting surface and transfer objects from one hand to the other, but they will offer an object and not release it. Around 12 months a baby goes through the voluntarily dropping stage and achieves a proficiency — too much for most mothers — at this once difficult operation. But he still has much to learn in positioning objects accurately, as in building a tower of bricks, and one of his difficulties is through an inability to release the object at the right time.

Adults trying to perform similar precise manipulations with the limb anesthetized or in conditions of extreme cold show similar clumsiness. Here the adult is denied the usual tactile cues and has to rely upon vision to indicate the position of the object in relation to his fingers. He performs clumsily under such conditions. It is tempting to think that an infant also is too dominated by vision at this stage and is only slowly acquiring the skill of relying upon internal signals to give him more immediate information to control his manipulative and release responses.

G. THROWING

Skills such as block building which depend upon visual-spatial perception, motor manipulation, positioning, and release show marked improvement from 3 to 5 years and, as we have seen, the whole task is made up of many subskills. If we take a more complex coordination such as throwing we appreciate how many subskills contribute to the action. The thrower not only has to grasp and release an object at a critical time, requiring control over his shoulder, arm, hand, and finger movement, but in order to carry out the throwing action he has to have command of his static and dynamic balance, involving leg, trunk, and head.

Wild (1938), using film analysis, demonstrates that a child does not use his body in throwing until between the ages of 4 and 5 years, when he starts to orientate himself in the direction of the throw. She stresses the increasing economy of effort which is a ubiquitous principle in the development of children's skills.

In addition a child requires accurate assessment of his visual-spatial environment if he is to hit his target, which may be moving. A fully developed throwing action is a high level skill and would seem to be well outside the range of a young child. Yet by 5 and 6 years a child, and here there is a marked sex difference in favor of the boys, has acquired many of the features of mature throwing. He places his feet and legs correctly; the stance allows him to twist his body and transfer its weight as he throws; he uses his shoulder, elbow, wrist, and fingers in the action and miraculously is on target. Here we have a highly coordinated pattern of complex responses that have been put together in a strict temporal sequence lasting only fractions of a second. They are an excellent example of a time-stressed problem — to which we shall return — where a child has to learn to preprogram a series of subskills and then integrate the resulting signals which are fed back to him from these varied sources.

H. INTERSENSORY SKILLS

Phylogenetically man does not show sudden differences from lower organisms in the number of the senses. As Sherrington (1951) reminds us, we might have surmised that a more complex nervous system would have been served by a greater number of sensory modes. What in fact has changed in phylogenesis is a vast increase in the complexity of intersensory interactions. The nervous system has not developed "new senses, but better liaison between old senses" so that behavior at the human level is dependent upon multimodal and intersensory control mechanisms (Birch & Lefford, 1963).

We are familiar enough with this system but the implications of it are sometimes blurred in the adult. For example, we assume that he can distinguish the necessary visual pattern if given the motor task of copying it. Yet we are sometimes mistaken and find out too late that inadequate performance is based upon inadequate visual discrimination. The complexity is much more apparent with children, where often the attainment of a skill may be impossible for them because of their inability to put together discrete experiences. We may suspect this to be so with 2- to 3-year-old children when trying to throw a ball. Their motor responses are often uncoordinated but their assessment of their visual-spatial surroundings may also be inaccurate. We have clearer indications of the difficulty in tasks such as drawing figures, where the problem of intersensory integration is directly examined.

I. VISUALLY GUIDED MOVEMENTS

Goodenough (1926) has described how, at the first stage, when children begin to copy two-dimensional shapes their scribbling has all the appearances of a primary motor expression totally unrelated to the presented visual form. Later during the second year a child begins to respond to what he himself has produced, that is, he interprets what he has scribbled. The query arises whether he now interprets what he sees he has done, or what he intended to do—but this is every artist's problem. Bender (1938) notes that the next stage is the scribbling of loops and she feels that at this age of 2 to 2½ years the actual pattern is not an exact guide to the child but rather a stimulus that evokes an almost reflexive (loop) response.

It is at the age of 4 that Goodenough claims a child's drawings are unambiguous responses to a visual form. Even here the reproductions are often strikingly inaccurate and we have to decide how far this is due to motor deficiencies per se or to an inability to use the visual information to control motor responses, if we assume that the visual perceptions are accurate in the first place. Experiments have been conducted to sort out these variables. In their 1967 monograph Birch and Lefford have studied the abilities of 5-, 6-, 7-, and 11-year-old children to draw simple geometric shapes, such as triangles and diamonds, under a variety of conditions. The easiest was where the subjects had to trace directly over the shapes and here there was a marked improvement between the ages of 5 and 6 years. Indeed, as shown in Fig. 3 there is as much improvement between these two age groups from 6 to 11 years. A similar relationship between the age groups was found in the results for drawing the shapes over line grids, which was a more difficult task than the tracing, and for drawing the shapes freehand. As expected, all age groups found the freehand task difficult but again the marked improvement is between the 5 and 6 year olds. On the other hand it is of note that 50% of the 11 year olds made some errors and scored less than 16 out of 20 on the test as is evident in Fig. 4.

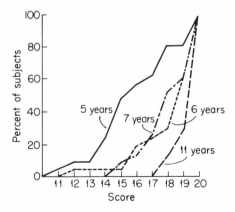

Fig. 3. Tracing: cumulative percentages at different ages of subjects who obtain a given total tracing score. (From Birch & Lefford, 1967.)

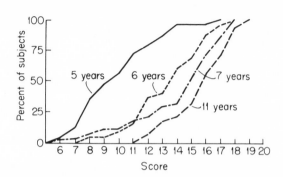

Fig. 4. Freehand drawing: cumulative percentage at different ages of subjects who obtain a given total drawing score when drawing is made on a blank answer sheet. (From Birch & Lefford, 1967.)

To what do we attribute the difficulty in this apparently simple copying task? And why is there improvement with age? The 5-year-old group does not trace the drawings satisfactorily so that at this age it would seem as if motor performance itself often contributes to individual variation and errors. Indeed, when the drawings of the 5-year-old children were analyzed in detail it was found that their tracing errors were mainly in terms of the formation of angles and straightness of line, and that all age groups had some difficulty with tracing angles. We can say, then, that under these conditions of tracing where the visual guidance component is reduced to a minimum the younger children of 5 years do not always control their motor responses and that all the children had some difficulty in tracing more complex shapes involving angles. This may be expressed by saying that in the tracing experiment the visual signal is as compatible as it is possible to make it with the motor responses. Under such conditions performance is relatively successful, particularly after 6 years. But the evidence makes it clear that children, and especially 5 year olds, experience difficulty in monitoring manual responses even where the visual feedback is presented as unequivocally as it is in the tracing condition. It is, therefore, not surprising that where the responses involve copying from a visual figure placed not immediately underneath the response (as in tracing) but slightly away from it, the children find the drawing task much more difficult. Now they have both to translate the visual pattern in front of them to a different location and carry out the appropriate motor responses.

Many perceptual motor tasks require a subject to integrate the signals from an external source against those from his own limbs. If, as may happen with a child, he is unsure how to interpret such signals arising from his own responses, the task will indeed be complex for him. Townsend (1951) emphasizes that the ability of children to copy geometric forms correlates more highly with form perception than with motor ability. Yet it is well known that children perceive differences between shapes before they can copy them satisfactorily, as allowed in the Stanford-Binet Intelligence Test.

Connolly (1968) examined this problem by requiring children of 4, 5, and 6 years to recognize simple line drawings, as shown in Fig. 5. All age groups could do this. It was then demonstrated in a freehand drawing experiment that all the children could draw vertical, horizontal, and oblique lines. Finally the children were given two copying tasks. In the one they were asked to draw the line figures; in the other they had to make them with matchsticks. The 4-year-old children found both the drawing and the construction task very difficult. There was a significant improvement in both at 5 years. There was no further improvement at 6 years for the construction task but the drawing was better.

From observing how the task was carried out it appeared the construction as opposed to the drawing problem allowed the children

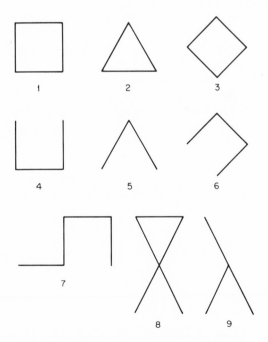

Fig. 5. Line drawings for recognition, copying, and construction. (From Connolly, 1968.)

much more opportunity to manipulate the situation. When construct-ing many would refer back, visually, to the stimulus card and then adjust their own matchstick copy. The visual feedback allowed a di-rect comparison between display and response with the opportunity for adjustment of the response. It is a straightforward correlation prob-lem: Does the proposed orientation of the matchstick agree or not with the display? But in the drawing task a child has to decide where he wishes to draw a line. He has to infer how it will appear and then he has to select the appropriate motor response to draw it. He may be wrong at either point and he may feel dissatisfied with what he has drawn but there is not the same opportunity for correction as in the construction task. Thus there is much more emphasis in the line draw-ing task upon translating the visual pattern into an appropriate motor response. For the adult, drawing a line in a preselected area is suffi-ciently easy for us to expect no errors between a construction and drawing task under these conditions, but for a child the visual-spatial task alone is difficult and the drawing requirements add to the com-plexity.

In an earlier experiment Birch and Lefford (1963) compared the efficiency with which children aged 5 to 11 years could recognize geometric forms when using either visual, kinesthetic, or haptic sense modalities. They defined haptic as the "complex sensory input ob-tained by active manual exploration of a test object." The exploration gave rise to tactile, kinesthetic, and surface movement sensations from the fingers and hand. Kinesthetic information was provided by placing the subject's arm behind a screen and with the arm out of sight pas-sively moving it through a path describing the geometric form. Eight blocks from the Seguin Form Board were used as stimuli: a triangle, square, cross, star, hexagon, semicircle, diamond, and circle. Three cross-modality interactions were examined for intersensory equiva-lence: (1) visual and haptic interaction; (2) visual and kinesthetic in-teraction; and (3) haptic and kinesthetic interaction. Throughout the experiment paired stimuli were presented for comparison, the first member of the pair to one sense modality and the second to the other modality.

It is, perhaps, not surprising that for judgments of both identical and nonidentical forms the visual-haptic discriminations were the most accurate. It was found that the ability to make these intersensory judg-ments definitely improved with age, the improvement following a typ-ical logarithmic growth curve. By the eleventh year there was a mini-mum of errors under all experimental conditions. Subjects found the diamond and hexagon the two most difficult forms to judge in all conditions and in general made more errors on their intersensory judgments of identical forms than of nonidentical.

Such experiments bring out the complexity of intersensory judgments and how much a child has to acquire in the first few years of life. An adult has learned to expect a certain pattern of stimulation for a square or circle, whether that be visual or tactile. He has categorized shapes in terms of their predominant features — straightness of line, size of angles, equality of length, etc. — and is looking for these characteristics. His task is more one of matching or recognition when he compares the stimulation from one sensory mode with that from another. But the child may often be trying to make the wrong comparison because he has the wrong hypothesis, or, in the case of a complicated shape, he may have formed no hypothesis at all and just be vaguely trying to distinguish some salient feature. Here, then, with intersensory comparisons, as with so many examples in skills, we see that the child has a more difficult task than the practiced adult.

There is another point that could be worthy of further investigation. The intersensory discrimination may be poorer in children because the actual discrimination of any one sensory mode is inferior to that of an adult. This should be investigated both in terms of their ability to make an initial discrimination upon new material and their rate of improvement when they have had the opportunity to practice.

We have not stressed the importance for learning of interaction between the sensory-perceptual functions and the motor system. But this classic field of study (Stratton, 1897) has recently been much influenced by von Holst's (1954) concept of reafferentation, particularly as discussed by Held (1965) and his colleagues (Held & Bossom, 1961; Held & Hein, 1958; Held & Rekosh, 1963; Held & Schlank, 1959). The stimulation affecting an organism, such as a kitten, as a result of its own movements was shown to be necessary for new perceptual learning to be achieved. Held and Hein (1963) have also demonstrated the need for kittens to make postural adjustments to changes in visual stimulation if they are to develop the ability to make the complex visual differentiation required in the visual cliff situation of Walk and Gibson (1961). The significance of this form of feedback is brought home to us when we work with handicapped children, where there is no limb to supply the normal tactile-kinesthetic sensations, or with cerebral palsied children (Abercrombie, 1964), or in the case of blind children who cannot match their motor responses against a visual environment.

By contrast, in normal development we are studying a correlational process whereby the motor sensory feedback loop enables us to match responses with visual perception. It would seem that here we have one of the basic mechanisms for allowing a child to make visual and motor adjustments. His world changes as he literally grows bigger in it but the feedback he receives from his responses enables him to make perceptual adjustments to these changes in himself. It is of note that in many processes such as the matching of head or eye movements with visually perceived objects, or as here in the matching of feedback from responses with perception, we find that a correlational mechanism enables the child to reach rapid agreement and consistency in his sensory judgment. Without the consistency he would be lost in his sensory world; without the cross-correlational techniques there are doubts whether he could achieve consistency (Maccoby & Bee, 1965).

J. SERIAL ORDERING OF EVENTS

So far we have discussed motor responses in terms of everyday categories — reaching, grasping, walking, and so on. For the remainder of this discussion let us consider the skills more in terms of their psychological constituents. After Lashley's (1951) famous paper psychologists are not likely to underestimate the significance of the temporal ordering of events. But work with children does emphasize the supreme importance of carrying out the right actions at the right time. So often we see a child with the right responses but unable to execute them when he should. It is almost as if it is all there but he has too much to sort out in the allotted time. We begin to appreciate the significance of having certain subroutines preprogrammed so that they can be run off quickly with the minimum of attention. Again, some responses are made too late because a child is uncertain how to carry them out. He has not practiced the response and is still at the stage of finding out the best way to execute it. We find some interesting interactions between speed and accuracy in a number of experiments where it appears as if one component is deliberately sacrificed for the other.

K. SPEED AND ACCURACY

It is one of the features of adult skills that the two components of speed and accuracy are complementary qualities of performance. The accomplished craftsman works with precision but amazingly fast. Many experiments have shown a relationship between these variables and Fitts (1954) proposed a simple way of assessing the information-processing rate in a motor response based upon the two constraints of time taken and accuracy of response. Several other workers have examined its consistency in unpracticed tasks (Annett, Goldby, & Kay, 1958) and with practiced subjects (Kay, 1962).

Connolly, Brown, and Bassett (1968), using a similar type of task, asked children, aged 6, 8, and 10 years, to dot with a pencil between two circles, each with a radius of 1 inch with centers 5 inches apart. Children were told to put their dots as near to the middle as possible and to do so as quickly as they could. Table I gives the main findings: when analyzed the results show that older children are quicker, that girls are faster than boys, and that there is a practice effect which is more pronounced with the older children. There is no difference between the age groups for accuracy nor does accuracy increase with practice within the limit of this experiment. Two points should be stressed. The 6-year-old children had achieved a level of muscular control enabling them to perform their motor response efficiently. Second, "the fact that accuracy decreases with practice, while speed increases, indicates that the two components are compensatory, and this suggests that the older children may have sacrificed some potential extra accuracy in favor of the extra speed which they actually achieved. It is not therefore possible to conclude that 10 year old children could not have been more accurate than the 6 year olds."

The authors go on to stress the qualitative difference between how the older subjects performed the task as a smooth and unitary whole compared with the apparently discrete components with two marked end points of the younger children. There is a need for detailed analysis of how children do put together the components of a task. In an assembly operation similar to the Fitts (1954) and Annett *et al.* (1958) studies Connolly (1968) has found marked improvement with practice in the *movement empty* component, in contrast to the findings of previous experiments with adults. And, as might be expected, after practice the grasp component also improves with children. The position is that we have sufficient evidence from normative studies of child de-

Table I

MEAN NUMBER OF DOTS AND MEAN ACCURACY SCORE PER SUBJECT
PER TRIAL FOR EACH AGE AND SEX GROUP[a]

Age	Mean No.			Accuracy score		
	Male	Female	Both	Male	Female	Both
6	11.40	13.41	12.40	2.93	2.94	2.94
8	15.73	17.53	16.63	2.78	2.89	2.83
10	20.21	23.04	21.63	2.93	2.68	2.80
All	15.73	17.99	16.88	2.88	2.84	2.86

[a]Accuracy scale 0–4: 0 = off target; 4 = on target.

velopment to accept the improvement which takes place with age. We now need to carry out more studies which examine the details of performance so that we can find out where improvement takes place and understand the underlying mechanisms controlling such progress.

L. A Time-Stressed Skill: Catching

One of man's happiest skills is his ability to coordinate his movements in time to catch an object. It is, of course, a time-stressed skill. The ball, let us say, is only in the air for a limited time, it may be going to fall a long way from the catcher, and it may be traveling very quickly. Yet with mathematic nicety the skilled player arrives at the right spot at the right time and takes the catch.

A young child does no such thing. Roll the ball a little away from a 1 year old and no movement is made to stop it. The writer made a film analysis of children aged 2, 5, and 15 years old catching a ball. For the youngest children a 4-inch diameter ball was thrown gently from a distance of 3 feet. The hands were held together with palms upward. When the ball fell into them there was no immediate closing of the fingers to retain the ball. The two hands would move together, very slowly, and cuddle the ball against the body, with little coordination of fingers. Often the ball just rolled off the hands. The eyes did not follow the flight of the ball but tended to watch the hands or the thrower. If the ball was thrown slightly away from the hands no response was made to it, and the ball had fallen to the floor before the child was aware of it.

There was marked improvement in the 5 year old. The fingers were more flexible and were cupped to try to retain the ball. The child now moved the hands to meet the ball when it was going to fall short and though there was little anticipation there was a quick appreciation of what had happened. The child's eyes now began to observe the whole scene and watched the ball in flight, though a lot of attention was still given to the hands. By contrast the 15 year old watched the throwing action and the flight of the ball and ignored his own hands which were moving to anticipate the point of contact. The fingers were outstretched and closed quickly on the ball once it fell into the palm.

The striking feature lay in the contrast between the performances. It was difficult to imagine the beginnings of the highly coordinated, anticipatory, high speed but smooth action of the 15 year old in the performance of the 2 year old. But appearances are deceptive, and it was quite clear that at the intermediate age the foundations of the adult performance were being laid. It was also apparent that the nature of the task was changing and that the whole task was a much more unified skill.

III. Summary and Future Work

Contrary to popular belief the significance of human skills lies not in their uniqueness but their ubiquity. The preeminently interesting skills are those which we all learn to perform, not those that are mastered by only a few. And one phase that is most revealing is where we are all learning to perform them, namely, early childhood.

In this chapter we have not attempted to give an exhaustive account of the work in this field. Rather, we have selected certain manifestly widespread characteristics of motor development that hold over many years of childhood and underlie adult skills. This outline has indicated that considerable advances have been made in understanding both when and how we acquire the beginnings of motor control. We have avoided well-known arguments such as the contribution of maturation and learning to the process, the significance of handedness (Thompson, 1962), and have deliberately eschewed speculative and descriptive theorizing.

From the evidence we have considered it would seem that for the immediate future the following lines would be worth pursuing.

A. DETAILED ANALYSIS OF PERFORMANCE

Overall time measures showing improvement with age and practice are useful but it is the detailed analysis revealing such features as how the skill is being conducted, how the role of the limbs progressively changes, and how anticipatory responses are established which are now required. The earlier photographic records were important signposts but we now require a stricter measure of the time sequence of the constituent parts to evaluate their contribution to the total skill. This will be particularly relevant in establishing the role of vision as against tactile-kinesthetic cues in many skills.

B. PRACTICE: THE USE OF INTERNAL SIGNALS

Studies of skills have shown that the signals used by an operator in the early stages of practice may be ignored in the later, and, vice versa, that those he either ignores or is unaware of at first may become all important in the practiced performance. This is always a challenge to any training schedule — how to teach the new operator to use the signals, and particularly the internal signals, which will become important in the final stages of performance. With children, there is the added difficulty that the very nature of their naive performance prevents them from receiving such signals; for example, head or arm movements might be so random that internal signals cannot give a consistent pattern of information. It would be very much to the advantage of the subject if we could reduce the random variation in the early stages of practice and thereby make it possible to attend to the appropriate internal source of signals at the earliest opportunity (Annett & Kay, 1957).

C. PRACTICE: LONG-TERM EFFECTS

Many studies have revealed how simple information processing skills continue to improve "even over millions of cycles of practice" (Fitts, 1964; Crossman, 1959). Most of the data agree with Snoddy's (1926) finding that logarithmic increments in the number of trials result in logarithmic gains in speed. These findings raise important questions about the nature of such improvement. Are the signals coded differently after so much practice? How is increased muscular control attained over these specific actions? What is the relationship of the compatibility between display-response and practice? Can practice compensate for incompatibilities?

Young children's performances, on the other hand, have rarely been practiced to any extent. We know very little about their rate of progress in comparison to adults, but because their subskills are fewer and less practiced it might be supposed that both their initial and longer term rates of progress will differ from those of an adult.

D. COMPLEXITY OF TASKS

Experiments with children offer a unique opportunity for examining how we acquire the skills to cope with increasingly complex situations. We need to study how a subject makes a number of rapid translations in order to code information from a display to a motor output. Fitts and Switzer (Fitts, 1964), for example, studied the response time to pictures in terms of the number of mediating processes that the subjects had to make, such as stimulus → familiar object name → vocalization. He emphasizes the close link between verbal learning and perceptual motor learning and the fact that skill learning often continues far beyond the point of verbal learning studies. It would be valuable to examine the complexity of children's skills in a similar way and to continue until performance was fully practiced.

E. INTERSENSORY FACILITATION

The excellent work in this area has opened up this problem. The whole issue of how a child builds up his idea of the body schema and how this accords with his spatial environment is fundamental. A child has to monitor his motor responses more than an adult; he often needs vision to inform him where his hand is, to tell him whether he is holding a cup horizontal, and so on. He gradually learns not to require these visual cues, and knows where his limbs are in relation to his environment. But we are now beginning to appreciate some of the details of this complex process. The senses interact and the feedback from responses correlates with our perceptions of the external environment. We match the internal and external worlds. The child has to face an environment that is more complex than that of the adult because it is less familiar, less stable (for the younger child), and less constant. Just as the changes for a child are particularly apparent in the first years of life where he has to adapt to a changing leg-body ratio, or weight-strength ratio, so too he has to adapt to an environment that is becoming increasingly demanding in its temporal-spatial ratio. A child literally changes shape and grows bigger in a world where he has less time to cover more ground, as he moves into an adult environment.

It is indeed an intriguing problem. It might appear that man is born into a world where he is at first a passive recipient of sensory information. He becomes a quick moving, coordinated, anticipatory body who has learned to stand asymmetrically to meet the contingencies in his environment. But, as we have noted, the early picture is misleading. The beginnings of adult skills are discernible in the child and when we observe closely they add considerably to our understanding of human motor performance.

References

Abercrombie, M. L. J. *Perceptual and visuo-motor disorders in cerebral palsy: A survey of the literature.* London: Spastics Society and Heinemann, 1964.

Ames, L. B. The sequential patterning of prone progression in the human infant. *Genetic Psychology Monographs,* 1937, **19**, 409–460.

Annett, J., Goldby, C. W., & Kay, H. The measurement of elements in an assembly task — the information output of the human motor system. *Quarterly Journal of Experimental Psychology,* 1958, **10**, 1–11.

Annett, J., & Kay, H. Knowledge of results and skilled performance. *Occupational Psychology,* 1957, **31**, 69–79.

Bartlett, Sir F. C. The measurement of human skill. (Oliver Sharpey Lectures to the Royal College of Physicians in London) *Occupational Psychology,* 1948, **22**, 31–38, 83–90.

Bayley, N. Development of motor abilities during the first three years. *Monograph, Society Research Child Development,* 1935, No. 1.

Bayley, N. Comparisons of mental and motor test scores for ages 1-15 months by sex, birth order, race, geographical location, and education of parents. *Child Development*, 1965, **36**, 379-411.

Bender, L. A visual motor gestalt test and its clinical use. New York: American Orthopsychiatric Association, *Research Monographs*, 1938, No. 3.

Birch, H. G., & Lefford, A. Intersensory development in children. *Monograph, Society Research Child Development*, 1963, **28**, 1-48.

Birch, H. G., & Lefford, A. Visual differentiation, intersensory integration, and voluntary motor control. *Monograph, Society Research Child Development*, 1967, **32**, 1-87.

Burnside, L. H. Coordination in the locomotion of infants. *Genetic Psychology Monographs*, 1927, **2**, 281-372.

Connolly, K. J. Some mechanisms involved in the development of motor skills. *Aspects of Education*, 1968, **7**, in press.

Connolly, K. J., Brown, K., & Bassett, E. Developmental changes in some components of a motor skill. *British Journal of Psychology*, 1968, **59**, 305-314.

Crossman, E. R. F. W. The measurement of discriminability. *Quarterly Journal of Experimental Psychology*, 1955, **7**, 176-195.

Crossman, E. R. F. W. A theory of the acquisition of speed-skill. *Ergonomics*, 1959, **2**, 153-166.

Crowell, D. H. Infant motor development. In Y. Brackbill (Ed.), *Infancy and early childhood*. New York: Free Press, 1967.

Fitts, P. M. The information capacity of the human motor system in controlling the amplitude of movement. *Journal of Experimental Psychology*, 1954, **47**, 381-391.

Fitts, P. M. Perceptual motor learning. In A. W. Melton (Ed.), *Categories of human learning*. New York: Academic Press, 1964.

Gesell, A. The ontogenesis of infant behavior. In L. Carmichael (Ed.), *Manual of child psychology*. (2nd ed.) New York: Wiley, 1954.

Gesell, A., & Amatruda, C. S. *Developmental diagnosis: Normal and abnormal child development*. (2nd ed.) New York: Hoeber, 1947.

Goodenough, F. L. *Measurement of intelligence by drawings*. Chicago: World Book Co., 1926.

Halverson, H. M. An experimental study of prehension in infants by means of systematic cinema records. *Genetic Psychology Monographs*, 1931, **10**, 107-286.

Halverson, H. M. Studies of the grasping responses of early infancy. *Journal of Genetic Psychology*, 1937, **51**, 371-392. (a)

Halverson, H. M. Studies of the grasping responses of early infancy. *Journal of Genetic Psychology*, 1937, **51**, 393-424. (b)

Halverson, H. M. Studies of the grasping responses of early infancy. *Journal of Genetic Psychology*, 1937, **51**, 425-449. (c)

Halverson, H. M. Motor development. In A. Gesell (Ed.), *The first five years of life*. New York: Harper, 1940.

Held, R. Plasticity in sensory-motor systems. *Scientific American*, 1965, **213**, 84-94.

Held, R., & Bossom, J. Neonatal deprivation and adult rearrangement: Complementary techniques for analyzing plastic sensory-motor coordinations. *Journal of Comparative and Physiological Psychology*, 1961, **54**, 33-37.

Held, R., & Hein, A. V. Adaptation of disarranged hand-eye coordination contingent upon re-afferent stimulation. *Perceptual and Motor Skills*, 1958, **8**, 87-90.

Held, R., & Hein, A. V. Movement-produced stimulation in the development of visually guided behavior. *Journal of Comparative and Physiological Psychology*, 1963, **56**, 872-876.

Held, R., & Rekosh, J. Motor-sensory feedback and the geometry of visual space. *Science*, 1963, **141**, 722–723.

Held, R., & Schlank, M. Adaptation to disarranged eye-hand coordination in the distance-dimension. *American Journal of Psychology*, 1959, **72**, 603–605.

Illingworth, R. S. *The development of the infant and young child.* Edinburgh and London: Livingstone, 1966.

Irion, A. L. A brief history of research on the acquisition of skill. In E. A. Bilodeau (Ed.), *Acquisition of skill.* New York: Academic Press, 1966.

Kay, H. Channel capacity and skilled performance. In F. A. Geldard (Ed.), *Defence psychology.* New York: Macmillan (Pergamon), 1962.

Lashley, K. S. The problem of serial order in behavior. In L. A. Jeffress (Ed.), *Cerebral mechanisms in behavior.* New York: Wiley, 1951.

Leonard, J. A. Tactual choice reactions: I. *Quarterly Journal of Experimental Psychology*, 1959, **11**, 76–83.

Maccoby, E. E., & Bee, H. L. Some speculations concerning the lag between perceiving and performing. *Child Development*, 1965, **36**, 367–377.

McGraw, M. B. From reflex to muscular control in the assumption of an erect posture and ambulation in the human infant. *Child Development*, 1932, **3**, 291–297.

McGraw, M. B. Development of neuromuscular mechanisms as reflected in the crawling and creeping behavior of the human infant. *Journal of Genetic Psychology*, 1941, **58**, 83–111.

McGraw, M. B. *The Neuromuscular maturation of the human infant.* New York: Columbia Univer. Press, 1943.

Mowbray, G. H., & Rhoades, M. V. On the reduction of choice reaction times with practice. *Quarterly Journal of Experimental Psychology*, 1959, **11**, 16–23.

Munn, N. L. *The evolution and growth of human behavior.* (2nd ed.) London: Harrap, 1965.

Peiper, A. *Cerebral function in infancy and childhood.* (3rd ed.) New York: Consultants Bureau, 1963.

Sherrington, C. S. *Man on his nature.* London and New York: Cambridge Univer. Press, 1951.

Shirley, M. M. *The first two years: A study of twenty-five babies.* Vol. I. *Postural and locomotor development.* Minneapolis: Univer. of Minnesota Press, 1931.

Snoddy, G. S. Learning and stability. *Journal of Applied Psychology*, 1926, **10**, 1–36.

Stratton, G. M. Vision without inversion of the retinal image. *Psychological Review*, 1897, **4**, 341–360, 463–481.

Thompson, G. G. *Child psychology: Growth trends in psychological adjustment.* (2nd ed.) Boston: Houghton Mifflin, 1962.

Townsend, E. A. A study of copying ability in children. *Genetic Psychology Monographs*, 1951, **43**, 3–51.

von Holst, E. Relations between the central nervous system and the peripheral organs. *British Journal of Animal Behavior*, 1954, **2**, 89–94.

Walk, R. D., & Gibson, E. J. A comparative and analytic study of visual depth perception. *Psychological Monographs*, 1961, **75**, 1–44.

Welford, A. T. The measurement of sensory-motor performance: Survey and reappraisal of twelve years' progress. *Ergonomics*, 1960, **3**, 189–230.

White, B. L., Castle, P., & Held, R. Observations on the development of visually-directed reaching. *Child Development*, 1964, **35**, 349–364.

Wild, M. R. The behavior pattern of throwing and some observations concerning its course of development in children. *Research Quarterly*, 1938, **9**, 20–24.

Sustained Performance[1]

EARL A. ALLUISI
University of Louisville

I. Introduction

By "sustained" performance we mean the more-or-less continuous performance of tasks, sets of tasks or jobs, during four or more hours a day over several weeks, months, or even years. The performances of interest belong principally to the domain of work behavior. They differ from the test behaviors covered in most of the other chapters of this book.

A. CHARACTERISTICS OF WORK BEHAVIOR

How do test and work behaviors differ? They differ in many ways that stem basically from differences in the tasks presented to the subjects, operators, or workers in the two situations. The tasks presented in typical test situations tend to be simple and unitary (cf. those described in other chapters here or in Woodworth & Schlosberg, 1954), relative to the complex multidimensional tasks that comprise job or

[1]Based in part on materials previously published in *Acta Psychologica* (Alluisi & Chiles, 1967) and in *Human Factors* (Alluisi, 1967), and on the presidential address made by the author at the sixtieth annual meeting of the Southern Society for Philosophy and Psychology, Louisville, Kentucky, 11–13 April, 1968. Although the author accepts full responsibility for the presentation of the material in this chapter, he wishes to acknowledge his substantial debt to his colleagues and co-workers, especially to Drs. O. S. Adams, W. Dean Chiles, Glynn D. Coates, Ben B. Morgan, Jr., and John B. Thurmond.

work situations (cf. Bills, 1943; Ryan, 1947). They tend to depend on single channels of sensory input and motor output, whereas work typically demands the time-sharing of many different stimulus and response elements. Speed or accuracy scores are usually employed in the measurement and evaluation of test performance, but no simple solution has been found for the problems involved in the selection of criteria for the assessment of complex and sustained performance (cf. Chiles, 1967; Dunnette, 1963).

Relative to the postacquisition, highly skilled performances of trained operators or experienced workers, the behavior observed in many test situations is essentially unskilled. It is true that even the highly skilled may continue to show improvements with sustained performances of complex tasks, but the levels of skill involved are still several orders of magnitude different from those required to master simpler tests. Motor skills in particular have been shown to continue to improve over years of practice (Hovland, 1951; Woodworth & Schlosberg, 1954); piano playing is a good example.

The motivation of the subject or operator is likely to be different in test and work situations. Although he may appear to work steadily in the test situation, the subject's performance is not likely to represent the kind of maximum effort that is made only at the expense of some physiological cost. In the work situation, on the other hand, the operator may pause frequently during typical performance sessions, but he will exert a maximum of effort when an emergency condition makes it necessary. Perhaps because of these differences, test and work situations appear to be differentially sensitive to temporal influences and stressful conditions; more will be said on this point later.

B. Interests in Sustained Performance

The closely related topics of sustained performance and work behavior have been of greater concern to personnel and industrial psychologists (e.g., Fleishman, 1967a; Gilmer, 1961, pp. 283–380) than to experimental psychologists (e.g., Seashore, 1951; Woodworth & Schlosberg, 1954, pp. 798–813). This has been the case for quite some time (cf. Ghiselli & Brown, 1955; Maier, 1955; Robinson, 1934; Tiffin & McCormick, 1958; Viteles, 1932). Of course, these topics have been of concern to others, for example, to industrial engineers especially in the context of time-and-motion studies (Barnes, 1958; Gilbreth, 1919), as well as to those interested in the effects of fatigue (Bartley & Chute, 1947; Crowden, 1932; Floyd & Welford, 1953; McFarland, 1953, pp. 326–368; NRC Committee on Work in Industry, 1941), sleep (Kleitman, 1939, 1949, 1963), and work-rest cycling (Ray, Martin, & Alluisi, 1961).

The situation has begun to change; recently more than a dozen different laboratories were represented at a conference on the assessment of complex performance (Chiles, 1967). Although there had been isolated signs of experimental psychology's increased concern with work behavior as early as 10 to 15 years ago (e.g., Fitts, Schipper, Kidd, Shelly, & Kraft, 1958), it took the expansion of our aerospace programs and of psychology's roles and responsibilities therein (Grether, 1962) to accelerate the change. Interest has grown particularly in the measurement and evaluation (or assessment) of sustained, complex performance, especially in the operation of modern man-machine systems.

C. THE ASSESSMENT OF SUSTAINED PERFORMANCE

"Performance assessment" is one of the most important and difficult areas of behavioral experimentation. It is important in its own right, as any supervisor who has been called upon to justify the ratings of his workers can attest. It is important also because it is the crux of the "criterion problem" for so much other work (cf. Fleishman, 1967a, pp. 81-161). The final validation of selection and training techniques depends upon the assessment of the performances of men who have been differently selected and trained. The final validation of an improved, human engineered man-machine system depends upon it. The evaluation of the effects of various stresses, the measurement of performance decrements, the establishment of limits and optimum conditions and procedures – these, and many other tasks depend upon the measurement and evaluation, or assessment, of sustained performance.

As indicated earlier, the assessment of man's work behavior has challenged physiologists, engineers, and psychologists for many years. The task has been recognized as a difficult one; the problems uncovered have been formidable, and the solutions have been ephemeral. The typical researcher has responded by concentrating in subareas related to the specific skills of his discipline. For example, a physiologist might translate the problems of performance assessment into problems of measuring the output, impairment, or recovery of muscles. An industrial engineer might concentrate on time-and-motion study or on the measurement of productivity. Psychologists have generally concentrated their efforts in different ways, depending upon their specific subspecialties: industrial and personnel psychologists on selection and training, engineering psychologists on the design of equipment, and experimental psychologists on one or more of the traditional areas of learning, perception, psychomotor performance, etc.

The basic difficulty is that we do not now know how to assess sustained performances of complex meaningful tasks—to measure and evaluate work behavior. Thus, we have no criterion measure(s) about which to design our research, and because of this we are forced to do research on the criterion—to do research to discover how sustained performance can be assessed.

II. Three Approaches to Performance Assessment Research

Three techniques have been used in the direct research attempts to solve the problems of performance assessment. They have been discussed in detail elsewhere (Chiles, 1967) and will only be touched upon here. They represent a dimension of possible approaches, with the techniques of full-scale mission simulation at one end (cf. Grodsky, 1967), the methods of factor-analytically identified specific laboratory tests at the other end (cf. Fleishman, 1967b; Parker, 1967), and a synthetic-work approach placed intermediately between the two (Alluisi, 1967).

A. FULL-SCALE SIMULATION

Full-scale, integrated, mission simulation (e.g., Grodsky, Mandour, Roberts, & Woodward, 1966) represents the highest degree of fidelity possible in the simulation of "real" work. As Grodsky (1967) has pointed out, it calls for performance in real time, rather than in compressed or extended time, with the experimental or simulative environment, facilities, equipment, man-machine system dynamics, and task sequence matching the real world of events as closely as possible. Actual workers (operators, pilots, or astronauts) are usually employed so that the performance of the simulated mission is made with operational realism, and at high levels of skill.

There are, of course, other kinds of simulation (cf. McCormick, 1964, Chapter 18), and both part- and whole-task simulation techniques have been used in training and training research (J. A. Adams, 1961; Fleishman, 1967a, pp. 216–227), in performance appraisal (Fleishman, 1967a, pp. 96–114), and in human engineering and systems research (Fitts *et al.*, 1958). The principal advantages of full-scale mission simulation are that it provides a maximum of face validity and involves the subject in situations that resemble closely the operational conditions to which generalization is desired. Both of these are important advantages.

It is important to have face validity because there will be little opportunity to establish a final empirical validity until the criterion problem is solved. It is important to have the test and operational situations resemble one another, because then the subject's or operator's behavior may tend to be the same in the two. This is particularly important and will remain so until we are better able to assess the effects of some of the less well controlled operator variables such as his motivation, his personal weighting of the various aspects of his job, his sense of personal commitment to the work, etc.

There are, unfortunately, two important disadvantages to the use of full-scale simulation techniques — and these are apart from the questions of economic feasibility that arise from the relatively high cost of simulation studies. First, there is the difficulty of assessing the operator's performance in the simulated system. If we could assess this, then we should be able to measure and evaluate it in the operational situation; if we cannot assess it in the operational system, there is little likelihood that we could do so in the simulated system.

Second, there is the difficulty of generalization from the simulated system. The more faithful the simulation, the greater the generalization of results to the *specific* operational system or work situation that has been simulated, but the less the generalization to other systems. That is to say, to the extent that the results of the simulation include variances based on specific factors, generalizations can be made to operational systems which also include these specifics, but not to other systems.

Full-scale mission simulations are used more often, not to assess man's performance in a given system, but rather to assess the performance of the entire man-machine system. System-performance measures are typically employed, and especially when obtained from complete systems "exercises," such data are invaluable to the designer and systems manager in the testing, evaluation, and modification of specific systems (e.g., see McCormick, 1964). System-performance measures are of limited usefulness in the assessment of sustained *operator* performance, however, because we would need to know just how the man and the machines interact in the man-machine system before we could interpret the significance of meaning of such measures *vis-a-vis* the performance of the subject or worker. Such man-machine interactions, at best, are only infrequently known and specifiable (cf. Morgan, Cook, Chapanis, & Lund, 1963, pp. 1–50).

B. SPECIFIC-TEST TECHNIQUES

The disadvantages of full-scale simulation techniques can be overcome by the use of test batteries that consist of a number of appropriately selected or designed individual tasks. First, the subject's performance on each individual task can be assessed rather exactly. Second, these performances should be generalizable to other situations in which the tasks are used. Complete generality of performance on the test battery will depend only on (1) the availability of a taxonomy of the tasks that go to make up complex performances in operational systems, (2) a task analysis of specific systems in terms of this taxonomy, and (3) appropriate weightings of the representative tasks in the test battery in accordance with their relations with the taxonomy and task analysis. The need for research to develop a task taxonomy has been recognized (cf. Fleishman, 1967b, pp. 361–364).

The disadvantages of specific-test techniques, like those of full-scale simulations, are great. First, they have little or no face validity; we can compute no empirical validity coefficients. This means that we have little or no evidence at all of their validity as performance-assessment instruments.

Second, the resemblance of the test situation to the operational is likely to be minimal, and this leads to some serious questions concerning the behavior observed. That is to say, if the operator or worker approaches the test and operational situations differently, it is only reasonable to expect that his behavior might be influenced. If he is more highly motivated in the one than in the other, the results obtained in the test situation may not generalize to the operational; if he takes one situation seriously, but responds to the other as to a parlor game, the generalization of results would be sorely limited!

The better specific-test techniques are factor-analytically based, in the sense that they call for the use of tests that have been identified as related to the pertinent features or factors involved in the complex task (e.g., Fleishman, 1967b; Parker, 1967). Their use, however, as sequentially performed individual tests misses one of the principal features of sustained performance; namely, the time-sharing requirements that characterize the multiple responsibilities and complex behavior called "work."

C. Synthetic Work

In an attempt to minimize the disadvantages of the other two techniques, a synthetic-work approach has been developed. It is based on the measurement of multiple-task performance in a synthetic work situation, rather than a simulated one like that employed by Fitts and his colleagues (Fitts *et al.*, 1958). It is designed for use under controlled laboratory conditions, but it could also be used in controlled "field" experimentation. Its principal advantage is that it has none of the disadvantages of the other two techniques—or, at least, none to the same degree. Its principal disadvantage is shared by both of the other techniques; namely, there is little information regarding its empirical validity, and only a low likelihood of obtaining such information before the criterion problem has been solved.

The essential feature of this approach is the use of time-shared tests that are combined into a multiple-task performance (MTP) battery. The tests or tasks should be generalizable to a wide variety of systems, although it is recognized that their final generality may be dependent on the same sorts of taxonomy, task analysis, and weightings discussed previously. The tasks, as combined into the MTP battery, should have high face validity both in terms of content and user acceptance.

The content validity is required to assure the proper generality. The user acceptance is required because without it the operator's view of the test situation will be different from his view of the operational, and his behavior will differ in the two. Only one will be in the domain of work behavior; the other will be in a different behavioral domain.

III. Synthetic Work and Multiple-Task Performance

In modern psychological terms, the kinds of functions required of man in sustained-performance or work situations include (1) the discrimination and identification of sensory inputs, (2) the receiving, processing, storage, and retrieval of information, and (3) the exercise of control actions that range from discrete binary key-presses to continuous-control guiding or steering actions (tracking).

These, then, constitute functions that must be measured by any MTP battery that claims some measure of content validity. They represent the areas of sustained performances required of workers, or of subjects in work or synthetic-work situations. They are stated in terms mostly of intellectual activities, but it *is* man's intellectual ability that is usually first thought of when his role as an operator or worker in a man-machine system is described or defined (cf. Morgan *et al.*, 1963) —e.g., his ability to perceive and evaluate the cogent conditions of the situation in which he finds himself, to identify problems where they exist, to make decisions concerning the necessary actions to be taken (and even to improvise solutions to problems, where necessary), to effect the actions, and to monitor their accomplishment. Most of the functions involved in the "routine" operations of the system are automated in one way or another; e.g., by use of automatic equipment such as an automatic choke on a truck, an autopilot in an aircraft, or an automatic control system in an aerospace vehicle. Even in these cases, however, man is expected to back-up the system by monitoring the subsystem operations, and to assume full control where and when necessary.

The performance functions will be categorized, for convenience, into seven major areas as follows: (1) watchkeeping, vigilance, and attentive functions, including the monitoring of both static (discrete) and dynamic (continuous) processes; (2) sensory-perceptual functions, including the discrimination and identification of signals; (3) memory functions, both short- and long-term; (4) communication functions, including the reception and transmission of information; (5) intellectual functions, including information processing, decision making, problem solving, and nonverbal mediation; (6) perceptual-motor functions, especially to the extent that special skills such as aiming, tracking, swimming, driving, typing, and similar motor skills are necessary to the operation of the system; and finally (7) procedural functions that include such things as interpersonal coordination, cooperation, and organization.

These seven areas are represented either directly or indirectly in each of several similar MTP batteries that have been used.[2] One of these batteries will be described in detail to show how its tasks measure these functions.

A. A MULTIPLE-TASK PERFORMANCE BATTERY

The front view of an operator panel used in one MTP battery is shown in Fig. 1. We shall use the term "performance battery" when speaking of this specific one, and reserve the term "MTP battery" to represent the general class of such multiple-task performance instruments. Behavioral measures are obtained from the subject's performance of the six tasks presented with the panel and a pair of earphones. The tasks are generally displayed at each of five identical work stations — one for each member of a 5-man crew.

[2]The development of the initial multiple-task performance battery, and most of the early research conducted with it and its modifications (see Section IV, A), was completed in the Human Factors Research Laboratory of the Lockheed-Georgia Company with the support of the U.S. Air Force under Contract Nos. 33(616)-3745, -6050, -7607, and 33(657)-10506. Most of the later research (see Section IV, B) has been conducted by the Performance Research Laboratory of the University of Louisville with the support of the U.S. Army Medical Research and Development Command, Department of the Army, under Contract No. DA-49-193-MD-2567, and the National Aeronautics and Space Administration under Research Grant No. NGR-18-002-008.

Fig. 1 (opposite.).   Operator's panel from a multiple-task performance (MTP) battery. The tasks are described in the text. (Adapted from Alluisi *et al.*, 1963.)

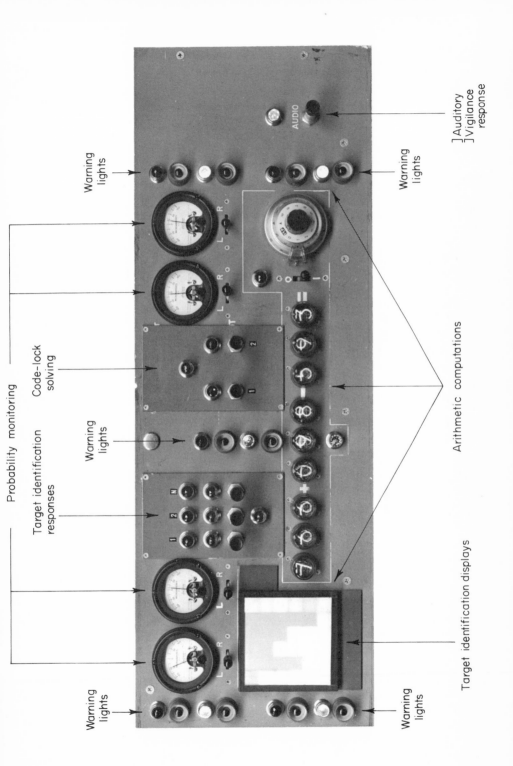

Probability monitoring

Warning lights

Code-lock solving

Target identification responses

Warning lights

Warning lights

Warning lights

Warning lights

AUDIO

] Auditory
] Vigilance response

Arithmetic computations

Target identification displays

67

Three watchkeeping tasks are used to measure the subject's performance of watchkeeping, vigilance, and attentive functions (auditory vigilance, warning-lights and probability monitoring). Three active tasks are used to measure the operator's performance of memory functions (arithmetic computations), sensory-perceptual functions (target identifications), and procedural functions (code-lock solving).

Communication functions are not measured directly, although they are involved to some extent in the performance of all three active tasks. A task designed to measure directly certain nonverbal-mediational aspects of intellectual functioning is under development (see Alluisi & Coates, 1967), and some versions of the MTP battery have employed tracking tasks to measure perceptual-motor functions (e.g., Adams, Levine, & Chiles, 1959; Chambers, Johnson, van Velzer, & White, 1966).

As will be indicated in the descriptions that follow, each of the tasks has been used and is fully described elsewhere. All of the tasks show very high reliabilities (Alluisi, Hall, & Chiles, 1962; Passey, Alluisi, & Chiles, 1964; Alluisi, 1967), and have done so since their earliest use (Adams *et al.*, 1959). They are nearly identical to the tasks employed in other MTP batteries (cf. Adams & Chiles, 1960, 1961; Alluisi, Chiles, & Hall, 1964a; Alluisi, Thurmond, & Coates, 1967; Chambers *et al.*, 1966).

1. Arithmetic Computations

Three 3-digit numbers are displayed along the lower central portion of the panel (see Fig. 1) by means of nine 1-digit numerical indicators. The operator is required to subtract the third 3-digit number from the sum of the first two. He is not allowed to use paper and pencil or any other aid. He indicates his answer by a lever switch and three concentric rotary decade switches located immediately to the right of the numerical indicators. If his answer is correct, a blue indicator light located immediately above the lever switch will be lit for a half-second interval as the problem is removed and just prior to the presentation of a new problem. An amber indicator light, located immediately below the center of the numerical indicators, is lit 30 sec prior to the presentation of the first problem and remains lit throughout the presentations of arithmetic-computation problems. Problems are usually presented at a rate of 3 per min during a 30-min interval of a 2-hr work period.

The arithmetic-computations task (Adams & Chiles, 1960, 1961; Adams *et al.*, 1959; Alluisi, Chiles, Hall, & Hawkes, 1963; Alluisi *et al.*, 1964a, 1967; Passey *et al.*, 1964) measures both short- and long-term memory functions. Of course, it also involves information handling, and to a certain extent, intellectual functions. Thus, it is not a pure measure of memory functioning, but rather it is heavily involved with memory in a manner quite similar to real work. It is also an excellent user of channel capacity and permits realistic loadings of the operator.

2. Auditory Vigilance

The auditory-vigilance task (Adams & Chiles, 1960, 1961; Adams *et al.*, 1959; Alluisi *et al.*, 1963, 1964a; Passey *et al.*, 1964) is presented through one side of a headset worn by the subject. The sensory input is provided by a 1175-Hz tone that recurs once every 1.20 sec under normal conditions. The beeping tone has a normal on-period of 0.25 sec and an off-period of 0.95 sec. The critical signal to be detected by the subject is a lengthening of a single off-period by about 50%, i. e., to 1.40 sec. When the subject detects the occurrence of a critical signal he is to report it by depressing a push button on the extreme right side of the panel (see Fig. 1) within 30 sec of the occurrence. He is not provided knowledge of results concerning the correctness of his response on this task, nor is he informed regarding missed signals.

3. Code-Lock Solving

As presently constituted, the code-lock task (Alluisi *et al.*, 1962, 1963, 1964a, 1967; Passey *et al.*, 1964) is a group-performance task that primarily involves procedural functions. The task requires a crew of 5 men to discover the proper sequential order for depressing their push buttons – one for each crew member. Three jewel indicator lights (red, amber, and green) and two push buttons (one of them a spare) are located on each panel in the right-of-center section above the numerical indicators (see Fig. 1).

Illumination of the red light is the signal that a problem is present and unsolved. The amber light is illuminated when any operator depresses his push button, but with no indication as to which operator it was or whether it was just one or more than one who did so. The problem is solved only when each of the five push buttons has been depressed in the correct sequential order for the specific problem.

Thus, the red light is extinguished when the correct first operator in the sequence depresses his push button, and it will remain extinguished until an incorrect response is made. When this occurs, the red light is reilluminated, and the programming apparatus is reset automatically to the beginning of the sequence. In order to recommence the search for a solution, then, the correct first subject must depress his key first, then the correct second operator must depress his key, etc. When all five push buttons have been depressed in the correct order, the green light is illuminated as a signal that the problem has been solved.

Following a between-problem pause of 30 sec, the green light goes off, the red light comes on, and the crew is presented with a replication of the problem previously solved. This requirement for a second solution has been included to increase the sensitivity of the task to performance decrements. Following the second solution and a between-problem pause of 30 sec, the green light goes off, the red light comes on, and the crew is presented with a new sequence or code to solve.

The elements of this code-lock task have been used in the development of a code-transformation (COTRAN) task that appears to provide performance measures of nonverbal mediation (Alluisi & Coates, 1967). The acquisition of the problem-solving skill involved in the COTRAN task has been studied, as has also the ways in which this task can be combined with other tasks in an MTP battery (Alluisi & Morgan, 1968).

4. Probability Monitoring

The four meters with semicircular scales located along the upper portion of the panel (see Fig. 1) are used in displaying the probability-monitoring task (Adams & Chiles, 1960, 1961; Adams *et al.*, 1959; Alluisi *et al.*, 1963, 1964a, 1967; Passey *et al.*, 1964). A pointer on each scale is driven by a random program generator. The pointer settings are normally distributed with a mean of zero (12 o'clock position on the scale) and a known standard deviation. Introduction of a signal or bias to the programming device causes the mean of the distribution on one of the four scales (different on different panels) to shift by a specified amount. This shift in the mean does not affect the variability of the pointer positions.

When the subject detects a shift in the mean, he indicates this by moving a horizontally placed lever switch under the meter in question — to the left if he has detected a bias to the left, or to the right if he has detected a bias in that direction. Whenever the subject moves any of the probability-monitoring lever switches, the pointer of the meter in question will move to, and stabilize at, the mean of its current distribution (i.e., either zero, or biased right or left). If a bias is present, then release of the switch causes the scale to be reset to the zero-bias condition.

5. Target Identifications

In the lower left of each operator panel (see Fig. 1) there is a 4-in square array of 36 close-butted, square lights. These lights, forming a 6-by-6 matrix, are used in presentation of "metric histoforms" that are employed in the target-identification (or target-ID) task (Alluisi *et al.*,

1963, 1964a, 1967; Passey *et al.*, 1964). These are contoured figures consisting of lit and unlit elements giving the appearance of solid bar graphs (cf. Alluisi, Hawkes, & Hall, 1964b; Fitts, Weinstein, Rappaport, Anderson, & Leonard, 1956).

A finite set of 240 metric histoforms has been drawn at random from the 720 possible 36-element constrained figures; i.e., figures in which each of the six possible column heights appears once and only once. Each of these 240 figures is programmed to appear with its base at 6 o'clock, with its columns rising, as was shown in Fig. 1. These figures are described to the subjects as representing noisefree "stored target" images. Another set of figures, drawn from the same basic set of 720, is used to represent "sensed target" images; these are usually perturbed, either with random visual cell noise (Alluisi *et al.*, 1963, 1964a, b) or random positioning (rotation in 90-deg steps) relative to the stored target image (Alluisi *et al.*, 1967).

The task as presented to the subject is as follows: There will be a 5-sec display of the noisefree (or upright) figure or stored target image. This will be followed by a 5-sec off-period. Then there will be a 2-sec display of a noisy (or randomly positioned) image, "sensed target-A," a 2-sec off-period, and a 2-sec display of a second noisy (or randomly positioned) image, "sensed target-B." After a response period of 14 sec, the cycle will be repeated with new stored and sensed images.

Each subject is required to respond by use of one of three large push buttons (on the panel shown in Fig. 1, these are slightly above and to the right of the target-ID display). His response indicates whether in his judgment the stored target image was the same as the first, second, or neither of the sensed target images. One of the three amber lights in the row just above the push buttons is lit as soon as the subject makes his response and remains lit until the problem is cycled and a new problem presented. The light serves merely as an aid to memory; it indicates to the subject which of the three possible responses it was that he made. Just prior to the presentation of a new problem, a blue knowledge-of-results indicator light in the row above the amber lights will be lit for a half-second interval to inform the subject either of the correct response to the problem (e.g., Alluisi *et al.*, 1967) or of the "final decision" made by the crew commander on the basis of information regarding the responses made by all five crew members (e.g., Alluisi *et al.*, 1963, 1964a, b).

6. *Warning-Lights Monitoring*

The third of the three watchkeeping tasks is presented on the panel (see Fig. 1) with five pairs of warning lights, each pair consisting of one green and one red light (Adams & Chiles, 1960, 1961; Adams *et al.*, 1959; Alluisi *et al.*, 1963, 1964a, 1967; Passey *et al.*, 1964). The subject is required to turn any green light on should it go off, and any red light off should it come on, by depressing the push button located immediately below the light in question. If he fails to respond within 2 min, the nonnormal condition is corrected automatically, and the subject is scored with a missed signal.

B. Content Validity: Functions Measured

At the beginning of Section III we listed seven operator functions as major areas that should be represented in any MTP battery that was to be used to create a synthetic-work situation. Then, in the preceding subsection (Section III,A) we described one of the MTP batteries that has been used, the "performance battery," as we called it. Now we shall take another look at both the functions and the tasks in the performance battery to see how well the tasks represent the functions, at least on a logical basis. Only in this way can we judge the extent to which the performance battery can claim to have content validity.

1. Watchkeeping Functions

Three tasks are employed in the performance battery to measure the operator's performance of watchkeeping functions: two for the monitoring of static processes (auditory vigilance and warning-lights monitoring) and one for the monitoring of a dynamic process (probability monitoring). They differ also in terms of the conspicuity of the onset of the critical signal. In auditory vigilance, the critical signal is a discrete, single occurrence of an extended off-period, or pause, in a temporal string of beeping tones. The subject responds simply to the occurrence of the signal. Likewise, the onset of a red warning light is rather conspicuous, and it is probably the onset to which the subject responds rather than to the presence of the signal. On the other hand, the onset of the signal in the probability-monitoring task is completely masked by a kind of visual noise — the random fluctuations of the pointers — and the subject is forced to respond to the presence of the signal. Thus, although all three are watchkeeping tasks, or "passive" tasks as they are sometimes called, they represent attempts to measure different aspects of the watchkeeping, vigilance, and attentive functions of man.

2. Memory Functions

Both long- and short-term memory functions are measured with arithmetic computations. Of course, as we have said previously, the performance of mental arithmetic computations also involves information handling and, to a certain extent, intellectual functions. We do not believe that arithmetic computations provide a pure measure of memory functioning, but rather that they are heavily involved with memory in a manner quite similar to real work. Also, they are an excellent user of channel capacity and permit realistic loadings of the operator.

3. Sensory-Perceptual Functions

Of all the tasks that could be used to measure sensory-perceptual functions, the performance battery employs just one — the target-identification task. It is not that sensory-perceptual functions are difficult to measure, granted a logic for selecting their specific representations in a test battery, but rather that such a logic is especially difficult to devise for "general" tasks. It is difficult to abstract meaningful representations of these functions because most jobs are now designed so as not to tax man unnecessarily in these areas (the same goes for perceptual-motor functions). Where these functions do appear as problems, it is usually because of excessive demands made of the operator or worker in ways that are highly specific to the work or job in question. For example, man-machine systems are generally designed so as not to press man with regard to his visual acuity. Where visual acuity is a problem, it is likely to be so only because of some specific aspect of the particular system. It might be a problem in the case of a newly designed critical task that has not yet been instrumented with "necessary" optical aids; or, it might be a problem for the astronaut during those brief periods in which high g forces are acting on him and his vehicle. Thus, because of the specificity of the sensory-perceptual (as well as the perceptual-motor) performance problems, it is difficult to design general tasks to represent them properly in an MTP battery, even though these functions are relatively easy to instrument and measure. The target-identification task in the performance battery represents at least one general aspect of the sensory-perceptual functions.

4. Procedural Functions

Group performance and procedural functions are measured principally with the task of code-lock solving. This task also taps short-term memory and, to a lesser extent, intellectual functions. In addition, the target-identification task has been used in some studies (Alluisi *et al.*, 1963, 1964a) as a group-performance task that included both procedural functions and decision-making or intellectual functioning of the crew commander.

The three tasks just listed — arithmetic computations, target identifications, and code-lock solving — are often referred to as active tasks. They are to be distinguished from the watchkeeping or passive tasks.

They require a more active participation on the part of the subject for highly successful performance, and they are somewhat more likely to show relatively little impairment with highly motivated subjects under mildly stressful conditions.

5. *Communication Functions*

The first-order communication functions are not measured directly in the performance battery. However, certain aspects of these functions, such as information-handling performances of the operator, can be developed with use of the arithmetic-computations and code-lock solving displays, and laboratory research has been started in this area (cf. Alluisi & Coates, 1967; Alluisi & Morgan, 1968).

6. *Intellectual Functions*

None of the tasks in the performance battery provides a specific, direct measure of intellectual functions. All three active tasks obviously tap at least some aspects of intellectual functions, but not to any significant degrees. Laboratory research is underway to develop a modification of the code-lock task which will provide a direct measure of the nonverbal-mediational aspect of intellectual functioning (Alluisi & Coates, 1967; Alluisi & Morgan, 1968). Both individual- and group-performance versions of this new task are being tested, with the group version's showing some promise of providing a direct measure of communication functions.

7. *Perceptual-Motor Functions*

Perhaps the greatest shortcoming of the performance battery is its lack of a perceptual-motor task such as tracking. Some of the difficulties encountered in trying to develop a meaningful yet reliable general test of perceptual-motor functions are similar to the difficulties encountered with sensory-perceptual functions (see Section III,B,3). A tracking task was once tried with the performance battery, but it proved to be unreliable (Adams *et al.*, 1959). Of the other MTP batteries in use, one does include a tracking task (Chambers *et al.*, 1966), whereas the other does not (Alluisi *et al.*, 1967).

IV. Research on Sustained Performance

An historical presentation will be used to summarize the results of the research on sustained performance that has been complete with use of various versions of the MTP battery. This research was initially aimed (1) at the development of a performance-assessment technique based on the concept of synthetic work, (2) at the measurement of the effects of working in a volumetrically restrictive environment, and (3) at the determination of optimum work-rest schedules. More recent work has continued the emphasis on the development of performance-assessment techniques, and (4) has begun to measure the behavioral effects of infectious diseases. In addition, the data collected have contributed to our knowledge of the effects of certain of man's diurnal rhythms.

The program of research began in 1956 with a concern about the effects on aircrew performance of confinement in the anticipated volumetrically restrictive work environment of a proposed nuclear aircraft. It was estimated that the crew area of the nuclear bomber, with a 5-man crew, would provide no more than 23 ft² per man. In contrast, 64 ft² per man was provided for the 14-man crew of a Navy blimp (ZPG-2W), and 66 ft² per man was provided for the 114-man crew of the nuclear submarine; yet, the blimp and submarine were considered to present volumetrically restrictive work environments, especially for long-duration missions (cf. Panel on Psychology and Physiology, 1949).

A crew-compartment mock-up was designed and constructed to the scale of the nuclear aircraft. However, because of classification and because plans for the nuclear aircraft were shelved about the same time that support for the space program was increased, the mock-up was changed to accommodate the operator panels that were then being developed for the performance battery (Adams, 1958). The crew-compartment mock-up that was subsequently employed is shown in an artist's conception cut-away view in Fig. 2. The section with a round top, containing the 5-station work area and the leisure area, was the original scaled section; the square-topped section containing the 6-bunk sleeping area was a later addition. The total volume was approximately 1100 ft³, divided about equally between the two sections.

A. Early Experimentation: The Work-Rest Phase

The initial plan of study aimed to measure the effects of various work-rest schedules on sustained performance. An MTP battery had been designed to provide a synthetic-work environment. That is to say, the battery required that several different tasks could be combined to provide for multiple-task performance. Synthetic work requires the concurrent performance of several tasks at once; the intent is to synthesize the several different tasks of an MTP battery into a

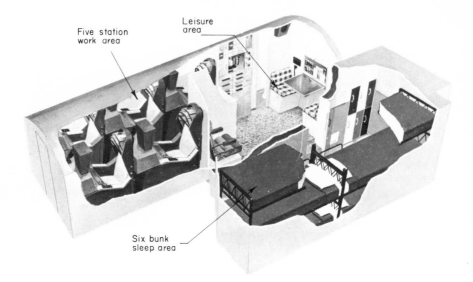

Fig. 2. Cutaway view of a crew-compartment mock-up employed with the perform-ance tests in studies of sustained performance. (Adapted from Alluisi *et al.*, 1962.)

reasonably realistic work-like situation—a situation that requires an operator to be responsible for more than merely a single function and that permits a variation in his work load.

Although there have been some differences among the studies completed, especially where different MTP batteries have been used, the typical sort of multiple-task performance employed is shown in Table I. The work is divided over a 2-hr performance period so that the operator or subject is responsible for the watchkeeping tasks all of the time, but he is responsible for the active tasks only part of the time. Thus, relative demands on performance can be low, interme-diate, or high, depending on whether the watchkeeping tasks are pre-sented alone, with only one of the active tasks, or with two (or more) of them.

With the completion of an initial version of the performance battery and the crew-compartment mock-up (Adams, 1958), data collection began (Adams *et al.*, 1959). Much of the research was influenced by constraints imposed by the operational or work situation to which generality was desired; namely, (1) crews of men rather than individ-uals would be needed, (2) the work would have to be performed 24 hours around the clock on a high-alert basis for 5 days or longer, and (3) the work environment would remain volumetrically restrictive. With these constraints in mind, the first study was designed to be a technical investigation of multiple-task performance.

1. A Technical Study

The questions asked in the first study conducted with the performance battery (Adams *et al.*, 1959) were concerned with such things as the rates at which operators became proficient on the tasks, the test-retest reliabilities of the measures of performance obtained, the interactions among the tasks when performed in various multiple-task combinations, and the intertest correlations. The panel employed in this initial experiment differed from that previously described (and shown in Fig. 1) in that it did not include the target-identification nor code-lock tasks, which had not yet been designed. Instead, it had a pattern-discrimination task, a compensatory-tracking task, and a scale-position monitoring task, in addition to arithmetic computations, auditory vigilance, probability monitoring, and warning-lights monitoring.

Certain changes were made in the panel's configuration as a result of the data obtained in the study. Five tasks were retained — three of the watchkeeping tasks (auditory vigilance, probability and warning-lights monitoring), and two of the active tasks (arithmetic computations and pattern discriminations). The tasks that were retained had demonstrated impressively high reliabilities, and they imposed relatively minor training requirements. The performance battery appeared to provide measures of essentially orthogonal functions, and it was capable of being programmed in numerous ways to make possible the study of a broad range of operator work loads (Adams *et al.*, 1959). The presentation of these tasks was integrated into a 2-hr work period similar to that which was given earlier in Table I; probability monitoring was not presented during the first and last 15-min intervals of the 2-hr period, arithmetic computations continued for an additional 15 min, code-lock solving did not occur at all, and pattern discriminations (instead of target identifications) began 15 min earlier than indicated for target identifications and continued for 45 min. The important thing to note is that time-shared performances were still required during each 2-hr performance period.

Table I
TYPICAL 2-HOUR PROGRAM FOR MULTIPLE-TASK PERFORMANCE[a]

Task	Minutes								
	000	015	030	045	060	075	090	105	120
Auditory vigilance	xxxxxxxxxxxxxxxxxxxxxxxxxxxxxxxxxxxxxxxx								
Probability monitoring	xxxxxxxxxxxxxxxxxxxxxxxxxxxxxxxxxxxxxxxx								
Warning lights	xxxxxxxxxxxxxxxxxxxxxxxxxxxxxxxxxxxxxxxx								
Arithmetic computations		xxxxxxxxxx							
Code-lock solving			xxxxxxxxxxxxxxxxxxx						
Target identification							xxxxxxxxxx		

[a]Each x represents 3 min; so 15 min is represented by xxxxx.

2. Four-Day (96-Hour) Studies

The plan of research about to be started was conceived of as follows: There was to be a number of 4-day or 96-hr studies in which investigations would be made: first of the effects of the lengths of the duty and rest periods with their ratio held constant, then of the effects of the ratio of duty to rest with the use of a single rest-period duration, namely, the briefest one acceptable to the subjects. Subsequently, the most efficient work-rest schedule was to be selected and tested over a 15-day period of performance.

In accordance with this plan, a second experiment was designed. It sought to measure the effects of the durations of the work and rest periods over a 4-day (96-hr) interval. A unit work-to-rest ratio was used, with work-rest cycles of 2-hr on-duty and 2-hr off, 4 on and 4 off, 6 on and 6 off, and 8 on and 8 off. Sixteen male college students served as subjects, with four subjects assigned to each of the four work-rest schedules. The principal data were obtained with the measures of the performance battery, but additional data were gathered in an experimenter's record (log book) and with a questionnaire administered to the subjects after the test.

The results indicated that the performance scores continued to improve throughout the 96 hr with each of the four work-rest schedules, and no significant difference among the schedules was obtained. The data of the experimenter's log and the questionnaires suggested, however, that the 2- and 4-hr cycles resulted in more favorable adjustments by the subjects than did the 6- and 8-hr schedules (Adams & Chiles, 1960).

From these data it appeared that subjects could follow a work-rest schedule that permitted rest (or sleep) periods as brief as 2 or 4 hr in duration. Indeed, the questionnaire data suggested that the subjects preferred the shorter work periods and that they were willing to trade off the length of the rest period to obtain briefer work periods. On the basis of this conclusion, it was decided to use the brief 2-hr rest period in studying the effects on performance of work-to-rest ratios of 2:1 and 3:1.

Twenty male college students served as subjects. They were divided into four groups of 5 subjects each. Two of the groups followed a work-rest schedule of 4-hr on-duty and 2-hr off, around the clock for 4 days, whereas the other two groups followed a schedule of 6-hr on and 2-hr off for the same length of time.

The performance data gave clear evidence of diurnal cycling with 24-hr periodicity on all measures with both schedules. Once again, however, the differences in the performances obtained with the battery did not permit any conclusion to be reached concerning which of the two schedules was the better.

Fortunately, there was a clear indication that the 4-2 schedule was preferred over 6-2 schedule by the subjects. In addition, the experimenter's log indicated that the subjects who followed the 4-2 schedule averaged about 5-1/2 hr of sleep per 24-hr period, whereas those who followed the 6-2 schedule averaged less than 4 hr of sleep (Adams & Chiles 1961, pp. 29–34).

All of the 4-day studies had one feature in common: they failed to produce differences in performance that could be used to reach meaningful decisions concerning the efficacy of the various work-rest schedules employed. This appears to be a function more of the total duration of the studies — i.e., the 4-day or 96-hr periods — than of any lack of effect of the schedules or lack of sensitivity of the performance measures (cf. Ray *et al.*, 1961). Man apparently has the necessary resiliency to meet the demands of quite stressful work-rest schedules over relatively brief 4-day intervals. Presumably, he has performance reserves that he can use to help him over such brief stressful periods. Studies of longer duration appear to be necessary to demonstrate work-rest schedule effects on sustained performance.

3. *Studies of Longer Duration*

The results of the 4-day studies had suggested that a work-rest cycle of 4-hr on-duty and 2-hr off might provide a highly efficient schedule for operators who had to perform the kinds of functions included in the performance battery's tasks. The results did not indicate whether the subjects could maintain acceptable performance over prolonged periods of, say, 15 days or more. This was measured in the first of several long-duration studies of sustained performance (see Adams & Chiles, 1961).

Two crews of operational Air Force personnel each followed a 4-2 work-rest schedule for 15 days. There were 5 subjects in one crew and 6 in the other. Both physiological and performance data clearly demonstrated diurnal cycles of about 24-hr periodicity throughout the 15 days. In general, the performance cycles lagged about 2 hr behind the physiological. Also, there appeared to be slight shifts in the cycles during the course of the study — shifts that could be interpreted as indicating slightly lengthened cycles of greater than 24-hr periodicity. These shifts can be seen in the data of Figs. 3 and 4 with heart-rate levels and correct arithmetic computations, respectively. The performance cycle's lag can also be seen, for example, by comparing the

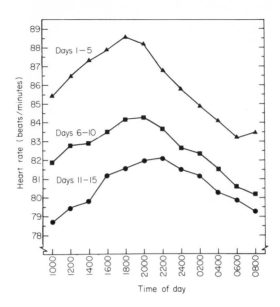

Fig. 3. Average heart rates at different times of day during three 5-day periods of a 15-day study of 11 subjects (4-2 work-rest schedule). (Data of Adams & Chiles, 1961.)

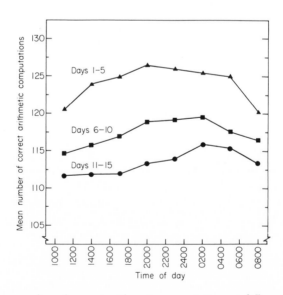

Fig. 4. Average number of correct arithmetic computations at different times of day during three 5-day periods of a 15-day study of 11 subjects (4-2 work-rest schedule). (Data of Adams & Chiles, 1961.)

times of peak performance and peak physiological activation indicated by the cycles.

The apparent shift in the performance and physiological cycles is tentatively interpreted as an indication of fatigue, or a work-rest schedule stress; namely, as a result of the accumulated fatigue produced by the demands of the schedule, the subjects were reaching their physiological and performance peaks slightly later each day. This hypothesis may provide some interesting measures of fatigue and work-stress effects, if it is validated in other long-duration studies of sustained performance.

In general, the data supported the hypothesis that the 4-2 schedule could be used over fairly long durations. Specifically, it was concluded that with some selection, highly motivated crews could maintain acceptable performance levels while following a 4-2 work-rest schedule for a period of 2 weeks, and possibly for longer durations. The conclusion was based principally on the fact that two of the eleven subjects were able to maintain high performance levels throughout the 15 days. In addition, the majority of subjects indicated during posttest interviews that they could have continued the test for at least an additional 15 days if it were necessary and important for them to have done so.

The crew-performance code-lock task was subsequently developed, and the pattern-discrimination task was replaced with target identifications (Alluisi *et al.*, 1962, 1963). The resultant panel was the one shown earlier in Fig. 1, and the 2-hr performance periods employed with this panel were the same as that given previously in Table I. In addition, the target-identification task was provided with a secondary display at the crew commander's position so that it reflected certain aspects of crew performance; this did not interfere with the individual-performance aspects of the task.

Then, with the addition of these crew-performance tasks and measures to the performance battery, the 15-day study of the effects of the 4-2 work-rest schedule was replicated. The subjects were 6 highly motivated Air Force Academy cadets — probably the most highly motivated subjects this experimenter has ever encountered! The subjects were asked to do whatever they could to prevent the expected diurnal cycling in performance by expending "extra effort during those work periods that seem to be hard on you — usually those in the early morning hours between, say, 2:00 and 6:00 A.M."

The physiological data (self-determined axillary temperatures and pulse rates) gave clear indications of a diurnal rhythm with 24-hr periodicity; the performance data of this group of subjects who were referred to with the code name, "HOPE-II," gave essentially no indications of diurnal cycling (Alluisi *et al.*, 1963). There was one important exception, but that will not be presented until after a description is given of the subsequent study, "HOPE-III," in which a group of 10 subjects followed a work-rest schedule of 4-hr on-duty and 4-hr off for a 30-day period.

All 10 subjects in HOPE-III were Air Force pilots. They were divided into two 5-man crews that followed the 4-4 work-rest schedule for the entire 30-day duration of the study. The subjects had been led to believe, however, that the confinement for the experiment would extend for 40 days, and since they did not learn otherwise until the study ended on the thirtieth day, it can be assumed safely that their data show no end effects.

As in the previous studies, the physiological data of HOPE-III gave clear evidence of diurnal cycling. This is illustrated in Fig. 5, where the self-determined axillary temperatures are shown for the 30-day period. Here, as in the remaining figures in this chapter, rolling means are used to minimize the effects of variations attributable to differences among individuals and work activities. Thus, each point has represented in it all 10 subjects and an equal number of subjects who have just risen from sleep, who are in the midst of a 4-hr work period, and who have just completed a 4-hr work period.

Several conclusions appear to be supported by the data of Fig. 5. First, the diurnal cycling with 24-hr periodicity in axillary temperature is clearly evident. Second, the drifting or lagging of the diurnal cycle – suggestive of a cycle that is slightly longer than 24 hr – is also evidenced; this is shown in the peaks of the broken line's being slightly displaced to the right of the peaks of the solid line. Third, it can be seen that the diurnal cycling in temperature apparently continued without much abatement for the first 20 or 25 days of the study. Only during the last 5 to 10 days does the diurnal variation appear to be somewhat flattened (statistically significant during the last 5 days only). This suggests that physiological adaptation to atypical work-rest schedules will take at least 20 days, and perhaps as long as 25 or 30 days on the average – even where the environment is controlled and the variations due to activity are removed by means such as the rolling-mean techniques used here. There is additional support for this conclusion in the literature (cf. Ray *et al.*, 1961).

The HOPE-III subjects, like those in the HOPE-II study of the 4-2 schedule, had been shown the data of the earliest 15-day experiment in which diurnal variations in performance had been noted. They, too, were instructed to expend extra effort when necessary to preclude such performance cycling effects. They were apparently able to do so, but not quite as well as the HOPE-II cadets had done. Thus, although

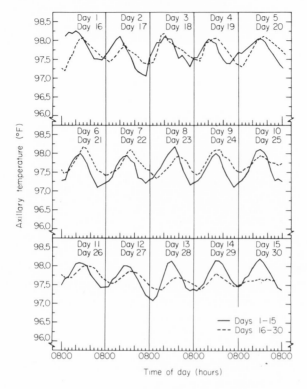

Fig. 5. Average axillary temperatures of 10 subjects (HOPE-III) during 30 days of sustained performance on a 4-4 work-rest schedule. (Data of Alluisi *et al.*, 1963.)

the HOPE-III subjects did exhibit statistically significant performance cycling on some of the tasks, the magnitude of the effect was not great, and the *lowest* levels in their cycles still represented substantially better performance than that generally exhibited by the 11 subjects in the earlier 15-day study of the 4-2 schedule.

The one important exception that was alluded to earlier, and which had been noted in the HOPE-II data, is shown in Fig. 6 with the data of arithmetic computations when performed concurrently with the code-lock task. The data given are those of the second 4-2 study (HOPE-II) and the 30-day 4-4 study (HOPE-III). The data indicate a condition of performance stress for both groups during the first several days of experimentation, apparently while they were still learning to time-share the tasks in the performance battery.

Performance stress may be said to exist when on the introduction of an additional task, performance on all tasks (including the newly in-

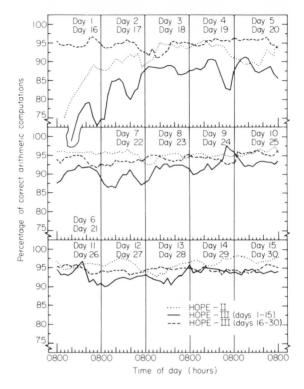

Fig. 6. Average percentage of correct arithmetic computations by 6 subjects in a 15-day study (HOPE-II) and 10 subjects in a 30-day study (HOPE-III) with 4-2 and 4-4 work-rest schedules, respectively, performed *with* code-lock problems. (Data of Alluisi *et al.*, 1963.)

troduced one) falls below the levels attained without the additional task. This was the case during the early days of performance when the code-lock task was added to the demands of the arithmetic-computations and watchkeeping tasks. For example, it is apparent from the bottom panel in Fig. 6, where the data of the third and sixth 5-day periods of HOPE-III are shown along with the third period of HOPE-II, that the subjects did eventually learn to time-share these tasks. Also, since these levels of performance are essentially identical to those obtained without concurrent performance of the code-lock task, it can be concluded that the condition of performance stress no longer existed.

Rather, it was during the first several days that the performance stress was evidenced. During those days, the diurnal cycling of performance was clearly indicated in the data (see the uppermost panel of Fig. 6). This is interpreted to mean that even when the subjects are generally able to overcome diurnal-cycling effects in their performances, they are able to do so only within limits. A physiologically determined diurnal rhythm is present and underlies all performance; information and motivation can be employed to overcome the tendency for performance to exhibit the same rhythm, but only to a point. If the subjects are overloaded — if they have more than they can do, as in the performance-stress condition — the diurnal-cycling effects are likely to reappear in the performance data.

The results of the 30-day study otherwise indicated that the 4-4 work-rest schedule was less demanding than the 4-2 schedule (Alluisi *et al.*, 1963). It was concluded that whereas with proper control of selection and motivational factors, crews can work effectively for at least 2 weeks (and probably longer) using a schedule of 4-hr on-duty and 2-hr off, crews can work even more effectively for periods of at least a month (and quite probably for 2 or 3 months) using a schedule of 4-hr on-duty and 4-hr off. Also, the latter schedule would apparently require less demanding controls of the selection and motivational factors.

4. Effects of Sleep Loss

The conclusions just listed were further supported by the results of four 12-day studies of the combined effects of sleep loss and the two work-rest schedules (Alluisi *et al.*, 1964a). This is illustrated in Fig. 7 in terms of the percentage of correct responses in the arithmetic-computations task when it was presented without concurrent presentation of the code-lock task. The solid curve represents the data of the two groups (20 subjects) who followed the 4-4 work-rest schedule, and the broken line represents the two groups (12 subjects) who followed the 4-2 schedule.

Performance was generally inferior on the 4-2 schedule as compared with the 4-4, and the stress of sleep loss (40 and 44 hr of wakefulness with the two schedules, respectively) resulted in greater performance decrements for subjects on the 4-2 schedule than for those on the 4-4 schedule. Diurnal cycling in the performance measures of the 4-4 subjects was generally not apparent, except during the period of sleep-loss stress. The performance of the 4-2 subjects also showed increased diurnal cycling during the sleep-loss period. Thus, it again appears that the extent to which motivation can be used to overcome the physiological rhythm is limited; as Bloom (1961) has concluded, there is reason to respect the normal diurnal body rhythms.

5. Control Studies

Although direct reference has not been made to them, several control studies have been conducted. In one (Adams & Chiles, 1961, pp.

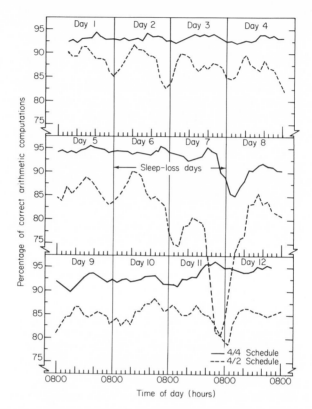

Fig. 7. Average percentage of correct arithmetic computations (*without* concurrent presentation of code-lock problems) by 12 subjects on a 4-2 work-rest schedule and 20 on a 4-4 schedule during the 12 days of a sleep-loss study. (Data of Alluisi *et al.*, 1964a.)

35–39), 6 college students were tested 4-hr per day, 5 days per week, for 6 weeks (120 hr of performance). When their performance was compared with that of the earlier 15-day 4-2 study, it was generally found that the controls continued to improve and were superior to the experimental subjects on most tasks (specifically, on arithmetic computations, auditory vigilance, and warning-lights monitoring).

A second control study (Hall, Passey, & Meighan, 1965) was concerned with an evaluation of performances on the three watchkeeping tasks (auditory vigilance, probability, and warning-lights monitoring) when they occurred with and without concurrent performance of the three active tasks (arithmetic computations, target identifications, and code-lock solving). After familiarization and preliminary training given over a 4-day period, two groups of 5 college students were tested for 4 hr per day on 6 successive days. It was concluded that concurrent presentation of the active tasks has a detrimental effect on the operator's performance of his watchkeeping duties (see also Hawkes, Meighan, & Alluisi, 1964). The effects are similar to those of performance stresses, in that removal of the concurrently presented active tasks invariably resulted in the recovery of the watchkeeping performances back to the previously attained levels.

A more recent control study was conducted at the University of Louisville with a slightly different version of the MTP battery — a version that is essentially the same as the performance battery that was shown earlier (in Fig. 1) except that the auditory-vigilance task has been replaced with a blinking-lights monitoring task. In this study (Alluisi *et al.*, 1967), 10 Air Force ROTC cadets followed a work-rest schedule of 4-hr on-duty, 4-hr off, 4 on, and 12 off, for 11 consecutive days. These subjects were not restricted in their activities except, of course, during the 8 hr of work per day; during the remaining 16 hr per day they were free to conduct their normal activities (school was not in session).

The dotted line in Fig. 8 presents the control group's percentage of correct responses in the arithmetic-computations task, when this task was worked without concurrent presentation of code-lock solving. The broken line presents the comparable data of the first 12 days of performance of the ten pilots in the 30-day study of the 4-4 work-rest schedule (HOPE-III).

It is apparent from the data of Fig. 8, as it was in all the data obtained, that the two groups performed at essentially identical levels. From this it can be concluded that the 4-4 schedule under the conditions of the 30-day study (i.e., with controlled environmental conditions) produced performances that were as good as those obtained with a less demanding 4-4-4-12 schedule under the more nearly normal working conditions in which the operators, subjects, or workers are free during their off-duty hours to do what they care to do.

B. LATER RESEARCH: THE EFFECTS OF ILLNESS

Men are subject to illnesses — to infection — as long as they live, and their work or sustained performances may be expected to show the effects of such illnesses. A large part of the biomedical literature is devoted to infectious diseases, and a great deal of medical practice is devoted to the prevention of infection and the treatment and cure of infected individuals.

Relatively little of the psychological literature, however, has been concerned with the effects of infectious diseases on behavior. If only little is known of man's behavioral reactions to infection, essentially

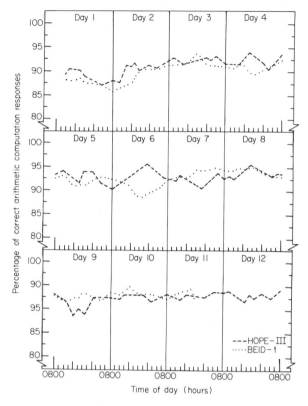

Fig. 8. Average percentage of correct responses (to arithmetic-computation problems presented without concurrent code-lock problems) by a 10-man control group (BEID-1) and a 10-man experimental group (HOPE-III) working 8 and 12 hr per day, respectively. (Data of Alluisi *et al.*, 1967.)

nothing is known regarding the quantitative effects of infectious diseases on his sustained performance or work (cf. Warm & Alluisi, 1967).

There is little doubt that this dearth of knowledge concerning the behavioral effects of infectious diseases has been based in great measure on the more basic needs for suitable methods of assessing man's sustained performances. It was not unnatural, therefore, that the present line of synthetic-work research on the general question of sustained performance turned specifically to the study of the effects of illness.

1. Effects of Tularemia

In one experiment (Alluisi *et al.*, 1967), of 10 volunteer subjects, 8 were infected with respiratory *Pasteurella tularensis* (commonly called "tularemia" or "rabbit fever") and 2 served as uninfected controls. The subjects worked on a schedule of 4 hr on-duty, 4-hr off, 4 on, and 12 off, during each of 12 successive days. Exposure occurred on the morning of the fifth day of testing. As indicated by the rectal temperatures shown in Fig. 9, the experimental subjects were febrile by the eighth day, remained so during the ninth day when treatment was started, were normal on the tenth day, and were slightly subnormal in temperature on the last two days of testing. The broken curve in Fig. 9 presents the rectal temperatures of the two control subjects; the dotted line presents the self-determined axillary temperatures of 10 subjects in the University of Louisville control group discussed

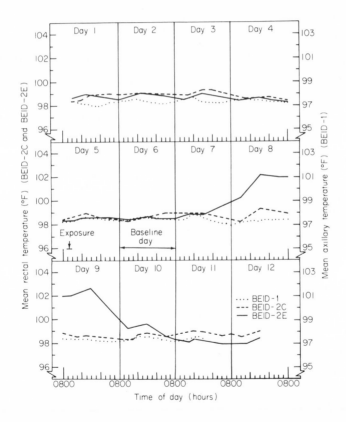

Fig. 9. Average temperatures of 20 subjects working 8 hr per day, 10 subjects for 11 days (BEID-1) and 10 for 12 days (BEID-2); the axillary temperatures of BEID-1 are read from the ordinate on the right, and the rectal temperatures of BEID-2 are read from the ordinate on the left (both for the controls, C, and the experimental subjects, E). (Data of Alluisi *et al.*, 1967.)

previously (and identified in the figure as BEID-1). The experimentals are identified in the figure as BEID-2E, and the hospital controls are identified as BEID-2C.

Respiratory tularemia is a febrile disease based on infection with the *P. tularensis* bacterium. It is characterized by severe headache, photophobia, nausea, myalgia, and depression. All eight of the experimental subjects became symptomatic on either the seventh or eighth day of testing, and chemotherapy was begun on each either during the eight or ninth day. Both of the double-blind controls remained asymptomatic throughout the period of testing.

Decrements in the performances of the experimental subjects were measured during the period of illness with each of 13 scores that are based on the six tasks employed in the MTP battery used. In addition, a general index of performance was derived in order to represent in a composite score the general performance of the subjects on all tasks. This index of general performance is the mean percentage of baseline performance—where each subject's performance with each of the 13 measures during the sixth day of testing was taken as the baseline and set at 100%. The results obtained with this index of general performance are shown in Fig. 10.

As is indicated by the data of Fig. 10, average efficiency fell about 25% during the period of illness. Recovery 3 days after treatment had begun was incomplete, with performance averaging 10 to 15% below that of control subjects.

In terms of the individual tasks, illness-related decrements in performance appeared to be evidenced more clearly in the active tasks relative to the watchkeeping tasks, but the recovery to baseline performance following treatment was less nearly complete in watchkeeping than in the active tasks. The recovery in watchkeeping was found to be better, not worse, than the recovery in the active tasks, during an extended 15-day replication of the tularemia experiment (Thurmond, Alluisi, & Coates, 1968). Since the illness-related decrements in performance were again more clearly evidenced in the active tasks, the difference in the recovery patterns of the two studies is specific. It demonstrates an effect that cannot occur where time-sharing is not required, and it emphasizes both the advantage and the potential danger implicit in the use of a composite measure such as the index of general performance.

On the average, there was a 6% drop in performance efficiency with each 1°F rise in rectal temperature during the period of illness (8% per °F in the later study, where average efficiency fell 33%). Differences among individual subjects were very great; the decrements in performance ranged from essentially none to about 20% per degree in

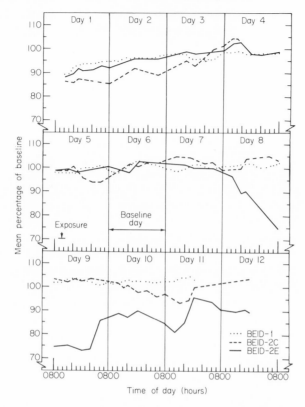

Fig. 10. Average percentages of baseline performances of 20 subjects working 8 hr per day, 10 subjects for 11 days (BEID-1) and 10 for 12 days (BEID-2); 8 experimental (E) and 2 control (C) subjects are included in the latter group. (Data of Alluisi *et al.*, 1967.)

both studies. Additional research will be required to identify the psychological and biomedical correlates of such performance decrements. Hopefully, such research should lead not only to an explanation of the wide range of differences among individuals in their behavioral reactions to illness, but also to continued advances in our development of techniques for the assessment of sustained performance and in our understanding of man's work behavior.

2. Effects of Other Infections

The effects of phlebotomus fever (commonly called "sand-fly fever") on sustained performance have been studied in two 15-day experiments similar to the tularemia studies described in the previous section. Although it is a viral infection (*Phlebotomus papatasii*, Sicilian strain) normally contracted through the bite of a sand fly, phle-

botomus fever is characterized by symptoms that are nearly identical
to those of tularemia, a bacterial infection (*Pasteurella tularensis*):
fever, severe headache, photophobia, malaise, and leukopenia. It is
not fatal, and recovery will occur in a few days without chemotherapy.
The results of these studies have not yet been published.

Only one other study can be cited (cf. Warm & Alluisi, 1967) as
having dealt experimentally with the effects of infection on human
performance; this is the excellent and extensive study of Frankenhaeuser (1958) on the behavioral effects of primary aseptic meningo-
encephalitis. Although multiple-task performance was not measured,
nor a synthetic-work situation employed, the results are relevant to
our interests in sustained performance because of the functions
measured with the tests used. They included measures of visual
recognition, spatial discrimination, visual-motor coordination, reasoning, verbal ability, and numerical skill.

In general, the adult patients who had suffered from the viral encephalitis were inferior to a group of control subjects who had been
matched for age, sex, social class, and education. The differences were
statistically significant in tests that involved speed of performance —
such as target identification, multiplication, letter cancellation, and
color naming — and it has been suggested that response time may be
adversely affected by meningoencephalitis in adults.

C. RELATED PERFORMANCE ASSESSMENT RESEARCH

As we indicated earlier (cf. Section II), there have been numerous
attempts in recent years to conduct experimental research on sustained performance. We cited the excellent work of Grodsky and his
colleagues (Grodsky, 1967; Grodsky *et al.*, 1966) in full-scale, integrated, mission simulation as representing one of the best examples of the
good work being done at one end of a dimension of possible approaches to research on performance assessment — the end at which
the highest possible degree of fidelity is achieved in the simulation of
an actual work situation. The definitive work of Fleishman (1967b)
and Parker (1967) was cited as representing the other end of the dimension, where individual tests of factor-analytically identified primary abilities are used, and where no attempt is made to have the test
situation simulate faithfully any work situation. The synthetic-work
approach that falls somewhere between the two ends of this dimension has been described in detail here.

Other approaches have also been used. The pioneering work of
Fitts and his colleagues at the Ohio State University (Fitts *et al.*, 1958;

also published in Fleishman, 1967a, pp. 676–692) with the use of an air traffic control simulator for laboratory experimentation on the operation of a generalized air traffic control system falls between the synthetic-work and full-scale simulation techniques. In fact, the Ohio State work laid the groundwork for the step to be taken from "a generalized air traffic control situation" to the even more general "synthetic-work situation." The debt should be recognized and acknowledged.

Finally, by way of example it should be noted that others have employed techniques that fall between synthetic work and the specific-test end of the dimension (Hartman & Cantrell, 1967; Steinkamp, Hawkins, Hauty, Burwell, & Ward, 1959). In one such experiment (Hartman & Cantrell, 1967), 13 subjects followed one of three different work-rest schedules on each of 12 successive days (4 hr on-duty and 2 hr off, 4 and 4, or 16 and 8), except for days 8, 9, and 10, when all the subjects worked continuously without sleep. The subject's work consisted of 2-hr blocks of testing in which five devices were used: (1) the *Complex Coordinator* developed during World War II (a discontinuous pursuit tracking task); (2) the *Multidimensional Pursuit Test* also developed during World War II (a 4-element compensatory tracking task); (3) the *Neptune*, a multiple-task device recently developed at the Air Force School of Aerospace Medicine to include four tasks (watchkeeping, short-term memory, arithmetic computations, and tracking); (4) the *Multiple Reaction Time Task*, also developed at the School of Aerospace Medicine (both simple- and choice-reaction tasks are included); and (5) the *Complex Discrimination Reaction Time Test* (a problem-solving and reaction task). In general, the data corroborated and extended those of the work-rest studies reported earlier in this chapter (cf. Section IV,A); the major differences among the schedules occurred during the period of the stressful wakefulness.

The synthetic-work approach to the study of sustained performance is being employed in several different laboratories. In addition to the work cited (nearly all from the Human Factors Research Laboratory of the Lockheed-Georgia Company and the Performance Research Laboratory of the University of Louisville—the only active laboratories in this area until recently), MTP batteries are now being used in the Training Research Division of the Aerospace Medical Research Laboratories at Wright-Patterson Air Force Base, at the Missile and Space Systems Division of the Douglas Aircraft Company, and at the Federal Aviation Administration's Civil Aeromedical Institute in Oklahoma City. Progress on the assessment of sustained performance is being made.

V. Criteria for Task Selection and Validity

In a recent conference on the methodological problems associated with performance-assessment research (Chiles, 1967), it was noted that the greatest of the problems faced with the synthetic-work approach are those related to the selection of tasks for inclusion in the multiple-task performance battery (Alluisi, 1967, p. 383). A discussion of the criteria that can and should be employed for the selection of the tasks will show why this is true, especially an examination of the validity criterion.

A. VALIDITY

We have a problem with regard to predictive validity. As we indicated earlier (cf. Section I), we shall not be able to measure the predictive validity of any of the MTP batteries until we have a suitable criterion; i.e., until we are able to assess the operator's or worker's performance of real work in operational systems. Thus, the tasks in the performance battery described (in Section III, A) were not preselected for predictive validity. With the assistance and advice of numerous associates and consultants (see Adams, 1958, p. ii), they were selected on the basis of content validity. This was discussed previously (Section III, B). Also, evidence that they have at least some construct validity has been presented elsewhere (Alluisi, 1967, pp. 381–382).

An attempt could be made to measure concurrent validity by correlating the results obtained with the MTP batteries with those obtained by other approaches, but this has not yet been done. Concurrent validity is a meaningful concept only when there is agreement in the field concerning standard tests and procedures (e.g., the Binet as a test of intelligence). The performance battery described in this chapter (in Section III, A) comes closest to a standardized battery, at least in terms of the amounts of data collected with its use, but its self-correlation would provide evidence of reliability, not concurrent validity.

In summary, the performance battery has content validity and some construct validity — its tasks appear to include the desired content, and to measure the desired functions orthogonally. We see no immediate possibilities of obtaining direct measures of predictive or concurrent validity, and this constitutes one of the greatest methodological problems in attempts to study the assessment of sustained performance.

B. OTHER CRITERIA FOR TASK SELECTION

The usual criteria of validity and reliability are not sufficient for the selection of tasks to be included in an MTP battery that is to be used to create a synthetic-work situation. Other criteria must be met. Among the most important of these are the eight listed below.

1. Face Validity: Operator Acceptance.

To the subject or operator, the test battery and each task in it must appear to measure important aspects of performance. This is important because if a task fails to convince the operator of its importance and validity, his performance on that task may reflect fluctuations in his interest and motivation independently of the parameters under study. In fact, one seemingly invalid task could so change the attitude of the subject as to make invalid all of his performance – it could lead him to behave differently in the test situation than he would behave in the actual work situation. It is frequently difficult to meet the requirements of this criterion.

2. Sensitivity

The task must reflect the genuine performance changes that occur under the conditions of study. It should not be so sensitive as to suggest a serious impairment, for example, when none actually exists. It should not be too sensitive to incidental or accidental events, yet it must be sufficiently sensitive to reflect appropriate changes created by relevant experimental conditions. This criterion has caused difficulty in past years, especially in the study of fatigue where individual, isolated tests of functions have been insensitive (cf. Fraser, 1967).

3. Engineering Feasibility

Equipment suitable for programming, presenting, and scoring the task should be available, or within design and construction capabilities, at reasonable cost and without major delay. Furthermore, the equipment must be sufficiently reliable to permit sustained use for periods comparable to lengthy mission durations – like the 15- and 30-day durations studied in the experiments reported here (see Section IV).

4. Task Reliability

In addition to the equipment or hardware reliability, of course, each task must demonstrate suitably high statistical reliability.

5. Flexibility

Each task in an MTP battery, and the battery itself, must be easily modifiable in terms of the programming of stimuli and the recording of responses. For example, watchkeeping tasks should be designed to permit their use with a variety of signal metrics. Programming of the

tasks in multiple-task performance conditions should be uncon-
strained so that various combinations of the tasks can be used in different studies — as might be demanded by the attempt to represent different amounts of the basic functions when "synthesizing" different
work situations. This criterion will become even more important if
ever a taxonomy of tasks is developed.

6. Work-Load Variability

A range of work loads must be available with the performance or
MTP battery, and it must include both realistic loadings of the operator and the demand for time-sharing among the tasks. Both theory and
practice have demonstrated that man can rise to meet the demands of
the occasion whenever the occasion is represented by a single task or
by a set of tasks that falls short of presenting a realistic work load. Also,
it appears that when man is forced to time-share among a number of
tasks (a characteristic condition of most, if not all, operational or work
situations), his performance provides one of the earliest indications of
incipient impairment. Thus, the work loads that can be imposed with
the MTP battery should range from the relatively light to conditions of
near or actual operator over-load.

7. Trainability

Asymptotic levels of performance should be attainable with the selected tasks after a minimum of training, and preferably with nothing
more than familiarization training. "Learning" should not be a major
variable in the tasks selected, unless the tasks are selected to measure
changes in this function per se. This criterion must be met if realistic
levels of skill are to be presented; in the operational situation, the
operator is not expected to learn to perform his functions while carrying out a mission. All the tasks in the performance battery should,
therefore, reflect the high level of skill of the man in the operational
man-machine system.

8. Control-Data Availability

Reliable control data should be available, and it must be feasible to
collect additional control data with the entire MTP battery and with
each of its separate tasks. The tasks must be adaptable to laboratory
investigations; they should be equally well suited to the undergraduate college student, to volunteer military subjects, and to samples of
operators who represent appropriate subpopulations of workers.
Where differences in performance are obtained with different samples
of subjects, the differences must be specifiable and capable of being
related to expected results with other populations.

VI. Concluding Comments and Summary

The assessment of sustained performance or work behavior involves problems that are obviously complex, but the problems are not impossible to solve. We believe it to be of great importance to the science of psychology that concentrated efforts be made toward their solution. The final tests of the validity of a science's theories lie in the utility of the technologies based on those theories. In the present case, the further development of technology awaits the creation of appropriate and valid behavioral theory (or theories).

We have attempted here to present the philosophy, techniques, and data of a program of research on the assessment of sustained performance or man's work behavior. The methodology developed has employed a synthetic-work situation in which it is possible to measure and evaluate the performances of subjects or operators who are required to work at the time-shared tasks presented with a multiple-task performance (MTP) battery. The tasks themselves were selected to measure certain behavioral functions that man is called upon to perform in a variety of work situations in the complex man-machine systems of today. Specific research studies have dealt with confinement in a volumetrically restrictive environment (see Adams, 1958), sustained performance, work-rest scheduling, and diurnal rhythms in man (see Alluisi & Chiles, 1967), and with the behavioral effects of infectious diseases. The results of these studies provide perhaps the best basis on which to judge both the synthetic-work techniques and the possibility of experimental psychology's contributing significantly to our knowledge of man's work behavior.

The general conclusions supported by the results of experimentation are as follows: (1) Crews consisting of as many as 10 men can be confined in a space as small as 1100 ft³ for as long as 30 days or more without observable detriment. (2) Men apparently can follow a work-rest schedule of 4 hours on-duty and 4 hours off for very long periods without damage to their performances. (3) For shorter periods of 2 or possibly 4 weeks, selected men can follow a more demanding 4–2 work–rest schedule with reasonable maintenance of performance efficiency. (4) In following the more demanding schedule, man uses up his performance reserve and so is less able to meet the demands of emergency conditions such as those imposed by sleep loss. (5) The diurnal rhythm which is evidenced in physiological measures may also be evidenced in the performance, depending on the information given to, and the motivation of, the subjects, and depending also on the total work load. (6) Even where motivation is sufficiently high, the diurnal cycling of performance may be demonstrated when the operator is overloaded or stressed. (7) The average performance efficiency of a crew of men will drop between 25 and 33 % during a period of illness with a febrile disease such as tularemia. (8) During such an illness, the average drop in performance efficiency is between about 6 and 8 % per 1°F rise in rectal temperature, but (9) individual differences will be very great and may be expected to range from essentially no decrement to one of about 20 % per degree.

In short, the synthetic-work methodology and its MTP batteries appear to yield measures of sustained performance that are sensitive to the manipulation of both obvious and subtle experimental variables. They have provided a means for the conduct of experimental research on sustained performance or work behavior, and the data collected have led to inferences and conclusions like those listed in the preceding paragraph. Even in this small way, progress is being made; psychology is advancing.

References

Adams, J. A. Some considerations in the design and use of dynamic flight simulators. In H. W. Sinaiko (Ed.), *Selected papers on human factors in the design and use of control systems.* New York: Dover, 1961.

Adams, O. S. Aircrew fatigue problems during extended endurance flight. Phase I: Planning. *USAF WADC Technical Report*, 1958, No. 57–510.

Adams, O. S., & Chiles, W. D. Human performance as a function of the work-rest cycle. *USAF WADC Technical Report*, 1960, No. 60–248.

Adams, O. S., & Chiles, W. D. Human performance as a function of the work-rest ratio during prolonged confinement. *USAF ASD Technical Report*, 1961, No. 61–720.

Adams, O. S., Levine, R. B., & Chiles, W. D. Research to investigate factors affecting multiple-task psychomotor performance. *USAF WADC Technical Report*, 1959, No. 59–120.

Alluisi, E. A. Methodology in the use of synthetic tasks to assess complex performance. *Human Factors*, 1967, 9, 375–384.

Alluisi, E. A., & Chiles, W. D. Sustained performance, work-rest scheduling, and diurnal rhythms in man. *Acta Psychologica*, 1967, **27**, 436–442.

Alluisi, E. A., Chiles, W. D., & Hall, T. J. Combined effects of sleep loss and demanding work-rest schedules on crew performance. *USAF AMRL Technical Documentary Report*, 1964, No. 64–63. (a)

Alluisi, E. A., Chiles, W. D., Hall, T. J., & Hawkes, G. R. Human group performance during confinement. *USAF AMRL Technical Documentary Report*, 1963, No. 63–87.

Alluisi, E. A., & Coates, G. D. A code transformation task that provides performance measures of nonverbal mediation (COTRAN). *NASA Contractor Report*, 1967, No. CR–895.

Alluisi, E. A., Hall, T. J., & Chiles, W. D. Group performance during four-hour periods of confinement. *USAF AMRL Technical Documentary Report*, 1962, No. 62-70.

Alluisi, E. A., Hawkes, G. R., & Hall, T. J. Effect of distortion on the identification of visual forms under two levels of multiple-task performance. *Journal of Engineering Psychology*, 1964, **3**, 29–40. (b)

Alluisi, E. A., & Morgan, B. B., Jr. Effects of practice and work load on the performance of a code-transformation task (COTRAN). *NASA Contractor Report*, 1968, No. CR-1261.

Alluisi, E. A., Thurmond, J. B. & Coates, G. D. Behavioral effects of infectious diseases: Respiratory *Pasteurella tularensis* in man. *Univer. of Louisville Performance Research Laboratory Report*, 1967, No. ITR-67-6.

Barnes, R. M. *Motion and time study*. New York: Wiley, 1958.

Bartley, S. H., & Chute, E. *Fatigue and impairment in man*. New York: McGraw-Hill, 1947.

Bills, A. G. *The psychology of efficiency*. New York: Harper, 1943.

Bloom, W. Shift work and the sleep-wakefulness cycle. *Personnel*, 1961, **38**, 24–31.

Chambers, E. S., Johnson, L. O., van Velzer, V. C., & White, W. J. Standard operational tasks for assessment of human performance—COMPARE design specification. *Douglas Missile and Space Systems Division Paper*, 1966, No. 4136.

Chiles, W. D. (Sp. Ed.) Conference proceedings: Assessment of complex operator performance. *Human Factors*, 1967, **9**, 325–392.

Crowden, G. P. *Muscular work, fatigue and recovery*. London: Sir Isaac Pitman, 1932.

Dunnette, M. D. A note on *the* criterion. *Journal of Applied Psychology*, 1963, **47**, 251–254.

Fitts, P. M., Schipper, L., Kidd, J. S., Shelly, M., & Kraft, C. Some concepts and methods for the conduct of system research in a laboratory setting. In G. Finch & F. Cameron (Eds.), *Air Force human engineering, personnel, and training research*. Publ. No. 516. Washington, D.C.: National Academy of Sciences-National Research Council, 1958. Pp. 174–187.

Fitts, P. M., Weinstein, M., Rappaport, M., Anderson, N., & Leonard, J. A. Stimulus correlates of visual pattern recognition: A probability approach. *Journal of Experimental Psychology*, 1956, **51**, 1–11.

Fleishman, E. A. (Ed.) *Studies in personnel and industrial psychology*. (Rev. ed.) Homewood, Ill.: Dorsey, 1967. (a)

Fleishman, E. A. Performance assessment based on an empirically derived task taxonomy. *Human Factors*, 1967, **9**, 349–366. (b)

Floyd, W. F., & Welford, A. T. (Eds.) *Symposium on fatigue*. London: H. K. Lewis, 1953.

Frankenhaeuser, M. Psychological investigation. In R. Mueller, I. Nylander, L. Larsson, L. Widen, & M. Frankenhaeuser, Sequelae of primary aseptic meningo-encephalitis: A clinical, sociomedical, electroencephalographic and psychological study. *Acta Psychiatrica et Neurologica Scandinavica*, 1958, **33**, 91–109. (Monograph Suppl. No. 126, Pt. III).

Fraser, D. C. Recent experimental work in the study of fatigue. In E. A. Fleishman (Ed.), *Studies in personnel and industrial psychology*. Homewood, Ill.: Dorsey, 1967. Pp. 540–545.

Ghiselli, E. E., & Brown, C. W. *Personnel and industrial psychology*. New York: McGraw-Hill, 1955.

Gilbreth, F. B. *Applied motion study*. New York: Macmillan, 1919.

Gilmer, B. von H. (Ed.) *Industrial psychology*. New York: McGraw-Hill, 1961.

Grether, W. F. Psychology and the space frontier. *American Psychologist*, 1962, **17**, 102–108.

Grodsky, M. A. The use of full scale mission simulation for the assessment of complex operator performance. *Human Factors*, 1967, 9, 341–348.

Grodsky, M. A., Mandour, J. A., Roberts, D. L., & Woodward, D. P. *Crew performance studies for manned space flight.* ER 14141. Baltimore: Martin Co., June 1966.

Hall, T. J., Passey, G. E., & Meighan, T. W. Performance of vigilance and monitoring tasks as a function of workload. *USAF AMRL Technical Report*, 1965, No. 65–22.

Hartman, B. O., & Cantrell, G. K. MOL: Crew performance on demanding work/rest schedules compounded by sleep deprivation. *USAF SAM Technical Report*, 1967, No. 67–99.

Hawkes, G. R., Meighan, T. W., & Alluisi, E. A. Vigilance in complex task situations. *Journal of Psychology*, 1964, 58, 223–236.

Hovland, C. I. Human learning and retention. In S. S. Stevens (Ed.), *Handbook of experimental psychology.* New York: Wiley, 1951. Pp. 613–689.

Kleitman, N. *Sleep and wakefulness.* Chicago: Univer. of Chicago Press, 1939.

Kleitman, N. The sleep-wakefulness cycle of submarine personnel. In Panel on Psychology and Physiology, *Human factors in undersea warfare.* Washington, D.C.: National Research Council Committee on Undersea Warfare, 1949. Pp. 329–341.

Kleitman, N. *Sleep and wakefulness.* (Rev. ed.) Chicago: Univer. of Chicago Press, 1963.

McCormick, E. J. *Human factors engineering.* New York: McGraw-Hill, 1964.

McFarland, R. S. *Human factors in air transportation.* New York: McGraw-Hill, 1953.

Maier, N. R. F. *Psychology in industry.* (2nd ed.) Boston: Houghton Mifflin, 1955.

Morgan, C. T., Cook, J. S., III, Chapanis, A., & Lund, M. W. *Human engineering guide to equipment design.* New York: McGraw-Hill, 1963.

National Research Council Committee on Work in Industry. *Fatigue of workers.* New York: Reinhold, 1941.

Panel on Psychology and Physiology. *Human factors in undersea warfare.* Washington, D.C.: National Research Council Committee on Undersea Warfare, 1949.

Parker, J. F., Jr. The identification of performance dimensions through factor analysis. *Human Factors*, 1967, 9, 367–373.

Passey, G. E., Alluisi, E. A., & Chiles, W. D. Use of the experimental method for evaluations of performance in multi-man systems. *USAF AMRL Memorandum*, 1964, No. P-67.

Ray, J. T., Martin, O. E., Jr., & Alluisi, E. A. *Human performance as a function of the work-rest cycle.* Publ. No. 882. Washington, D.C.: National Academy of Sciences-National Research Council, 1961.

Robinson, E. S. Work of the integrated organism. In C. Murchison (Ed.), *A handbook of general experimental psychology.* Worcester, Mass: Clark Univer. Press, 1934. Pp. 571-650.

Ryan, T. A. *Work and effort.* New York: Ronald Press, 1947.

Seashore, R. H. Work and motor performance. In S. S. Stevens (Ed.), *Handbook of experimental psychology.* New York: Wiley, 1951. Pp. 1341–1362.

Steinkamp, G. R., Hawkins, W. R., Hauty, G. T., Burwell, R. R., & Ward, J. E. Human experimentation in the space cabin simulator: Development of life support systems and results of initial seven-day flights. *USAF SAM Technical Report*, 1959, No. 59-101.

Thurmond, J. B., Alluisi, E. A., & Coates, G. D. An extended study of the behavioral effects of respiratory *Pasteurella tularensis* in man. *University of Louisville Performance Research Laboratory Report*, 1968, No. ITR–68–8.

Tiffin, J., & McCormick, E. J. *Industrial psychology.* Englewood Cliffs, N.J.: Prentice-Hall, 1958.

Viteles, M. S. *Industrial psychology.* New York: Norton, 1932.

Warm, J. S., & Alluisi, E. A. Behavioral reactions to infection: Review of the psychological literature. *Perceptual and Motor Skills,* 1967, **24,** 755–783 (Monograph Suppl. No. 4–V24).

Woodworth, R. S., & Schlosberg, H. *Experimental psychology.* (Rev. ed.) New York: Holt, Rinehart & Winston, 1954.

CHAPTER 4

Cybernetic Theory and Analysis of Motor Learning and Memory[1]

KARL U. SMITH
HARVEY SUSSMAN
University of Wisconsin

I. Introduction

This chapter describes the concepts and methods of experimental systems research in the scientific study of human learning. The expression *experimental systems research* refers to the laboratory investigation of learning as a variable, feedback-determined process. It also includes application of the principles and findings of feedback research to the design of learning, training, and educational devices. In systems studies, we are concerned with the cybernetic or variable control factors that determine the relationships between learning, memory, and performance. Such control factors can be understood by experimental feedback analysis of motor-sensory interactions.

In the two decades of its existence, experimental feedback study has corrected past limitations of experimental psychology by theoreti-

[1] The research in this chapter has been supported by the National Science Foundation for a project on Multivariate Feedback Analysis of Feedback Delay and Intermittency in Performance and Learning, by the Social and Vocational Rehabilitation Administration for a project on Experimental Cybernetic Analysis of Body Motions, and generally, under a training grant provided by the Biological Sciences Section, National Institute of Mental Health.

cally clarifying learning and training factors in physical behavioral science (K. U. Smith, 1967). Specifically, development of feedback research methods has made possible for the first time a systematic investigation of the human factors involved in the design of machines, training devices, and educational processes and techniques. More recently, advances have been made in applying practice-related feedback theory and methods to research on physical rehabilitative processes (K. U. Smith & Henry, 1967).

As used in research on learning, the term *cybernetics* means guidance and control of behavior. Two points of view have developed in the last two decades about the field of cybernetics. The first, represented by Wiener (1948) who coined the term cybernetics, emphasized the mathematical study and modeling of living control mechanisms through computer or servomechanism simulation (Ashby, 1963). During this same period, an experimentally oriented sector of cybernetic study has developed. This approach is based on laboratory experimentation in which the variable space, time, force, and signal feedback variables of motor-sensory systems have been investigated as determinative factors in learning and performance (K. U. Smith & Smith, 1966).

The experimental concept of feedback emphasizes several aspects of psychophysiological regulation: (1) reciprocal interaction between motion and sensory input; (2) closed-loop regulation by dynamic movement of both self-generated input and environmental stimulation; (3) positive and negative regulation of different patterns of error of sensed input; and (4) multidimensional feedback control by different levels of postural, transport, and articulated movement (Fig. 1). In this approach, vital closed-loop regulation is not limited to the simple servomechanism model of negative feedback control. Rather, we emphasize the positive and negative feedback and feedforward aspects of closed-loop control of continuously guided and organized response. Motion, physiological processes, and learning are linked together as closed-loop operations which can guide, start, stop, modulate, vary, transform, and integrate internal organic and external skeletal-motor behavior. Learning and memory capabilities are defined directly by the significant properties of closed-loop, motor-sensory interactions *within* a living system, not by extraneous associations or reward-and-punishment reinforcements acting on the system.

Past views emphasized that learning is determined by time-contiguity and associative factors *between* different responses, or by reward, punishment, or drive reduction effects which occur *after* some

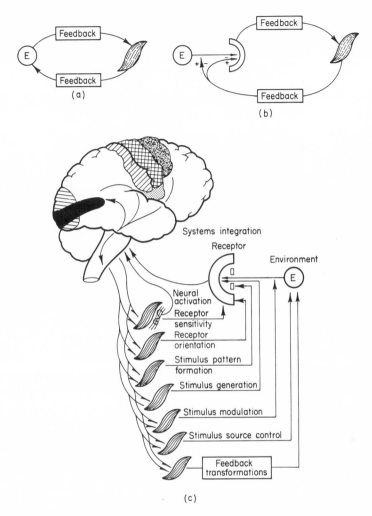

Fig. 1. The dimensions of dynamic feedback control. (a) Reciprocal feedback regulation. (b) Self-governed feedback control of the environment. (c) Systems feedback regulation of neural activation, receptor sensitization, and stimulus control.

critical response that is to be learned. In contrast, a systems concept states that learning is determined by the direct sensory effects of movement or stimulation which accompany the response to be learned and does not require reinforcing aftereffects or associated reactions. In our view, the concept of learning reinforcement is incompatible with a feedback doctrine because the former stresses open-

loop factors of reward, punishment, anxiety reduction, and drive
reduction as associated contingencies of learned response and does
not recognize the significance of intrinsic motor-sensory factors in
guiding response and determining learning.

II. Experimental Systems Design in Learning Research

Experimental cybernetic methods are based on the view that
variable space, time, force, and signal feedback factors determine performance, learning, and memory (Fig. 2). The top diagram in this figure denotes the fact that in unaided response, different modes of reactive and operational feedback are produced by motor-sensory activity.
The feedback received from movement itself is designated *reactive
feedback*. Such sensory effects of movement are *always* dynamic and
typically serve to define the feedback compliance between kinesthetic, interoceptive, and exteroceptive factors in performance and learning. Besides these effects, the individual also receives *operational*
feedback from action of movement on the environment. Such sensory
effects are of a tactual, visual, or auditory nature and may be *dynamic*
or persist as *static aftereffects* of movement. For example, in moving
his hands through the sand, a child sees the marks in the sand as they
are made as well as the static trace of these marks for some time after
the movement has been completed. In doing systems analysis of
learning, we are concerned with all of these modes of movement-controlled feedback and their critical properties as determinants of learning. In the present view, the serious fault of past associative and reinforcement doctrines is that they have attempted arbitrarily to limit the
determination of learning and memory primarily to the static aftereffects of response, as such effects can be defined in terms of mass-
action concepts of temporal contiguity, reward-and-punishment reinforcement, and drive reduction.

A. FEEDBACK COMPLIANCE AND TOOL-USING

As suggested in Fig. 2b, modes of feedback in unaided behavior can
be added to and transformed by tools and machines. Such implements
add a dimension of *instrumental* feedback to behavior and learning
which is distinct from the reactive and operational components of
motor-sensory activity. Instrumental feedback is provided through
exteroceptive stimulation to give the human operator both the feel of

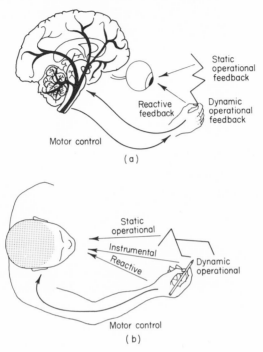

Fig. 2. Modes of dynamic feedback regulation of sensory input. (a) Unaided closed-loop regulation involving reactive and operational feedback. (b) Instrumental feedback control involving reactive, instrumental, and operational feedback.

an implement as well as its critical motions in performing typical activities of marking, cutting, smashing, shearing, forming, pushing, lifting, or throwing. The implement serves to transform the feedback factors involved normally in unaided motor-sensory interactions. It thus makes possible magnification of behavior in performing tooling functions that can be carried out only in limited ways with the hand.

In systems theory, the main determinants of both performance and learning relate to the space, time, force, and signal *compliance* or *coherence* between the modes and levels of feedback defined in Fig. 2. To learn rapidly and to achieve efficiency in performance, the reactive, instrumental, and operational feedback factors must be yoked dynamically and continually in terms of time, force, and spatial patterning of movement and sensory input. When such compliance is reduced, the demand for practice to achieve some standard of efficient performance is increased and the potential level of effective action is reduced.

B. EXPERIMENTAL CYBERNETIC METHODS

Feedback compliance is far more than generalized factors of stimulus-response compatibility. To study feedback compliances in detail, it has been necessary to devise new methods of altering quantitatively the variable space, time, force, and signal factors which define the modes and conditions of feedback in motor-sensory systems. Some of the main experimental cybernetic methods now in use are illustrated in Fig. 3. These methods include electronic, electromechanical, optical, magnetic-tape, television, and hybrid-computer methods to vary the space, time, force, and signal characteristics of feedback parameters of most of the known response systems in the human body.

In all of the methods illustrated in Fig. 3, the experimental devices are inserted in some part of the closed-loop circuit linking motor response and sensory input. The subject does not see, feel, or hear the effects of his responses directly, but only after the feedback properties of these movements have been varied by the electronic, optical, or computer systems. Using different methods, spatial inversion and distortions, time delays and interruptions, force amplifications and reductions, and signal variations and distortions can be introduced into given sectors of a motor-sensory feedback loop and the variable feedback determinants of learning and memory systematically investigated. In contrast to past general methods used in motor learning research, the techniques described in Fig. 3 permit experimental control of the intrinsic interacting motor and sensory factors that characterize the dynamic functions of response mechanisms, and can be used to vary the space, time, force, and signal characteristics of particular motor-sensory interactions. They are not limited to the study of conditional, temporal, and reinforcement associations *between* different reaction systems.

III. Systems Determinants of Learning

The cybernetic approach defined here creates the concept of systems determinants of learning. Rate and scope of learning in a living system depend on the extent to which the organism can establish self-governed, continuous control over its own movements and on the extent that different modes of feedback regulation are compliant with one another.

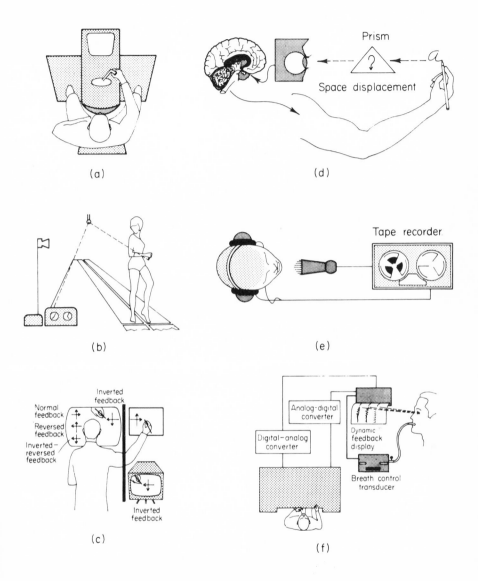

Fig. 3. Experimental cybernetic methods. (a) Electromechanical tracking system. (b) Electronic behavior sensing and auditory feedback in the study of locomotion. (c) Laboratory television system used for inverting and reversing the visual feedback of motion. (d) Optical system for study of space-displaced feedback. (e) Magnetic tape recorder with a storage loop for delaying sensory feedback. (f) Hybrid-computer experimental laboratory system. (Based on K. U. Smith & W. M. Smith, 1962 and K. U. Smith & M. F. Smith, 1966.)

A. MULTIDIMENSIONALITY OF RESPONSE COMPONENTS IN LEARNING

Figure 1 indicated that several closed-loop factors, such as the continuity and multidimensional characteristics of feedback control, define the pattern of any particular response to be learned. Specifically, we assume that every motion system, such as locomotion, hand motion, eye movements, and speech, involves at least three levels of closed-loop control corresponding to postural, transport, and manipulative or articulative movements, and that neural integration of behavior is based on specialization and interaction of these different closed-loop circuits. Postural movements maintain the body's position in space by means of feedback loops which incorporate the receptors that are sensitive to the pull of gravity, for the earth's gravitational field is the primary spatial reference system for the behaving organism. Transport movements propel the legs in walking and the arms in moving the hands from one position to another. The transport movement system has dual representation on both sides of the midline to control the body's bilaterally symmetrical parts. The manipulative or articulative feedback circuits control the highly specialized and refined movements of the hands, feet, mouth, face, and the mobile receptors. Manipulative movements usually define the focal activities of the individual, such as his manual or verbal skills, so that detailed precise motions can be guided to perform highly precise, stimulus control operations. Smooth coordination of these diverse bodily activities is possible only because of the closed-loop nature of the responding system.

Special electronic behavior sensing systems which separately time the manipulative and transport components of response have been developed to measure the changes in duration of manipulative and transport movements when the visual feedback of response was displaced or delayed by optical and laboratory television techniques (Fig. 3b). Results of one study (K. U. Smith, 1966b) indicated that learning curves for manipulative components were quite different from those for travel movements in a drawing task involving optical inversion of feedback. This difference was significant when learning was distributed over 20 days with one-half hour practice each day, as well as when practice was massed in a single day.

B. MOVEMENT-PRODUCED FEEDBACK AS A DETERMINANT OF LEARNING

A main issue raised by a feedback theory of learning is whether direct sensory effects of motor activity induce learning. Gould and

Smith (1963) tested this issue by using television methods to control angular displacement of visual feedback in maze tracing and circle-drawing motions. Methods and results of the experiment are shown in Fig. 4. The design consisted of practicing 24 subjects in the two tasks. During each day of training, each subject traced one maze pattern and drew three circles under each of four conditions of feedback displacement. Order of displacement of conditions was varied by subject.

Underlying this experiment was the assumption that the circle drawing task would show fewer learning effects because the subject received no direct sensory effect of his accuracy in drawing a circle under the four displacement conditions, whereas the maze task, by giving continuous information to the subject for guidance of his hand movements, would produce significant learning changes. In the circle drawing task, the subject received an elliptical distortion of the actual pattern he was trying to draw. Since he could never tell the extent of this distortion, he never got an accurate indication of the guidance of his motion in drawing a true circle.

The results, summarized in the graphs in Fig. 4, confirmed the assumptions on which the experiment was based. The maze task gave significant learning effects at all angles of displaced feedback, whereas the circle drawing task did not. This experiment showed that movement-controlled dynamic feedback from a given response was not only a sufficient but an essential condition for learning that response.

C. Dynamic versus Static Feedback as a Determinant of Learning

Figure 2 indicated that the feedback determinants of learning may be either dynamic or static in nature. Dynamic feedback represents the active components of reactive, instrumental, and operational effects of movement, whereas static feedback represents the persisting delayed *aftereffects* of a response on the environment. Earlier, we noted that static feedback of motion represents in part what traditional learning theorists have designated as *knowledge of results* in learning. The term *informational feedback* also has been used to designate these static operational aftereffects of a given motion in learning (Bilodeau, 1966).

K. U. Smith, Ansell, and Smith (1963) compared the relative effects of delayed-dynamic and delayed-static feedback effects of target location responses on learning. Using a single large videotape recorder connected with a laboratory television setup, visual feedback of the tracing motions was stored for a period of performance and then

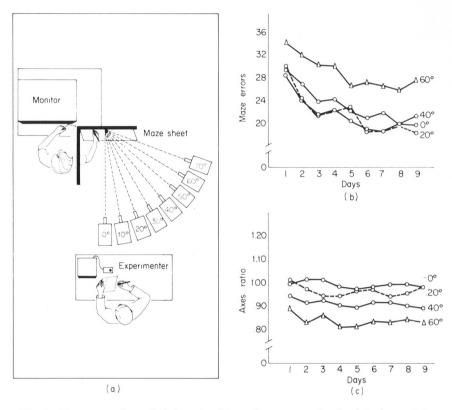

Fig. 4. Experimental proof of the role of immediate sensory feedback in determining human learning. (a) Method of angularly displacing the visual feedback of maze tracing and circle-drawing motions. (b) Learning curves for maze tracing. (c) Learning curves for circle drawing in which the subject had no indication of error in drawing. (Based on Gould & K. U. Smith, 1963.)

played back to the subject as a consecutive delayed sensory effect. The subject did not see his movement directly but had to view them in a television monitor. Images of 30 seconds of performance were stored on videotape and after this interval were played back to the subject in two ways — i.e., as a static fixed picture of the tracing pattern made by the subject (static feedback pattern), and as a dynamic replay of the actual movements as made in the performance period (dynamic feedback condition). In addition, the dynamic and static conditions of learning were compared under conditions of normal orientation and inversion of feedback. Four groups of 7 subjects each separately practiced one of the four sensory conditions used. Dynamic feedback conditions gave the highest level of performance throughout the learning period. In this condition, the dynamic upright condition was superior to all other conditions. Time of performance was lowest for the dynamic upright and static upright condition. A slight negative effect of practice was found in the static upright condition. Normally, these differences would be exaggerated in favor of the dynamic condition because it is not delayed, whereas the static conditions of feedback are always delayed. Results of the experiment, which represents just one example of several studies that have been done in this area, fully confirm the view that there are different sources of movement-controlled feedback in learning and that the immediate dynamic sources are the most significant for determining acquisition.

D. STIMULUS SELECTION IN MOTOR PERFORMANCE AND LEARNING

An experimental systems theory defines motor performance and learning as specialized aspects of stimulus selection and control which are generally involved in behavior. In this view, perception and motion are one and the same thing: both involve response control of stimulus selection and input. The terms *motor skill* or *psychomotor skill* generally have been used to depict more overt levels of stimulus feedback selection (Fig. 1c), which may involve at least eight levels of neural activation and regulation of receptor sensitivity, guidance of receptors, and dynamic control of stimulation that are normally involved in motor performance and learning as well as in perceptual activities.

One issue raised by a systems concept of stimulus selection is whether the primary functions of determination of receptor sensitivity and orientation are feedback controlled. A number of critical experiments have indicated that these functions are in fact based on closed-loop regulation. Results of stabilization of the retinal image indicate that periodic flick movements of the eye are required to maintain sensitivity of the visual system to continuous stimulation, and that when these movements are eliminated by image stabilization, the system quickly adapts to incident illumination.

Another experimental example (K. U. Smith, 1966b) has suggested that visual orientation is regulated by feedback control. This experiment consisted of mounting a small dove prism on a scleral contact lens, which served to invert or reverse visual feedback of eye movement itself. The effect of wearing such an *ocular prism* was to cause *skittered vision* or continual jumpy movements of the eyes, with corresponding unstable control of seeing. This effect persists as long as one can tolerate wearing the prism. Experiments carried out with hybrid-computer inversion of stimulus feedback of eye movement have confirmed the findings of this optical study.

These experiments on dynamic control of stimulus selection prove that effective coordination of motion and receptor input during learning depends on normal feedback compliance between receptor movements and receptor input. When such dynamic motor-sensory spatial and temporal compliance is lacking, sensory input cannot be coordinated with more generalized motor activities of the body.

E. SELF-GENERATED ACTION IN MOTOR LEARNING

One of the most critical differences between traditional associative and reinforcement theories and a systems doctrine of learning is represented by the distinction between *open-loop, environmental* determination, and *closed-loop, self-generated* regulation of movement and learning. In accounting for learning, traditional ideas stress environmental determinism by open-loop association between different responses or between stimuli of different responses. Systems doctrine states that one of the most critical determinants of learning is the degree of self-governed action that can be imparted to the learning situation. Constraint on continuous, self-regulated control of action during learning constitutes a major stress factor leading to fatigue, boredom, satiation, and loss of motivation, as well as a discoordinating effect which impairs motor-sensory interaction.

Newly developed hybrid, real-time, laboratory computer systems have created an entirely new level of experimental science in research on the self-governed systems determinants of learning. Figure 5 illustrates how the components of a hybrid-computer laboratory have been arranged to explore the feedback factors of learning and performance in a great variety of motion and physiological systems of the human body. The central parts of an analog-digital-analog computer system have been related to numerous specialized experimental stations for research on feedback factors in learning eye movement tracking, head movements, visual-manual motion, speech, posture, brain rhythms, breath control, and cardiac action. These motor-sensory mechanisms involve continuous response regulation of sensory input and are studied by means of the analog sector of the bimodal computer system.

In addition, the laboratory is designed so that the same computer setup can be used to control motor-sensory interactions in learning

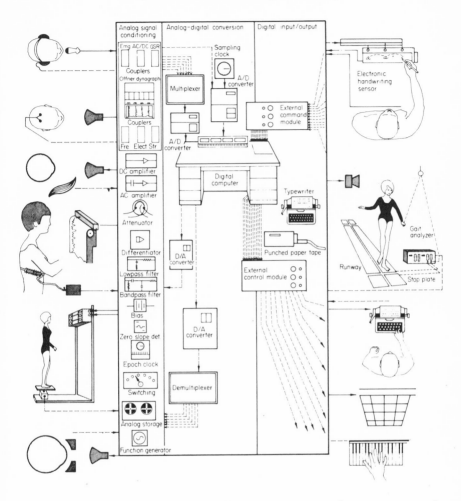

Fig. 5. Experimental stations, signal conditioning equipment and conversion, control, and actuating components of the hybrid-computer system.

discrete movements, as shown on the right in Fig. 5. Experimental stations for study of discrete mechanisms include typewriter, keyboard operations, keyboard-light-cell devices, and apparatus to study handwriting, locomotion, object manipulation and assembly motions. Analog sectors of the laboratory are shown on the left in Fig. 5, while the discrete or digital parts are indicated on the right. The second column from the left describes signal conditioning equipment used with analog inputs and outputs. The central part of the laboratory is indicated by the analog-digital and digital-analog conversion equipment used with the analog components and by the external command and control modules for the digital experimental stations.

F. AUTOMATION OF FEEDBACK DESIGNED EXPERIMENTS

The diagram in Fig. 6 illustrates how experimental operations were performed with the hybrid-computer system. In an experiment on breath-control motion, the subject viewed the action of an oscillograph cursor which was actuated by breath pressure. The subject's breath motions were transduced by a strain-gage pressure sensor and the electrical analog of the movements amplified. They were then sampled, converted to digital form, and their digital voltage level measured by an analog-digital converter. These measured digital signals were selected by the digital computer and programmed for feedback variations. The signals were then reconverted to analog form by the digital-analog converter and amplified and used to drive the oscillograph feedback display which the subject viewed. Comparable experimental computer control of discrete input-output operations can be achieved by the computer system for many different types of behavioral-physiological feedback systems.

An experiment on breath control illustrates how the laboratory computer system shown in Fig. 6 can be used to investigate self-generation of movements in learning motor skills, such as those used in musical instrumentation. This experiment also illustrates how advanced real-time computer systems of the sort just described represent a new level of experimental automation of all aspects of research operations in learning and training. The subject's breath-pressure movements were transduced to their electrical analog by means of a strain-gage pressure sensor which was connected to a mouthpiece. The breath-pressure signals were then put through the conversion and experimental programming steps described above and displayed as an oscillograph feedback source to the subject.

This experiment was designed to demonstrate to what extent practice changes the continuously generated properties of magnitude, frequency, and velocity of movement which characterize continuous, self-generated control of sensory feedback during learning. The computer system was programmed to automate all aspects of the observations on individual subjects. The oscillograph record in Fig. 6 indicates the different types of experimental programming used and how the different programs affected the feedback display which the subject observed . In controlling his breath pressure, the subject viewed the

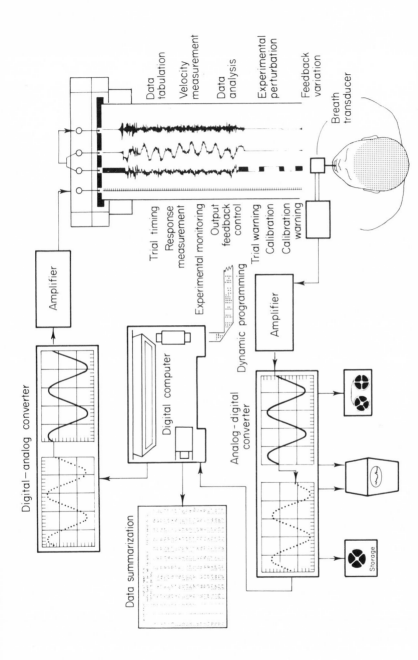

Fig. 6. Techniques of dynamic programming for experimental automation in psychophysiological feedback research on motor skill. (Based on K. U. Smith, 1965.)

117

response line on the left of the oscillograph record and did not see the remaining parts of the record. This line represented error in keeping the breath pressure at a constant level or in compensating variations in feedback which were introduced by the computer system. The middle response line indicates the appearance of such perturbation of the feedback of the breath-control movements, as combined with error of the subject's performance. The response line to the far right represents velocity of the breath-control movements, as obtained by programmed action of the system in computing the first derivative of the input movement signals.

The captions related to the oscillograph feedback display indicate the types of experimental automation used in the experiment. Each of the operations indicated required a distinctive program. In addition to these program-controlled, automated operations, the system also read out the input analog and digital signals on magnetic tapes and displayed these signals on an oscilloscope.

The breath-control records obtained on subjects during learning (K. U. Smith, 1966b) indicated that the essential basis of motor learning is continuous, self-generated activity, and that learning proceeds in terms of change in this productive regulation of response. This self-produced activity consists of oscillatory movements of different frequency and magnitude. With practice, magnitude and frequency characteristics of the movements are gradually changed. The records indicate that learning feedback control of breath pressure involves changes similar to those that occur in learning visual-manual tracking.

The computer system may be used to automate measurement of velocity of movement during learning. During learning, velocity of continuous control movements are generally reduced. However, we have observed marked individual differences in the pattern of velocity changes (K. U. Smith, 1966b). In some cases, changes in velocity are closely associated with improvement in control accuracy, but in other cases no such relationship could be seen.

G. FEEDBACK DETERMINANTS OF PHYSIOLOGICAL MOTIVATION IN LEARNING

In classic thinking, physiological motivation of motor learning is supposed to be produced by conditioned derivation from physiological drives, which serve at some stage of acquisition as a basis of reward reinforcement by drive reduction. This centrifugal concept of physiological drive always has been suspect because it attempts to reduce motivation to episodic drive states of hunger, thirst, and sex, and because it contains no specification of the known dynamic roles of skeletal-motor activity in regulating energy exchange, respiration, cardiac activity, and metabolism.

Two major researches have been done on physiological motor-sensory interaction in learning (K. U. Smith, Putz, & Molitor, 1966). One of these compared the extent of learning in visual-manual tracking under unperturbed and perturbed conditions. Two types of perturbation were compared. In one study, the subject's own respiration signal was admixed with his hand motion signal. In the second, the computer system generated a perturbation wave of the same magnitude and frequency as the subject's respiratory cycle. Results showed that subjects learned to control the respiratory perturbation at a higher level of precision than they governed the computer-generated external perturbation. Tracking with both types of perturbation was less accurate than nonperturbed performance. The learning curves under the three conditions of perturbation were comparable in form, but displayed the differences in levels of accuracy just indicated. This fact suggests that the primary determinant of the learning function was the motor-sensory feedback interactions involved in the tasks, not the sources of physiological perturbation and motivation as would be specified in a reinforcement model. Overall, the results suggest that a significant human factors consideration in any learning situation must be the extent to which the devices and conditions of learning permit effective integration and control over internal organic functions that can perturb performance.

IV. Response Guidance in Motor Learning

One of the major limitations in past theories of motor learning is that they contain no ideas whatsoever about the guidance mechanisms of motor response. We are supposed to believe that association and reinforcement processes impart directionality and space guidance to movement and govern the mechanisms of directional control. This assumption of past learning theory has been negated by findings that there are a number of fundamental directional stereotypes in behavior which always precede learning. The observations described earlier, namely, that the eye operates as a direction-specific motor-sensory system, negate almost all claims of reinforcement learning theorists that mammalian behavior has no form or pattern prior to learning but can be "shaped" by reinforcement.

A. THEORY OF DIRECTION SPECIFICITY OF RESPONSE

A cybernetic concept of learning is based on the view that behavior mechanisms are always directionally controlled, both before and during learning. However, the servomechanism (Wiener, 1948) and informational engineering or sampled-data models (Ashby, 1963) have attempted to reduce this directionality to time sampling factors in information exchange between external stimuli (targets) and perception in detecting and governing error. In reinforcement theory, reduction of tracking error is supposed to act as knowledge of results which induces a drive-reduction reinforcing effect.

In our view, cybernetic doctrine was incomplete until a psychophysiological concept of response guidance was developed through experimental research on tracking (Lincoln & Smith, 1952) and on space-displaced sensory feedback in behavior (K. U. Smith & Smith, 1962). This work indicated that all movement systems of the body are intrinsically direction-specific as neurogeometric control systems, which can be modified in their directional control through learning.

The beginnings of a spatial or neurogeometric theory of direction specificity in behavior was established with the recognition that classic studies on inversion and displacement of the retinal image represent an historical background of current research on feedback factors in perception and motion (K. U. Smith & Smith, 1962; W. M. Smith, Smith, Stanley, & Harley, 1956). This past research on displaced vision indicates that individuals can never really adapt to inversions and reversals of vision in a completely normal way, and that partial adaptation to spatial distortions of visual feedback requires long periods or even weeks or months of practice and exposure. A survey of all the literature on this subject (K. U. Smith & Smith, 1962) brought out the fact that capability of compensating for space-displaced vision through compound movements is absent in invertebrates and vertebrates below the mammals, but has been expanded in limited ways in lower mammals and primates.

A systems theory of direction specificity in behavior and learning has been developed through extensive research on different conditions of inverted, reversed, and angularly displaced visual feedback of different body motions. This theory refines the general doctrine that learning is determined by particular properties of sensory effects of dynamic movement, and states, in particular, that the effectiveness of both self-generated and external stimulus patterns in guiding motion depends directly on the spatial compliance between movement and sensory input. Two postulates of this theory are indicated in Fig. 7— i.e., the concepts of *critical ranges of angular displacement* in guid-

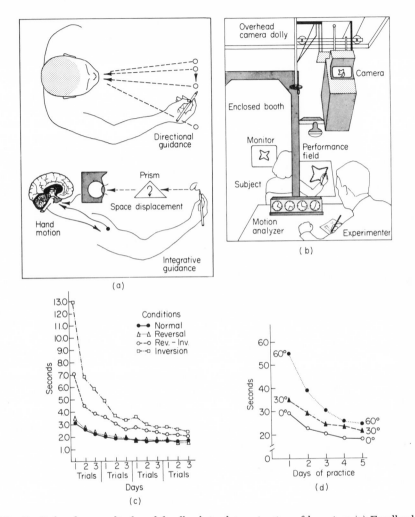

Fig. 7. Role of space-displaced feedback in determination of learning. (a) Feedback theory of the guidance of motion through space-displaced feedback. (b) Laboratory television system for inverting, reversing, and angularly displacing the visual feedback of motions. (c) Learning curves for different conditions of inversion and reversal of visual feedback of star-tracing motions. (d) Learning curves for comparative effects of angular displacement of target location motions.

ance of motion, and of *directional specificity* of axes of movement and receptor input. The upper left diagram shows the postulate that guidance of, and feedback compliance in, every motor-sensory system depends on detection of three critical ranges of angular displacement of movement and sensory input: (1) an indifference range in which there is no detection; (2) a direction-specific range in which movement can be guided without disturbance before and during learning; and (3) a breakdown range in which movement is interrupted and must be guided as discrete or irregular movements. In the breakdown range, the amount of learning needed to integrate movement and sensory input depends on the magnitude of displacement.

The postulate of direction specificity of axes of displacement states that the effects of different directions of disorientation vary as a function of the body axes affected. That is, axes of motor-sensory control of perception and motion generally are related to postural control of the vertical and bilateral transport regulation of the horizontal axis of the body. It is assumed that such intrinsic direction-specificity of behavior determines reaction and adaptation to particular conditions of inversion and right-left reversal of sensory feedback in motion. In general, the theory specifies that inversions affect precision and extent of learning more than right-left reversal of feedback.

B. Determination of Learning by Spatial Feedback Factors

Figure 7 also illustrates laboratory television methods which have been used to test the validity of the concepts of direction specificity and guidance of response in learning. The laboratory television methods used are like those shown in Fig. 3 and depend on the use of a specially wired television camera to angularly displace or invert and reverse the visual feedback which a subject gets from his own motions in tracing stars or doing other tasks. The camera views the movements made and its circuits can be switched to invert, reverse, or both invert and reverse the visual feedback of the subject's movements. To angularly displace the visual feedback of movement, the camera is moved to different positions around the performance situation, thereby in effect changing the location of the subject's eyes in space in viewing the task area and his own hand movements.

Figure 7(c) and 7(d) illustrate results of two major researches on the effects of axial and angular displacement of the televised feedback of responses. In the first study, the pattern of visual feedback of star-tracing motions was inverted, reversed, and both inverted and reversed, and the effects of these displacements compared with normally oriented feedback. The four learning curves shown in Fig. 7(c) give the results of this comparison. In exact keeping with theoretical expectations, the inversion condition disturbed star-tracing performance most and required the most learning to reapproximate normal performance. The effects of combined inversion and reversal were next and those of reversal of effect were no different from normal orientation of the televised feedback. The less-marked effect of the combined inversion and reversal condition, as compared with that of inversion alone, can be understood by the fact that the relative configural relations between the vertical and horizontal axes of motion were not disturbed when both axes of motor-sensory guidance were reversed.

The curves in Fig. 7(d) illustrate the comparative effects of angular displacement of target location motions. In this experiment, the subject was required to touch a series of small metal targets that were arranged in a vertical plane facing the camera, and the camera was then moved to the different displacement angles. Results showed that the learning curves varied in an orderly way as a function of the angles of displacement, much as predicted by theory. Generally, the zero angle of displacement had only limited effects on the duration of movements in hitting the targets, whereas the other angles impaired coordination even after 5 days of practice.

These two experiments have been augmented by at least ten other major investigations, which proved that all the main response systems of the body — eye movements, head movements, posture, locomotion, various types of hand motion including handwriting, compound object manipulation, and panel-control motions — were directionally guided and specialized in terms of critical ranges of angular displacement and direction-specific axes of displacement of movement-produced sensory feedback. Some movements, such as eye movements, have very small critical angles of displacement beyond which accuracy of movement guidance is seriously impaired on a permanent basis. Generally, the possibility of compensating the effects of any breakdown range of angular displacement depends on the number of articulated dimensions of movement control which are available for reorienting and governing the displaced sensory input. Additional evidence indicates that all binocular and bilateral movements are integrated in terms of displacement of differences in stimulation on bilaterally symmetrical points on the body.

In a systems approach, the hundreds of thousands of distinct motions that the human individual can learn and perform in skilled athletic, tool-using, orientative, speech, musical, artistic, object manipulation, and social activities are specialized in ontogenetic development and adult learning as direction-specific responses. These

movement patterns are based on detection of relative, dynamic space-
displacement of movement and sensory input, and on detection of relative space-displacements of sensory input in bilateral activities. This
view has been tested by measuring the number of significantly different, direction-specific movements which are created by a combination
of eight directions of movement in star tracing and four different conditions of inversion and reversal of feedback of these movements.
Results (K. U. Smith, 1966b) of the study gave a complete substantia-
tion of the assumptions used in setting up this research.

V. Temporal Feedback Determinants of Learning and Memory

In traditional doctrine, learned behavior is described in terms
of time association between discrete stimulus-response (S-R) units or
by time linking of a discrete response to be learned and some reinforcing aftereffect (reward or drive-reduction effect). However, the S-R
unit hypothesized in such views is a conceptual entity which is accepted by learning psychology but which has not been analyzed as a
sensorimotor process. Moreover, the determinative temporal contiguity between responses that is assumed in such theory cannot be
exactly defined and is interpreted in different ways in particular reinforcement doctrines. More importantly, the temporal interval between a response and the stimuli generated by that response — that is,
the feedback interval — is not recognized in the S-R model. Thus, an
important area of cybernetic research — the study of feedback timing
and its role in learning — has never been defined or investigated in
conventionalized S-R learning research. An experimental systems
study of learning is based prominently on the investigation of feedback delay, intermittency, and other closed-loop timing factors in
acquisition and memory.

A. Delayed Feedback and Learning

Cybernetic research on delayed feedback has been most important
in shedding new light on the determinative time factors of sensorimotor learning. In its *real-time analysis*, such research has defined new
ways of measuring and specifying the meaning of temporal variations
such as delay and intermittency in controlling feedback patterns, and
by analyzing such temporally organized characteristics of feedback

systems as clocking, time marking, memory recording, and feedfor-ward-control processes as critical determinants of learning.

By *feedback delay* we mean a temporal lag between a movement and the controlling sensory feedback that is generated by the move-ment. Delayed feedback is a feature in most categories of machine performance, such as automobiles, aircraft, tractors, and high-speed implements, where the design or momentum of the machine intro-duces a lag between the operator's movements and perceived action of the device. Delayed sensory feedback can be produced experimen-tally by interrupting the controlling feedback loop in a closed-loop performance situation.

The effects of delayed feedback on performance and learning were first noted in studies of military tracking systems during and subse-quent to World War II, when it was observed that transmission lags were detrimental to performance accuracy and learning. In another type of experiment, Lee (1950) used a dual magnetic-tape recording and playback system to delay the auditory feedback of speech and other sound-producing motions. The critical issue of learning science raised by research on feedback delay is whether real-time factors defining the motor-sensory interactions *within* a response system ac-tually determine the rate and course of learning in a significant way. The assumption is that if they do, such factors take precedence over time relationships and undefined contiguities *between* responses as determinants of learning (K. U. Smith, 1962).

Figure 8 describes use of the memory circuits of the hybrid-computer system as a time machine to control the feedback delay of different motion systems of speech, breath control, and visual-manual tracking. In these experiments, the different motor responses of a sub-ject were transduced with appropriate sensors and the electrical analogs of these movements amplified and sampled by the analog-digital converter. The digital computer selected the sampled input signal and, according to a special program, stored this input signal in memory for a predetermined period of time. After this programmed variable delay was put into the signal, it was outputted to the digital-analog converter, deconverted to dc form, and displayed as a visual or auditory delayed feedback of response to the subject. Using special programs, many different delay values can be introduced into the closed motor-sensory loops of the different responses and the effects on learning and performance investigated.

Oscillograph records of three subjects shown to the right in Fig. 8 give an overall idea of the comparative effects of feedback delay on different motor-sensory systems. Delay values in seconds are given in

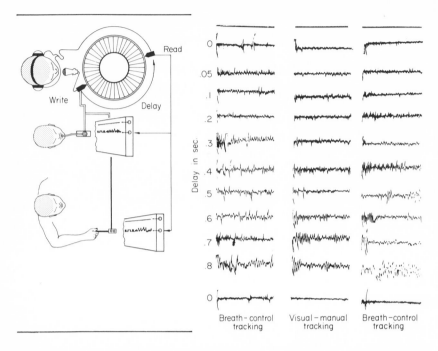

Fig. 8. Comparison of the effects of feedback delay in different motion systems. Left: Techniques of using the hybrid-computer system as a universal, real-time laboratory machine for comparing effects of feedback delay on movement error and rhythm of different motion systems. (Based on K. U. Smith, 1965.)

the column to the left. As indicated by the magnitude of variation in each of the records, increase in delay magnitude produced a marked decrease in accuracy of the responses measured. Breath control was affected just as much as visual-manual tracking. Increase in delay magnitude caused a change in the basic rhythm of each movement so that the dominant wavelength was increased in duration as the delay value was increased. This finding underlies our view that the rhythm and synchronism of continuously controlled movement, including the rhythm of respiration, was determined by closed-loop delays involved in the different reactions.

Observed effects of feedback delays indicate that little or no learning actually occurs in most response systems with feedback delays longer than 0.4 second, or if limited learning occurs, it is likely to be unstable. These and other findings indicate that every motion system of the body is specialized in terms of the temporal feedback compliances that regulate it. Speech and eye movement tracking display the most distinctive closed-loop temporal characteristics. Speech is affected most by temporal lags around 0.2 second and less affected by delay values above and below this value. Eye movement tracking may be seriously impaired by feedback lags of 0.1 second or less. The general rule is that the more accurate and precise the motor-sensory system, the more it is affected by small magnitudes of feedback delay.

Studies of feedback delay effects in learning substantiate the view that intrinsic, motor-sensory, *feedback timing* is a far more significant determinant of learning than the so-called association, conditioning, and reinforcement intervals which have been studied in traditional learning theory. First of all, the magnitudes of feedback delay which, to all intents and purposes prevent learning in precisely controlled motion systems, have no counterpart in past learning research.

The effects of learning with a feedback delay of a given magnitude may be manifest as positive transfer effects in responding to sensory lags of lower magnitude. Such transfer effects may be evident even though no consistent learning was observed with the longer delay values. No positive learning transfer effects have been found between practice with small delay magnitudes of less than 1.0 second and subsequent performance with longer delay magnitudes.

A highly significant factor in learning with feedback delay is the insidious, unseen, and unexperienced effects of time lag on reaction and perception. No matter how experienced and sophisticated the subject in the delayed reaction experiment, effects of the time lag remain subtle and hidden. A subject can never grasp and predict what is going on and what to do about it. Anticipation and feedforward projection of response through learning and memory are possible only when the space and time factors in feedback control are compliant with one another. When spatial factors may be used to guide and mark response over time — i.e., to encode time — the effects of feedback delay on learning and feedforward prediction in response are minimized.

B. Feedback Delay and Intermittency in Learning and Memory

In an experimental systems concept, learning and memory are interrelated as dynamic feedback and feedforward control processes. Memory is more than a static storage mechanism which makes possible recall or recognition of past perceptions and movements. Its more significant dynamic property consists of time spanning on-going events of perception and motor response and projecting these events into the future by *feedforward control* of movement. According to this *dynamic theory*, memory emerged and was refined first in evolution as a mechanism of neural coding for feedforward guidance of posture, locomotion, and orientation movements. In the vertebrates and man, these time-spanning and feedforward regulatory mechanisms of learning have been extended to productive control of articulated movements and to formation of long-term memory based on encoding of time by use of tools, architecture, and symbols.

Experimental systems studies of memory have been carried out by using hybrid-computer methods to produce delay and intermittency in the sensory feedback of response during both learning and dynamic recall. This research was based on the concept of investigating learning and memory as visual and visual-manual tracking processes. As indicated in Fig. 9, subjects either manually tracked or observed by visual tracking the action of an oscillograph cursor whose motion was controlled by a computer-generated signal. When this path had been tracked or observed for 15 seconds, the subject was asked to reproduce the stimulus path by operating a small hand control that transduced the handmotions by means of a strain-gage sensor. This dynamic reproduction of the observed path was made under two conditions — i.e., under variable conditions of feedback delay and intermittency. Five temporal delay and intermittency conditions, 0.0, 0.2, 0.4, 0.6, and 0.8 second, were used.

The experimental design also varied the persistence or operational record of the observed stimulus pattern during learning. Two experiments were done to encompass the different variables. In the first or primary experiment, using a repeated-measures design the order of persistence conditions was varied by subject among 12 subjects who practiced for forty 15-second trials. There were five trials under each display condition for each learning mode, where learning mode refers to the procedures of visual tracking and visual-manual tracking of the stimulus pattern. In the second experiment, the five conditions of delayed and intermittent feedback were varied in a random way by subjects among 16 practiced subjects.

Results of the effects of such variations in spatial persistence of the stimulus pattern during learning on dynamic reproduction of the stimulus pattern are shown in Fig. 9. Error level in reproduction of the stimulus pattern varied in a linear way as a function of degree of persistence of the pattern during learning. This error function was relatively higher when the stimulus pattern was visually tracked than when it was manually tracked. Overall, error level increased by about 300% when the persistence of the display was varied between 0 and 100%.

Error in reproduction of the observed or tracked stimulus pattern varied as a linear function of both intermittency and delay magnitude. There were no significant differences between the two temporal vari-

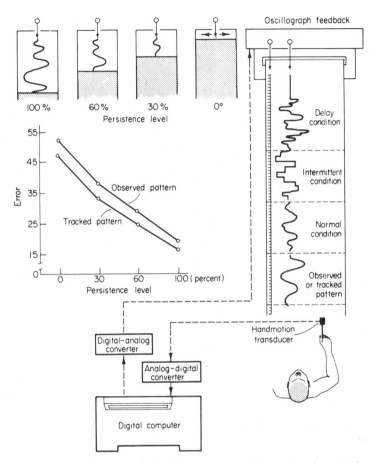

Fig. 9. Experimental systems study of memory as an interacting dynamic feedback and feedforward process. (Based on Sussman & Smith, 1967.)

ables in affecting the reproduction of the stimulus pattern. Error level in reproduction increased by about 250% between 0.0 levels of delay and intermittency and the maximum times of 0.8 second. Mode of learning had no differential effect on error level of reproduction under the intermittency and delay conditions.

These results point up the fact that all aspects of motor learning and memory can be studied as interacting dynamic processes of feedback and feedforward control of behavior. The findings confirm the belief that learning and memory function as time-spanning mechanisms, which depend heavily on the spatial persistence of the operational or observed stimulus patterns. There are definitely two dynamic ways of learning—i.e., by sensory or perceptual tracking, and by overt motor tracking. Either can produce highly accurate reproductions of stimulus patterns through dynamic motion. Feedback delay and intermittency affect feedforward control in dynamic reproduction of stimulus patterns just as they influence other more generalized forms of learned response. The main conclusion is that both learning and memory of motor skills can be comprehended scientifically only when they are more extensively investigated as time-spanning control processes in both perceptual behavior and overt activity.

The findings just described represent an experimental evaluation of the meaning of the intermittency phenomena in accounting for motor behavior. The intermittency hypothesis (Craik, 1947) holds that behavior is basically an error-correcting discrete process that depends on sampling external stimuli. Although the intermittency hypothesis has been given great prominence by traditional perceptual and learning theorists (Bertelson, 1966), and by informational engineers as a binary, *sampled-data* theory of visual-manual and eye movement tracking (Young & Stark, 1963), its proponents have not developed actual real-time methods for controlling intermittency in motor control of sensory input. To evaluate past theory in a direct experimental way, we have created a number of experimental feedback methods for analysis of intermittency in behavior, such as those described above. Research on performance and learning with these exact methods of computer control of real-time intermittency has indicated that there are many modes of dynamic intermittent variation in feedback. These include periodic *blanking, averaging, displacing, extraneously interrupting, differentiating,* or *transforming* the feedback of response. The concept of some kind of generalized control of intermittency in motor response is meaningless from an experimental cybernetic standpoint.

VI. Determination of Learning in Implemental and Social Behavior

Figure 10 illustrates the behavioral cybernetic concept of motor-skill learning in implemental and social behavior. The theory is that the amount and rate of learning needed to acquire instrumental and social motor skills are determined by feedback compliances between the motor and sensory circuits of an individual and the design of implements which he uses, as well as the behavior of other individuals which are interposed in his motor-sensory circuits. Instrumental

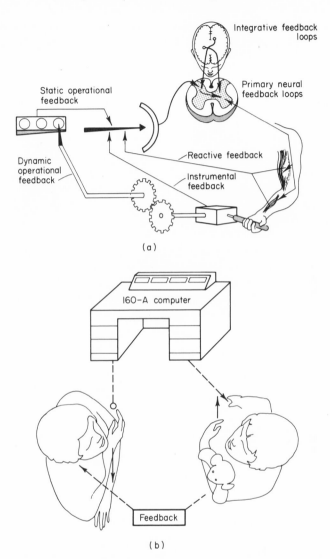

Fig. 10. Behavioral cybernetic theory of determination of learning instrumental response and social tracking. (a) A tool or machine is composed of several components — a master or control sector, an actuator sector, and a slave sector. (b) Diagram illustrating social tracking in which two organisms are locked or yoked together in a mutual feedback circuit. (Based on K. U. Smith, 1967.)

and social behavior are closely related psychophysiologically. In instrumental behavior, the individual becomes feedback yoked to a tool or machine to govern his sensory inputs. In social behavior, he becomes feedback yoked to movements of another person to guide his own movements and to govern his sensory inputs. In this systems concept, instrumental and social behavior have evolved in man as closely related, interlocked modes of structuring and controlling the environment by tools, machines, architecture, social forms, and language.

A. Determinants of Instrumental Learning

Learning and performance with tools and machines are generally determined by the design of implements in conforming to the motor and sensory mechanisms which control a device and sense its operational effects on the environment. We designate this conformation in human and instrumental design as the *feedback compliance* of the tool or machine.

Implements alter the status of human learning because they introduce special modes of transformation of feedback control into motor-sensory activities, thereby changing the feedback compliances which normally exist between overt response and receptor input. We illustrated previously in Fig. 2 that, in addition to the normal sources of reactive and operational feedback in unaided behavior, the tool or machine creates a variable pattern of instrumental feedback which the operator must govern compliantly in relation to the other sources of sensory input.

As suggested in Fig. 10a, a tool or machine may be considered as being composed of several components—a master or control sector, an actuator section, and a slave sector. The master component is attached to the operator's effector system and must conform in definite ways to the part of the body controlling the tool. The slave component performs the actual operations of the tool and its actions must be compliant, not only with the materials and objects that are operated on, but with the dynamic actions of the operator's receptor systems. The actuator section of the tool or machine transforms the actions of the control mechanism to slave action. In complex machines, it serves to integrate sources of multiple response control to effect slave action, and must be compliant with the way that these multiple effector actions of the operator are normally integrated.

Various technological devices, from simple hand tools to complex computerized machine systems, differ in terms of the way in which the master, actuator, and slave components of devices are arranged to transform the space, time, force, and signal characteristics of unaided feedback. Simple tools preserve all of these parameters of normal feedback while amplifying one or another dimension of control. Compound machines amplify one or another dimension of control in order to automate and magnify all dimensions of feedback control.

Studies on the human factors in learning and performance on complex machines have been carried out in design research on various types of *anthropomorphous machines*. Anthropomorphous machines are man-like manipulators, walking machines, eye movement machines, head movement implements, and exoskeletons which preserve in exact ways the space, time, force, and signal feedback compliances of the motor-sensory systems to which they are attached while amplifying the power of the system to exert force or to control space and time (Mosher, 1965; K. U. Smith, 1966a). Thus manipulators have been built which expand the reach and power of the human arm by several times while still giving the operator a delicate sense of the force needed and of the space displacement involved in manipulating lethal materials at distances 30 or 40 feet removed from the body. Tests of effective design of such machines have clearly demonstrated that the amount of learning needed to become efficient in their operation is dependent almost entirely on the extent to which the machine's main components comply with the normal force, space, time, and signal feedback characteristics of operator motion. When such compliance is achieved in design of a machine, complex operations with the implement can be learned in a matter of minutes.

Research on anthropomorphous eye movement machines has been carried out to determine the human factors in design which are required to effect integration of continuously controlled and discrete movements of a perceptual system such as the eye (K. U. Smith, 1967). Effective design of perceptual machines follows the same basic rules of feedback compliance and integration as hand-controlled implements. Studies of this eye movement machine indicated that feedback delay can interfere just as seriously with the operation of perceptual machines as it can in the learning and control of other implements.

B. Motor Learning Factors in Social Tracking

In the experimental feedback approach, social behavior of man and animals is achieved in all of its detail and organization by a specialized form of tracking, called *social tracking* or *biosocial tracking*. Such tracking is not simply a discrete response of one animal to another which serves as a stimulus. Rather, as suggested in the diagram in Fig. 10b, two organisms become locked or yoked together in a mutual feedback circuit so that the motor response of one serves as a stimulus analog for response-controlled sensory input for the other, and vice versa. The two individuals thus become locked together by crossed-yoked motor-sensory feedback circuits much as the action of the individual's hand can be yoked in a closed control circuit with the eye movement system. When mutual motor-sensory yokes between two or more individuals are established, they can follow and track one another through sustained activity as a closed social system. According to this theory, all significant social behavior, including reproductive activities in animals, sexual intercourse, communication, emotional expression, parent-child interaction, teaching, and the various forms of grouping, are basically motor-sensory skills based on social tracking. In the present view, all forms of competitive interaction also are based on social tracking.

The challenge faced by experimental science in the study of social behavior is to comprehend theoretically both the elaborate patterns of organization and the vast detail of human or animal activity that gives substance to the overall social patterns. Our view is that only an experimental systems concept of social tracking will resolve this dual enigma of biosocial behavior. The first issue raised by this point of view is whether particular theoretically guided experimental models of social tracking can be established, and whether performance and learning in such tracking follow the rules of feedback guidance and regulation.

Numerous experimental studies of different patterns of social tracking in man have now been completed. These studies were based on use of optical, television, magnetic tape, and hybrid-computer devices to yoke individuals together in cross-circuited motor-sensory loops so that the accuracy of individuals in mutually tracking the responses of one another could be measured both individually and on a systems basis. Design of these experiments follows exactly the theoretical construction of social tracking behavior—i.e., the responses of one subject are transduced and their analog displayed as a feedback source to the second individual. This second subject tracks these signals and his movements are transduced and their analog transmitted as a feedback source back to the first subject. By interposing the hybrid-computer system or other methods of feedback variation and measurement of the tracking into the closed social yoke, the accuracy of this yoke as a system and of the individual subjects can be measured. Studies with optically yoked setups have indicated that children from 2 to 6 years can perform dynamic social tracking long before they can trace or reproduce static forms. Using a dual television circuit to yoke two subjects together, it has been shown that feedback delays and displacements affect social tracking behavior and learning just as they do individual behavior. A series of major experiments with the hybrid-computer system have indicated that the various modes of positive and negative feedback regulation, the different systems arrangements of the subjects in receiving information from one another and from the environment, the kind of individual and systems feedback that each individual gets relative to his own performance, the occurrence or nonoccurrence of an indication or error in systems performance, and the magnitude of the feedback delays and displacements involved in a person's tracking determine efficiency of performance and rate of learning in the social tracking yoke. A definite finding has been that effective social behavior is never based on simple stimulus-response *social chaining*, in which the response of one individual acts as a sequential stimulus to the second, and vice versa. All such social chaining involves variable feedback delays which preclude effective response and learning. To perform efficiently, two or more people must function as closed motor-sensory systems wherein each person gets immediate feedback of the social *systems performance* as well as of his own response. Learning in social systems is influenced by the same space, time, force, and signal feedback compliances which link machine action to the individual. Efficiency in social interaction is not determined by fixed anatomical factors, but by dynamic motor-sensory compliances which can dynamically link two or more people together in an organized feedback yoke possessing distinctive systems errors and sources of sensory control.

VII. Motion Organization in Training Design

The experimental systems study of motor skill leads not only to a new science of human learning, but to fresh concepts of motion organization and training design for human development and rehabilitation. In the present approach, all motion systems of the body, such as posture, transport movements, hand-arm motions, locomotion, head-eye movements, and speech, may be analyzed as multidimensional, closed-loop control systems in which particular components and levels of movement are specialized as space-time feedback circuits for control, generation, and selection of sensory inputs. In functioning as closed-loop mechanisms, given motion systems are guided by self-generated stimulus feedback patterns and compliances. Each movement creates directional space displacements in feedback patterns, which are formed and modulated in a particular geometric way in time to form space-time patterns of sensory input that may be differentially detected by brain cells. It is this space-time patterning of movements that determines their learning and their relations and integration with other motions. In the dynamic, closed-loop control of motions, the potentials for variable feedback timing are most limited while the potential plasticity for variable spatial control is relatively very great. Learning and memory function mainly to organize movements on a space-time feedback basis by recording the course of past movements of perception and motion and be projecting this course as a feedforward control process in future action. Mainly, memory in motor skill is the retention of the directional specificity of movement-controlled receptor tracking and overt regulation of stimulus selection which may be used for feedforward regulation of both perception and skilled overt movement.

The experimental feedback methods which have been discussed in the present research to obtain substantiating data for a cybernetic interpretation of motion and learning also constitute basic instrumental designs for development of feedback training mechanisms and automation of learning and instructional techniques. The optical, electronic, television, and computer methods used for the detailed research described here can be adapted with minor variations to feedback training designs in optometry, physical medicine, athletics, the performing arts, education, rehabilitative training, social training, and other sectors of physical behavioral science. This potential for feedback research methodology and the theory of experimental systems analysis lying behind it define what we mean by a practice-related doctrine of learning and educational design: the same ideas and implements which can be applied to the analyses of organized behavior and learning can be used to guide the design and evaluation of training procedures in both education and rehabilitative medicine.

VIII. Summary

1. This chapter has defined an experimental systems theory of motor learning in which motor-sensory feedback factors within responses, rather than associative or reinforcement time contiguities between responses, are postulated to be the main determinant of learning.

2. In a systems theory of learning, several modes of reactive, instrumental, and dynamic and static feedback factors operate in terms of space, time, force, and signal compliances to indicate systems error in motor control of sensory input, and thus determine the rate and course of learning in motor skill.

3. Experimental systems methods of studying learning include electronic, electromechanical, optical, television, magnetic tape, and hybrid-computer laboratory methods which can be interposed between the motor and sensory mechanisms of responses and used to vary experimentally the feedback compliances which determine performance and learning.

4. Proof of the multidimensional role of movement components in determining learning has been indicated by the fact that transport and manipulative movements show significantly different learning functions in a variety of response systems.

5. Motor learning has been found to be absent in learning tasks in which dependable feedback guidance of movement fails to occur and to be present in comparable tasks in which immediate sensory feedback occurs.

6. Dynamic feedback has been found to be superior to static feedback in determining learning. The observed superiority is probably increased many times in ordinary learning situations in which dynamic feedback is not artificially delayed as it was in the study described.

7. Several levels of response-controlled stimulus selection occur in both observational or perceptual learning and motor skill learning. Integration of these dimensions of selection are necessary because the absence of any one of them precludes overall effective motor regulation of sensory input.

8. That learning depends on continuous, self-generated production of compound movements has been indicated by the fact that hidden velocity and accelerative properties of motion change during learning in ways quite distinct from specific amplitude and frequency characteristics of response patterns.

9. A new level of multivariate research on learning has been reached through design of hybrid-computer laboratory systems which can be used to automate all aspects of experimental operations in variable feedback research on all the major motion and physiological systems of the body.

10. Research based on hybrid-computer control of psychophysiological interaction has indicated that a major factor in feedback determination of learning involves the immediate closed-loop effects of external motor-sensory control of physiological perturbation on precision and efficiency of external behavior.

11. Overall organization and detailed specialization of response in learning is assumed to depend on directional guidance of different component movements, as produced by relative space displacement of movement and sensory input. Studies on learning with different

conditions and modes of space displacement of motor-sensory feedback and spatial specialization of response in learning have confirmed
this central concept of the experimental cybernetic approach to motor
skill.

12. Contrary to classic thinking, the critical temporal factors determining learning are those of feedback delay and intermittency which
define the temporal compliances of motor response and sensory input.

13. The experimental systems approach to motor learning can be
characterized as a practice-related doctrine in that the laboratory feedback methods used in this orientation also may be applied in detailed
ways to new methods of feedback-controlled training in education,
physical medicine, rehabilitation, the performing arts, athletics, and
other sectors of physical behavioral science.

References

Ashby, W. R. *Cybernetics*. New York: Wiley, 1963.
Bertelson, P. Central intermittency twenty years later. *Quarterly Journal of Experimen-
tal Psychology*, 1966, **18**, 153-163.
Bilodeau, I. McD. Information feedback. In E. A. Bilodeau (Ed.), *Acquisition of skill*.
New York: Academic Press, 1966. Pp. 255-296.
Craik, K. J. W. Theory of the human operator in control systems: I. The operator as an
engineering system. *British Journal of Psychology*, 1947, **38**, 56-61.
Gould, J., & Smith, K. U. Angular displacement of the visual feedback of motion. *Per-
ceptual and Motor Skills*, 1963, **17**, 699-710.
Lee, B. S. Some effects of side-tone delay. *Journal of the Acoustical Society of America*,
1950, **22**, 639-640.
Lincoln, R. S., & Smith, K. U. Systematic analysis of factors determining accuracy in
visual tracking. *Science*, 1952, **116**, 183-187.
Mosher, R. S. Exoskeleton prototype. *Technical Proposal*, Department of the Navy,
Office of Naval Research. Schenectady, N.Y.: General Electric Company, 1965.
Smith, K. U. *Delayed sensory feedback and behavior*. Philadelphia: Saunders, 1962.
Smith, K. U. Cybernetic foundations of learning science. *Proceeding of the Association
Computing Machinery.*, 1965, **20**, 8-26.
Smith, K. U. *Review of principles of human factors in design of the exoskeleton and
four-legged pedipulator*. Madison, Wis.: Univer. of Wisconsin Behavioral Cyber-
netics Laboratory, 1966. (a)
Smith, K. U. Cybernetic theory and analysis of learning. In E. A. Bilodeau (Ed.), *Acquis-
ition of skill*. New York: Academic Press, 1966. Pp. 425-482. (b)
Smith, K. U. Cybernetic foundations of physical behavioral science. *Quest*, 1967, **8**,
26-89.
Smith, K. U., Ansell, S., & Smith, W. M. Sensory feedback in medical research: I. Delayed sensory feedback in behavior and neural function. *American Journal of Physical Medicine*, 1963, **42**, 228-262.
Smith, K. U., & Henry, J. Cybernetic foundations for rehabilitation. *American Journal of
Physical Medicine*, 1967, **46**, 379-467.

Smith, K. U., Putz, V., & Molitor, P. *Experimental systems analysis of yoked vision: Cybernetic foundations of visual rehabilitative science.* Madison, Wis.: Univer. of Wisconsin Behavioral Cybernetics Laboratory, 1966.

Smith, K. U., & Smith, M. F. *Cybernetic principles of learning and educational design.* New York: Holt, Rinehart & Winston, 1966.

Smith, K. U., & Smith, W. M. *Perception and motion: An analysis of space-structured behavior.* Philadelphia: Saunders, 1962.

Smith, W. M., Smith, K. U., Stanley, R., & Harley, W. Analysis of performance in televised visual fields: Preliminary report. *Perceptual and Motor Skills,* 1956, **6,** 195–198.

Sussman, H., & Smith, K. U. *A cybernetic analysis of dynamic memory.* Madison, Wis.: Univer. of Wisconsin Behavioral Cybernetics Laboratory, 1967.

Wiener, N. *Cybernetics.* New York: Wiley, 1948.

Young, L. R., & Stark, L. Variable feedback experiments testing a sampled-data model for eye tracking movements. *IEEE Transactions on Human Factors Engineering,* 1963, **HFE–4,** 38–51.

CHAPTER 5

Differential Processes in Acquisition[1]

MARSHALL B. JONES
The Pennsylvania State University

I. Introduction

In an article in the *Psychological Review* Edgar F. Borgatta (1954) announced to psychology and to the world a theory for the explanation of all behavior. This theory was absolutely general and capable of formulation with full mathematical rigor. Borgatta called it the General Theory of Equilibrium, and said:

> This theory states that for a given system composed of two or more elements, the average performance of the elements may be assessed. Then, it will be found that the performance of the *individual* elements may be specified as a direct *function* of their distance from the average performance. Further, if the direction of difference is maintained, *the sum of the differences will total to zero*. In no case will it be negative. The beauty of this theory is that *it has fitted all sets of data to which it has been applied.*

Borgatta, of course, was spoofing. Nevertheless, the distinction upon which his theory rested makes a difference. Individual behavior can always be analyzed into typical or mean behavior and the individual's deviation from it. This difference, between mean and deviant behavior, is the root fact from which have stemmed what Cronbach

[1]Research sponsored by the Air Force Office of Scientific Research, Office of Aerospace Research, United States Air Force, under AFOSR Contract No. F44620-68-C-0072.

(1957) called "the two disciplines of scientific psychology." From it, all other differences between experimental and differential psychology are derived.

Any experiment on motor behavior involves at least two experimental conditions. The experimental variation may be distribution of practice, knowledge of results, the order in which two tasks are practiced, or many other things, but always there must be more than one experimental condition if conclusions are to be drawn.

The purpose of an experiment is to determine the effects of the experimental conditions upon other variations which may be dependent upon them. In the analysis, therefore, the dependent data are always grouped according to the experimental conditions under which they were collected; there are always at least two sets of data. The task of analysis is to compare these sets of data and to compare them as sets. However, in order to make these comparisons the analyst must first determine which of the various behaviors that appeared under a given condition was characteristic or typical of it. This behavior is always a behavior of central tendency; almost always it is the mean behavior.

For many years psychological tests were called "experiments." The usage was incorrect because the administration of a psychological test involves a single test condition. It makes no difference how standardized or how objective the test may be, nor how many tests there are; it is not an experiment. From it nothing can be learned about the determinants of mean behavior on the test. In the administration of one or more tests under one test condition, it is impossible to study mean behaviors because there is nothing with which to compare them. In psychological testing deviations from the mean are all that can be studied.

By the same token, the experimentalist cannot study deviant behaviors. To him behaviors which deviate from the mean are "errors." In calling them errors he certainly intends no reflection on anyone else, because they are *his* errors. Deviations from mean behavior are caused by circumstances which the experimenter has not controlled. To the extent that they exist the experimenter has chosen to study experimental conditions which are relatively unimportant determinants of the dependent behaviors.

It must be recognized, of course, that there are many determinants which an experimenter cannot control, in the narrowest sense of this word. Since every experiment must be performed at some time, the experimenter cannot manipulate any event which took place before the experiment began. He cannot manipulate the genotype of his subjects, or their childhood experiences, or what happened to them in school. An experimenter can only manipulate present variations, and not all of them.

For the most part, it is precisely those things which experimenters cannot control that most interest differential psychologists. Genetic variations and early experience are the essence of their concern. It is a mistake, of course, to suppose that these matters cannot be studied experimentally. In animals they are, even today. However, in an experimental area which works primarily with adult human subjects the genotypes and previous experiences of these people are the principal source of individual variation within experimental conditions.

In the study of motor learning the hiatus between experimental and differential psychology is slowly being filled; but it is still deep. The experimenters are still primarily concerned with mean differences; they manipulate conditions of learning, and their results are referable to those conditions. The differential psychologists study deviations from the mean; they manipulate conditions only on occasion, and their findings are referable to events which happened before the experiment began.

About these central differences a host of others have accumulated. Experimental method is almost always some variety of analysis of variance. Differential method is almost always correlational analysis. Experimental workers think in terms of retroactive and proactive interference, fatigue, and habit strengths. Students of individual differences think in terms of abilities, genetic contributions, and personality factors.

Even the moods of the two disciplines are different. Differential psychology is passive, speculative, and leisurely. Its data are given; they are found, not produced. In a burst of activity the differential psychologists make their observations and analyze them; then they relax into their armchairs. The experimentalists are active, hardboiled, and harried. Worlds are waiting to be conquered and their would-be conquerors perform experiment after experiment in an undignified scramble to discover them.

Many people have lamented this division of psychological labor and called for a "united discipline" which can speak to Nature with a "single voice." "In both applied and general scientific work," said Cronbach (1957, p. 683) in his presidential address to the American Psychological Association, "psychology requires combined, not parallel, labors from our two historic disciplines. In this common labor, they will almost certainly become one, with a common theory, a common method, and common recommendations for social betterment. In the search for interactions, we will invent new treatment dimensions and discover new dimensions of the organism. We will come to realize that organism and treatment are an inseparable pair and that no psychologist can dismiss one or the other as error variance."

I do not despise prophecy, but the existing division will not be easily bridged. It may be that we already have common recommendations for social betterment, but we most certainly do not have common methods and common theories. And it is not at all clear how we might go about getting them. Perhaps, we should look for interactions, as Cronbach suggests. It may be that parallel labors will not suffice; but it may also be that the very parallelism of our labors offers the best promise of a dialogue between the two disciplines.

In motor learning mean changes occur with practice, within a single condition of learning. Since it is misleading to talk of these changes as experimental (when no experiment may have been performed), I will use the word *normative* when I wish to speak of them. In this chapter *normative* refers to mean behavior, regardless of the context in which it occurs.

Some normative events are not subject to experimentation. All human beings must walk before they can run; and it is not likely that we will soon arrange things so that running comes first; nor is there any individual variation in the order in which the two behaviors are acquired. In the sense that I use the word, walking and running are normatively ordered. Since all men must walk first and run later, walking first is also the mean behavior.

In motor learning differential changes also occur with practice. They occur at the same time, in the same place, and in the same subjects. Because they do, there exists a possibility that there may be relationships between the two kinds of events. It may be that there are correspondences between normative changes in learning and the differential process that accompanies them. There may be correspondences between the two kinds of events in the development of motor behavior or in training.

Were relationships of this sort to be found, they would not explain the results obtained in either line of inquiry. They would be empirical correspondences and no more. Nevertheless, science begins with correspondences. If we can find them in motor learning and motor behavior, we may find ourselves in need of new methods with which to study them. Someday we may even need new theory with which to explain them.

II. The Superdiagonal Forms of Practice

Whatever its theoretical interpretation may be, learning is accomplished through trials of practice. On each trial every subject generates a score; and between scores on any two trials there exists a correlation. Since correlation is a symmetrical relationship, a correlation matrix which sets forth all these relationships contains $n(n-1)/2$ correlations, where n is the number of trials. Matrices of this description play a central role in the differential study of learning.

The first correlational analysis of practice was carried out by Perl in 1934. She used 4 tasks and 20 trials on each task. In order to simplify the computational problem, she singled out the 1st, 6th, 12th, and 19th trials for analysis. "The intercorrelations of scores on these different trials of the same task were computed," wrote Perl, "and we found that for each test they tended to be arranged in an hierarchy, i.e., the 1st trial correlated higher with the 3rd than it did with the 6th, it correlated higher with the 6th than with the 12th, and so on. The nearer together in the series trials fall the higher the intercorrelations between scores on these trials" (Perl, 1934, p. 210).

Since 1934, this finding has been repeated many times (Adams, 1953; Edgerton and Valentine, 1935; Fleishman, 1953a; Fleishman & Parker, 1959; Greene, 1943; Houston, 1950; Melton, 1947, p. 1022; Reynolds, 1952a,b; Viteles, 1933). A study (E. A. Bilodeau, 1952) with the Two-Hand Coordination Test is a good example. The subjects were 152 basic airmen; the trials were 60 seconds long, with 30-second rest intervals between trials. The correlations between the eight trials of practice appear in Table I. Each trial correlates strongest with the trials which immediately precede or follow it. The further we move across the rows (to the right) or up the columns the greater the sequential separation and the smaller the correlation between the trials. For example, moving across the third row the correlations are .91, .89, .87, .85, and .86. Along the fourth row they are .91, .88, .86,

Table I
MEANS, STANDARD DEVIATIONS, AND
INTERTRIAL CORRELATIONS FOR THE TWO-HAND
COORDINATION TEST

Trial	1	2	3	4	5	6	7	8	$\overline{X}$	σ
1	—	.79	.77	.74	.73	.71	.71	.70	34.9	11.8
2		—	.87	.87	.84	.82	.82	.82	42.9	14.9
3			—	.91	.89	.87	.85	.86	46.1	15.8
4				—	.91	.88	.86	.88	50.4	16.2
5					—	.89	.90	.90	54.7	18.9
6						—	.93	.93	58.1	18.1
7							—	.94	61.0	18.6
8								—	63.3	18.7

and .88. In both rows there is an inversion in the last column. The last correlation in the third row should not be greater than .85; nor should the last correlation in the fourth row be greater than .86. However, with these two exceptions, and they are both minor, the matrix is organized according to the sequence in which the trials succeed one another.

This pattern is called the *superdiagonal form*. It is named after the $n - 1$ correlations between neighboring trials, $r_{i, i + 1}$, which make up the superdiagonal. Each superdiagonal correlation is bottom-most in one of the vertical columns. The superdiagonal form is an ordinal pattern. It requires only that the correlations decrease or remain the same across the rows and up the columns. The magnitude of these decrements is not specified. For example, the correlations in the fifth column are .91, .89, .84, and .73. The third of these correlations might have been .85, .86, or .87 instead of .84, and the requirements of superdiagonal form would still have been met. There is no quantitative law which the correlations must satisfy.

In the superdiagonal forms of practice, however, there is more than ordinal pattern. Most of these matrices are ruled by an exact regularity, *the law of single tetrad differences*. This law states that every sequence of four trials satisfies the equality

$$r_{ik}r_{jl} - r_{il}r_{jk} \approx 0 \qquad (i < j < k < l)$$

This law is demanding. For every distinct combination of four trials there is a tetrad difference which must approximate zero. Therefore, there are as many tetrad equations to be satisfied as there are ways of selecting four different trials from the n there are in the matrix. In the case of an eight-trial matrix, as in Table I, there are 70 tetrad equations which must be satisfied. Two of these tetrad differences are

$$r_{13}r_{27} - r_{17}r_{23} = .77 \times .82 - .71 \times .87 = .014$$
$$r_{27}r_{38} - r_{28}r_{37} = .82 \times .86 - .82 \times .85 = .008$$

In the matrix of Table I, the largest of the 70 tetrad differences is .027. The average difference, in absolute value, is .010.

The name of the single tetrad law derives from Spearman's law of tetrad differences. Spearman (1904) worked with another correlational hierarchy. It too was ruled by an exact regularity which involved tetrad differences. In Spearman's hierarchy there are two tetrad differences which must be satisfied for every sequence of four trials, instead of just one. In addition to the equality in the single tetrad law, the correlations must also satisfy the equality

$$r_{ij}r_{kl} - r_{il}r_{jk} \approx 0 \qquad (i < j < k < l)$$

In superdiagonal forms generally but most emphatically in the correlation matrices of practice this second equality is not met. In the correlation matrices of practice only one set of tetrad equalities is satisfied; hence, the name.

The law of single tetrad differences is purely descriptive. No theoretical ideas are anywhere involved. There are no unknown quantities or hypothetical factors. The law applies directly to observed data.

III. Exceptions to Superdiagonal Form

The meaning of any generalization is best determined by examining the conditions under which it breaks down. A regularity is itself a variation like any other, and holds or does not hold according as the conditions which sustain it are present or absent. In the case at hand we need to discover tasks which do not show superdiagonal form or, better yet, learn how to modify tasks so that superdiagonal form is abolished.

Exceptions to superdiagonal form are not easy to come by, but they do exist. E. A. Bilodeau (1953a) had subjects practice a task in which turning the knob of a micrometer was translated into a linear scale, 25 points for each full turn of the knob. The subjects, 40 basic airmen, were told after each trial how many scale points one way or the other they were from target, which was eight full turns of the knob or 200 points on the linear scale. The knob was shielded from visual contact and the subjects were unaware of the conversion formula. The results for the 16 trials of practice appear in Table II.

In some tasks the effect of practice may be to eliminate reliable individual differences. All subjects approach a common level of performance except for random departures. In tasks of this sort the intertrial correlations should show superdiagonal form early in practice. As practice continues, however, reliable differences among subjects at any one trial are eroded away until little or nothing is left but error. As this point is reached, correlation level falls close to zero and patterning all but disappears.

The results for the micrometer task conform closely to this description. The average absolute error is high initially, falls sharply in the next three trials, and approaches asymptotic values around the ninth trial. The standard deviations are maximal at the second trial; the first trial, it should be remembered, is "free" in the sense that the subjects have no knowledge of previous results; thereafter, it drops sharply and also reaches asymptotic values at or about the ninth trial. Mean-

Table II
MEANS, STANDARD DEVIATIONS, AND INTERTRIAL
CORRELATIONS FOR MICROMETER READING[a]

Trial	1	2	3	4	5	6	7	8	9	10	11	12	13	14	15	16
1	–	.30	.33	.29	.12	.14	-.16	.07	.05	.10	-.00	.04	.03	-.16	-.06	.05
2		–	.72	.56	.43	.20	-.10	.34	.11	.15	.22	.08	.01	-.02	.13	.06
3			–	.72	.66	.47	.15	.34	.17	.31	.20	.03	-.08	.06	.03	.18
4				–	.57	.57	.26	.08	.06	.29	.20	.10	.13	.13	-.05	.20
5					–	.77	.44	.14	.23	.48	.09	-.10	-.04	-.05	.00	-.04
6						–	.65	.15	.30	.62	-.01	.11	.01	.02	-.09	.14
7							–	.19	.36	.60	-.08	.22	.17	.13	.09	.23
8								–	.19	.09	-.04	.28	.33	.27	.27	.42
9									–	.47	.14	-.08	.20	.04	.12	.05
10										–	.08	-.00	.19	.20	.27	.20
11											–	-.16	.17	.09	.19	-.03
12												–	.09	.38	.20	.41
13													–	.09	.06	.12
14														–	.52	.31
15															–	.22
16																–
X̄	178	73	41	32	26	23	18	20	13	15	14	11	13	14	12	11
σ	6.8	53.9	42.2	44.4	31.6	29.7	17.2	18.2	11.0	15.4	8.9	8.6	11.7	11.0	9.4	9.2

[a] From E. A. Bilodeau (1953a).

while, the correlations start off in an unmistakably superdiagonal pattern. The correlations among Trials 2 through 7 are almost perfectly regular. However, at the eighth trial, correlation level drops precipitously and the matrix becomes completely disorganized.

Line drawing is another exception to superdiagonal form. E. A. Bilodeau and Ryan (1960) taught 48 blindfolded undergraduates to draw a 3-inch line. Errors were reported back to the subjects in sixteenths of an inch "long" or "short" of the target. Altogether, the subjects received 35 trials. However, both means and standard deviations reached asymptotic values by the sixteenth trial. Table III contains the results.

The correlations in Table III are generally low and their pattern is extremely ragged. Nevertheless, some elements of superdiagonal form are present. The average correlation in the superdiagonal is .346. In the next diagonal over the average correlation is .211; in the third diagonal it is .195. In succeeding diagonals the average is .082, .090, .097, and continues to follow a generally decreasing course. In short, there is a tendency for the correlations to become weaker as the trials are more and more separated in practice, but it is only a tendency. In a developed superdiagonal form this regularity appears in each row and column. Here it appears only on the average. Reading across the rows or up the columns there are many departures from the superdiagonal rule.

All in all, the correlation pattern in Table III is vestigial. This description, moreover, applies to the last 19 as well as to the first 16 trials of practice. Correlation level remains at the same level throughout; and there are traces of superdiagonal form through all 35 trials, but these traces are no more or less apparent later than early in practice. Superdiagonal pattern does not disappear in Table III because it never appears, except in vestigial forms which are equally distributed at all stages of practice.

Still another exception to superdiagonal form is lever positioning.[2] E. A. Bilodeau (1953b) trained his subjects, 41 basic airmen, to move a lever through a 26° arc. The maximal arc through which the lever

Table III
MEANS, STANDARD DEVIATIONS, AND INTERTRIAL
CORRELATIONS FOR LINE-DRAWING[a]

Trial	1	2	3	4	5	6	7	8	9	10	11	12	13	14	15	16
1	—	.68	.34	.24	−.14	.21	.25	−.05	.07	.17	.28	.23	.06	.08	.10	.11
2		—	.21	.03	−.13	.04	.20	.07	.13	.24	.09	.17	.22	.19	.06	.09
3			—	.39	.10	.41	.13	−.22	.24	−.08	.03	.18	−.22	.03	−.05	.08
4				—	.21	.42	.31	−.00	−.08	−.10	.14	−.03	−.22	−.15	−.25	−.06
5					—	.46	.16	.33	.34	−.04	.07	.12	−.09	−.08	−.04	−.11
6						—	.33	.05	.08	−.02	.04	.25	−.21	−.09	.05	.09
7							—	.01	.23	.23	.09	.04	−.27	−.11	.07	.04
8								—	.26	.04	.21	.15	.07	−.06	.18	.03
9									—	.34	.39	.36	.13	.13	.18	.23
10										—	.43	.13	−.08	.10	.26	.34
11											—	.51	.24	.23	.10	.38
12												—	.26	.14	.16	.07
13													—	.47	.25	.19
14														—	.20	.44
15															—	.43
16																—
X̄	16.4	11.3	9.8	6.8	6.9	4.1	5.3	4.7	5.2	4.9	5.1	5.0	4.5	3.6	4.8	4.6
σ	8.2	7.4	6.5	5.5	4.9	3.9	4.2	4.1	3.9	3.6	4.1	3.9	3.2	2.9	3.7	3.2

[a]From E. A. Bilodeau & Ryan (1960).

[2]See Chapter 9 and especially Chapter 6 for extensive coverage of lever-positioning studies. Note too that the apparatus used by E. A. Bilodeau (1953b), though similar, differed in several significant respects from the more developed lever-positioning apparatus used in later studies, for example, E. A. Bilodeau and Bilodeau (1958) and E. A. Bilodeau, Bilodeau, and Schumsky (1959).

could be moved was 42°, and the subjects had no visual contact with the lever. Information was fed back to the subjects in degrees of arc past or short of the target. The results were virtually the same as in line drawing, a vestigial superdiagonal pattern that showed no tendency to weaken or strengthen with practice.

In 1962 Jones pointed out that if practice were understood as a process of simplification, the superdiagonal pattern of intertrial correlations could be explained. According to Jones, any ability or other differential element which was active at any point in practice was active at the outset, at the first trial. With each new trial some of these elements dropped out, not to return. As practice progressed fewer and fewer abilities, fewer and fewer differential elements remained; those that did tended to be peculiar to the task being practiced. Differentially, practice was a process of simplification. From this hypothesis, Jones was able to derive the superdiagonal forms of practice and, more particularly, the single-tetrad law. The theory was also congruent with the common observation (see Section VIII) that the later trials of practice are more specific to the particular task than those at the beginning.

The results with the micrometer task are congruent with Jones' theory. It is only necessary to suppose that in some tasks the process of simplification converges on pure error. The only differential elements which are present at the beginning and which remain throughout practice are errorful; all of the reliable elements drop out sooner or later. As they do, correlation level drops toward zero and correlation pattern degenerates into disorganization. Line drawing and lever positioning are not so easily explained.

The most obvious feature of these two tasks is their extreme simplicity; in both cases a trial consists of a single, self-contained motion. It is possible to argue that superdiagonal form is lost or almost lost under these conditions because the task is already so simple that there is nothing to simplify. The process of simplification aborts because it is required to begin at its end.

There is, however, an alternative, in fact, an antithetical explanation. The tasks which show strong superdiagonal patterning are all of them fairly complex. Tasks like Two-Hand Coordination and the Complex Coordination Test require many, continuous, and coordinated behaviors. It may be, therefore, that line drawing and lever positioning lack superdiagonal form because they require a single discrete motion which, though it may be perfected, cannot substitute for a gathering complex of interrelated behaviors. In this view, the superdiagonal forms of practice reflect the assembly and organization of a complex skill. Practice, so far from being a process of simplification, is a process of complication. This view of the matter is equally competent to explain the superdiagonal forms of practice. It can explain the failure of patterning in line drawing and lever positioning. And it can explain the usual finding that later trials are more specific, less related to external tests and variations than earlier ones; the specificity lies in the particular organization that characterizes an accomplished skill.

On the existing evidence it seems to me most adequate to regard practice as a process of both simplification and complication. In a typically complex task the earlier stages are given over mainly to simplification as preexisting habits and understandings give way before the demands of practice; at the same time, however, the skill itself is cumulating and coming together and in the later stages of practice complication predominates. In some tasks, for example, the micrometer, there is no complication, no complex assembly that can, according as the subjects build it well or poorly, spread them out into reliably different levels of performance. Learning is a matter of settling into the task, but the task once learned is everywhere the same because it is not so much built as it is freed from proactive effects.[3]

IV. Invariance

Correlational analysis was developed and is generally used as a one-sample, nonexperimental method of investigation. It is never the method of choice, if there is a choice. Differential psychologists do not use it as much as they do because they consider it a better or more powerful form of investigation than experimental method but chiefly because they have no alternative. The things that interest differential psychologists do not lend themselves to experiment, partly for technical and partly for moral reasons. At the same time, it is also true that some differential psychologists have become so used to correlational analysis that they turn to it when an experimental alternative exists. For the same reason, perhaps, differential psychologists have generally failed to notice that correlations themselves are often open to experimental study.

In experiments on human learning it is usual to administer more than one trial of practice to the subjects; it is also usual to examine only the means in each experimental group. In some groups the rate of increase, asymptotic level, or some other variation reflected in the

---

[3]This chapter is limited to differential processes in *acquisition*; but differential processes also take place in retention, where they are equally important. For discussion of retention generally including some differential aspects, see Chapter 6.

means are different than in others. However, the correlation between any two trials is also defined in each experimental group and may also vary from one group to another. What is true, moreover, of individual correlations is also true of the general pattern into which they fall. Unless the task is exceptional, the individual correlations will arrange themselves in a superdiagonal pattern in all groups; and just as individual correlations may vary from one group to the next so may the properties of the correlation pattern as a whole. In any case the correlations themselves, individually and in the pattern they form collectively, are functions of the experimental conditions. At least they may be. There is no necessity that a particular experimental manipulation will have any effect whatever on the intertrial correlations, even though it may have dramatic effects upon the means. The correlations may remain identically the same in all experimental groups. This possibility, moreover, is not hypothetical. There exists evidence that a traditional, important, and extensive class of experimental variations, namely, those that are mediated in their effects by fatigue, for example, distribution of practice and the effort required to make a response, have no effect whatever on intertrial correlations.

An example of this invariance was first reported by Kientzle (1946) in an experiment on properties of the learning curve under different distributions of practice. "Correlations between scores on specific trials," said Kientzle (1949, p. 532) in retrospect, "were associated with the ordinal numbers of the trials, but not with the amount of rest between them. In other words, intertrial correlations were invariant under spacing."

In a second study Kientzle (1949) addressed herself to the invariance of the intertrial correlations under different distributions of practice. Two groups of college students practiced writing the inverted alphabet for fifteen 1-minute trials with no rest between trials. One group continued practice without rest, while the other received 60 seconds of rest before each of the last five trials, i.e., Trials 16 through 20. Two additional groups practiced the first 15 trials with 60 seconds of rest before each trial. One group continued on this schedule, while the other completed practice without rest. Kientzle calculated the correlations between Trial 15 and Trials 16 and 20. Both correlations, i.e., $r_{15, 16}$ and $r_{15, 20}$, took substantially the same values in all four groups. "Although changing conditions of spacing late in practice materially affected mean scores and standard deviations," Kientzle concluded, "it did not affect correlations with the 15th trial" (Kientzle, 1949, p. 536).

Effects upon mean performance produced by distributing practice in different ways are mediated by reactive inhibition or, more generally, fatigue effects, at least, so it is that the psychological consensus has it (Osgood, 1953, p. 507). Kientzle's findings suggested that intertrial correlations might be independent of experimental variations other than distribution of practice which affect performance through fatigue. Jones (1968) carried out a test of this suggestion, using the force required to make a response on the Manual Crank.

Two identical experiments were performed. Each experiment involved a total of 160 basic airmen who were divided into four groups of 40 subjects each. In all four groups the subjects stood before the handle and rotated it as fast as they could for a continuous practice period of 5 minutes. Group I practiced with minimum, Group 4 with maximum load; Groups 2 and 3 were alternated between minimum and maximum loads after each minute of practice, Group 2 beginning with minimum and Group 3 with maximum load. The number of crank revolutions in each 20-second period was recorded.

Each group generated a 15-variable correlation matrix, and the average correlation in each matrix was calculated. In the original experiment the difference between the largest and smallest average correlation was .08; in the repeat experiment this difference was .10. However, the largest difference for a single group between experiments was of the same order, .08. The differences between experiments were as large as the differences between groups within an experiment. Variations in effort had no effect on the *level* of intertrial correlation.

Nor were there any differences in pattern. Table IV sets forth the correlations between each period and every other, averaged over all four groups in both experiments; the correlations are patterned into a rough superdiagonal form. The pattern in Table IV is not perfect; it was still less so in the eight matrices which were averaged to produce Table IV. Nevertheless, in all eight matrices this same pattern appeared and with comparable degrees of roughness.

A detail of patterning which suggested itself for particular attention was the contrast, in the two alternating groups, of correlations among periods in which the subjects were working against the same load and correlations between periods in which they worked against different loads. The correlations between periods with different loads were fully as large as those between periods with the same load.

In discussing her findings on distributed practice, Kientzle (1949, p. 537) wrote:

If intertrial correlations depend on number of trials, but not on the amount of intervening rest, and if the invariance of correlations means an invariance of component abilities, then rest does not change a subject's standard score on a specified trial. That is, if it

Table IV

CORRELATIONS AMONG 20-SECOND PERIODS ON THE MANUAL CRANK
AVERAGED OVER THE FOUR GROUPS AND TWO EXPERIMENTS

Period	1	2	3	4	5	6	7	8	9	10	11	12	13	14	15
1	—	.65	.51	.47	.47	.44	.51	.48	.44	.43	.42	.39	.44	.42	.39
2		—	.83	.69	.69	.63	.61	.63	.58	.55	.56	.52	.53	.55	.51
3			—	.85	.78	.76	.72	.73	.71	.66	.63	.64	.61	.64	.61
4				—	.88	.84	.77	.74	.70	.77	.73	.70	.66	.64	.50
5					—	.91	.80	.83	.78	.81	.82	.76	.68	.72	.72
6						—	.84	.84	.80	.83	.82	.81	.72	.73	.75
7							—	.88	.85	.81	.79	.79	.84	.79	.78
8								—	.89	.81	.83	.80	.81	.83	.80
9									—	.80	.82	.81	.80	.82	.81
10										—	.84	.85	.77	.75	.77
11											—	.89	.77	.82	.82
12												—	.77	.78	.81
13													—	.83	.80
14														—	.88

were possible to observe, say, two 15th trials from the same group of subjects, the one trial under massed conditions and the other under spaced, each subject's standard score would be the same on both trials. He might earn a higher score with rest, but he would keep the same standing on both trials.

The same language applies to the Manual Crank study. The evidence suggests that a subject's standard score in the kth period would not have been different, if he had been assigned to a different experimental group. If we imagine an (obviously hypothetical) analysis of variance in which each subject works the Manual Crank under all four conditions but the ordering of the conditions is irrelevant, then individuals and trials interact, to produce a nonunitary correlation matrix, but individuals and conditions do not.

Another way to make the same point is to say that loading on the Manual Crank does not affect the differential structure of the task. Insofar as individual differences are concerned, the task remains the same no matter what the loading is. Mean performance changes with loading, while the subjects' relative standing remains invariant.

Individual differences in performance are usually ascribed to events and variations which antedate the experiment. Differential psychologists think in terms of genetic differences and abilities, habits, and factors which are shaped by the past experience of the subject and which he brings with him, in some form, into the laboratory. If this view is correct, it follows that some experimental manipulations may not interact with the genetic-experiential tangle the subjects evolved prior to the experiment. The variation affects each individual in the same way.

To date, we have only begun to explore the problem of differential invariance. We know that it exists for a few variations in one or two tasks. We do not know how far this invariance extends or, for that matter, whether there may not be experimental variations that have nothing to do with fatigue under which the intertrial correlations are also invariant.

V. Differential Definition

A. THE CONCEPT

Beyond differential invariance lie all those experimental manipulations which affect the intertrial correlations. Fortunately, these outer regions are not as uncharted as they might seem at the outset. If the correlations fall into a superdiagonal form, at least roughly – and this limitation excludes only a small number of very simple tasks – the number of ways in which the correlations *can* be affected is sharply limited. The correlations may differ in the precision with which they obey the single tetrad law. They may differ in level, i.e., whether the correlations are generally large or small. And they may differ in the slope of the pattern as it falls away from the superdiagonal. Two matrices may be equally regular and have the same level yet differ markedly in pattern-slope. One matrix may be almost flat while the other has larger correlations in the superdiagonal and smaller ones in the upper right-hand corner with a steep gradient between the two extremes. If two superdiagonal patterns are alike in level, slope, and regularity they may still differ but only in relatively subtle ways, of which the most important is the course of differential change (see Section VI).

The idea of differential definition is composed of these three variations: level, pattern-slope, and regularity. The better defined a task is, the higher the level of correlation, the flatter the pattern-slope, and the more regular it is. In the extreme case all correlations equal unity; every trial is differentially identical with every other. A poorly defined task shows a low order of correlation and falls off steeply from the superdiagonal or is highly irregular. In a well-defined task, every trial is roughly equivalent with every other, while in a poorly defined task the trials are various in their differential contents.

The three components of differential definition are all capable of precise formulation. In order to formulate slope and regularity with precision, we must first fit a theoretical superdiagonal pattern, i.e., one which obeys the single tetrad law exactly, to the empirical correlations. The differences between corresponding empirical and best-fitting theoretical correlations are irregularities in the superdiagonal pattern. Unfortunately, the residual correlations, as these differences are called, are partly determined by correlation level; the higher the level, the smaller the residuals are likely to be. The best way to correct for this interaction is to express the residuals in terms of Fisher's z transformation. The root mean square of the transformed residuals may then be taken as an inverse measure of regularity, the smaller the root mean square the more regular the superdiagonal pattern.

Pattern-slope is best formulated as

$$\delta = 1 - \left(\frac{\rho_{1,n}}{\rho_{n-1,\,n}}\right)^2$$

where ρ_{ij} is the best-fitting theoretical correlation between Trials i and j. The theoretical correlations between the first and last trials, $\rho_{1,n}$, and between the last two trials, $\rho_{n-1,n}$, determine the slope of the pattern. The smaller $\rho_{1,n}$ is in relation to $\rho_{n-1,n}$ the steeper the slope. In a perfectly defined task the slope is flat and $\rho_{1,n}$ equals $\rho_{n-1,n}$. Correlation level is simply given as the average correlation in the matrix.

Two of the components of differential definition, level and slope, impose mathematical limits on each other. If level is high, better than .80, then slope must be fairly shallow, because no correlation can exceed unity. At the same time, slope must also be shallow when correlation level is low, less than .20, because a superdiagonal pattern consists of positive correlations only. The technical possibilities for a steep gradient between the superdiagonal and the upper right-hand corner are maximal when correlation level is in the neighborhood of .50.

In principle, it is possible for intertrial correlations to take some pattern other than superdiagonal form but, as a matter of fact, they never do. If an intertrial matrix has any pattern at all, it is superdiagonal. Hence, absence of superdiagonal pattern is materially synonymous with little or no definition. Tasks like lever positioning and line drawing lack definition. Absence of superdiagonal pattern is a qualitative extreme of poor definition. At the other extreme is perfect definition, in which all intertrial correlations equal unity. In between lie moderate levels of correlation with greater or lesser degrees of regularity and widely varying pattern-slopes.

B. TARGET SIZE

The Two-Hand Coordination Test measures a subject's ability to guide a pin around a track by manipulating control handles. Turning

the right-hand control moves the pin away from or toward the operator; turning the left-hand control moves the pin left and right. The
object is to drive the pin over the pathway as quickly as possible.

I. McD. Bilodeau (1965) divided 114 basic airmen into three groups
of 38 subjects each. All three groups worked on a clover-shaped track
that was flush with the plate in which it was set. The differences
among the groups concerned the play that was tolerated in the control
handles. Group P (precise) was the standard condition; the handles
could be turned 187.5° before the pin went off the track; in Group M
(moderate) the play was 860°; and in Group F (free) it was 1626°. In
Groups P and M the contacts had to be made consecutively; in Group
F a subject who jumped the track was permitted to bring the pin back
further along the track. Each subject practiced five one-minute trials a
day for 6 days. Performance was analyzed in number of contacts made
per day, so that the analysis rests on a 6-variable matrix.

Table V contains the results for Group P, and Table VI the results
for Group F. The results for Group M are not presented. However,
Groups P and M were much alike. Correlation levels in the two

Table V
MEANS, STANDARD DEVIATIONS, AND CORRELATIONS
IN THE TARGET-SIZE EXPERIMENT, GROUP P[a]

Trial	1	2	3	4	5	6	$\overline{X}$	σ
1	—	.84	.80	.83	.78	.73	69	20.5
2		—	.90	.86	.81	.75	103	29.5
3			—	.91	.86	.80	139	43.9
4				—	.89	.85	171	53.3
5					—	.93	208	61.7
6						—	241	68.9

[a]From I. McD. Bilodeau (1965).

Table VI
MEANS, STANDARD DEVIATIONS, AND CORRELATIONS
IN THE TARGET-SIZE EXPERIMENT, GROUP F[a]

Trial	1	2	3	4	5	6	$\overline{X}$	σ
1	—	.68	.54	.40	.32	.23	367	89.9
2		—	.87	.70	.58	.51	553	96.4
3			—	.89	.82	.74	665	104.1
4				—	.91	.87	741	94.1
5					—	.90	790	88.3
6						—	829	91.4

[a]From I. McD. Bilodeau (1965).

groups were .84 and .86, respectively. Pattern slope in Group P was slightly shallower, δ equaled .40, than in Group M, δ equaled .52. Root mean errors in Groups P and M were .05 and .08, respectively.

Group F, in contrast, is plainly less well defined than either of the other two groups. Pattern slope is very steep, with correlations ranging from the low .90s in the superdiagonal to .23 in the upper right-hand corner. Correlation level is .67, δ equals .86, and root mean error .09.

In this experiment, enlarging target size by allowing more play in the control handles and permitting the subjects to come back on the track as best they could greatly weakened differential definition. It permitted the subjects to register many more contacts per day than in either of the other two groups, but it also modified the task in a way which called for much greater differential change over the 6-day period.

C. Transfer of Training

Differential definition and its components may also be affected by prior training on another task. Fleishman (1953a) gave standard and experimental forms of the Rudder Control Test to two groups of air cadets. One group took the standard and the other the experimental test first. Since there were six trials of practice on the standard and four on the experimental test, there were 15 correlations within the standard test, 6 within the experimental, and 24 between the tests, under either order of administration. In Table VII, the averages for each of these groups of correlations are presented.

With respect to differential relationships the standard test was more disturbed by following the experimental test than vice versa.

For both tests the average within-test correlation was lower when the test came second than when it came first; but the drop was greater for the standard test.

The average correlation between tests was greater when the standard test came first than when it came second.

The patterns of within-test correlations are not presented, but they were superdiagonal forms for both tests under both administrations. However, the pattern was rougher for the standard test when it came second than when it came first, while the patterns of correlation within the experimental test were smooth superdiagonal forms under both administrations.

When the standard test came first, the pattern of between-test correlations was very regular; in fact with the standard test first, the *whole* matrix had regular superdiagonal form. However, with the experimental test first, the pattern of between-test correlations was rough.

It is significant that in neither of these studies did Fleishman report any normative results. The usual thing is the opposite; normative results are reported but not differential. Nevertheless, in any experimental study of motor learning both kinds of information are available. We know a great deal about the normative effects of many experimental variations; but we know next to nothing about the differential consequences of the same variations. And there may be relationships between the two orders of events. It may be, for example, that the disturbances of differential definition produced in one task when it follows upon another bears a relationship to transfer of training between the two tasks.

Table VII

AVERAGE CORRELATIONS WITHIN AND BETWEEN
STANDARD AND EXPERIMENTAL FORMS OF THE RUDDER CONTROL TEST
WHEN THE STANDARD FORM WAS ADMINISTERED FIRST AND WHEN THE
EXPERIMENTAL FORM WAS ADMINISTERED FIRST[a]

Correlation	Standard first	Experimental first
Standard – standard	.64	.48
Experimental – experimental	.76	.83
Standard – experimental	.43	.32

[a]From Fleishman (1953a).

VI. The Course of Differential Change

Traditional learning curves are plots of mean performance (or some other behavior of central tendency) against trials. Ordinarily, these curves are increasing and negatively accelerated. In the early stages of practice the curve rises sharply. As practice proceeds, the steps between trials become smaller. Toward the end of practice the curve rises very slowly as it approaches the asymptote.

A correlation coefficient reflects (inversely) differences in the alignment of individuals on two variables. The stronger the correlation the more nearly individuals are aligned alike; the weaker the correlation the greater the differences between the two arrays. A correlation, therefore, between neighboring trials of practice reflects the magnitude of the differential step between them. It measures differential change from one trial to the next.

In the matrix of Table I these (superdiagonal) correlations are .79, .87, .91, .91, .89, .93, and .94. With one exception, the correlations increase steadily. This increase in the superdiagonal correlations means that the differential process which accompanies practice on the Two-Hand Coordination Test is negatively accelerated; as practice proceeds, the differential steps between successive trials get smaller.

Since the superdiagonal correlations are inversely related to the magnitude of the steps between neighboring trials, the process of differential change is more clearly pictured if the correlation coefficient is transformed into its inverse, the coefficient of alienation, i.e.,

$$\text{Alienation} = \sqrt{1 - r^2}$$

We need also to remember that the superdiagonal correlations (or alienation coefficients) are not measures of differential status but of change in differential status, without regard to sign. They are comparable, therefore, not with mean performance but with absolute change in mean performance.

In Fig. 1 the coefficients of alienation and absolute changes from trial to trial in the mean and standard deviation of performance on the

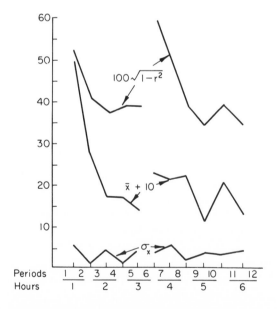

Fig. 1. Superdiagonal coefficients of alienation and changes from one trial to the next in the mean and standard deviations on the Complex Coordination Test.

Complex Coordination Test are presented. Practice in this study (Reynolds, 1952b) was distributed into six 1-hour sessions. In each hour, performance in the first and in the last 20 minutes is plotted. There was a lunch break between the third and fourth hours.

In Fig. 1 the curve for differential alienation parallels the one for mean change. Both start high, between the first and second periods, and decrease through the third hour.

Over the lunch break there was a major change in mean performance (a drop) which was followed by generally decreasing changes (improvements) in the afternoon.

The same changes took place differentially, except that the differential effect of the lunch break was greater than its effect upon the means.

Meanwhile, the changes in standard deviation follow an irregular but level course.

In the case of the Complex Coordination Test normative and differential changes during acquisition are roughly parallel. Nevertheless, there is in Fig. 1 a difference between the two processes which in some other tests is more marked and more sustained.

The smallest differential change during the morning hours occurred between the third and fourth periods. Between the fourth and fifth and again between the fifth and sixth periods differential changes were somewhat larger. Between the same periods changes in the mean continued to decline.

In the Rotary Pursuit (Fleishman, 1960) and Discrimination Reaction Time Tests (Fleishman & Hempel, 1955) the course of differential change undergoes a clear change of sign. Mean change continues to decline throughout acquisition, but differential change after a pronounced initial drop increases slowly through the terminal phases of practice.

The significance of these discrepancies is that differential change may continue, in fact, it may increase, at stages of practice in which mean performance is nearing its asymptote and practice seems no longer to be having appreciable effects.

VII. Inheritance

If there is any one book with which differential psychology may be said to have begun, it is Francis Galton's *Hereditary Genius*. The bulk of Galton's text was concerned with the inheritance of those intellectual and personal qualities that make for eminence in judges, commanders, literary men, musicians, scientists, painters. However, Galton (1887) also considered familial tendencies in two distinctly motor vocations, rowing and wrestling.

He said:

> In respect to oarsmen, let me assure the reader that they are no insignificant fraction of the community, – no mere waifs and strays from those who follow more civilized pursuits. A perfect passion for rowing pervades large classes. At Newcastle, when a great race takes place, all business is at a standstill, factories are closed, shops are shut, and offices deserted. The number of men who fall within the attraction of the career is very great; and there can be no doubt that a large proportion of those who are qualified to succeed brilliantly, obey the attraction and pursue it (p. 305).

Galton compiled information on all men who had rowed with distinction on either the Tyne or the Thames in the preceding 26 years. "The names," said Galton, "are not picked and chosen, but the best men have been taken of whom any certain knowledge could be obtained." Galton classified his oarsmen into two broad categories of eminence: good and excellent. He calculated that not 1 man in 10 attained the lower rank and less than 1 in 1000 became an excellent oarsman.

Galton found a total of 35 men who had attained a degree of eminence as oarsmen sufficient to rank them in either of these two grades. Of these 35 men 33 were related to one or more of the other eminent oarsmen. There were 6 families with 2 eminent oarsmen, 2 with 3, 1 with 5, and 1 with 10. The most remarkable of these was the family of Henry Clasper. "He was," wrote Galton, "for many years stroke of a four-oared crew, and frequently the whole crew, including the coxswain, were members of the Clasper family. For eight years this crew won the championship of the Tyne. Six times Henry pulled stroke for the crew winning the championship of the Thames, and Coombes declared that he was the best stroke that ever pulled." Henry's brother, Richard, was only slightly less distinguished, and another brother, Edward, ranked as a good rower despite the disadvantage of having lost a leg.

Galton's studies of inheritance have been criticized principally on the grounds that familial tendency is not conclusive evidence of hereditary gifts. In a family like Clasper's rowing must certainly have dominated the ambitions of all its male members. At a very early age they must have prepared for an oarsman's career. And this preparation may have had a bearing on their phenomenal success.

The figures on oarsmen may also be questioned on technical grounds. According to Galton's estimates, the ratio of good to excellent oarsmen was roughly 100 to 1. Nevertheless, in the list of names he gave the ratio was 1 to 1; there were as many excellent as good oarsmen. The most likely reason for this discrepancy is that it was more difficult to obtain "certain knowledge" about less distinguished men. Still if the 1600-odd good oarsmen which Galton was not able to locate had also been listed, it is possible that Galton's figures would have been less impressive.

With human subjects it is not easy to distinguish familial from genetic transmission. An approach which reduces the extent of the problem is to study young children. Individual differences in behavior are present in the first few months of life and persist without much change through the first two years at least (Thomas, Chess, Birch, Hertzig, & Korn, 1964). Some of these differences, like activity or the responsiveness of a child to external stimulation, involve heavy motor components.

The study of young twins carries the argument further. Freedman and Keller (1963) followed 11 pairs of fraternal and 9 pairs of identical twins on a monthly basis through the first year of life. The twins' behavior was evaluated on the Bayley Mental and Motor Scales and the Bayley Infant Behavior Profile. Within-pair differences in all scales were much smaller between identical than between fraternal twins.

In twin studies environmentalists usually advance the argument that identical twins tend to imitate each other, to identify with each other, and that their observed likeness to each other is secondary to these psychological processes rather than their genetic identity. However, in Freedman and Keller's study this argument does not apply. In the first year of life infants do not respond to each other at all, much less imitate each other.

Similar differences between identical and fraternal twins have also been observed at the adult level. In 1933 McNemar studied the performance of 46 pairs of fraternal and 47 pairs of identical twins on the Koerth pursuit rotor, steadiness, speed-drill, spool-packing, and card-sorting tests. Holzinger heritability coefficients appear in Table VIII; these coefficients state the proportion of the variance within families which is attributable to genetic variations. For the pursuit rotor, steadiness, and speed drill tests the heritabilities are high; for card sorting heritability is moderate and for spool packing, it is low.

On three of these tests, pursuit rotor, spool packing, and card sorting, the twins were given seven trials of practice. In Table IX Holzinger heritabilities for the first two and the last two trials are presented. In all three cases these heritabilities tend to be lower at the end of practice than at the beginning. In the case of the pursuit-rotor and

Table VIII
Holzinger Heritability Coefficients (Corrected for Age)
In 46 Pairs of Fraternal and 47 Pairs of Identical Twins
on Five Psychomotor Tests[a]

Test	Heritability
Pursuit rotor	.90
Steadiness	.80
Speed drill	.69
Spool packing	.25
Card sorting	.46

[a]From McNemar (1933).

Table IX
Holzinger Heritability Coefficients (Corrected for Age)
in 46 Pairs of Fraternal and 47 Pairs of Identical Twins
on Trials 1, 2, 6, and 7 in Three Tests of Motor Skill[a]

Test	1	2	6	7
Pursuit rotor	.78	.74	.64	.67
Spool packing	.28	−.02	−.17	−.02
Card sorting	.43	.51	.31	.43

[a]From McNemar (1933).

card-sorting tests the decline is relatively slight and easy. In the spool-packing test, there is no heritable variance except on the first trial; thereafter, it disappears altogether.

There is one other study in the literature which concerns itself with the magnitude of genetic contributions at different stages of practice (Brody, 1937); it found no change with practice on the Minnesota Spatial Relations Test.

It appears, therefore, that genetic contributions tend to be more prominent at the beginning of practice than later on. However, these twin studies are now almost 30 years old; it might be profitable to take up these questions again.

VIII. Correlations with Other Tests

Most of the differential work on psychomotor performance as a dynamic process is relatively recent. In the main, psychomotor performance has been treated as a whole; if more than one trial was administered, a subject's scores were averaged over them.

And the principal effort has been to classify psychomotor tasks into coherent differential groups, i.e., so that subjects who do well on one test in the group can be expected to do well on the others too.

This effort has been carried out almost exclusively by means of factor analysis. In this technique the variance of each test is resolved into the test's loadings on several hypothetical factors. There has always been some doubt as to what it is that factor-analytic resolutions assert about the correlations from which they are derived; but this chapter is an inappropriate place in which to attempt a clarification of the question. However the matter is put, factor analysts have reached agreement with respect to several factors which operate in psychomotor tasks (Fleishman, 1953b, 1954). I will describe only six of them.

A factor called *wrist-finger speed* has been identified in several tapping and aiming tests. Its loadings suggest that it is independent of eye-hand coordination. For example, the speed with which a person can tap a pencil, without regard to where he taps it, loads high on the factor. However, if taps are scored only when they fall within a small circle, tapping speed loads low; and the smaller the circle the lower the loading.

Aiming is supplementary to *wrist-finger speed*. It also involves speed, but tests which require precise positioning of each tap load highest on the factor. Eye-hand coordination appears to be essential. The factor appears in printed tests only.

The Purdue Pegboard and O'Connor Finger Dexterity Tests have high loadings on *finger dexterity*. Both tests require precise manipulation of small objects, like pegs or pins. Sensing with the fingertips is essential.

Manual dexterity is like finger dexterity except that it concerns larger objects. Tests which load on it do not require sensing with the fingertips.

Tests which require a subject to hold an object stationary, for example, to hold a stylus so that it does not touch the sides of a small hole, load heavily on *steadiness*. The factor also appears when subjects are asked to move an object in a highly controlled manner, for example, in a track so that the stylus does not touch the sides.

Psychomotor coordination is found almost exclusively in apparatus tests, like the Rotary Pursuit, Rudder Control, and Complex Coordination Tests. The normative basis of this factor has been rather vaguely described as "representing either coordination of the body, in movements of moderate scope, or coordination of such movements with the perception of a visual stimulus."

In the early days of psychological testing it was thought by some that a compensatory mechanism might be built into human nature.

People who were poor at reading made up for it by being good at something else. People who had unusual intellectual gifts had poor motor coordination. However, it became apparent early in the use of psychological tests that nature was not equalitarian. People who did better than average in one area could be expected to do better than average in all other situations which called for maximal performance from the subjects. It was this fact which gave rise to Spearman's two-factor theory. Spearman hypothesized that all tests of ability depended in part upon a general factor, which he called g, that was responsible for the positive correlations among tests of ability.

In the mid-thirties Herbert Woodrow raised a related question. Everybody improves with practice on any test, but some people improve more than others. Woodrow wondered whether there might not be a general positivity among improvement scores in the same way that there was among raw scores on unpracticed tests. If there was, he reasoned, the fact would have important implications for the theory of intelligence.

Woodrow carried out several studies in this connection. In one of them (Woodrow, 1939) 82 subjects were given 66 trials of practice on four tests: horizontal adding, substitution, two- and four-digit cancellation. The same subjects were also administered 21 other tests without practice. For each individual and for each of the four tests which were practiced, Woodrow calculated an improvement score, which equaled the individual's score at the end of practice minus his score at the beginning. He found that the correlations among improvement scores were low, on the order of .20 to .30. The correlations, moreover, between improvement scores and the other tests were also low. As often as not they were negative. He concluded that there was no general factor common to improvement scores.

In the same study Woodrow also reported the correlations between the 21 unpracticed tests and initial and final performance on each of the practiced tests. The results appear in Table X. In the case of all four tests, initial performance tended to correlate better with the unpracticed tests than did final performance.

The examination of psychomotor performance in relation to external tests was deferred for 20 years. In the 1950's, however, a series of studies from the Air Force confirmed and extended Woodrow's earlier results with printed tests. The principal study in this series was carried out by Adams in 1953.

The subjects in Adams' study were 197 basic airmen. They were administered 32 printed tests, 13 simple psychomotor tests, and 7 complex psychomotor tests. All of the complex psychomotor tests

Table X
AVERAGE CORRELATIONS OF 21 UNPRACTICED TESTS
WITH INITIAL AND FINAL PERFORMANCE ON FOUR PRACTICED TESTS[a]

Test	Average correlation	
	Initial	Final
Horizontal adding	.30	.19
Substitution	.22	.13
Two-digit cancellation	.15	.10
Four-digit cancellation	.18	.16

[a]From Woodrow (1939).

were practiced and none of the others. Practice was most extensive on the Complex Coordination Test (CCT), which served as the focal point of the investigation.

Adams' results are presented in Table XI. On the average, the printed tests correlated better with initial performance than with final performance on the CCT. The 13 simple psychomotor tests maintained their relationship to initial performance on the CCT, even increased it a little. Initial performance on the six complex psychomotor tests other than the CCT behaved like the printed tests; it correlated better with initial than with final performance on the criterion test. However, final performance on the same six tests correlated better with final performance on the CCT than with initial performance.

These results have been repeated by several investigators using many different psychomotor tests. The results have uniformly confirmed Adams' findings. If two tests are widely dissimilar, practice on one of them generally serves to reduce the correlation between the two tests. If they are alike, practice tends to increase the relationship between the tests.

As practice proceeds on a psychomotor task the proportion of variance which is specific to the task, i.e., which cannot at present be related to external variables, increases. In the Complex Coordination Test, for example, the proportion of specific variance increases from 6% at the beginning to 38% at the end of practice (Fleishman & Hempel, 1953). In psychomotor tests generally, most of the variance at the end of practice is specific to the task. This finding has tended to focus attention for the first time in many years on specific variance.

In one analysis of psychomotor test relationships (Fleishman, 1954) the proportion of variance which was specific to the tests averaged 49%. This result is typical. In field and criterion behaviors the proportion of specific variance is much larger. Usually, at least 75% of the variance is specific to the tasks, frequently as much as 90%.

Table XI
Average Correlations of 32 Printed, 13 Simple Psychomotor,
and 6 Complex Psychomotor Tests with Initial and Final
Performance on the Complex Coordination Test[a]

Kind of test	Average correlation with the CCT	
	Initial	Final
Printed	.38	.25
Simple psychomotor	.24	.27
Complex psychomotor		
Initial	.45	.38
Final	.41	.49

[a]From Adams (1953).

In his presidential address to the American Psychological Association, Cronbach characterized experimental psychology as a "tight little island" and differential psychology as a "Holy Roman Empire." In the case of experimental psychology the plural might have been more descriptive. In any experiment there is a great deal of unexplained variance within experimental conditions. Known experimental relationships exist as many islands in a sea of within-group error. And the same is true of differential psychology. Its findings are so many islands surrounded on all sides by expanses of specific variance.

References

Adams, J. A. The prediction of performance at advanced stages of training on a complex psychomotor task. *USAF Human Resources Research Center Research Bulletin*, 1953, No. 53–49.

Bilodeau, E. A. Transfer of training between tasks differing in degree of physical restriction of imprecise responses. *USAF Human Resources Research Center Research Bulletin*, 1952, No. 52–54.

Bilodeau, E. A. Speed of acquiring a simple motor response as a function of the systematic transformation of knowledge of results. *American Journal of Psychology*, 1953, **66**, 409–420. (a)

Bilodeau, E. A. Acquisition of two lever-positioning responses practiced over several periods of alternation. *Journal of Experimental Psychology*, 1953, **46**, 43–49. (b)

Bilodeau, E. A., & Bilodeau, I. McD. Variable frequency of knowledge of results and the learning of a simple skill. *Journal of Experimental Psychology*, 1958, **55**, 379-383.

Bilodeau, E. A., Bilodeau, I. McD., & Schumsky, D. A. Some effects of introducing and withdrawing knowledge of results early and late in practice. *Journal of Experimental Psychology*, 1959, **58**, 142–144.

Bilodeau, E. A., & Ryan, F. J. A test for interaction of delay of knowledge of results and two types of interpolated activity. *Journal of Experimental Psychology*, 1960, **59**, 414–420.

Bilodeau, I. McD. Transfer of training across target sizes. *Journal of Experimental Psychology*, 1965, **70**, 135–140.

Borgatta, E. F. Sidesteps toward a nonspecial theory. *Psychological Review*, 1954, **61**, 343–352.

Brody, D. Twin resemblances in mechanical ability, with reference to the effects of practice on performance. *Child Development*, 1937, 8, 207–216.

Cronbach, L. J. The two disciplines of scientific psychology. *American Psychologist*, 1957, **12**, 671–684.

Edgerton, H. A., & Valentine, W. L. A factor analysis of learning data. *Psychological Bulletin*, 1935, **32**, 719.

Fleishman, E. A. A factor analysis of intra-task performance on two psychomotor tests. *Psychometrika*, 1953, **18**, 45–55. (a)

Fleishman, E. A. Testing for psychomotor abilities by means of apparatus tests. *Psychological Bulletin*, 1953, **50**, 241–262. (b)

Fleishman, E. A. A factorial study of psychomotor abilities. *USAF Personnel & Training Research Center Research Bulletin*, 1954, No. 54–15.

Fleishman, E. A. Abilities at different stages of practice in rotary pursuit performance. *Journal of Experimental Psychology*, 1960, **60**, 162–171.

Fleishman, E. A., & Hempel, W. E., Jr. Changes in factor structure of a complex psychomotor test as a function of practice. *USAF Human Resources Research Center Research Bulletin*, 1953, No. 53–68.

Fleishman, E. A., & Hempel, W. E., Jr. The relation between abilities and improvement with practice in a visual discrimination reaction task. *Journal of Experimental Psychology*, 1955, **49**, 301–312.

Fleishman, E. A., & Parker, J. F., Jr. Prediction of advanced levels of proficiency in a complex tracking task. *USAF WADC Technical Report*, 1959, No. 59–255.

Freedman, D. G., & Keller, B. Inheritance of behavior in infants. *Science*, 1963, **140**, 196–198.

Galton, F. *Hereditary genius.* New York: Appleton, 1887.

Greene, E. B. An analysis of random and systematic changes with practice. *Psychometrika*, 1943, 8, 37–53.

Houston, R. C. An evaluation of the predictive properties of measures of variability of performance on three psychomotor tasks. Unpublished doctoral dissertation, Univer. of Maryland, 1950.

Jones, M. B. Practice as a process of simplification. *Psychological Review*, 1962, **69**, 274–294.

Jones, M. B. Intertrial correlations under variations in effort. *Ergonomics*, 1968, 175–181.

Kientzle, M. J. Properties of learning curves under varied distributions of practice. *Journal of Experimental Psychology*, 1946, **36**, 187–211.

Kientzle, M. J. Ability patterns under distributed practice. *Journal of Experimental Psychology*, 1949, **39**, 532–537.

McNemar, Q. Twin resemblances in motor skills, and the effect of practice thereon. *Journal of Genetic Psychology*, 1933, **42**, 70–97.

Melton, A. W. (Ed.) *Apparatus tests.* Washington, D.C.: U.S. Govt. Printing Office, 1947. (AAF Aviation Psychology Program Research Report No. 4.)

Osgood, C. E. *Method and theory in experimental psychology.* London and New York: Oxford Univer. Press, 1953.

Perl, R. E. An application of Thurstone's method of factor analysis to practice series. *Journal of General Psychology*, 1934, **11**, 209–212.

Reynolds, B. Correlation between two psychomotor tasks as a function of distribution of practice on the first. *Journal of Experimental Psychology*, 1952, **43**, 341–348. (a)

Reynolds, B. The effect of learning on the predictability of psychomotor performance. *Journal of Experimental Psychology*, 1952, **44**, 189–198. (b)

Spearman, C. General intelligence, objectively determined and measured. *American Journal of Psychology*, 1904, **15**, 201–293.

Thomas, A., Chess, S., Birch, H. G., Hertzig, M. E., & Korn, S. *Behavioral individuality in early childhood.* New York: New York Univer. Press, 1964.

Viteles, M. S. The influence of training on motor test performance. *Journal of Experimental Psychology*, 1933, **16**, 556–564.

Woodrow, H. Factors in improvement with practice. *Journal of Psychology*, 1939, **7**, 55–70.

CHAPTER 6

Retention under Free and Stimulated Conditions[1]

EDWARD A. BILODEAU
Tulane University

I. Historical Comment

Ebbinghaus (1964) and his successors have dominated the study of retention for most of the twentieth century. Gradually and steadily a stock of methods and materials has accumulated. Improvements on the honorable and old tradition of Ebbinghaus seem desirable to a number of recent investigators. One especially important new issue is that the shape of the curve of forgetting, long thought to be well known, is not really well described for human beings.

Most modern research has dealt with acquisition curves, not retention curves, and it should not be assumed that retaining is the opposite of learning. Retention research has been in doldrums for decades and until 1957 neither independent nor dependent variables had been evolved or reexamined as in the field of acquisition. The prevailing opinion was that retention fell very fast in verbal learning and that retention hardly failed at all in motor learning. There were exceptions to the majority view; data obtained by McGeoch (1932) led him to con-

[1] The principal part of this chapter is devoted to a discussion and overview of work originating in the Tulane Laboratory. The work of other laboratories is reviewed where it seems especially relevant, but does not get the detailed coverage it deserves. The preparation of this chapter was supported by the Air Force Office of Scientific Research, Office of Aerospace Research, United States Air Force, under AFOSR Contract No. F44620-68-C-0072.

tradict the generalization that skilled motor acts are better retained than are verbal materials and Hunter (1934) spoke of the failure to recall a motor skill minutes after a correct execution and went out of his way to state that there is no one curve of forgetting.

There are many reasons why a voluminous literature fails to tell us much about the observed or the theoretical curves of forgetting. (1) Much of the pre-World War II data cannot stand examination by contemporary research design. (2) The duration of rest is not examined in most studies, one value being common. (3) Much effort is directed to short-term processes and an overall shape is difficult to assess by extrapolation. (4) The methods of measuring retention have evolved very slowly. (5) Curves showing the forgetting of component (single) events within trials are in short supply. (6) There has been much variation of the conditions of learning, but not of recalling.

Until recently, research in *verbal* learning has stressed the Ebbinghaus task of serial rote learning, the paired-associate task, and the many experimental variables which they imply. This situation changed rapidly after the work of Peterson and Peterson (1959) and Underwood and Postman (1960), who have introduced major new techniques and ideas to alter our thinking on portions of the curve for verbal materials. Indeed the whole field of memory has undergone an explosive growth in the last decade, some of it being reviewed by Melton and others in a special issue of the *Journal of Verbal Learning and Verbal Behavior* (1963, pp. 1–119) and in other places (Bilodeau & Bilodeau, 1961; Bilodeau & Levy, 1964; Keppel, 1968; Naylor & Briggs, 1961; Posner, 1967a; Postman, 1964). Selected readings of journal articles can be found in Kausler (1966) and Slamecka (1967). Important project work employing new tasks is being done by a number of productive investigators: Bahrick (Bahrick, Clark, & Bahrick, 1967), Broadbent (1963), Bousfield (Bousfield & Puff, 1964), Conrad (1967), Cofer (1965), Deese (1965), Lloyd (Lloyd & Johnston, 1963), Murdock (Murdock & vom Saal, 1967), Posner (1967b), Reid (Reid, Brackett, & Johnson, 1963), Shepard (Shepard & Chang, 1963), Tulving (1967), Wickelgren (1966), and Yntema (1963). Since this chapter stresses motor retention, relatively little can be said here about verbal retention even though it will be touched upon from time to time.

II. Retention Curves for Verbal and Motor Tasks Compared

Students are often taught that the retention curve is like the one shown in Fig. 1, which is plotted after data collected by Ebbinghaus

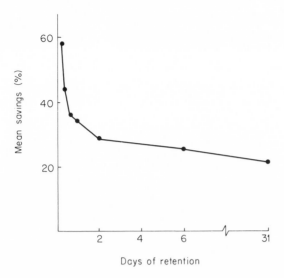

Fig. 1. An example of a common concave retention curve. (Data from Ebbinghaus, 1885; see 1964 translation.)

in the last century. Here, a measure of savings in number of nonsense syllables recalled, based upon the method of relearning, is plotted against the duration of the retention interval. The curve has a concave appearance and looks exponential. Accordingly, the classic description is that forgetting proceeds rapidly at first, and later more slowly. Substantial limitations to the classic view were raised by Underwood (1957), who suggested that a major portion of the bow was attributable to uncontrolled proacting agents. More recently, Bahrick (1964, 1965) has added other reservations and states that the shape is an artifact; it is the result of several factors, only one of which is the rate at which associations weaken in time. The form of the curve of Fig. 1 also depends upon the Ebbinghaus procedure for collecting the data, most notably the nonsense syllable material and the relearning procedure. Some people have assumed that these procedures would give a curve-shape typical of human memory in general. This assumption, as we shall see, is not a good one.

Some recent ideas about the shape can be traced to Underwood (1957), and his asking why the classic curve in verbal learning fell so fast and so far. The best answer to date is his own, namely, that much, if not most of the early forgetting, comes about through the interference generated by the prior learning by the subject of many lists. The target list is susceptible to forgetting to the extent of previous training with materials of the same sort and all probably learned in the same situation as well. This is a proaction effect. Earlier, McGeoch (1942) tried to establish interpolated learning as the culprit, but with modest success. An experimental design employing a task interpolated between training and recalling is a retroactive one in that the effect of interpolation on the recall of the training task is studied.

After making a deduction for the contribution of proaction to the amount forgotten, Underwood reported that verbal materials were much less sensitive to forgetting than earlier investigators had said. Underwood calculated that, instead of forgetting the greater part of a list of words within just a few minutes, an individual might retain as much as 90 % after 24 hours and produce a far shallower curve than in Fig. 1. This allowance for proaction, of course, altered our orientation toward the classic retention curve because most experiments on rote memory had used the same subject over and over. Repeated use of the same subject from one retention interval to another can be a methodological flaw unless one is interested in the phenomena of proaction for themselves. Since most verbal experiments of the earlier era have used this design, their data are limited to that use. Subjects who are given many lists to learn develop positive transfer in learning; in relearning they do poorly at first (negative transfer) and with additional practice trials regain original proficiency rapidly (delayed positive transfer). Ebbinghaus' curve must be thought of as a shape which results from a certain set of laboratory procedures. If we are curious about other procedures, we find other shapes produced.

In the area of motor-skills retention, a historical survey of the field yields a few studies with some forgetting (see Noble, Trumbo, Ulrich, & Cross, 1966, for instance) and a great many studies where no evidence for forgetting is found (e.g., Bell, 1950; Reynolds & Bilodeau, 1952; Battig, Nagel, Voss, & Brogden, 1957; Ammons, Farr, Bloch, Neumann, Dey, Marion, & Ammons, 1958; Fleishman & Parker, 1962; Roehrig, 1964). In the foregoing cases, the curve is equal to a constant. Every failure to find forgetting makes it that much more difficult to speak of the variables that produce more or less of it. There is much laboratory data to confirm anecdotal sayings about motor skills being highly resistant to forgetting. For more of the history of motor-skills retention, Chapter 1 by Irion should be read.

Only one or two of the null experiments need concern us in any detail. The one by Ammons *et al.* will be considered first since it was the most resourceful. The apparatus was the Airplane Control Test, a device that presents the operator with a small, moving model airplane mounted on a universal joint. The subject is required to compensate for the erratic movements of the plane as it simulates flight through

rough air. He does this with hand stick and foot pedals as he might in a real vintage airplane. In a standard airplane simulator, the pilot enters the craft and operates it from the inside. In the test used in this experiment, the operator looked at the model and operated it from the outside. Several hundred college subjects were trained to steady the model well, and then retrained up to two years later. No evidence of forgetting was produced even with the extreme temporal intervals. The question is whether Ammons *et al.* have failed to find forgetting, which some might believe to lie uncovered by their techniques or whether we can accept the data at face value.

Another study with the same leaden result was the one by Fleishman and Parker (1962). This null outcome resulted after the use of substantial laboratory facilities and a tracking task simulating display and control characteristics of an air-borne radar attack in an interceptor airplane. That is, the subject learned to coordinate the action of stick and rudder controls. Nothing at all seemed to be forgotten with a year of layover; after 2 years of layover, proficiency was, at most, slightly inferior at first, but certainly mastery was reacquired in a few minutes. The authors also attempted to predict retention performance from ability measures estimated from scores available on 44 printed and psychomotor tests. Their best two predictors, *spatial orientation* and *multilimb coordination*, did not correlate significantly with the retention scores on the trainer and their conclusion about finding negligible results has been accepted.

Actually, instead of doing worse with time, the subject may perform better after resting. This is particularly true if the initial practice period is massed, the finding being called the reminiscence phenomenon. Reminiscence is common, powerful, and it might even mask tendencies to forget. The experiment by Koonce, Chambliss, and Irion (1964) on the rotary pursuit test is a good example of the power of reminiscence. Several lengthy values of retention, including 1 and 2 years, were used after a period of relatively massed training at tracking the target. At the beginning of retraining, every rest group exceeded a no-rest control group and all the rested groups did equally well. When initial practice is spaced in time, as it was in Bell's (1950) study, there is no reminiscence effect with a year of layover. There was a nominal loss in proficiency which was quickly overcome during retraining. If the subject is allowed a brief period to readjust and warm up, we can conclude that the pursuit rotor is not a suitable device for demonstrating forgetting. We can also conclude that it is an admirable device for showing reminiscence.

The studies reviewed above are unlike the Ebbinghaus procedure in that the subject is used in one condition only and, therefore, proactive effects are at a minimum. Further, no special activity was interpolated between training and retraining and the subject was not assigned any experimental skills to master during the layover. If he were assigned to performing the reversed form of the task or some other variant of control-display changes, the chances of producing forgetting through the medium of retroaction might be enhanced. Lewis (see Lewis, McAllister, & Bechtoldt, 1953) is especially well known for his long-term project on many aspects of this procedure. After working variables such as different motor tasks, levels of ability or achievement, response measures, etc. the Lewis findings can be summarized as follows. Retroactive interference is (1) difficult to produce, (2) obtained in small amounts when produced, and (3) rapidly converted to positive transfer upon the resumption of a relearning period.

In summary, over a period of several decades in the investigation of training and retraining of skills involving continuous responding, we find insufficient forgetting to cast up a forgetting curve. There are still reservations around, for the investigators themselves would be reluctant to board a jet liner with a pilot returning from a 2-year furlough. Certainly, his recall of cockpit procedures would have deteriorated so far as to make immediate certification most unlikely. His control-column skills would seem to be far better recalled, but there being a narrow tolerance for error among high performance aircraft, not to mention passengers, we had better admit the need for some retraining on manual skills too.

Next we move on to the forgetting of especially simple skills, those of a positioning variety. These, it turns out, are forgettable.

III. Retention Curves for Simple, Positioning Skills

Figure 2 shows a lever task for learning a simple positioning response similar to line drawing. The task is usually one of learning how far to move the lever and later recalling the move under instruction to repeat an earlier response. A series of studies with the lever is surveyed in detail below, and so the task will be carefully described.

The subject is asked to reach into the box and to move the lever (blind) through several degrees. After the move is completed, the experimenter records the amplitude of response in degrees of arc, and says something to the subject such as, "You were 54 units short of the target." The subject, then, has made one response called R_1 and the experimenter has administered one knowledge of results, or information feedback; the latter is designated IF.

The lever presented in Fig. 2 has been employed extensively for studies of feedback and its effect on learning in general. All kinds of numerical and temporal transformations of feedback were investigated in a program resembling schedules of reinforcement and with much the same objective—to see how changes in response depend upon the conditions of feedback. The studies of feedback are reviewed in detail in Chapter 9.

In a series of studies with variations in the temporal point of administering IF, it was found that the temporal position of IF between R_1 and R_2 had no effect on accuracy whatsoever (Bilodeau & Bilodeau, 1958). Feedback was delayed by seconds, minutes, hours, days, and weeks, and even so, learning was not dependent upon its temporal position. Instead, it was found that the longer the time between R_1 and R_2, the poorer the learning. To make a long story short, the ex-

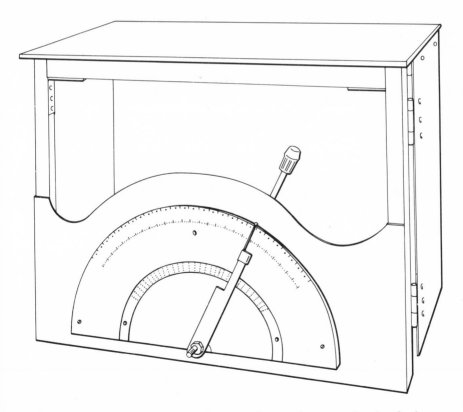

Fig. 2. An experimenter's view of the Manual Lever Apparatus showing the lever within the box and a scale for measuring amplitude of lever displacement outside the box. (From Bilodeau, Jones, & Levy, 1964.)

planation of the poor learning with spaced responses held that subjects with long intervals between responses were forgetting some
things of importance. Three basic events of training, not one as is the
usual view, were being forgotten, it was thought. These events were
(1) R_1, (2) IF, and also (3) any planned response or response alternative (R^a) the subject might have made at the time of training. So it
turned out that a project on learning and feedback produced some
basic questions about the role of memory.

A *verbal* component to levering, of course, was present from the
start because experimenters in motor studies often use "long" and
"short" and numbers such as "27" and "54" for verbal feedback.
These IF's are administered as *some* function (f) of a previous response, and indeed, are deliberately arbitrary and preprogrammed. If
the subject, for example, moves 35° toward a 30° goal the true error or
error score is +5°, but the IF administered is not necessarily equal to
+5°. Since IF is by definition equal to f(true error), the score reported
might be anything at all, say $5 \times 5°$, $5 + 5°$, etc. In this formulation,
R and IF are different events.

The transforming is done in order to examine the relationships between IF and the response it arouses. In a simple case, for example, an
IF of 100 (purporting to be the response error in a task such as the
lever) should yield a lever displacement different from an IF of 10 and
generally the latter would produce a smaller movement change the
next time. Here, it is assumed that the subject will enter a larger
correction when administered a larger apparent error. There ought to
be both levering and numerical associative hierarchies to IF whatever
its form or code — numbers, signs, units, etc., in the same way that various words are associated with a stimulus word in the familiar word
association tests. If the reader tends to make the error of equating the
IF term with the response term, instead of defining it as some function
of the response term, he should refer to Chapter 9.

Generally, three component events within a trial (R_1, IF, R^a) can be
discerned. These should not be ignored, confounded, or left unelabo-
rated. Forgetting curves are needed for each component just as much
as for the standard curve of relearning of R_1. In the standard experiment on retention, whether verbal or motor, the subject is almost always asked to do his best during the retraining phase, and is even
overtly asked to improve as in relearning; he has not been asked to
repeat anything such as a component of training. Requesting a person
to improve does not set him to the basic memory task. Beyond the
issue of repetition, methods which introduce special stimulus associates into the recall environment seem promising. That is, a more ac-

tive acknowledgment of training context or preexperimental context might well be made by the experimenter in order to deliberately intervene in the retrieving process. No such special conditions are introduced into what can now be called the standard recall (free) environment. In short, on balance most of the operations characterizing a standard retention study have been in common with the design of a learning study. The high degree of similarity in procedure may have been a function of the prevailing conception of learning and forgetting, that is, one is the inverse of the other. If one believes this, the experimenter will surely design the recalling environment in an ordinary way. The test period will be a replicate of training procedures, is to be called *relearning*, and the experimenter would not dare to change the testing environment.

The study of the within-trial events which might be liable to forgetting was initiated by Bilodeau, Sulzer, and Levy (1962). The basic events are shown in Fig. 3 where positioning a lever will illustrate the task. Here, R_1 is the first and the only levering response of Training, R^a is the alternative response or the response that the subject could make in place of R_1, and IF is the feedback pertaining to R_1 or to R^a at the experimenter's discretion. During Pretraining, the subject can be shown $0, 1, 2 \ldots n$ targets or places to move. Let us suppose he is guided to just two alternatives. If we allow the subject to move to one place and not to the other, the move executed is what is called R_1 and the other possible move, the one not yet executed is called R^a. The experimenter is now in a position to ask recall of three different kinds of prior events, namely R_2, R^a, and IF_r, respectively. The R_2 is, naturally, the subject's attempt to repeat R_1; R_2 is not an attempt to improve upon R_1 or an attempt to relearn R_1. Indeed, if R_1 is in error, to

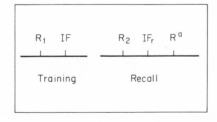

Critical events of memory

Fig. 3. Identification of the two major events of a trial of training and the three major events of a trial of recalling. (From Bilodeau & Levy, 1964.)

repeat it is to remember an error. IF_r stands for the recall of feedback and R^a is the first unguided movement toward the alternative place.

As a hypothetical example to illustrate the notation, for the three events, let us use 20° and 30° as Targets 1 and 2, respectively. Suppose the subject moves to 17° for his blind selection of target and the experimenter tells him that he has moved to the wrong target, that he is low by 10 units. During Recall, the experimenter can request (1) R_2, in which case the subject should try to repeat 17° as best he can perhaps achieving 18°; (2) IF_r, in which case the subject should try to repeat "low by 10 units" or −10; and (3) R^a, and the subject should move the lever toward 30°, perhaps achieving 32°. R_2 calls for repeating a response previously identified by the experimenter as in error, R^a calls for executing a free response previously performed under guidance, and IF_r calls for repeating the experimenter's IF about R_1 and R^a. In scoring tracking behavior, on the other hand, the recall of IF and R^a has not been requested. Only the reading-out of the correct response over several trials is called for.

Figure 3 should be used by the reader to make *inter*trial and *intra*-trial comparisons for this will be useful. One should examine the figure with the idea that learning is an increasing consistency in repeating the required response, and forgetting is a decreasing consistency in repeating the response. Relating the individual events of the recall trial of those of the training trial and to each other is the general objective. To take one problem, will the subject's recall of R^a depend more upon (a) the recalled feedback (IF_r) or (b) the administered feedback (IF)? Most readers would answer correctly. We do perform more in accord with what we remember to be correct and incorrect than what was actually so.

The levering data show much forgetting of this simple skill, provided the data are examined in the right way. If we look for a difference between the average scores of Training and Recalling, we find small ones, a finding consistent with earlier studies of the mean over many years. Yet in learning our descriptive statistics we were told that means can remain constant while major changes occur in the consistency of scores from one distribution to another. Also, the mean may vary, yet still fail to describe the major changes occurring within and between distributions of scores. Certainly forgetting is a far richer phenomenon than implied by the finding that a subject averages fewer responses in recalling than in training. A systematic error trend over time might well be evidenced or perhaps even a random error trend.

A. MEASURES OF MEMORY

Changes between two arrays of scores such as produced by one trial of Training and by one trial of Recalling of many subjects can be measured by the mean, variance, and correlation. A change in one, two, or all three of these statistics can signify that forgetting is taking place. If a subject correctly anticipates Items 1–4 of a 10-item list during Training, and Items 5–10 during a trial of Recalling, his Recalling score by simple tally exceeds that of Training even though there is no overlap in the items produced. Though this example is extreme, it brings out the paradox associated with merely counting the events of Training and Recalling. The subject in question can be said to remember more than he learned (2 items more) or said to remember nothing (no items of Training repeated in Recalling). In levering, when the mean of R_2 is equal to the mean of R_1, we must not assume that the responses were repeated. Perhaps, not a single one of them was since the mean does not imply anything about repetition. If memory is to be viewed as persistence and forgetting as inconsistence, statistics of change and communality ought to be used.

Figure 4 illustrates hypothetical cases and was made to show how forgetting may occur without changes in the means. In (a), the distribution of the first response of a large number of subjects is shown

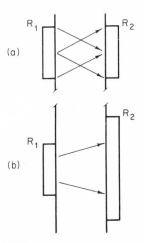

Fig. 4. (a) R_2 represents a distribution of responses where many subjects attempt to repeat their prior responses (R_1). Here, forgetting leads to a correlation of zero, but mean and variance hold constant. In (b), forgetting leads to an increase in variance, but mean and correlation hold constant. (From Bilodeau & Levy, 1964.)

under the label R_1. The distribution labeled R_2 represents the attempt of each subject separately to repeat R_1. The arrows show what might happen to four hypothetical and inconsistent subjects. In short, they do so badly at recalling R_1 that the correlation (r) between the two arrays of scores ($R_1 \cdot R_2$) falls to zero. Of course, a portion of this change in time is to be attributed to experimental error and some other portion to forgetting. By comparing the two distributions of the figure still further, we see clearly that the means and variances remain unchanged and insensitive to the forgetting taking place.

Figure 4(b) represents the hypothetical case with a change of variance, no change in mean, and no change in correlation. Here, the subjects as a group are especially inconsistent, yet z scores and means remain the same from Training to Recalling. Only a comparison of the standard deviations or variances of the distributions would tell us about what is changing and by how much.

The ideas illustrated in Fig. 4 show memory treated in terms of response consistency. It is for this reason that the more frequent use of variance, correlation, or any other statistic that will describe consistency and lack of consistency has been urged. This recommendation is easily applied to motor-skills data where the magnitude of the error of response is calculated as a matter of course. When variances and correlations are not calculated, valuable information about process may be lost.

B. DATA

Figure 5 shows an example of how the forgetting of R_1 is measured by plotting the magnitude of R_2 against the magnitude of R_1. The scatter plot on the left side of Fig. 5 shows forgetting after a 20-minute retention interval; the one on the right, showing even greater deterioration, is for a 6-week period of layover. In 6 weeks, the correlation (r) dropped from .74 to .20 indicating that a great deal of common variance has disappeared.

Figure 6 illustrates the use of variance. The question is simply, "What happens to the variance of the second response with respect to the first over time?" In 6 weeks' time, the variances rise in size by factors of 4 or 5, and, as usual for levering, the variances take a positive acceleration.

Figure 7 shows how IF administered verbally has been forgotten 28 days after its administration. The value of r is about .30, showing how little there is in common between the number administered and the number remembered. For example, suppose the administered IF to be −297; that is, the experimenter told some subjects they were "low

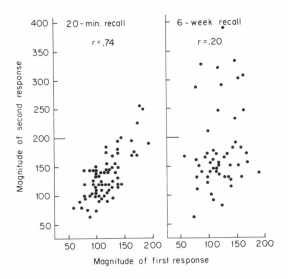

Fig. 5. Scatter plots showing the deterioration of R_2 with respect to R_1 after 20 minutes and after 6 weeks. (After Bilodeau & Levy, 1964.)

by 297 units" and that a month later four of them remembered IF as follows: "−300," "+297," "low," "I don't remember," respectively. Forgetting feedback has several aspects, including changing the absolute value, changing the sign, recalling the sign but not the number, and not responding in kind. Incidentally, the levering recalls (R_2 and R^a) are strongly related to the value of IF_r. The associations among the different components of recall are an important phenomenon of recall and vary in strength with the length of the retention interval. This phenomenon suggests many ideas, including the one that the subject's memory for one event (A) can be altered by administering a reminder of another event (B). That is, if we can change a person's recall of B, have we changed his recall of A?

Figure 8 was made to illustrate the plotting of r as a dependent variable. The correlations between R_1 and R_2 remain high and stable around .75 for at least 2 days of retention and then fall rapidly. At 6 weeks the value is near .25, the variance in common having declined 50 percentage points.

The analyses of consistency of levering in Figs. 6, 7, and 8 from Training to Recalling have shown that individuals become more variable over time and that they change position relative to one another. Both of these changes occur in a lawful way. The means also change, but they do not appear to be the most important measure for levering.

184 Edward A. Bilodeau

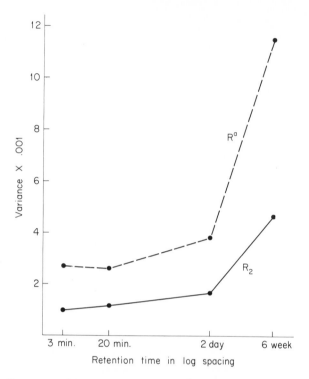

Fig. 6. An illustration of increasing variance in the recalled response as a function of retention time for response repetition (R_2) and response alternative (R^a). (After Bilodeau & Levy, 1964.)

The levering procedures have not been tried with tracking tasks and they should be. Now, however, it will be necessary to examine more closely how a given association fares over time.

C. ANALYSIS OF SHAPE

The curves shown in Figs. 6 and 8 are not like the ones produced from Ebbinghaus data as in Fig. 1.[2] Of course, the mean performance under relearning and not variances and correlations under conditions of repetition was plotted on the ordinate of Fig. 1. Actually, there are so many differences between the experimental procedures that the reasons for the shape variation cannot be pinpointed. On the other

[2]The shape of the curves in Figs. 6 and 8 is unaffected by taking the logarithm of time. Logarithms were used so that both ends could be well seen by eye.

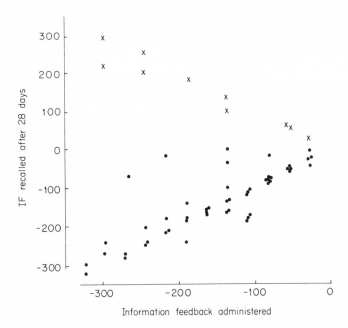

Fig. 7. Information feedback recalled (IF_r) has been plotted against information feedback administered (IF) for 60 subjects verbalizing a number and a sign. The X's represent the subjects who recalled the wrong sign. (After Bilodeau *et al.*, 1962.)

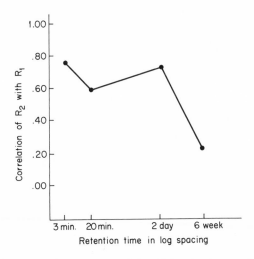

Fig. 8. An illustration of decreasing correlation between the events of recalling and training with increasing value of retention time. (After Bilodeau & Levy, 1964.)

185

hand, there has been criticism of the variance and correlation plots, and the student may wish to refer to Bahrick (1966) for objections to plots as in Figs. 6 and 8.

If the degree of response consistency from one moment to the next is known, we have, in effect, an estimate of the amount of skill acquired and so are in a good position to set up a retention curve. Having done this, we can begin to phrase our retention questions better. A good question is the simple one: what happens to response consistency after we have established a given level of consistency? We have seen from the lever series and its data that the answer is: nothing much happens over the short term, then later on the relationship deteriorates. In other words, forgetting on the lever is slow at first, then proceeds faster and faster; much later, it seems plausible to suppose it must slow up when there is little left. On the other hand, if we are talking about misrecall, the trend is upward because with time there is more and more of it, not less.

After examining a great deal of lever data, Bilodeau and Levy (1964) proposed a two-stage curve of forgetting in retention of R_1, R^a, or IF. Looking back on the data plotted in Figs. 6 and 8 we can find what they saw. First, some forgetting seemed to have taken place even before the first retention test. This early forgetting was called Stage 1. Second, the later, negatively accelerating kind of forgetting, they called Stage 2. Stage 2, for our purposes, is the more important or extensive period and it is most unlike the Ebbinghaus curve in that it is bowed in the opposite direction.

In the theoretical curve illustrated in Fig. 9, the intercept (Y) has been arbitrarily fixed at unity so that at t_0 recall is perfect. Recall is perfect in the sense that (a) the ratio of close-by variances (R_1/R_2) is unity or (b) the correlation for R_2 with R_1 is unity. This value of unity (or whatever it is) tells us how much learning there was prior to the retention test. The communality in variance (r^2) between Training and Recalling can be estimated from the figure, thereby increasing its usefulness. This is done by reading the value of r corresponding to t and squaring the value of r. The statistic r^2 tells the amount of variance shared by two variables. In the case of $r = .70$, for example, $r^2 = .49$ and Recalling and Training have 49% of their variance in common.

Certain important activities were deliberately interpolated between Training and Recalling in the experiments illustrated in Figs. 6 and 8 even when the interval was only 3 minutes long. These activities underlie Stage 1. All subjects released their grip on the lever, moved the resting arm away from the top of the lever box, changed foot position, moved out of the room, and moved back into position in front of the lever. These events occurred between R_1 and R_2 and under these

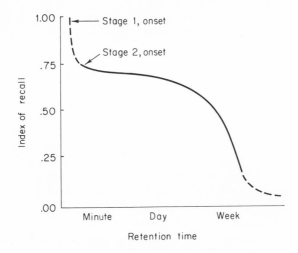

Fig. 9. Two stages of forgetting hypothesized by Bilodeau and Levy. The longer, solid section is called Stage 2 and is preceded by a brief period called Stage 1. (After Bilodeau & Levy, 1964.)

circumstances the correlations were about .70. In an earlier study some subjects did not disengage themselves from the training environment and these correlations were up over .90. The interrupting acts associated with moving away after the execution of R_1 probably were responsible for the correlation dropping about 25 units and nearly doubling the variance, an hypothesis later deliberately checked out by evaluating disengaging and nondisengaging treatments (Boswell & Bilodeau, 1964). Disengaging the subject could produce (*a*) responses that interfere with the recall of R_1, or (*b*) changes in postural and environmental cues used by the subject to reproduce R_1 more exactly. If the changes in stimuli and responses associated with disengagement took rather sudden effect and then no more, Stage 1 could be explained as a warm-up phenomenon or as a loss of set. Posner (1967a) has also been able to manipulate short-term memory on the lever by having the subject classify digits during brief interpolated activity.

   Perhaps on occasion the retention curves of rote memory for verbal materials have also been dealing with Stage 1 through the action of disengagement or loss of set. Stage 1 might also be deepened by proaction, as supposedly happened to Ebbinghaus, who abused himself with the repeated learning of many different lists. Data plotted by Keppel and Underwood (1962) in verbal retention suggest the concave bow to be absent when proaction is a minimum and other data too have indicated that short-term memory can be good when the right circumstances obtain.

Data lying along the concave Ebbinghaus function are generally explained by referring to exponential-like decay processes. This explanation is popular and seems natural because so many different kinds of data have been fitted by the exponential function. Stage 2 is novel in shape and its convexity needs elaboration and rationalization. If the idea of reliability of responding is used, however, the unique naturalness to the exponential explanation disappears, and we can feel more comfortable for there is an attractive way of rationalizing any convexity. Given that the subject can repeat a response from one moment to the next, he should be able to repeat nearly as well if the attempt at repetition is delayed by an extra moment. Said another way, if the probability of repeating a response after an instant is high, there is no reason to assume that something unusual will happen to change things greatly during a second instant. The probability of repetition across the two instants should also be high though somewhat less than for the first one. Perhaps the starting of a car can be used for an analogy to the question of response reliability over intervals t and Δt. Assume the car is started every morning and that no failures at starting are ordinarily encountered. What is the probability of success after the interpolation of a morning without attempting a start? It is a lesser probability for two days than for one to be sure; the greater decrement in probability should occur in the second day of layover inasmuch as we assumed a relatively troublefree start with the 24-hour situation and expect trouble the longer we wait.

Stage 2 amounts to a situation without the deliberate introduction of proaction or loss of set by the experimenter, or a situation where, because of previous training, they have been overcome by the subject. Both retroaction and proaction ideas can be worked into a probability model of the second stage. A theory of memory must account for the delayed interference of previous events and for the way interference is to be encountered from future events. In other disciplines there are examples of effects temporally displaced from their initial cause. There is the odor trend of a rotting egg, a process of growth set in motion by earlier events. An updating of pro- and retroaction concepts is required and the updating is based on the general idea that the probability of the occurrence of interfering events should rise in keeping with the expectation of events randomly distributed in time and that the growth of their effect is ogive-like as in Stage 2. How this might be set up for both proaction and retroaction is described below.

1. Proaction: past experiences can act upon established response reliability, not necessarily immediately and totally as suggested by a concave curve, but corrosively and progressively as suggested by convexity in the curve. The reason might be that the probability of encountering proactive sources rises in time in a fashion analogous to the ogive-like accumulation of chance events. The interference need not be immediate but may even be delayed to the point of recalling.

2. Retroaction: the effect of new experiences upon response consistencies established in the past is not necessarily total and immediate, but can be rather slow and accelerating. The reason might be that the probability of encountering retroactive sources rises in time in a fashion analogous to the ogive-like accumulation of chance events. Again, we see that the source may not be encountered right after learning and its effect may not be felt until recall is underway.

Here is a retention problem for the reader to think about. Suppose our subject is an amateur meteorologist interested in hurricanes in the North Atlantic, learning their names fairly well, and following tracks for several seasons, including the year 1970 in which we will take special interest. If it is not reasonable to believe that almost all the names will be forgotten upon the close of the season, then what might be the events responsible for any forgetting which will eventually take place? New names cannot be the responsible agent until the arrival of 1971 series. Do the names previously stored in 1969, and even those reaching farther back, have their greatest effect right away, i.e., while 1970 names are in store between 1970 and 1971 and yet to be read-out? Can any effect be ascribed to time *qua* time? Is it likely that much of the subsequent forgetting of a proactive nature will not take place until attempts to read the 1970 names out of store are made?

There are no compelling data to indicate that suggestions (1) and (2) above on pro- and retroactions are correct. We can anticipate other models which could account for the various shapes of retention curves now being discovered and it is urged that we begin to think about how one might account for shapes different from the classic one. The following pages take a much closer look at what happens where events of Recalling are manipulated and the application of a model of random events to explain the data.

D. REPEATED RECALLING

In the lever studies considered so far the subject retrieved the event just once; there was no request to read it out again and again. As much as 6 weeks intervened between R_1 and R_2, but there was no additional call for the repetition of R_1. If R_2 had been scheduled for day 2 and a third read-out (R_3) at 6 weeks, we might wonder about the effect of the earlier retrieval on the later retrieval. That is, what is the effect of a read-out on a subsequent read-out or is $R_3 = f(R_2)$? There are many modes and efficiencies by which responses may be read out of store. With a computer, the mode does not matter except that it is correct or incorrect. The reading *qua* reading from store does not ordinarily have implications for the next read-out unless there is some accident with the memory tape or something like that. With a human subject, the search *qua* search or the conditions under which the read-out is made does seem to matter. An elderly subject reminiscing about earlier events may actually substitute more recent recalls for the earlier original events. Out in the street or in the laboratory, then, a recollection might be traced to a previous recollection, to the original events, or even to both. Bilodeau, Jones, and Levy (1964) initiated the examination of this substantial question. The matrix of intertrial correlations for learning tasks was used as a point of departure.

Reynolds (1952), Fleishman (1953), Jones (1962, 1966), and others have cast up a great many correlation matrices for motor-skills learning tasks. These tasks usually involved learning to stay on target as with rotary-pursuit apparatus. Jones summarized and evaluated this literature, concluding that a particular pattern of r's, the superdiagonal form, is generally observed in tracking types of tasks. In this pattern a trial correlates most strongly with its neighbors, most weakly with the first and last trials of the series, and so on, as shown schematically in the upper part of Table I. The superdiagonal pattern is obtained under ordinary procedures of training a complex skill. That is, the dominant theme is to obtain a better and better score from trial to trial. Especially at first, when the subject is naive, were he to repeat an earlier response, it would imply a partial failure of learning because the subject would be repeating an error. Rather than repeating, the objective of the subject is to modify the response in order to reduce errors and to maximize time on target, etc. Toward the end of the training period, after learning has taken place, the process of response change will have gradually arrested and the process of repeating successful responses will be replacing it. Here, then, in the latter part of a training session *repetition* instead of *change* characterizes the process. The situation is actually a complicated one, for the within-trial events should show both acquisition-like and recall-like properties at one and the same time (see also Murdock, 1960; Tulving, 1964).

Repetition, it should now be recalled, is the key word for the lever series of retention studies. It is important to distinguish between the procedure of repeated recalling (reading-out or retention testing) and of repeated practice (reading-in or acquisition training), the repeated

Table I
MATRIX PATTERNS FOR ACQUISITION AND RETENTION TRIALS

	X_1	Superdiagonal form X_2	X_3	X_4
X_1		Med ———————————→		Lo
X_2				↑
X_3				Hi

	X_1	Monotonic hierarchy[a] X_2	X_3	X_4
X_1		Hi ———————————→		Med
X_2				↓
X_3				Lo

[a]Note, for example, $X_1 \cdot X_4 > X_3 \cdot X_4$.

recalling referring to repetitions with no improvements required and the repeated practice to a series of improvements with no repetitions required. In an experiment on the effects of repetition *qua* repetition (Bilodeau *et al.*, 1964), the subject was instructed to read-out the training response (now to be called R_0) not once, but four times. The retention intervals for successive repetitions (called R_1, R_2, R_3, and R_4) were 3 minutes, 20 minutes, 2 days, and 6 weeks, respectively.

The resulting pattern of r's is shown in the lower half of Table I, and it was a curious one, the monotonic hierarchy. Neighboring trials do not correlate highly, except for the earliest repetitions, and the last two terms of the series produce the lowest r. According to Jones (1962), the monotonic hierarchy cannot be rationalized in the same way as the superdiagonal pattern. The latter he interprets as the consequence of a process of simplification in the required skills. That is, progressively fewer factors are required to explain the variances over a series of learning trials. But for the monotonic hierarchy, only one factor is required from the start and less and less of it is used to explain later attempted repetitions. The data showed the one factor to be the recall of R_1 (note, not R_0), and signifies that the first read-out is the especially critical event. Its progressive dilution was attributed to increasing amounts of accumulating random variance as discussed earlier in connection with Fig. 9. Thus, it was concluded that the repeating process was neither the same as nor the inverse of the learning process. The repetition process did not appear to be one of unlearning.

The conclusion, it should be noticed, is not directly tested. It is based on lever data for a repetition schedule during retention testing and an earlier reserve of rotary-pursuit data (and the like) for an ac-

quisition schedule. It is not certain that repetition was the sole variable responsible for the monotonic structure. The conclusion is more
an interesting conjecture than a well-established principle. In Chapter 5 Jones shows that the correlational structure varies from task to
task and condition to condition. The superdiagonal form is not always
obtained from training data.

The subject of patterns of r seems especially promising and future
inquiries should start by looking for the training, interpolated task, and
retrieving variables that change the patterns. There are few experiments in the area. One of them (Bilodeau & Blick, 1965), intercorre-
lated retention trials for verbal materials, and here too, the pattern was
monotonic. Since sources of interference were deliberately inserted
into the reading-out phase by the experimenter, it was possible to
conclude that progressive complications characterized the retention
process.

One other finding in the lever series was of general importance, this
pertaining to the matrix for successive read-outs of IF. The IF matrix
tended toward the superdiagonal form; neighboring trials seemed
more alike than more separated ones, and the highest r's were between the terminal retrievals or 3 and 4. It could be that forgetting
verbal materials like numbers (for example, a subject might recall the
number 324 as 324, 320, 300, 300 over four successive read-outs) is
more systematic than forgetting levering, which was said to be dominated by accumulating random variance. However, not much is
known and so not much can be explained now. Again we see the need
for an extensive inquiry where the deliberate manipulation of patterns
in the matrices for learning, relearning, and repetition is the primary
objective. For additional discussion of intertrial structures see Jones,
Chapter 5 of this volume.

E. SUMMARY

Several new dependent and independent variables of memory have
been reviewed and this has led to the discovery of a curve shape different from the classic one. The lever data have given us curves for the
constituent events within trials: repetition of an earlier response, response alternative, and information feedback. It was concluded that
variance, correlation, and other statistics of change are good indices
for expressing the amount of forgetting taking place. This chapter
stressed memory as an issue of persistence or success at response repetition, and forgetting as an issue of response change. Response
change implies more than is conveyed by a simple tally of events retained. At least some forgetting seems a process different from learn-

ing and attributable to accumulating variance acting through proactive and retroactive sources. Theoretical explanations for retention curveforms which do not resemble that of Ebbinghaus were elaborated. It was speculated that interference processes are especially active at producing retention phenomena during reading-out phases.

IV. Stimulated Recall

A. HISTORICAL COMMENT

Research on retention with lever-positioning skills actually began with the study of the effects of delay of verbal feedback on learning lever positioning. This project grew into studies of the consequences of infrequent responding and infrequent feedback, effects that belong to the domain of forgetting. The impetus to a series of studies of memory for words came from a demonstration that the lever experiments could be done with verbal materials. This section deals with the verbal analogs as well as with levering. The knowledge gained in the motor domain has been usefully applied to the verbal one.

The first word study was innovative in several respects (Bilodeau *et al.*, 1962). It is called the *sweet-ugly* study because the two words *sweet* and *ugly* were shown side by side for a few seconds on a screen. In the instructions the subjects were told, "One of these two words is correct, write your selection on your card." The word the subject wrote was defined as his R_1; the word witnessed but not written down was defined as the alternative or R^a. Feedback was administered when the experimenter said, "You chose the correct (or wrong) word." The subject was not explicitly instructed to learn or remember sweet, ugly, or correct (or wrong). Five weeks after training, the experimenter asked for the recall of sweet, ugly, and correct or wrong, and found that all three events were forgotten to some extent and that the recall of one was dependent on the recall of the others. Figure 3, previously used to illustrate the use of the lever, can readily serve to schematize the experimental events and the design of the sweet-ugly study.

The sweet-ugly experimental design made good use of stimulated recall. Two of the original three events were readministered by the experimenter during Recalling and only after this briefing was the subject asked for the third event. For example, in one condition the instructions were, "Five weeks ago, you chose the word *sweet* and you were correct. What was the other word?" In this way memory for one event was measured after a reinstatement of the memory for the others. It might be said that the training context has been partly reconstructed by the experimenter for the subject. The procedure is to be contrasted with free recall where no special stimulus is introduced during the reading-out. In the example above, R^a, the incorrect word, is requested at recall after the subject has been reminded of R_1 and IF.

A complete program for the systematic variation of recall stimulation is reproduced in Table II. It shows the eight environments where forgetting may be found. These range from unstimulated recall (free recall) to completely stimulated recall. Rows 1, 2, 3 show two events used as stimulators; Rows 4, 5, 6 show one-event stimulation; Row 7 shows none; and Row 8 shows three. The sweet-ugly study used Rows 1, 2, 3 of the table for the experimental variable.

Table II
A CLASSIFICATION OF THE POTENTIAL TYPES
OF FORGETTING SITUATIONS[a]

Event reminded	Potential forgetting
R^a, IF	R_1
R_1, IF	R^a
R_1, R^a	IF
R^a	R_1, IF
R_1	R^a, IF
IF	R_1, R^a
None	R_1, R^a, IF
R_1, R^a, IF	None

[a]After Bilodeau *et al.* (1962).

One reminder was used in a lever study (IF, Row 6) as early as 1958 (Bilodeau & Bilodeau, 1958). The experimenter had said "When you were here yesterday, I told you that your move was low by X units. Now, let's try to improve upon yesterday's response." This instruction to the subject is actually a reminder of IF and a probe for the alternative response. The IF-stimulation design used in the lever study has become a small part of a much larger problem which is the theme of this section.

The forgetting of one event bears on the forgetting of other events. Conversely, the recall of one event has special implications for the recall of the others. Further, the recall of an event can be controlled by the introduction of new stimulus material into the retention environment. It has been found that the amount of bearing depends upon the strength of association between events. That is, the associative structure of the stimulus turns out to be the critical knowledge on which to base predictions about recall. The study of association structures is a search for rules which show how events are bound together or how one event entrains another.

The events R_1, R^a, and IF become interassociated during training for they are in close temporal contiguity. As in learning a list of paired associates, there are two types of associative processes occurring simultaneously during the acquisition phase: (1) the learning of the events *qua* events (responses or items) and (2) the learning to associate the events with one another. After training, both types of learning become susceptible to interference. If the subject is reminded of one event (or two), the remaining event (or events) is more readily produced, as the experimenter takes advantage of (or cues) the associative connections among events, hence the presumption that the recall of a given event is partly contingent on the recall of others.

In stimulated recall, a reminder of R^a and of IF can serve to arouse R_2 because of the connections $R^a \rightarrow R_2$ and IF $\rightarrow R_2$. An R_2 is not elicited in this way in the typical stimulus impoverished free-recall environment. In the free-recall experiment, events R^a and IF do not intervene or precede so explicitly and the ordinary antecedent to R_2 is merely the experimenter's call for it to be read out, no string of explicit reminders or stimulation being used to assist in the call. In the game of *Password,* as played on television, almost any common word in the language can be retrieved by the subject after the judicious application of only two or three stimulus words by the speaker. It is a very efficient process. Outside of the laboratory, people retrieve information in the presence of a great deal of contextual background as well as after multiple attempts. In the laboratory this background has been more often held constant than varied, and as a result, information about context or stimulation is scarce.[3]

In the recall of levering, the problem of stimulation has been expressed in this way. What happens if the forgetting of one event is

[3]There remains the necessity of measuring the retention of R^a and IF in more strictly verbal contexts than yet accomplished. The analysis of feedback, in particular, has been overlooked because feedback is so often confounded with the response term. In lists of paired associates, for example, x-y is exposed after the stimulus term x, y being ordinarily considered the response term. Indeed, it was observed long ago that y serves as a confirmation as well, but in fact, its informative aspects have been neglected.

In still another type of experiment, the R_1 term represents the correct response from one of several alternatives as with a multiple choice test. If items X, Y, Z were presented simultaneously, and the subject chose Z, it would be desirable to observe the forgetting of the alternatives (X and Y), and of the feedback (correct and incorrect) and their interdependencies.

permitted and at the same moment we assure that the other two associated events are recalled perfectly by each and every subject? To
assure the recall of the other two events is to hold relevant stimulus
variables constant. The manipulation of the recall environment may
be necessary to assure the proper control of powerful recall variables.
Lamentably often we find that the design of an experiment permits
the subject to forget all, a design corresponding to the seventh row of
Table II.

In the lever context, and patterning the design after the sweet-ugly
procedure, the plan called for the experimenter to tell the subject the
correct answers to two events before requesting recall of the third
event (Bilodeau, Levy, & Sulzer, 1963b). The levering response was
measured by its amplitude, and feedback was also expressed as a
number or variable quantity. This permitted the degree of recall to be
readily scaled and variance and correlation measures to express the
degree of change across the rest interval. It turned out that R_1, R^a, and
IF were associated, though only weakly. An extended discussion of
ideas about stimulation methodology, both motor and verbal was presented. In subsequent studies, particularly verbal ones, the S-R terms
were more strongly related and the effect correspondingly more grati-
fying. Obviously, better motor studies are awaited.

B. RECENT STUDIES OF VERBAL STIMULATION

The words *sweet* and *ugly* were selected for the first word study after much vacillation and were finally chosen from many word pairs
because they are not directly associated in word association norms;
that is, sweet does not ordinarily evoke ugly and ugly does not evoke
sweet. The choice of words with low interitem association strength
was a mistake for some purposes. On the other hand, *black* and *white*
might have been selected, but they were rejected because of high association strength, and a consequent overly high susceptibility to
effective stimulation.

If black and white had been used as training items, many subjects
with no recollection of them (black, white) might be found a year or so
later. But were the experimenter to begin the retention session by saying, "Last year you chose *black*, what was the other word?," the response *white* would be evoked and memory facilitated. White is the
strongest or primary free-association response to the stimulus black
and can be reconstructed through stimulation. The use of stimulation
has changed the task from the difficult one of the unaided or free recall
of white to an easier one of recognizing white because the administration of the stimulus evoked the associates of black. Because white is
the primary associate, it stands a particularly good chance of being

recognized as an appropriate recollection. By ascertaining the strength of the associations between a stimulus and its responses (and among the responses too), we would be in a strategic position to predict occurrences of responses with a knowledge of the stimulus.

A proper regard for word-association hierarchies and networks ended the search for words to replace sweet and ugly. The desired words were among the stimulus and response items of the norms on word association such as those collected by Russell and Jenkins (1954). However, Russell and Jenkins had not processed the strengths of association between their words sufficiently. The details of the computations and their uses are the subject of a recent article by Bilodeau and Howell (1968). Let us now briefly examine how the above efforts at regulating the events of recall during the read-out relate to some movements in other laboratories.

While reviewing 50 years of work on rote learning, Underwood (1957) invited investigators to focus their attention on the forgetting of a single association. Peterson and Peterson (1959) began a train of studies involving the retention of one nonsense syllable (a three-letter word made from a consonant, a vowel, and a consonant) after one trial of training, and the sweet-ugly story initiated a series of motor studies involving the limiting case for trials as well as events.

A shade of stimulated recall was used by Jenkins and Russell (1952) and Bousfield (1953) some time ago. The former broke up pairs of words consisting of stimulus and primary taken from word-association norms and trained the subject with a list containing these terms but in randomized order. For example, black and white would appear in the same list, but not as adjacent items. During free recall, they found that the subject tended to re-pair stimulus and primary in the read-out, or what is called the phenomenon of "associative clustering." It is as if the production of one item served as the stimulus for constructing or retrieving an associate, and so it can be said that the reorganization taking place during the retrieving phase is attributable to the subject's providing his own stimulus (see also Deese, 1959). In this case, it is a response produced stimulus and is not one under the experimenter's direct control. Rothkopf and Coke (1961) used a similar explanation for the word order imposed by the subject during the free recall of a large number of words of varying associative interdependencies. Free recall has always been operationally defined, and that is a good thing, for it has become quite clear that a great deal of what a subject will recall depends on what he has just recalled or said (Conrad & Hille, 1958; Murdock, 1963). Cofer (1965) provides a review of variables dealing with training materials and how they influence the sequential organization of the materials recalled during free recall.

In stimulated recall, the stimulation can be administered in any number of ways. For example, S-R₁ pairs may be split, with the responses used as training items and the stimuli introduced as memory aids during the retrieving period (Bilodeau, Fox, & Blick, 1963a). Note that the stimulus is employed during Recalling, not during Training as would be the case with a paired-associate task. If the right sort of stimulation were used during the read-out phase, the split-pair procedure could produce enhanced recall. To promote errors, stimuli that evoke associates to substitute for the training words, as can be done in recognition tests, could be introduced (Blick, 1965). These two ideas can quickly spread into a search for stimulus rules to produce facilitation and for other stimulus rules to produce interference. The search began with an analysis of the word-association process itself. It was found that rules of word association are indeed effective in foretelling what a subject retrieves in a stimulated recall environment. After all, the method of word association is an elementary method of memory along with free recall and stimulated recall.

In free association for words, the subject is asked to give the first word that comes to mind after the presentation of a stimulus word. Ordinarily, the subject is given no priming or practice nor is he likely to be asked to repeat his associates. In free recall, the retrieving session follows a session of training with the relevant materials, but the stimulus is dropped from the recall period. In stimulated recall, the stimulus appears only in Recalling and the subject is asked to retrieve items exposed during Training. The power of stimulated recall is derived from the preexperimental connections between one word and another. This power can always be increased by training with both stimulus and response terms.

For many years experimenters preferred to work with nonsense syllables because *cvc*'s were thought to be almost without associates (nearly meaningless). During the 1950's, after C. E. Noble's (1952) pioneering work on meaningfulness, considerable scaling of nonwords and words took place and work with common words gradually became more acceptable. Various measures of meaningfulness were used to predict one thing or another about the acquisition process. Here too came the Underwood and Postman (1960) frequency hypothesis about recalling which holds that newly learned connections were interfered with as older associates spontaneously recover with rest and take their place, words in more frequent use producing the most interference. This point of view finds an expression in paired-associate methods of training where the stimulus and response terms may be either high or low in frequency of use, but where no special attention is paid to the preexperimental strength of association between the S and R terms.

Head and hand are frequently used words of the language, for example, but word norms show that they are weakly associated.

Many people, including Cofer (1958) and Deese (1961), have emphasized the importance of working with the preexperimental associative strength between words. Garskof and Houston (1964) have pointed out that both association strength and associative overlap correlate with recall. Associative overlap refers to number of associates in common and the frequency of associates in common. Strength of association between S and R is the central issue in the discussions of the levering data and of the sweet-ugly study. Research progress has been swift and highly successful after suitable quantifications of the associative structures of stimulus terms (Bilodeau *et al.*, 1963a). The input to the analysis was preexperimental information about word arousal and the strategy was to use the normative information to anticipate what particular words the subject might retrieve in the recall session. The details of this procedure, however, are well beyond the subject matter of this chapter (Bilodeau & Howell, 1968).

C. Implications of Verbal Studies for Motor Research

The stimulus term is poorly identified in the average motor-skills article. This must handicap those individuals who wish to work with associative strength or to relate responses to stimuli in any molecular and precise manner. Studies on the lever seem to have made some progress on this difficult problem by identifying R_1, R^a, and IF as the within-trial events to which recall events can be related in a precise way. However, no basic distinction between motor and verbal events was really intended. Rather, the discussion turned on expected and obtained response associates of the training events. No S-R hierarchies of associative strength for levering responses are available for analysis and it is not possible to run word and levering analogs in any strict sense.

The psychometric assessment of associative structures, except for word–word hierarchies, is in its infancy and should be given every consideration in future projects. Probably, a knowledge of several hierarchies will be necessary to explain much variance for any given circumstance in any complex skilled act. The distinction between the motor and verbal domain was always thought to involve considerable overlap and now the distinction is even less useful. Chapter 11 on selective learning and Chapter 9 on information feedback, especially, emphasize the need to use S-R information from more than one source and show that the motor investigator must include more traditional verbal and perceptual stimuli and reactions in his prediction equation if he is to explain more of motor behavior. Alternatively, to explain response variance, several sources must be consulted, only one of which is motor.

D. SUMMARY

The stimulation technique is a broad and useful method for modifying tests of free recall in order to study how stored information is read out. Basically, stimulation has been or can be used during recalling when the subject is again presented with stimulus, response, and feedback material associated in various degree with the events to be retrieved. Response produced stimulation has or can be used when the recall environment is arranged so that responses occurring during read-out will themselves tend to call out additional events. The past few years have seen a marked increase in interest in associative structures, their measurement and experimental employment. This is especially true of verbal learning and memory. It is not true of motor learning and memory where normative data on associative hierarchies and networks are lacking. Much work lies ahead in comparing free association, free recall, and stimulated recall.

Until now, variations of stimulus, response, and information feedback have been largely confined to periods of training and interpolated training because the fashion during the past 60 years has been to stress the learning process. To be critical, all too often the recalling period has been treated as if it had little or no effect on retrieving. To use the method of free recall exclusively is to side with a passive interpretation of recalling as a process. Yet there is evidence that it is necessary to regulate the events of the recall environment as fully and as ingeniously as psychologists have done for the acquisition period. One way to begin, it was suggested in this chapter, is to consider the rules of free association as a cornerstone of memory and then proceed to elaborate the rules.

References

Ammons, R. B., Farr, R. G., Bloch, E., Neumann, E., Dey, M., Marion, R., & Ammons, C. H. Long-term retention of perceptual-motor skills. *Journal of Experimental Psychology*, 1958, **55**, 318-328.

Bahrick, H. P. Retention curves: Facts or artifacts? *Psychological Bulletin*, 1964, **61**, 188-194.

Bahrick, H. P. The ebb of retention. *Psychological Review*, 1965, **72**, 60-73.

Bahrick, H. P. Methods of measuring retention. In E. A. Bilodeau (Ed.), *Acquisition of skill*. New York: Academic Press, 1966. Pp. 351-360.

Bahrick, H. P., Clark, S., & Bahrick, P. Generalization gradients as indicants of learning and retention of a recognition task. *Journal of Experimental Psychology*, 1967, **75**, 464–471.

Battig, W. F., Nagel, E. H., Voss, J. F., & Brogden, W. J. Transfer and retention of bidimensional compensatory tracking after extended practice. *American Journal of Psychology*, 1957, **70**, 75–80.

Bell, H. M. Retention of pursuit rotor skill after one year. *Journal of Experimental Psychology*, 1950, **40**, 648–649.

Bilodeau, E. A., & Bilodeau, I. McD. Variation of temporal intervals among critical events in five studies of knowledge of results. *Journal of Experimental Psychology*, 1958, **55**, 603–612.

Bilodeau, E. A., & Bilodeau, I. McD. Motor-skills learning. *Annual Review of Psychology*, 1961, **12**, 243–280.

Bilodeau, E. A., & Blick, K. A. Courses of misrecall over long-term retention intervals as related to the strength of pre-experimental habits of word association. *Psychological Reports*, 1965, **16**, 1173–1192 (Monograph Suppl. No. 6–V16).

Bilodeau, E. A., Fox, P. W., & Blick, K. A. Stimulated verbal recall and analysis of sources of recall. *Journal of Verbal Learning and Verbal Behavior*, 1963, **2**, 422–428. (a)

Bilodeau, E. A., & Howell, D. C. Association rules in the prediction of recall from free-association matrices. *Psychological Bulletin*, 1968, **70**, 201–209.

Bilodeau, E. A., Jones, M. B., & Levy, C. M. Long-term memory as a function of retention time and repeated recalling. *Journal of Experimental Psychology*, 1964, **67**, 303–309.

Bilodeau, E. A., & Levy, C. M. Long-term memory as a function of retention time and other conditions of training and recall. *Psychological Review*, 1964, **71**, 27–41.

Bilodeau, E. A., Levy, C. M., & Sulzer, J. L. Long-term retention under conditions of artificially induced recall of related events. *Perceptual and Motor Skills*, 1963, **16**, 895–910 (Monograph Suppl. No. 8–V16). (b)

Bilodeau, E. A., Sulzer, J. L., & Levy, C. M. Theory and data on the interrelationships of three factors of memory. *Psychological Monographs*, 1962, **76**, No. 20 (Whole No. 539).

Blick, K. A. Cultural primaries as a source of interference in short-term verbal retention. *Journal of Experimental Psychology*, 1965, **69**, 246–250.

Boswell, J. J., & Bilodeau, E. A. Short-term retention of a simple motor task as a function of interpolated activity. *Perceptual and Motor Skills*, 1964, **18**, 227–230.

Bousfield, W. A. The occurrence of clustering in the recall of randomly arranged associates. *Journal of General Psychology*, 1953, **49**, 229–240.

Bousfield, W. A., & Puff, C. R. Clustering as a function of response dominance. *Journal of Experimental Psychology*, 1964, **67**, 76–79.

Broadbent, D. E. Flow of information within the organism. *Journal of Verbal Learning and Verbal Behavior*, 1963, **2**, 34–39.

Cofer, C. N. Comparison of word associations obtained by the methods of discrete single word and continued association. *Psychological Reports*, 1958, **4**, 507–510.

Cofer, C. N. On some factors in the organizational characteristics of free recall. *American Psychologist*, 1965, **20**, 261–272.

Conrad, R. Interference or decay over short retention intervals? *Journal of Verbal Learning and Verbal Behavior*, 1967, **6**, 49–54.

Conrad, R., & Hille, B. A. The decay theory of immediate memory and paced recall. *Canadian Journal of Psychology*, 1958, **12**, 1–6.

Deese, J. On the prediction of occurrence of particular verbal intrusions in immediate recall. *Journal of Experimental Psychology*, 1959, **58**, 17–22.

Deese, J. From the isolated verbal unit to connected discourse. In C. N. Cofer (Ed.), *Verbal learning and verbal behavior.* New York: McGraw-Hill, 1961. Pp. 11–31.

Deese, J. *The structure of associations in language and thought.* Baltimore: Johns Hopkins Univer. Press, 1965.

Ebbinghaus, H. *Memory.* 1885. (Translated by H. A. Ruger and C. E. Bussenius) New York: Dover, 1964.

Fleishman, E. A. A factor analysis of intra-task performance on two psychomotor tests. *Psychometrika,* 1953, **18,** 45–55.

Fleishman, E. A., & Parker, J. F., Jr. Factors in the retention and relearning of perceptual-motor skill. *Journal of Experimental Psychology,* 1962, **64,** 215–226.

Garskof, B. E., & Houston, J. P. Supplementary note: Recall as a function of word association strength and associative overlap. *Psychological Reports,* 1964, **14,** 185–186.

Hunter, W. S. Learning: IV. Experimental studies of learning. In C. A. Murchison (Ed.), *A handbook of general experimental psychology.* Worcester, Mass.: Clark Univer. Press, 1934. Pp. 497–570.

Jenkins, J. J., & Russell, W. A. Associative clustering during recall. *Journal of Abnormal and Social Psychology,* 1952, **47,** 818–821.

Jones, M. B. Practice as a process of simplification. *Psychological Review,* 1962, **69,** 274–294.

Jones, M. B. Individual differences. In E. A. Bilodeau (Ed.), *Acquisition of skill.* New York: Academic Press, 1966. Pp. 109–146.

Kausler, D. H. (Ed.) *Readings in verbal learning.* New York: Wiley, 1966.

Keppel, G. Verbal learning and memory. *Annual Review of Psychology,* 1968, **19,** 169–202.

Keppel, G., & Underwood, B. J. Proactive inhibition in short-term retention of single items. *Journal of Verbal Learning and Verbal Behavior,* 1962, **1,** 153–161.

Koonce, J. M., Chambliss, D. J., & Irion, A. L. Long-term reminiscence in the pursuit-rotor habit. *Journal of Experimental Psychology,* 1964, **67,** 498–500.

Lewis, D., McAllister, D. E., & Bechtoldt, H. P. Correlational study of performance during successive phases of practice on the standard and reversed tasks on the SAM Complex Coordinator. *Journal of Psychology,* 1953, **36,** 111–126.

Lloyd, K. E., & Johnston, W. A. Short-term retention as a function of contextual constraint. *Journal of Experimental Psychology,* 1963, **65,** 460–467.

McGeoch, J. A. The comparative retention values of a maze habit, of nonsense syllables, and of rational learning. *Journal of Experimental Psychology,* 1932, **15,** 662–680.

McGeoch, J. A. *The psychology of human learning.* New York: Longmans, 1942.

Melton, A. W. Implications of short-term memory for a general theory of memory. *Journal of Verbal Learning and Verbal Behavior,* 1963, **2,** 1–21.

Murdock, B. B., Jr. The immediate retention of unrelated words. *Journal of Experimental Psychology,* 1960, **60,** 222–234.

Murdock, B. B., Jr. Interpolated recall in short-term memory. *Journal of Experimental Psychology,* 1963, **66,** 525–532.

Murdock, B. B., Jr., & vom Saal, W. Transpositions in short-term memory. *Journal of Experimental Psychology,* 1967, **74,** 137–143.

Naylor, J. C., & Briggs, G. E. Long-term retention of learned skills: A review of the literature. *USAF ASD Technical Report,* 1961, No. 61–390.

Noble, C. E. An analysis of meaning. *Psychological Review,* 1952, **59,** 421–430.

Noble, M., Trumbo, D., Ulrich, L., & Cross, K. Task predictability and the development of tracking skill under extended practice. *Journal of Experimental Psychology,* 1966, **72,** 85–94.

Peterson, L. R., & Peterson, M. J. Short-term retention of individual verbal items. *Journal of Experimental Psychology,* 1959, **58,** 193–198.

Posner, M. I. Short term memory systems in human information processing. *Acta Psychologica*, 1967, **27**, 267–284. (a)

Posner, M. I. Characteristics of visual and kinesthetic memory codes. *Journal of Experimental Psychology*, 1967, **75**, 103–107. (b)

Postman, L. Short-term memory and incidental learning. In A. W. Melton (Ed.), *Categories of human learning*. New York: Academic Press, 1964. Pp. 145–201.

Reid, L. S., Brackett, H. R., & Johnson, R. B. The influence of relationships among items to be recalled upon short-term retention. *Journal of Verbal Learning and Verbal Behavior*, 1963, **2**, 86–92.

Reynolds, B. The effect of learning on the predictability of psychomotor performance. *Journal of Experimental Psychology*, 1952, **44**, 189–198.

Reynolds, B., & Bilodeau, I. McD. Acquisition and retention of three psychomotor tests as a function of distribution of practice during acquisition. *Journal of Experimental Psychology*, 1952, **44**, 19–26.

Roehrig, W. C. Psychomotor task with perfect recall after fifty weeks of no practice. *Perceptual and Motor Skills*, 1964, **19**, 547–550.

Rothkopf, E. Z., & Coke, E. U. The prediction of free recall from word association measures. *Journal of Experimental Psychology*, 1961, **62**, 433–438.

Russell, W. A., & Jenkins, J. J. *The complete Minnesota norms for responses to 100 words from the Kent-Rosanoff Word Association Test*. Technical Report No. 11, Contract No. N8onr-66216, Office of Naval Research and Univer. of Minnesota, 1954.

Shepard, R. N., & Chang, J. J. Forced-choice tests of recognition memory under steady-state conditions. *Journal of Verbal Learning and Verbal Behavior*, 1963, **2**, 93–101.

Slamecka, N. J. (Ed.) *Human learning and memory*. London and New York: Oxford Univer. Press, 1967.

Tulving, E. Intratrial and intertrial retention: Notes towards a theory of free recall verbal learning. *Psychological Review*, 1964, **71**, 219–237.

Tulving, E. The effects of presentation and recall of material in free-recall learning. *Journal of Verbal Learning and Verbal Behavior*, 1967, **6**, 175–184.

Underwood, B. J. Interference and forgetting. *Psychological Review*, 1957, **64**, 49–60.

Underwood, B. J., & Postman, L. Extraexperimental sources of interference in forgetting. *Psychological Review*, 1960, **67**, 73–95.

Wickelgren, W. A. Phonemic similarity and interference in short-term memory for single letters. *Journal of Experimental Psychology*, 1966, **71**, 396–404.

Yntema, D. B. Keeping track of several things at once. *Human Factors*, 1963, **5**, 7–17.

Transfer of Training

GEORGE E. BRIGGS
Ohio State University

I. Introduction

A. DEFINITIONS

Transfer of training refers to the effects of prior training on subsequent performance on a task, the latter differing in some way from the task utilized during the original training. It is of primary interest, therefore, to consider the ways that the training and the transfer tasks differ, and our main concern in Section II will be the influence on transfer of training of the several dimensions along which the two tasks can differ.

It follows from the above definition that the trainee or subject must first receive training and then be tested subsequently. This means, of course, that the study of transfer also involves the *retention* of skills — one cannot measure transfer effects independently of retention effects. In the laboratory we attempt to minimize retention effects by using rather short time intervals between the termination of original training and the beginning of the transfer task work. In real life, however, one may not begin his work on a transfer (or operational) task until weeks after he has finished training.

It follows also from the above definition of transfer of training that the characteristics of the original learning sessions themselves should have an influence on transfer task performance. For example, the amount of training clearly would be expected to influence the amount of skill exhibited in a later transfer task situation (Duncan, 1953), and likewise, the schedule of events during training should have an influence during transfer. The latter has been subjected to extensive study under the general title of part versus whole training. One may consider the transfer or operational task as composed of a complex of parts. Is it better, in terms of transfer task performance, to provide original training on the several parts individually or to provide whole-task training from the beginning? Unfortunately, we do not have space here to consider the part versus whole research literature. The reader is referred to Naylor (1962) for a recent review.

B. PARADIGMS

In the research literature there are several experimental designs for the study of transfer of training. In most cases there are two independent groups of subjects: an experimental group experiences first the training task and then is tested on the transfer task, while a control group experiences only the transfer task. To be fair, the two groups should be equated prior to training or be of sufficient size to assure equality between the two samples of subjects prior to training. One experimental design handles the equality problem by using a foretest on the transfer task which permits the experimenter to assign equally skilled subjects to the two groups. Then the experimental group experiences the training followed by the transfer task, while the control receives practice only on the transfer task.

There are other experimental paradigms, but most of them either are inappropriate for the study of skill transfer or they confound sequence effects with transfer effects. An example of the latter is the design wherein one group of subjects practices Task A then experiences Task B, while a second group practices Task B followed by Task A. Unfortunately, this A-B, B-A pardigm has been used in several studies to be reviewed here. One has to extrapolate from the training data to obtain an estimate of what such performance might have been at the time of transfer. Such extrapolation is undesirable, and the reader is encouraged to utilize a more adequate experimental design should he ever plan a transfer of training study.

C. MEASURES OF TRANSFER

Gagné, Foster, and Crowley (1948) describe and discuss the various ways to measure transfer of training. All nine measures presented assume two independent groups of subjects, and all provide an index of *relative* transfer: the transfer performance of an experimental (E) group is expressed in relation to the performance of a control (C) group or in relation to its performance on a foretest.

There are three basic transfer indices:

$$\frac{\text{E Group} - \text{C Group}}{\text{C Group}} \times 100 \tag{1}$$

$$\frac{\text{E Group} - \text{Initial C Group}}{\text{C Group on Trial N} - \text{Initial C Group}} \times 100 \tag{2}$$

$$\frac{\text{E Group} - \text{C Group}}{\text{Total Possible Score} - \text{C Group}} \times 100 \tag{3}$$

Each of the above three equations assumes that the basic performance measure for both groups will increase with practice, such as a measure of the number of correct responses. If one uses a measure which decreases with practice, such as the number of errors committed, the appropriate terms are reversed in Eqs. (2) and (3).

The possible range of the transfer indices will vary for the three cases. Equation (1) has a lower limit of minus 100 % transfer and no upper limit, while Eqs. (2) and (3) can range from minus infinity to plus infinity. In reality, of course, most indices are found in the range from minus 100 % to plus 100 % transfer. A negative transfer index means that whatever training experience the experimental group received, it penalized that group as its transfer task performance was less proficient than the control group which received no prior training. This is a situation wherein "nothing is better than something," a rather incongruous circumstance at first glance. Negative transfer has been found only rarely in skill performance tasks. Most often one finds some amount of positive transfer, and the question of interest, then, becomes how much positive transfer was obtained.

Equation (1) appears to be useful primarily when one is interested only in relative performance at the time of transfer for the E group. It has the disadvantage of being specific to the scoring units of the basic performance measure used, and different basic performance measures would not give comparable transfer indices even on the same subjects.

Equations (2) and (3) are somewhat more desirable indices in that not only is E group performance expressed relative to a control group, but also performance is expressed relative to some meaningful anchor points [initial and subsequent C group performance levels in the case of Eq. (2), and a total possible score in the case of Eq. (3)]. Gagné *et al.* (1948) favor Eq. (3) as that transfer index is independent of the basic performance scoring units [a problem with Eq. (1)] and it is independent of variations in learning scores [a presumed problem with Eq. (2)]. Actually, the latter criticism of Eq. (2) is the very point that makes this index particularly useful in applied research where one is interested in the amount gained (or lost) by some training procedure on a simplified task relative to direct practice on the more complex operational task. Further, Eq. (2) has the advantage of permitting a clear expression of the amount of *progress* being made by Group E relative to the progress in skill acquisition by Group C. Usually Trial N in Eq. (2) is the initial transfer trial or block of trials; thus, in this case the transfer index specifies initial transfer effects.

II. Functional Relationships in Transfer

This section deals with four major classes of task variables which have been found to influence performance in transfer of training situations: input variables, output variables, input–output relationships, and feedback variables. The reader may gain a perspective of these task variables by noting the servo model shown in Fig. 1 which indicates the locus of these variables.

The servo model has been quite useful in describing the situation imposed on a subject in a tracking task. As you can see in Fig. 1, the subject views a visual display and attempts to null out any difference between system input and system output, as shown on the display, by appropriate movements of a control device. The complexity of the tracking task can be varied by inserting various machine dynamics in the box labeled "machine controlled." Finally, the feedback loop conveys some kind or kinds of information about system output back to the display so that the subject can see the effects of prior control movements and the need for further action to reduce even more the difference between system input and system output. This difference is called system error.

We will be concerned here primarily with transfer of training in tracking tasks. Tracking is basic to vehicular control, and since ours is a "motorized" society, these skills are ubiquitous and therefore of interest to all of us.

A. INPUT VARIABLES

We will consider two classes of input variables in this section: input signal characteristics and display variables. Regarding the input signal we will be concerned with input *velocity*, first with simple

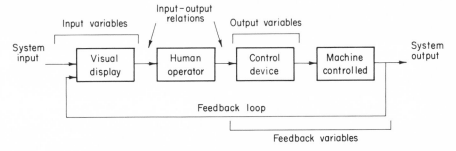

Fig. 1. A servo paradigm to describe human control of a closed-loop (feedback) system.

input signals and then with more complex signals. Now, input velocity is a function of two variables: the *frequency* aspect of the signal and its average *amplitude*. Typically, experimenters hold one of the two variables constant and vary the other aspect of the input signal to manipulate its velocity.

1. Input Frequency: Simple Signals

We will consider the most simple case first: amplitude is held constant while the speed of a constant-rate input is varied from training to transfer. Ammons, Ammons, and Morgan (1956) utilized the rotary pursuit apparatus and varied the speed of target rotation from 40 to 70 rpm. There were four target speeds during training and four during transfer with different groups of subjects under each training-transfer combination. The results, as revealed by Eq. (2), are summarized in Table I.

Note that high positive transfer occurred when the training to tranfer sequence was from lower to higher speeds, and that low positive (and one negative) transfer indices were obtained when the sequence was from high to low. Lordahl and Archer (1958) observed that Ammons' subjects received very little training prior to transfer, and examination of the Ammons data shows that very little improvement in performance occurred over both training and transfer for two thirds of the subjects. One may conclude, then, that the Ammons results are valid only for the initial phase of learning. What about the influence of simple input velocities for transfer at later stages of skill acquisition?

Lordahl and Archer (1958) provided their subjects with more extensive training prior to transfer. There were three groups: the control group experienced 60 rpm throughout, while one experimental group (40–60) trained at 40 rpm and transferred to 60 rpm, and the second experimental group (80–60) trained at 80 rpm and transferred to 60

Table I
TRANSFER INDICES [EQ. (2)] FOR THE CONDITIONS OF THE
AMMONS *et al.* (1956) STUDY

Training	Transfer speed (rpm)			
speed (rpm)	40	50	60	70
40		96	88	33
50	34		96	204
60	28	25		164
70	−13	53	85	

rpm. Both experimental groups yielded low positive transfer—54 % and 47 % for groups 40–60 and 80–60, respectively. Apparently these two groups did not differ at transfer; thus, unlike the Ammons results, there was no evidence of differential transfer, i.e., transfer from high to low speeds was not significantly different from transfer from low to high speeds.

It would appear, then, that with *simple* input signals differential transfer as a function of input speed may occur early in training, but not later. Further, from the Archer results it appears that more extensive training with an input frequency other than that used in transfer is detrimental in that transfer performance for both experimental groups was inferior to that of the control group. We must restrict these conclusions to situations like those where input velocity is varied for simple input signals. As we will see next, differential transfer is found with complex inputs even after rather extensive training.

2. Input Complexity

Jones and Bilodeau (1952) examined the influence of input complexity on tracking performance with a task requiring coordination of the two hands. The basic task was more complex than the pursuit-rotor device. During eight training trials two groups of subjects tracked a simple circular course, while another two groups tracked a more complex clover pattern. One group in each pair of original groups continued to track with the same input pattern for an additional eight trials (and so became control groups), while the other group in each pair of original groups transferred to the other condition (and so became experimental groups).

Initial transfer from clover to circle input patterns resulted in 89 % positive transfer in terms of total time to complete a circle, while transfer from circle to clover patterns produced only 77 % positive transfer in terms of total time to complete a clover pattern. These two indices are significantly different; therefore, here is a case where

transfer from difficult to easy versions of a task was superior to that
from easy to difficult versions. This finding has been confirmed by
Holding (1962) who used four different bandwidths of random signals
to provide inputs to a one-dimensional tracking task: 0–0.29 cps,
0–0.58 cps, 0–0.87 cps, and 0–1.16 cps. We will designate these as
bandwidths 1 through 4, respectively. Note that as the bandwidth is
increased, the complexity of the input increases. Holding's data were
published in graphic form and the present author read the transfer
indices from Holding's Fig. 3 (1962, p. 402); thus, these indices,
which are in the present Table II, are only approximate.

It can be noted that as with the Jones and Bilodeau results, transfer
from the more to the less complex inputs (the lower left section of
Table II) was superior, in general, to that from less to more complex
inputs (the upper right of Table II). We may conclude from these two
studies of input complexity that the subjects under the more complex
input conditions were able to learn most or all of the skill components
required under less complex input conditions, but the reverse was not
true; thus, the differential transfer. Holding (1962) proposed a formal
name for this situation: the principle of *inclusion*. The principle states
that if the training task includes most or all of the requirements present in a subsequent transfer task, then transfer performance will be
high; but if this inclusion is not present, then transfer performance
will be low. Obviously, the clover pattern used by Jones and Bilodeau
included all the characteristics of the circle but not vice versa, and a
higher bandwidth signal used by Holding contained all the frequencies of a lower bandwidth signal but not vice versa. Thus, the differential transfer found in both studies is consistent with the inclusion principle. It is worth noting at this point that when the inclusion principle
holds for a task, one would expect differential transfer favoring the
difficult-to-easy order of tasks because it is the difficult task that
usually includes the skill components to be required in the easy transfer task.

Table II
APPROXIMATE TRANSFER INDICES [EQ. (2)] FOR THE
CONDITIONS OF EXPERIMENT I OF HOLDING (1962)

Training bandwidth	Transfer bandwidth			
	1	2	3	4
1		38	58	−16
2	94		103	42
3	105	107		24
4	55	79	122	

3. Input Amplitude

We now have examined transfer (1) with an input consisting of single frequencies where the training frequency was higher or lower than that at transfer (Lordahl & Archer, 1958; Ammons *et al.*, 1956), and (2) with an input consisting of several frequencies at training and/or transfer (the clover pattern of Jones & Bilodeau, 1952; and all inputs used by Holding, 1962). It is clear that each of these studies manipulated input velocity since velocity is a function of input frequency when input amplitude is held constant, as it was within each of these four studies. Let us now consider the results of two studies in which input amplitude was manipulated systematically to vary input speed.

In a second experiment, Lordahl and Archer (1958) used the rotary pursuit task with rotation speed (and thus input frequency) set at 60 rpm, and they varied the radial distance from the center of the turntable to the target disc. All three groups transferred to a condition wherein the disc was set 3.5 inches from the center; the control group trained under this same condition, while one experimental group trained with the disc only 2.0 inches from center and the other group trained with the disc 5.0 inches from center. The latter condition involved the highest target velocity, the former experimental condition was the slowest target velocity, while the control group (and both experimental groups at transfer) experienced an intermediate input velocity. The transfer indices were both positive and were 82 and 90 % for the low-to-medium and high-to-medium input conditions, respectively. These two indices do not differ significantly; therefore, there is no evidence for differential transfer, but both are rather high (close to 100 % transfer) unlike the results from their first experiment.

In his second experiment Holding (1962) utilized two input amplitude conditions with half the subjects trained on the lower and transferred to the higher, while the other half experienced just the reverse order of conditions. Further, Holding ran the above two groups with a low bandwidth input signal (0–0.44 cps) and another two groups were run with a higher bandwidth input (0–0.87 cps). His results are summarized in Table III.

As you can see, differential transfer occurred under both bandwidth conditions. However, note that the pattern of this differential transfer was completely different for the two bandwidth conditions: with a low bandwidth signal superior transfer occurred from the lower to the higher input amplitude (velocity) conditions, while just the reverse occurred for the two groups who tracked the higher bandwidth signal. How can we account for the differential transfer found by Holding but not by Lordahl and Archer, and why should the pattern of differential transfer in the Holding experiment differ so decisively depending upon the frequency range of the input?

First, it should be emphasized that the Lordahl and Archer inputs were very simple and completely predictable, whereas Holding utilized complex, *random* inputs. Thus, the Archer subjects could predict the amplitude and rate of their inputs completely, but the subjects used by Holding could predict only in a statistical sense: they could learn the average velocities and accelerations and base some prediction of future response requirements on this information, but such predictions are far from the certainty enjoyed by the Archer subjects. It seems logical that differential transfer would not be found with a task so simple and predictable as that used by Lordahl and Archer, especially after substantial training. With sufficient training on a simple task, one can learn as much under one condition as under another, and apparently the Lordahl and Archer subjects did just that. With a more complex task, however, it is likely that one would learn more under one condition than under another, in part because there is more to be learned. Thus, it is not surprising that Holding found differential transfer, but why the difference in pattern of transfer for the two bandwidth conditions (see Table III)? Certainly the principle of inclusion holds for both bandwidth conditions: the smaller amplitudes occurred in both amplitude conditions, but only the larger amplitudes occurred in the high amplitude condition. Therefore, one can account for the pattern of differential transfer for the high bandwidth condition by the inclusion principle.

To account for the pattern of differential transfer found with the low bandwidth input, Holding (1965) suggested a hypothesis which he called *performance standards*. When working with a very easy task the subject will develop fairly high performance standards. If these high standards can be carried over to a "difficult" transfer task, this should promote good performance on the latter, thus favoring an easy-

Table III
TRANSFER INDICES FROM EXPERIMENT 2
OF HOLDING (1962)

Input bandwidth	Training to transfer amplitude conditions	
	Low to high	High to low
Low	141	73
High	65	121

to-difficult transfer sequence. Therefore, Holding accounts for the transfer pattern found for the low bandwidth condition. But shouldn't this same principle hold for the high bandwidth condition? Holding argues that it should not: the low-amplitude, high-bandwidth training condition here resulted in a much faster average velocity than in the comparable condition with the low bandwidth condition. Therefore, the subjects experienced a more difficult "easy" training task under the low-amplitude, high-bandwidth condition than under the low-amplitude, low-bandwidth condition, and thus they were not able to adopt high performance standards under this relatively easy condition.

These post hoc hypotheses leave much to be desired. Additional research needs to be performed to test their validity and to explicate the unexpected pattern of differential transfer found under the low bandwidth condition (see Table III).

4. Display Features

Typically, research on tracking performance has utilized either a pursuit or a compensatory display. Two moving elements appear in the former: a target element shows the input signal, and a cursor shows the output which the subject generates in his attempt to match the target element. On a compensatory display one observes a fixed element (the target), and the cursor moves in response to system error (the difference between input and output signals). Obviously, one receives more information from the pursuit than from the compensatory display since the former provides information separately on the input and output signals while only the difference between these two signals appears on the compensatory display. As one would predict, performance is usually better with a pursuit display. But what about transfer from pursuit to compensatory displays, and vice versa?

Andreas, Green, and Spragg (1954) trained subjects on one display condition and then transferred to the other display. While they did not provide a true control group, an estimate of C group on the initial transfer trial can be made for utilization in Eq. (2). Transfer to the compensatory display following training on the pursuit display resulted in approximately 52% initial positive transfer, while only about 17% positive transfer occurred upon transfer from compensatory to pursuit displays. These results would seem to indicate that greater transfer occurs from the pursuit to the compensatory display than vice versa. Unfortunately, Andreas *et al.* confounded input complexity with the display conditions such that the pursuit display condition also involved the more complex input. Therefore, we are unable to ascribe the observed differential transfer only to the display condition or only to the complexity variable. If the results are viewed in terms of input complexity, it is seen that the Andreas data are in agreement with the Jones and Bilodeau results described immediately above: transfer from complex to simple input conditions was superior to transfer from simple to complex. Therefore, we may better interpret the Andreas study as supporting the results and conclusions reached earlier on the matter of input complexity than as a contribution to the understanding of pursuit versus compensatory displays and transfer performance.

Briggs and Rockway (1966) provided a less equivocal test of the influence of display mode on transfer performance. In that study, all subjects experienced the same input signal during both training and transfer; thus, input complexity was not an issue. Two groups trained on a pure pursuit display and two groups trained on a pure compensatory display; one of each pair of groups then transferred to the other display condition (and thereby are experimental groups), while the other group of the original pairings continued on the same display condition as in training (and thereby served as control groups). The results showed 100% positive transfer for both experimental groups; thus, there was no evidence of differential transfer as a function of display mode.

The authors concluded, therefore, that the subjects learned no more during training on the pursuit display than was learned on a compensatory display. This was somewhat surprising for, as indicated earlier, a pursuit display provides more information than does a compensatory display. Presumably the *necessary* information was available in either display mode for skill acquisition in this tracking task.

5. Visual Noise

If subjects can acquire sufficient information from a compensatory display to match that skill which is acquired under the more informative pursuit display condition, what will happen to skill acquisition, as revealed during transfer, when compensatory display information is degraded by visual noise during training? Now, it has been demonstrated that tracking performance is lowered as visual noise is added to either a pursuit or a compensatory display (Howell & Briggs, 1959), so there is little question that such degradation of input information affects performance. But does visual noise affect learning as well as performance?

Briggs, Fitts, and Bahrick (1957a) studied training and transfer performance in a two-dimensional tracking task with complex machine dynamics in both dimensions of the task. One group trained with a noisefree compensatory display, while three groups experienced visual noise throughout training. The visual noise consisted of random movements of the cursor in two dimensions, which movements were uncorrelated with the system error signal. All groups during transfer experienced a five-trial block on the noisefree display plus one five-trial block on each of the three noise amplitude levels experienced by the three noise groups during training.

Figure 2 presents the results of both the training and the transfer trials. N_0 is the noisefree condition, while N_1, N_2, and N_3 refer to three (increasing) levels of visual noise amplitude. Note that Group 4 experienced five trials on each of the four noise conditions during both training and transfer and thereby serves as the control group as Groups 1–3 all transferred to this set of conditions. All groups performed comparably during transfer despite the wide and significant differences among groups during training. Thus, we may conclude that there was 100 % positive transfer for Groups 1–3.

The comparability of groups is shown even more dramatically for Groups 1 and 3 in Fig. 3. The top two functions are performance levels during transfer on the noisefree display, while the bottom two functions are performance on the second most extreme noise amplitude condition. What is particularly striking here is that even on the first block of transfer trials Group 3 performance is comparable to that of Group 1. You may note from Fig. 2 that Group 1 required 60 trials to attain this proficiency level and it appears that Group 3 attained the same level almost immediately upon transfer to the noisefree display. Thus, despite the very poor performance of Group 3 during training (see Fig. 2), these subjects learned as much about the basic tracking task as did Group 1. It follows, then, that visual noise influenced performance but not learning, the latter being revealed during transfer.

What is it that was learned even under conditions of visual noise? Briggs *et al.* noted that all subjects executed both large corrective movements of the control device and small "fine-tuning" adjustments, the latter being attempts to keep on target once the large movements eliminated most of the system error. Only Group 1 could receive uncontaminated feedback on the small corrections as the visual noise obscured this information for the other groups during training. However, all groups could see the effects of the large amplitude adjustments despite the presence of visual noise. This led the authors to the following conclusions: ". . . the attainment of skill . . . is dependent upon the opportunity to learn the skillful execution of primary, large amplitude corrections and (if necessary) secondary, small amplitude corrections. However, if practice on secondary adjustments is limited, . . . [as in the noise conditions] . . . then *overlearning* of only the

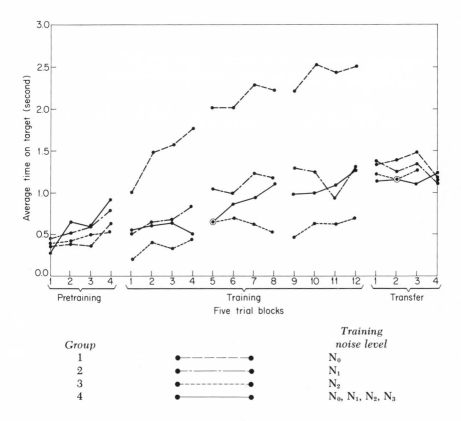

Fig. 2. Training and transfer performance as a function of visual noise. (After Briggs *et al.*, 1957a.)

primary corrections is sufficient preparation for maximum proficiency in a subsequent task requiring both primary and secondary corrections" (Briggs *et al.*, 1957a, p. 386).

6. Summary

We may conclude from the above research that transfer performance will vary as a function of input variables only to the extent that such variables influence what is learned during the training trials. Performance, as such, may be high or low during training but with no correlation to transfer task performance. Therefore, it becomes more important to determine *what* is learned (or learnable) during training than to simply seek relationships between input variables and transfer performance. The latter can serve as a first level of understanding transfer of training; the former is necessary for a more complete understanding.

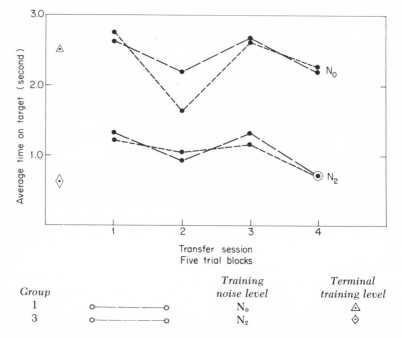

Fig. 3. Transfer performance on a noise (N_2) and on a noise-free (N_0) display. (After Briggs *et al.*, 1957a.)

B. OUTPUT VARIABLES

There are four physical characteristics of control devices which have been studied to determine their influence on tracking behavior: elasticity, viscosity, mass, and friction. Research reviewed by Bahrick (1957) indicates that elasticity (spring stiffness) facilitates positioning accuracy, viscous damping influences the control of the rate of movements, and mass affects the control of movement accelerations. Coulomb friction is independent of control device position, velocity, or acceleration; thus, unlike elasticity, viscosity, and mass, it cannot facilitate the accuracy of control movements. Rather, increasing coulomb friction merely increases the physical work required without providing useful feedback information via the kinesthetic sense mechanisms in the subject's arm. The other three physical characters do provide useful feedback information, via kinesthetic coding, as indicated above.

Thus, we can expect different control loadings (different amounts of spring stiffness, for example) to influence tracking *performance*. But in a transfer of training paradigm, will we observe differential *learning* as a function of control loading?

1. Coulomb Friction

Despite the fact that coulomb friction is noninformative in a feedback sense, it has been studied in several transfer experiments. Muckler and Matheny (1954) required subjects to track a simple sine wave input with a lever that could be loaded with 0 (actually 2.5 oz), 2, 4, 6, 8, 10, or 12 lb of coulomb friction. There were seven groups of subjects, then, and all transferred to the 6-lb condition following training. The authors utilized Eq. (1) for their transfer indices and found 86, 91, 90, 93, 90.8, and 89.7 % positive transfer for Groups 0, 2, 4, 8, 10, and 12, respectively. Of course, Group 6 obtained 100 % transfer as the control group. There were no significant differences among groups; thus, high, nondifferential transfer was obtained for all experimental groups. It would appear, then, that coulomb friction did not differentially affect transfer performance.

That this is an erroneous conclusion is indicated by a subsequent experiment by Gerall and Green (1958). These authors utilized two levels of coulomb friction: 2 and 14 lb. One group trained on 2 and transferred to 14 lb, while a second group experienced the reverse sequence. Thus, while there was no true control group, the authors extrapolated training performance to estimate what a control group would have done during the transfer trials. Using Eq. (2), the approximate transfer indices were both positive: 61 % for transfer to the 14-lb condition and 83 % for transfer to the 2-lb condition. Further, 61 % is significantly inferior to 100 % transfer but 83 % is not. Therefore, we may conclude that there is a differential transfer effect due to coulomb friction and the pattern is such that transfer from heavy to light friction is virtually complete, but transfer from light to heavy friction results in significant deterioration in transfer performance relative to continued experience with heavy friction.

Again, the influence of coulomb friction is primarily on performance as varying this friction does not affect the coding of useful feedback information. Thus, whereas normally we would interpret differential transfer as an indicant of an effect on learning, in this case the significantly low transfer index found for the light-to-heavy sequence most likely merely reflects an influence on performance, not learning.

2. Elasticity

Spring stiffness of a control device is the other control loading variable that has been studied in a transfer of training paradigm. Briggs, Fitts, and Bahrick (1957b) trained subjects in a complex two-dimensional tracking task under several levels of control loading. We are concerned here with two of these groups: the control group (Group 1) experienced an optimal control device throughout which provided elasticity of 1 lb/deg of deflection; an experimental group (Group 2) transferred to the above control device after training with a device that was loaded with a spring stiffness of only 0.25 lb/deg of deflection. This experimental group was significantly inferior to the control group during training, as expected, but there was no statistically significant difference between the two groups even at initial transfer. Thus, while elasticity produced a performance difference (training), there was no apparent learning effect (transfer). One might conclude that the difference in kinesthetic cues for the experimental group from training to transfer was of little consequence.

The latter is a premature and erroneous conclusion, as indicated by subsequent research by Briggs and Wiener (1966). These authors noted that the above results and conclusion ran counter to anecdotal evidence: kinesthetic cue changes obviously affect performance when one first encounters power steering in a car. For a fairly long period of time one cannot safely time share between the primary steering task and secondary tasks such as tuning the car radio, talking, or attending to an interesting scene off the road. Perhaps the Briggs *et al.* task was too insensitive to show transfer effects that really are present and due to control device elasticity.

To check this, Briggs and Wiener utilized two control groups and two experimental groups in a transfer of training paradigm. Both control groups experienced the same optimum control loading as that used by Group 1 in the previous study, and both experimental groups trained on the minimally loaded device used by Group 2 and then transferred to the optimum control device. One experimental and one control group tracked only the same two-dimensional task as was used previously, but the other two groups tracked also with a secondary task. The latter two groups, then, had a time-sharing requirement imposed on them which the authors predicted would result in significantly less than 100 % transfer for the experimental group; the other experimental group was expected to obtain almost 100 % transfer as in the previous study. The results confirmed these predictions with 70 % transfer for the time-sharing group (which was significantly inferior to 100 % transfer) and 86 % transfer for the experimental group not required to time share between the primary and secondary tracking tasks. The latter was not significantly different from 100 % transfer.

So, elasticity of a control device does influence transfer performance, but it is a complex not a simple learning effect: one can learn as much about a primary control task under one level of elasticity as under another, but his ability to time share between a primary and a secondary task is markedly affected by changes in control device elasticity. The latter is presumably due to the subject's learning to utilize a specific set of kinesthetic cues to permit visual time sharing between the two tasks, and if these cues are changed, as when the elasticity constant is modified, then the subject has lost the advantage of this previous learning and must learn anew a different set of kinesthetic cues.

3. Summary

From the above research on output variables we may conclude that performance as well as learning is differentially affected by control loading conditions. However, the learning effects seem to be rather more subtle than those noted earlier when we considered input variables. Of course, both visual (input) and kinesthetic (output) senses are involved in tracking performance, and so one must be concerned with both sets of variables when developing training tasks for optimum transfer performance. However, these results suggest, at least tentatively, that one could be relatively more concerned with input than with output variables in the design of training devices.

C. INPUT-OUTPUT RELATIONSHIPS

If the reader will refer back to Fig. 1, he will see that we now have considered transfer performance in terms of variations in the input and in the ouput of the human operator. We now will consider transfer performance as a function of certain relationships between input and output. Two such relationships will be discussed: (1) the ratio of control device gain to display gain, the C/D ratio, as it is called, and (2) the directional relationships between control movements and display movements.

1. C/D Ratios

If the subject moves his control device one unit of distance, say, and observes a cursor movement of three units, then the C/D ratio is 1/3. The smaller the C/D ratio, the more sensitive is the tracking system. Rockway and his associates performed a series of experiments in which subjects tracked a two-dimensional task with a particular C/D ratio and then transferred to a different C/D ratio. In the first study, Rockway (1955) utilized a control group which practiced for 50 trials on a C/D ratio of 1/3 and two experimental groups, one trained for 25 trials on a C/D ratio of 1/9 and the other on a C/D ratio of 1/27. Both experimental groups then transferred for 25 trials on the 1/3 C/D ratio condition. The transfer indices were 81 and 57 % for the 1/9 and 1/27 C/D groups, respectively, in terms of performance on the first transfer

trial. The 57% figure is significantly inferior to control group performance (100% transfer), but the 81% figure is not. Further, after the
first transfer trial there were no significant differences among groups.
Thus, we have only a mild suggestion that C/D ratio produces transfer
performance differences between experimental and control groups.

This conclusion was further supported in a subsequent study by
Rockway, Eckstrand, and Morgan (1956) in which the control group
experienced a C/D ratio of 1/27 throughout, while the two experimental groups transferred to this highly sensitive system after 25 training
trials on C/D ratios of 1/3 and 1/9, respectively. In this case, the experimental groups attained 83 and 89% positive transfer, respectively, on
the first transfer trial, and neither index is significantly different from
100% transfer.

However, the conclusion that C/D ratios during training make little
or no difference at transfer must be modified in light of a third study in
this series: Rockway, Morgan, and Eckstrand (1958) explored the
same ground covered in the first two experiments, but also they varied
the amount of training prior to transfer. Two experimental and two
control groups received 25 training followed by 25 transfer trials as
before, in essentially a replication of the first two studies, except that
C/D ratios of 1/3 and 1/18 were used. Two other experimental and two
additional control groups experienced 100 training trials prior to the
25 transfer trials.

Unfortunately, we cannot calculate transfer indices as in the first
two studies since Rockway *et al.* (1958) did not provide the training
data, but from visual inspection of graphs of their transfer data it is
clear that with the 25-trial experimental groups they obtained results
practically identical to those of the first two studies. However, with
the 100-trial experimental groups there is clear evidence that transfer
from 1/3 to 1/18 and transfer from 1/18 to 1/3 C/D ratio conditions *both*
produced performances significantly poorer than control group performance. Further, the 1/18 to 1/3 experimental group eventually
equalled control group performance (on Transfer Trial 25), whereas
the 1/3 to 1/18 group never did match its control group during transfer.

Several conclusions follow from these three studies: (1) C/D ratio
differences between training and transfer tasks can influence transfer
performance adversely but only after rather extended training. Why
might this be the case? Fleishman and Rich (1963) have shown that
kinesthetic cues from the control device do not begin to influence
skilled performance until after substantial training. Therefore, we can
interpret the above results by assuming that only the 100-trial groups
had sufficient time during training to develop use of the kinesthetic

feedback cues, and so when these cues were changed at transfer, the result was inferior transfer performance (compared to the appropriate control group). With less training, the 25-trial groups, there was not the opportunity to learn the use of kinesthetic cues for precise positioning of the control device; thus, a change in such cues at transfer made little or no difference in performance (again, compared to the appropriate control group). (2) But it did make some difference in those groups transferred from a low to a high C/D ratio condition, even after only 25 training trials. If you recall, these experimental groups were significantly inferior to their control groups on the first transfer trial. Further, in the third Rockway study, initial transfer performance for the low-to-high C/D condition was much worse (relative to the appropriate control group) than was transfer from high-to-low C/D ratios, both after 100 training trials.

Thus, we may conclude that there is differential transfer here: transfer to a less sensitive system (remember that a high C/D ratio means a less sensitive system) is more detrimental than transfer to a more sensitive system regardless of practice level. Why might this be? Tentatively at least, when transferring from a highly sensitive system to one of low sensitivity there will be a tendency to undershoot because during training one learns to make small movements. The opposite would occur when transferring from a low to a highly sensitive system, of course. Apparently, it is easier to adjust for overshoots than for undershoots of the target area. Certainly, the visual information on the display is more compelling in the case of a sensitive system, i.e., the cursor will take off "right now" for a control movement that is too large given the low C/D ratio, whereas with a low sensitivity system the visual information is "sluggish" since only large control movements will result in significant cursor movements on the display.

2. Directional Relationships

When a subject moves his control device to the left, say, which direction does the cursor on the display move? This is a matter of control-display directional relationship, and it involves the concept of stimulus-response (S-R) compatibility. S-R compatibility is a recognition that certain directional relationships are more "natural" (because of the biomechanics of the human operator—the way he is "built") or "expected" (because of overlearning in the past).

One of the first experiments on directional relationships and transfer was performed by Gibbs (1951). One group trained with an expected or compatible S-R arrangement in a one-dimensional compensatory tracking task and then transferred to a task with just the opposite relationship. A second group experienced the "unexpected" or incompatible S-R task first and then transferred to the expected relationship. Unfortunately, Gibbs did not publish the trial-by-trial data which would permit us to use any of the usual transfer index equations (he reported trials to criterion on the training and the transfer tasks), but we can see the pattern of results clearly.

In terms of training task performance, as one would predict, it took less time to reach criterion on the expected relationship (20.5 min) than on the unexpected relationship (30.0 min). Thus, the former was easier than the latter. In terms of transfer performance, the group which transferred from unexpected to expected tasks achieved very good transfer performance: they required only 1.9 trials to attain criterion on the same task which required 20.5 trials by the other group. However, the "expected-to-unexpected" group did very poorly at transfer: they required 25.7 trials to reach criterion, which was only 4.3 trials less than required by the other group in original training on the unexpected task. Therefore, there was evidence of some positive transfer for the expected-to-unexpected transfer group, but not much.

Adams (1954) noted the above study plus others and decided to investigate transfer of training utilizing limbs (the feet) which do not experience much overlearning of control-display relationships. In this way he could eliminate (partially, at least) the strong influence of learned expectancy noted by Gibbs, above. During training the control group saw the cursor move vertically downward (from $0°$ to $180°$) as the pedal controls were depressed. There were four experimental groups for which the displays were tilted to varying degrees during training to produce movements of the display cursor from-to: $315°$–$135°$, $270°$–$90°$, $225°$–$45°$, and $180°$–$0°$, respectively. All four experimental groups transferred to the $0°$–$180°$ condition.

There were no differences among groups during training, thereby indicating that overlearned expectancies were not present prior to this study, as they had been in Gibbs' research. But at transfer there were significant differences among the experimental groups. The approximate transfer indices from Eq. (2) were 106, 72, 56, and 38 % positive transfer for the $315°$–$135°$ through $180°$–$0°$ groups, respectively. As you can see, there was a direct relationship between the amount of change in directional relationship from training to transfer tasks and the amount of relative transfer. The least adequate transfer occurred for the experimental group which experienced a complete reversal of the directional relationship.

How can we summarize these results? In both studies a change from expected to unexpected relationships resulted in poor transfer performance when the change was a complete reversal of the control-display relationship. (The expectation in Gibbs' study was developed prior to the experiment in everyday experience; in Adams' study it was developed, apparently, during the training trials.) However, as shown by Adams, the change from expected to unexpected relationships is progressively less detrimental to transfer performance as the difference in the two relationships is diminished.

Therefore, directional relationships do influence transfer performance with a maximum detrimental effect occurring with complete reversal. But even with complete reversal, there is some degree of facilitation (positive transfer) on the initial transfer trials. Interestingly enough, Lewis, McAllister, and Adams (1951) showed that there was both some facilitation and some interference upon transfer from expected to a completely reversed, unexpected control-display relationship. That is, at initial transfer to a reversed control-display relationship the number of target acquisitions was higher than during initial training on the expected relationship, but also the number of directional movement errors was higher at transfer. Apparently, then, the facilitating and interfering effects combine to yield low positive transfer under completely reversed relationship conditions.

D. FEEDBACK VARIABLES

We will conclude this review of the empirical data with the influence of feedback effects in the man-machine paradigm (see Fig. 1) on transfer performance. There are two subtopics here: the influence of what are called quickening and aiding, and the influence of augmented feedback.

1. Quickening and Aiding

We have not discussed the fourth element in the servo paradigm of Fig. 1. In real-life tracking tasks the machine usually has complex dynamics which act upon the control device signals so as to make the system output a complex function of the control device movement pattern. This in turn makes life difficult for the human operator because he must relate movements of the control to the system output in order to make the latter match the input signal on the visual display. In theory, he must differentiate the function relating control device signal to system output signal, a complex "mental" feat. But with quickening or aiding, the necessary information on the derivatives of system output is sensed by the machine and inserted into the feedback loop along with the system output itself. This eliminates the need for the human operator to take any derivatives and so his job is greatly simplified.

For a more complete discussion of aiding and quickening, the reader
is referred to the classic paper by Birmingham and Taylor (1954).

So what happens when one transfers from quickened to unquickened (easy to difficult) systems and vice versa? Lincoln's doctoral dissertation (1953) involved either an aided or an unaided rate system
(system output was a constant velocity for a given position of the control device). There also was a simple positional control system, but we
are not concerned here with that task. One group trained on the unaided system and transferred to the aided system, while another group
experienced the reverse order of conditions. Transfer was positive for
both groups after 60 min of training over 6 days. The aided-to-unaided
transfer index was approximately 56 %, while that for the unaided-to-
aided group was approximately 52 %. Later, Holland and Henson
(1956) utilized a more complex set of machine dynamics with and
without aiding. Training was given for either 140 40-sec trials over 14
days or 260 40-sec trials over 26 days prior to transfer. For the lesser
amount of training the aided-to-unaided transfer index was 58 %,
while the unaided-to-aided group index was 64 %. For the comparable
groups with the greater degree of training the indices were 51 and
46 % transfer, respectively.

Finally, Dooley and Newton (1965) employed essentially the same
machine dynamics as used earlier by Holland and Henson, but they
attempted to score tracking error alone rather than tracking error plus
the derivatives of the output signal as in the two previous studies.
Unfortunately, it does not appear that they really measured system
error but rather they apparently measured system output, not the difference between output and input which is true system error. Nevertheless, their transfer indices after 100 min of training (4 days) were 46
and 79 % for the quickened-to-unquickened group and for the un-
quickened-to-quickened group, respectively. Further, at transfer the
former group exhibited very high variability in performance, while
the latter group was about one twentieth as variable. Therefore, from
this study, it seems that superior transfer occurs from unquickened to
quickened conditions. The same trend was found by Holland and
Henson, above; however, in none of these three studies were there
statistical tests of transfer differences between the experimental
groups, so for all we know, there may be no significance to the differences found at transfer.

At any rate, we can note that a modest amount of positive transfer
occurs as a function of aiding or quickening. Certainly the indices are
not as high as those found for the input, output, and relationship variables noted earlier in this chapter. Thus, some of what is learned under either aided or unaided tasks transfers to the opposite condition,

but not much. What is required in each condition? With both aided and unaided systems the response pattern is the same in general, but in detail, the response pattern under aiding tends to be more discrete —the subject generates a series of small step changes in control device position. So, something about the general response pattern can be transferred to either condition, especially in the studies of Holland and Henson and of Dooley and Newton where a single 3-cpm sine wave served as the input signal.

What is different in the two conditions is the complexity of the "mental" calculations required. In an unaided system, the subject must anticipate future control device movements by examining something analogous to the several derivatives of the relationship between system output and control device signals. However, with properly conceived aiding, the human operator need only respond directly to the amplitude of displayed error, and he is not required to anticipate future control movements. In fact, under aiding a subject will do worse if he tries to utilize self-estimated derivative information than if he simply responds with a control position which is directly proportional to displayed error.

Therefore, when going from aided to unaided systems, the subject must learn something "new"—how to anticipate future control positions—but he is assisted by something "old"—knowledge of the general pattern of control movements required. When going from an unaided to an aided system, the subject carried forward two old items —knowledge of the general response pattern required and acquired skill in recovering derivative information from the visual display of tracking error. The former helps, while the latter hinders transfer performance on the aided display. Apparently, then, the useful old information on the response pattern helps regardless of the order of conditions from training to transfer, while the new requirement hinders performance for the subject transferring from aided to unaided systems and the same requirement, which is old to the subject transferring from unaided to aided conditions, hinders him on the latter. It may seem incongruous that the same factor would be responsible for the relatively mediocre transfer performance of both groups but for different reasons. Apparently, such is the case. It may help to note that whereas initial transfer performance indices are comparable for the two groups, following initial transfer those subjects transferred from unaided to aided systems quickly improve to the same level as the appropriate control group, while the aided-to-unaided subjects approach control group performance very, very slowly (see Fig. 2 of Holland & Henson, 1956). Thus, the negative effect of the old requirement for the former subjects is quickly overcome whereas the learning of this as a new requirement is more lengthy. As usual, it is easier to discard an old habit than to form a new one, even though initially these effects may be comparable in terms of performance.

2. Augmented Feedback

As indicated in Fig. 1, the human operator receives what is called primary feedback directly in the tracking task. In addition, he may be provided with secondary or augmented feedback, as when an instructor comments upon the performance of the operator. In the laboratory augmented feedback has been provided by sensing system error (the difference between input and output) and comparing this to a criterion such as an on-target criterion. If the operator is on target, he receives an auditory or visual signal confirming that fact; if he gets off target, the signal ceases until he gets back on target. Such augmented feedback clearly is supplementary because the operator can see directly his tracking proficiency on the system display. Uniformly superior tracking performance has been found when augmented feedback is present. But what about transfer from an augmented feedback condition to one with no augmented feedback?

Bilodeau (1952), Goldstein and Rittenhouse (1954), Houston (1947), and Underwood (1949) all report research in which performance deteriorated following transfer to a no-augmented-feedback condition. On the other hand, Kinkade (1959), Minor (1958), Reynolds and Adams (1953), and Smode (1958), among others, have found that groups transferred to a no-augmented-feedback condition continued to perform at their previously acquired level of proficiency. Kinkade (1963) noted that the former researchers all used a tracking device called the Pedestal Sight Manipulation Task (PSMT), whereas the latter researchers used either a rotary pursuit task or the SETA apparatus (Gain & Fitts, 1959). He noted further that Barthol (1952) had observed the PSMT display is fuzzy at best and that visual cues for one of the three components of the task (ranging), in particular, are not very perceptible. The rotary pursuit and the SETA tasks both provide clear, noisefree visual displays.

Kinkade (1963) developed and tested the following hypothesis: if the operator sees clearly discernible primary feedback information on the tracking display, he will use augmented feedback only as confirmation of adequate performance; however, if the primary feedback information is obscured, he will attempt to utilize augmented feedback as a substitute for primary feedback. As a consequence, when augmented feedback is withdrawn completely, the latter operator's performance should deteriorate, while no such deterioration should occur in the former case.

Kinkade employed two experimental and two control groups. Both of the latter received the no-augmented-feedback condition throughout, while the experimental groups received 40 trials with augmented feedback present followed by 24 trials without augmented feedback. Figure 4 presents the results of both the training and the transfer trials along with a summary of the treatments of all groups. Note that Groups C_o and E_o experienced a noise-free tracking display throughout, while Groups C_n and E_n experienced noisy fundamental feedback (random movements of the cursor on the display as in the Briggs *et al.*, 1957a study) throughout.

As usual both experimental groups (E_o and E_n) were superior to their control groups (C_o and C_n, respectively) during training. Upon

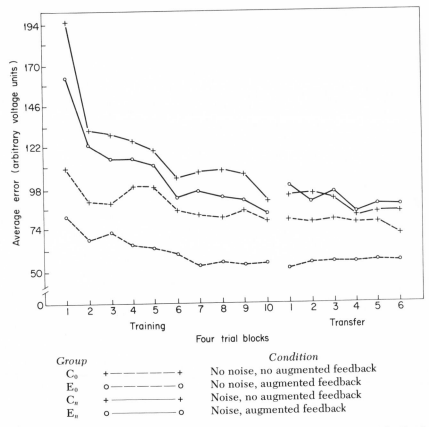

Group		Condition
C_o	+————————+	No noise, no augmented feedback
E_o	o————————o	No noise, augmented feedback
C_n	+————————+	Noise, no augmented feedback
E_n	o————————o	Noise, augmented feedback

Fig. 4. Training and transfer as a function of visual noise and augmented feedback. (After Kinkade, 1963.)

transfer, as predicted, Group E_n deteriorated immediately to the level of Group C_n but Group E_o continued to maintain its superiority to Group C_o. Note that the results are in terms of system error, so the lower the score, the better the performance. Therefore, Kinkade's data confirmed the hypothesis, and one may conclude that augmented feedback can result in superior transfer performance, provided the operator has not utilized it as a "crutch" earlier in training.

III. Interpretation

What general principles, if any, can one glean from the literature reviewed above? It is apparent that in most cases some amount of positive transfer occurs as a function of each of the independent variables manipulated. Negative transfer is the exception in transfer of skills. Thus, we may conclude that the human operator almost always acquires some skills that facilitate transfer performance regardless of the training task configuration. Such facilitation does vary in amount, however, and so we should be concerned with why some training conditions produce high positive transfer (equal to or greater than 100%) and others result in low positive transfer.

A. The Relative Difficulty Hypothesis

Day (1956) reviewed the literature prior to 1956 on the question of task difficulty and transfer performance. Based on a series of experiments, one of which is cited above, Gibbs (1951) concluded that "there may be greater transfer from the difficult to easy task . . . if the same kind of ability is required in both tasks . . ." (p. 109). The reason, as offered by Gibbs, refers to earlier writing by Bartlett (1947), who suggested that there is a central range over which an independent variable can be manipulated within which task difficulty, as measured by performance, is relatively constant. Variations outside this "optimum zone" are more difficult and require superior skill. Thus, transfer to the zone (difficult-to-easy) should be superior to transfer out of the zone (easy-to-difficult).

How well do the above studies bear out this hypothesis? Of the fifteen studies reviewed above which involved transfer both from difficult-to-easy versions of a task and vice versa, five resulted in superior transfer from difficult-to-easy versions, three showed superior transfer from easy-to-difficult tasks, six showed no differential transfer as a function of task difficulty, and in one study (Holding, 1962) differential transfer was found in both directions depending upon input frequency. This is not overwhelming evidence in support of the prediction that one should find superior transfer performance when transfer occurs from difficult-to-easy versions of a task. Nevertheless, the survey shows that the difficulty concept has some merit.

B. TASK SIMILARITY

In verbal learning tasks, which have not been considered here, there is evidence that transfer performance is systematically related to both stimulus and response similarity. This relationship has been summarized by Osgood (1949). The Osgood surface indicates increasing positive transfer if for the same response the transfer stimulus is made more similar to the training stimulus. Likewise, if the stimulus is held constant from training to transfer, increased similarity of the responses results in increased positive transfer. (In the latter case, most variation in response similarity results in negative transfer, but at least increasing response similarity moves transfer performance *toward* positive transfer.)

The use of the similarity concept in skilled tasks is more problematical than in verbal learning situations. One major reason is that scaling similarity is more easily accomplished with verbal materials. Another reason is that the information processing and the response selection and execution stages are more complex in skill tasks, and so a simple change in an independent variable can have complex effects on those intervening activities between stimulus and response in tracking. Note, for example, that in tracking there is no *single* correct response as in a verbal paired-associate task. Rather, the operator may select a particular response from a library of possible responses any of which may do the job adequately. Further, once a particular response pattern is selected, in a tracking task the execution of that pattern is monitored and subsequent adjustments may be required; with verbal responses, the output need be all or none without the fine-tuning control necessary in tracking responses.

Nevertheless, the similarity concept has been used in skilled performance tasks to explain the obtained transfer results. In this context the concept enjoys a fancy name "fidelity of simulation." This reflects the fact that skill training for a complex operational system, such as an aircraft, often is carried out partly in a simulator device. By referring back to the study by Muckler and Matheny (1954), one sees a trend toward increasing positive transfer as similarity of coulomb friction was increased from training to transfer tasks. A similar trend can be detected in some of the data of Table I.

Actually, of course, the similarity concept is central to the difficulty hypothesis discussed above: there it was pointed out that a particular independent variable can be varied over a range and result in relatively constant, optimum performance, but if the variation results in too dissimilar a condition, performance will deteriorate.

C. SKILL COMPONENTS

It may well be that one is stretching things a bit too far in trying to explain motor skill transfer simply in terms of a similarity concept. In skill tasks it may be more fruitful to ask what is learned during training and therefore what can be transferred given the demands of the transfer task. Fleishman has explored extensively the matter of skill components (see Fleishman, 1967, for a recent review). He has shown that human performance is not a unitary matter, but that it is related to a number of factors or abilities. Further, the relationships between performance and abilities vary systematically with practice. It would follow, then, that these abilities or skill components change in relative importance as a function of experience on a particular task. Further, Fleishman (1957) has shown that such skill components as perceptual speed, response orientation, and spatial orientation change systematically as the task itself is changed. Thus, in a highly compatible or expected display-control relationship, perceptual speed is an important determinant of task performance, but as the relationship between control and display becomes less expected, first spatial orientation and then response orientation assume greater importance, while perceptual speed becomes relatively unrelated to task performance.

Therefore, in a transfer of training situation one can assume from Fleishman's work that a transfer task requires certain skill components or abilities and that transfer performance will be a function of the extent to which such components have been acquired and utilized in the training task. This point was implicit in several of the interpretations offered above in this review of the literature.

What is needed, therefore, is a systematic analysis (à la Fleishman) of how changes in an independent variable affect the skill components of a task. Then one should be in a position to relate a transfer index to these skill requirements. While this has not been done systematically, Fleishman's work clearly indicates that such a procedure would provide an analytic understanding of skill transfer.

References

Adams, J. A. Psychomotor response acquisition and transfer as a function of control-indicator relationships. *Journal of Experimental Psychology*, 1954, 48, 10–14.

Ammons, R. B., Ammons, C. H., & Morgan, R. L. Transfer of skill and decremental factors along the speed dimension in rotary pursuit. *Perceptual and Motor Skills*, 1956, **6**, 43.

Andreas, B. G., Green, R. F., & Spragg, S. D. S. Transfer effects between performance on a following tracking task (modified SAM two-hand coordination test) and a compensatory tracking task (modified SAM two-hand pursuit test). *Journal of Psychology*, 1954, **37**, 173–183.

Bahrick, H. P. An analysis of stimulus variables influencing the proprioceptive control of movements. *Psychological Review*, 1957, **64**, 324–328.

Barthol, R. P. Errors in visual size-matching in the flexible gunnery task. *USAF Human Resources Research Center Research Note*, 1952, No. 52–2.

Bartlett, F. C. Some problems of "display" and "control." In A. Michotte (Ed.), *Miscellanea psychologica*. Louvain: Librairie Philosophique, 1947. Pp. 440–452.

Bilodeau, E. A. Some effects of various degrees of supplemental information given at two levels of practice upon the acquisition of a complex motor skill. *USAF Human Resources Research Center Research Bulletin*, 1952, No. 52–15.

Birmingham, H. P., & Taylor, F. V. A design philosophy for man-machine control systems. *Proceedings of the Institute of Radio Engineers*, 1954, **42**, 1748–1758.

Briggs, G. E., Fitts, P. M., & Bahrick, H. P. Learning and performance in a complex tracking task as a function of visual noise. *Journal of Experimental Psychology*, 1957, **53**, 379–388. (a)

Briggs, G. E., Fitts, P. M., & Bahrick, H. P. Effects of force and amplitude cues on learning and performance in a complex tracking task. *Journal of Experimental Psychology*, 1957, **54**, 262–268. (b)

Briggs, G. E., & Rockway, M. R. Learning and performance as a function of the percentage of pursuit component in a tracking display. *Journal of Experimental Psychology*, 1966, **71**, 165–169.

Briggs, G. E., & Wiener, E. L. Influence of time sharing and control loading on transfer of training. *Journal of Applied Psychology*, 1966, **50**, 201–203.

Day, R. H. Relative task difficulty and transfer of training in skilled performance. *Psychological Bulletin*, 1956, **53**, 160–168.

Dooley, R. P., & Newton, J. M. Transfer of training between quickened and unquickened displays. *Perceptual and Motor Skills*, 1965, **21**, 11–15.

Duncan, C. P. Transfer in motor learning as a function of degree of first-task learning and inter-task similarity. *Journal of Experimental Psychology*, 1953, **45**, 1–11.

Fleishman, E. A. Factor structure in relation to task difficulty in psychomotor performance. *Educational and Psychological Measurement*, 1957, **17**, 522–532.

Fleishman, E. A. Individual differences and motor learning. In R. M. Gagné (Ed.), *Learning and individual differences*. Columbus, Ohio: Merrill, 1967. Pp. 165–191.

Fleishman, E. A., & Rich, S. Role of kinesthetic and spatial-visual abilities in perceptual-motor learning. *Journal of Experimental Psychology*, 1963, **66**, 6–11.

Gagné, R. M., Foster, H., & Crowley, M. E. Measurement of transfer of training. *Psychological Bulletin*, 1948, **45**, 97–130.

Gain, P., & Fitts, P. M. A simplified electronic tracking apparatus (SETA). *USAF WADC Technical Report*, 1959, No. 59–44.

Gerall, A. A., & Green, R. F. Effect of torque changes upon a two-hand coordination task. *Perceptual and Motor Skills*, 1958, **8**, 287–290.

Gibbs, C. B. Transfer of training and skill assumptions in tracking tasks. *Quarterly Journal of Experimental Psychology*, 1951, **3**, 99–110.

Goldstein, M., & Rittenhouse, C. H. Knowledge of results in the acquisition and transfer of a gunnery skill. *Journal of Experimental Psychology*, 1954, **48**, 187–196.

Holding, D. H. Transfer between difficult and easy tasks. *British Journal of Psychology*, 1962, **53**, 397–407.

Holding, D. H. *Principles of training*. New York: Macmillan (Pergamon), 1965.

Holland, J. G., & Henson, J. B. Transfer of training between quickened and unquickened tracking systems. *U.S. Naval Research Laboratory Report*, 1956, No. 4703.

Houston, R. C. Knowledge of results in learning complex motor skills. Unpublished master's thesis, Northwestern Univer., 1947.

Howell, W. C., & Briggs, G. E. The effects of visual noise and locus of perturbation on tracking performance. *Journal of Experimental Psychology*, 1959, **58**, 166–173.

Jones, E. I., & Bilodeau, E. A. Differential transfer of training between motor tasks of different difficulty. *USAF Human Resources Research Center Research Bulletin*, 1952, No. 52–35.

Kinkade, R. G. Augmented feedback and tracking skill. *U.S. Naval Training Device Center Technical Report*, 1959, No. 508–3.

Kinkade, R. G. A differential influence of augmented feedback on learning and on performance. *USAF AMRL Technical Documentary Report*, 1963, No. 63-12.

Lewis, D., McAllister, D. E., & Adams, J. A. Facilitation and interference in perform-

Lewis, D., McAllister, D. E., & Adams, J. A. Facilitation and interference in performance on the modified Mashburn apparatus: I. The effects of varying the amount of original learning. *Journal of Experimental Psychology*, 1951, **41**, 247-260.

Lincoln, R. S. Visual tracking: III. The instrumental dimension of motion in relation to tracking accuracy. *Journal of Applied Psychology*, 1953, **37**, 489–493.

Lordahl, D. S., & Archer, E. J. Transfer effects on a rotary pursuit task as a function of first-task difficulty. *Journal of Experimental Psychology*, 1958, **56**, 421–426.

Minor, F. J. Analysis of tracking performance under varied schedules of achievement information feedback. Unpublished doctoral dissertation, Ohio State Univer., 1958.

Muckler, F. A., & Matheny, W. G. Transfer of training in tracking as a function of control friction. *Journal of Applied Psychology*, 1954, **38**, 364–367.

Naylor, J. C. Parameters affecting the relative efficiency of part and whole training methods: A review of the literature. *U.S. Naval Training Device Center Technical Report*, 1962, No. 950–1.

Osgood, C. E. The similarity paradox in human learning: A resolution. *Psychological Review*, 1949, **56**, 132–143.

Reynolds, B., & Adams, J. A. Motor performance as a function of click reinforcement. *Journal of Experimental Psychology*, 1953, **45**, 315–320.

Rockway, M. R. The effect of variations in control-display during training on transfer to a "high" ratio. *USAF WADC Technical Report*, 1955, No. 55-366.

Rockway, M. R., Eckstrand, G. A., & Morgan, R. L. The effect of variations in control-display ratio during training on transfer to a low ratio. *USAF WADC Technical Report*, 1956, No. 56-10.

Rockway, M. R., Morgan, R. L., & Eckstrand, G. A. Effects of variations in control-display ratio and amount of original practice on transfer of tracking skill. In G. Finch and F. Cameron (Eds.), *Symposium on Air Force human engineering, personnel, and training research*. Publ. No. 516. Washington, D.C.: National Academy of Sciences-National Research Council, 1958. Pp. 108–113.

Smode, A. F. Learning and performance in a tracking task under two levels of achievement information feedback. *Journal of Experimental Psychology*, 1958, **56**, 297–304.

Underwood, B. J. *Experimental psychology*. New York: Appleton-Century-Crofts, 1949. Pp. 414–416.

CHAPTER 8 _____

Supplementary Feedback and Instructions[1]

EDWARD A. BILODEAU
Tulane University

I. Introduction

In this chapter we are to highlight feedback experiments where the instructions to the subject are the experimental variable. The instructions may be given before, during, or after the response; there is a bewildering variety of ways of doing this. Speaking to the subject is the most simple and direct way of communicating with him. In the information-feedback chapter, the experimenter spoke to the subject quite specifically about his error, but in the present chapter, the information provided by the experimenter is less specific and more general. Moreover, substitutes for the spoken word have also been employed; mechanical devices that provide tones and working conditions that provide experience are illustrations. Since the procedural stress is on taking precise information out of the feedback, yet still communicating something to the subject about his success at performing, the outcomes of these studies are generally explained by hypothesizing changes in motivation. It has been a recurrent explanation over a long period of time (Ammons, 1956; I. McD. Bilodeau, 1966; Birch & Veroff, 1966; Brown, 1949; Cofer & Appley, 1964; Vroom, 1964). We shall begin by asking how motivation is treated by promi-

[1] The preparation of this chapter was supported in part by the Air Force Office of Scientific Research, Office of Aerospace Research, United States Air Force, under AFOSR Contract No. F44620-68-C-0072.

nent laboratory-oriented people and recent coverage in books on human learning. Afterward, we shall narrow the inquiry considerably and concentrate on motor-skills experiments as reported in journals.

A. The Status of Human Motivation

An important book on verbal skill was one edited by Cofer (1961), entitled *Verbal Learning and Verbal Behavior*. Nine chapters were contributed by such eminent psychologists as Deese, Melton, and Postman. No one chose to speak on the topic of motivation and, indeed, the topic is not even represented in the index. In 1966, two books of special importance appeared. The first was a revision of a prominent text in undergraduate teaching, *Experimental Psychology* by B. J. Underwood (1966). The 1949 edition contained a chapter devoted to motivation, but the revision has none. If we are to judge from this, it will not be until 1983 that undergraduate students might possibly see the chapter reappear in a further revision. In *Acquisition of Skill* (E. A. Bilodeau), the predecessor to the present book, with many contributors to the motor-skills area included, the word *motivation* was not listed in the index. The book nevertheless pretends to cover motor performance in a comprehensive way. Evidently, a considerable number of contemporary investigators get along somehow in covering attention mechanisms, feedback functions, tracking behavior, and the rest without invoking the term.

Some 25 years ago, Hull tried to show how incentive and motivation are related to the other principles of his conditioning system, such as habits, reward, etc. Motor- and verbal-skill investigators have not really borrowed seriously any of the details of these mechanisms. In the 1960's, the notion of motivation was still fairly primitive and was contained in the four assertions: it is necessary to initiate and sustain performance; it is potentially scalable; more of it might increase output; more of it might facilitate learning.

Despite the lack of inclusion in books at the present time, there is a continual undercurrent of interest in the topic of motivation and a few journal articles can be expected every year. The topic obviously waxes and wanes and the subject is included in this book as an acknowledgment of the undercurrent of interest.

B. Feedback and Motivation

Many authors treat feedback as if it were a cue, a command, a sign, or a bit of information in regard to the correctness of a particular past or future response. The subject learns to use the feedback and learns to execute responses more adequately. As an association-building variable it is said to strengthen the correlation between responses and stimulation. As a cuing variable, feedback acts upon already learned hierarchies of habits and serves as a selector mechanism. Emphases on habit processes are relatively new and the subject of the chapter, "Information Feedback"; the possible incentive value of feedback in arousing motivation is an older theoretical view.

If feedback is assignable to a motivational category, then it should serve as an incentive to stimulate performing in a more vigorous way or in an alternative way. Thus, the feedback may energize or activate already learned responses. Another aspect of the motivational point of view is that an increase in motivation augments response output which in turn is a more favorable condition for making new associations between responses and stimuli. Psychologists agree that changes in performance in a single experiment can come about through various agencies: increases in motivation, decreases in fatigue, increases in learning, and so on. The experimental problem has been to disassociate these in the laboratory.

II. Research: Contributions and Evaluation

A. PROMISING TECHNIQUES

There is no known way to alter motivation by a feedback technique which is beyond argument, but there are a few methods which do produce serviceable data and which bring out the issues.

One of the best-designed studies was reported by Willis (1967). The task was rifle marksmanship, the variable was level of recoil (2 or 25 foot-pounds), and the design was a double-shift transfer test. The subjects were unskilled and were given 60 hours of training before shifting load and testing for transfer. The 25-foot-pound load produces quite a bang, and flinching, trigger jerking, and other manifestations of recoilitis are common. The Hi load is said to be stressful and the Lo load is not. The design used four groups of subjects: Hi(training)-Hi(testing), Hi-Lo, Lo-Lo, and Lo-Hi. During training, the Lo outperformed Hi, and during testing the prior recoil level did contribute to the degree of skill exhibited. The study is exceptional in that (1) the task is not artificial yet interesting, (2) considerable training was administered, (3) the difference between stimulus levels was considerable, and (4) the design of the groups enabled the investigator to choose between alternative hypotheses.

The work studies of I. McD. Bilodeau (1953, 1955) on cranking and Saufley and Bilodeau (1963) on reversed alphabet printing bear on motivation-arousing procedures. I. McD. Bilodeau studied high-speed cranking and decrement in output when the subject was with and without experience about the working conditions of the experiment. Thus, the duration of work–time, duration of rest–time, and the amount of work-loading were the environmental variables manipulated. The subject was given experience with these or was told to expect certain values of these variables in a forthcoming cranking session. Rate of cranking was lawfully related to these stimulus variations. The conservation behavior exhibited was interpreted as an illustration of the action of habits — habits established during past experience with temporal and physical environments and the fatigue which they imply. But there is no especially compelling reason why the pacing behavior of men must be assigned to the habit class, only one of custom. The point is that here is a procedure with possible motivation properties which produces good, strong data. The cranking task, it should be said, is not a learning type of task in the conventional sense of learning to perform with more and more skill. It seems to be a situation where the subject learns how to regulate (downward) his output so that he can keep going under trying circumstances.

The method of supplementary information feedback (IF) or extra IF has also produced valuable data. Extra IF was first evaluated shortly after World War II. An electronic gunnery trainer was remade so that the subject was given achievement cues above and beyond the standard ones. Using the normal sighting station, the gunner is required to adjust his controls so as to frame or superimpose a number of dots upon a moving target airplane. In the standard situation, the feedback is the visual error or spatial difference between the dots and the target. In the experimental situation, the experimenter arranges to have the target change from standard white to red when the gunner's responses change from incorrect to correct. The reddening of the target for the experimental group is accomplished by a red filter and the redness signifies that ongoing tracking responses are proper, and so the standard white target means that ongoing responses are not correct. Tracking the target is difficult because the gunner is required to respond in three different ways, for example, parts called azimuth, elevation, and range. In a three-part task, there is a requirement to divide one's attention between the three sources of feedback. It was hoped that adding the red and not-red contingencies to the cues normally available would serve to boost the learning of good gunnery habits.

An unpublished study by Seashore, Underwood, Houston, and Berks (Underwood, 1949) showed that a group with the extra IF made higher scores than a group trained without. The writer (E. A. Bilodeau, 1952) was not satisfied that the higher scores meant higher learning, so he redid the study and added three special-purpose filter groups in a transfer of training design. One group was first trained for 4 days with the filter; then upon filter removal, it did no better than a no-filter control on the fifth day. A second group was given the filter on day 5 for the first time, and their scores then improved at the same fast rate as a control group had with the filter on the very first day. The third experimental group alternated from trial to trial between filter and no-filter conditions, and their scores also alternated, making wide swings between the level of the control group with the filter all the time and the other control group with no filter at all. Clearly, the extra cue improved gunnery scores over those of the standard cue, yet the operator had not learned how to take better advantage of the standard cues when trained with the filter.

The study shows that there was no extra transfer of the learning from filter-present conditions to the no-filter condition. It was concluded that the not-red-now state of the filter group served to cue the habit of searching for the correct response until the red-now state was obtained. But does the not-red-now state touch off habits which produce higher scores or does it trigger a motivation to do better? And for what it is worth, any subject will report that the filter condition is more interesting. Neither the state of the art nor the theory has enabled anyone to make a definitive answer. However, without the transfer groups, data from such studies as Seashore *et al.* are meaningless. Annett (1959) and Smode (1958) have worked on this problem, too. Smode concluded unhesitatingly that the extra IF does not set off a different habit, but that it motivates the subject to do more.

Another worthy technique, producing the data shown in Fig. 1, was that of Payne and Hauty (1955). These authors (see also Hauty & Payne, 1955) combined two good ideas in order to prepare the way for their phenomena. First, a 4-part tracking task was selected (the Multidimensional Pursuit Test presents the operator with an especially demanding task); it requires the operator to scan 4 meters and to nullify the frequent drifts of the indicators by entering appropriate corrections on 4 aircraft-like controls. Second, a considerable decrement in response was produced by requiring over 4 hours of work from the subject. Having assured themselves of a decrement phenomenon, the authors were in a good strategic position to determine if the decrement could be mitigated by various feedback operations. The control group or M_1 received no special information; M_2 represents a condition where the individual subject was told of his standing relative to an artificially high group norm for the last cycle; and M_3 includes all of M_2 procedures, but also displayed all the IF's of past cycles as well. IF's for M_2 and M_3 scores were displayed by means of

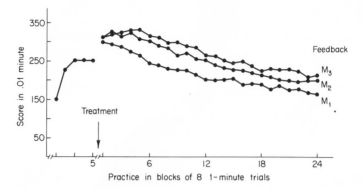

Fig. 1. Performance decrement with practice for different feedback (motivation) conditions. (After Payne & Hauty, 1955.)

colored pegs. The results show that conditions M_2 and M_3 had an immediate beneficial effect which grew larger and then smaller, and that M_2 and M_3 serve to postpone work decrement. Payne and Hauty labeled the conditions of their study *motivational* or *incitive* as opposed to *tuition*.

In the tuition treatments, extra IF was administered about which particular part response was wrong. This treatment was even better at sustaining a high level of proficiency (on the part). The authors say that "a very prompt and specific designation of the fact and locus of error might be said to promote proficiency largely because of its directive properties, even though the cues might acquire some drive value." This means that Payne and Hauty consider the tuition treatment as either cue, habit, drive, or all three. Had they retested their subjects several days later, after dissipation of all temporary work decrement and under standard feedback conditions, they would have been in a better position to separate habit from motivation, or at least to separate the transient effects from the more lasting ones. For example, if all groups performed equally well during the proposed delayed test period, any hypothesized better learning by the extra IF could be ruled out. We would, however, be unable to choose between the cuing and motivation roles of the extra IF. This is the very same impasse reached in the experiments with the red filter and the gunnery trainers.

An appreciable amount of direct verbal control over the subjects' responses on the Multidimensional Pursuit Test was achieved by E. A. Bilodeau (1955). After 20 days of practicing the four parts (A, B, C, D) of the tracking task, the subjects were proficient and had developed ways of scanning the four instruments to obtain error information. They also had developed ways of entering response corrections to compensate for errors detected. No one knows the precise ways or tactics that subjects come to employ, but we do know that a simple command on day 21 such as "Next, pay twice as much attention to instrument A" does in fact immediately lead to better performance in A and worse performance in B, C, and D. As a matter of fact, the sum of losses in B, C, and D equals the gain in A.

During the 20 days of training, three different supplementary IF schedules were evaluated. After each minute of practice, (1) the lowest of the four part scores was identified for one group of subjects, (2) one of the four parts was selected at random by the experimenter and represented to the subject as his lowest in a second group, or (3) nothing at all was said about the parts. Two findings stand out. First, the subjects receiving IF, whether true or random, improved more on the identified part on the next trial than if not informed. Second, on the whole, the three groups did equally well and by this is meant that the effect of feedback is transient. It has no lasting value and when the experimenter moves from representing A as worst to B as worst, there is a trade-off and performance at A suffers as B improves. No other study so keenly illustrates the transitory cuing role of this kind of instruction. We must conclude that the instruction improved the performance of the part, but not the learning of the part.

Using the method of extra IF does not guarantee that even augmented output will result. Some extra IF's are much too extra, e.g., too highly coded and meaningless to the subject. This observation is behind the fact that most skills investigators do not administer extra IF in their day-to-day studies. For example, the subject on the rotary pursuit test is not given his clock score nor is the subject turning blocks told the number of blocks overturned. The writer has engineered a spectacular failure with the rotary pursuit test which only justifies the standard procedure. One group was given time on target in percent plus a bonus ranging up to 40 percentage points after every trial; a second group was given time on target in percent minus as much as 40 percentage points; and the control group was given only the true percentage. All three groups performed and learned alike in spite of these severe score transformations. The null result suggests that the incentives provided by the general laboratory environment, and, too, the standard feedback represented by sight of stylus and target are quite sufficient for top performance. The experimental 40 percentage points do not necessarily inform the subject that he is superior or inferior, nor do they inform on the exact nature of error or proficiency. This would also be true of a tone or click administered for hits on the target of the rotor, it might be supposed.

Another failure of extra IF on the rotary pursuit test has helped to clear the air, especially in regard to reinforcement issues. Archer and Namikas (1958) administered a tone whenever the subject was on target for a prescribed length of time. Various groups received the tone after being on target for 0, 0.2, 0.4, 0.8, or 1.6 seconds. Group 1.6 earned fewer tones, of course, because the requirements were stiffer, and also each of the tones it did manage to earn was removed or delayed by 1.6 second from the onset of an on-target response burst. The results between groups were null, as were various similar operations by I. McD. Bilodeau and Rosenquist (1964), putting to rest (temporarily, to be sure) a notion that the tone might serve as a reinforcement. That is to say, there is an argument which holds that those rotary responses that precede the tone are strengthened because of the tone and those responses not followed by tones drop away with failure of tone to appear. Another part of the theory, not as widely accepted, would add that the learning produced by the tone comes about through a mechanism of drive reduction. This seems to mean that the tone satisfies some particular motivation, such as the one to hear the tone. It is never clear to some writers whether motor-skills studies fall within the boundary conditions set by writers of conditioning theory and so the preceding application of reinforcement language is certain to be out of bounds to many. A conditioning analysis of verbal and motor-skills learning was never popular and is even less so nowadays. Actually, many conditioning theorists wince when friendly and unfriendly students make irrelevant tests of conditioning theory in the contexts of verbal and motor skills.

B. More about Instructions to the Subject

Several types of feedbacks are especially hard to classify either for their stimulus characteristics or for their effects upon responses. The best we can do is to bundle them under the heading of instructions to the subject. An instruction can and has meant nearly everything. Table I presents a list of common procedures over which the cloak of instructions has been drawn. McGeoch and Irion (1952) cited and discussed more techniques than can be covered here. The list has grown since then, but otherwise there has been no progress (Surwillo, 1958). If we inspect Table I, we can see that it is by no means a certainty that the set is limited in any way, especially since the set remains undefined.

The first and most relevant question of all is whether the procedures in Table I have any effect. Some do and many do not. We can only be sure that the table deals with many things. Among those methods

Table I
LABORATORY TECHNIQUES OF INSTRUCTION ALLEGED TO CHANGE LEARNING

1. Before a response, the subject is:
   a. Admonished to try hard, try very hard, etc.
   b. Promised a nickel, a cookie, if he will . . .
   c. Told how important the experiment is
   d. Told that performance is related to intelligence
   e. Threatened with shock if . . .
   f. Told a rivalry or contest between subjects is established
2. After a response and before another, the subject is:
   a. Told, you were at the 60th (___) percentile
   b. Told, you were on target 40% (___) of the time
   c. At first told he is successful, later falls prey to failure trials
   d. Told: un ha, hmm, or that's a point
   e. Told a teammate's score
   f. Requested to set a goal, or the experimenter establishes one for him
   g. By verbal, mechanical, or electrical means, told that:
      (1) A particular error is in progress
      (2) A correct response is in progress
3. During continuous responding
   a. Most of the techniques under (1) and (2) above are possible
   b. Muscular tension is augmented by having the subject perform physical activity along with the main task
4. Uncommon instructions
   a. Told: go faster and make more errors
   b. Told: slack off, you don't have to do your best
   c. Told: pay no attention to instruments A and B, watch C instead

usually producing a null result are those that are highly verbal, highly coded, or nonspecific as to the act in question, and sort of trivial in any case. As a consequence of these and other shortcomings to be discussed later, the journals have published much inconsequential and null data. Most of these data are produced by investigators trying to show that incentives make a difference in the rate of *learning* a task. The fact of the matter is that psychologists know better the circumstances where these variables do not work than where they do. However, no one admits to this knowledge and no list can be found. Rather, there is an understandable tendency to act as if those investigators who report null results have, in effect, failed to find the phenomenon which is known to be true. Some of the more resourceful experiments are described below.

A study by Bayton and Conley (1957) used a block-turning task and a level of aspiration technique. A series of early successes was followed by a series of failure trials. The results were slim, if any. Further, one group was replicated and it gave results of opposite direction. Zimny (1956) used a nonsense syllable task and a task of sorting cards. He employed the incentive of an excused classroom assignment, a threat of electric shock, a statement that the task was a sign of intelligence, and a statement that the task afforded additional practice. These data were null. So were those of Bell (1959), who frequently exhorted the experimental group to do better at the pursuit rotor.

Perhaps a monotonous task, performed for an hour per day and over 24 days, would serve to bring out the incentive value in knowledge of performance. Chapanis (1964) used these temporal conditions with the task of punching random digits into a teletype tape. One group was given no extra information about their output of digits while in three other groups an electric counter provided a tally of output for the subject. In Group 2, the counter was never reset to zero and so the subject would have to process his count if he wished to make note of his daily progress. In Groups 3 and 4 the counter was reset to zero before the start of the hour, but in Group 4 the subject was requested to log his score onto a record card every 15 minutes, making his achievements more obvious. Special care was taken by the experimenter not to set quotas or to take notice of the output. All groups improved markedly over the 24 days and there were no differences among them. The design has been criticized by Locke (1967), who is attempting to establish motivational effects.

Noble, Fuchs, Robel, and Chambers (1958) reported two studies, using social competition as the variable, and the Rotary Pursuit Test and the Discrimination Reaction Time Test as apparatus. After the subjects practiced a while under social conditions, half were visually isolated from one another for the remaining trials. When run as individuals, the subjects using the Discrimination Reaction Time Test (a self-paced, response selection task) suffered a significant and uniform decrement in performance, but null results were obtained on the rotor. Noble *et al.* concluded that the motivational role of social competition is contingent upon as-yet-unanalyzed task factors.

Williams (1956) also used competition between groups and found that the quality of work performed was unaffected by competition. The quantity of work produced, however, was greater in the competitive condition. Noble *et al.* too, had obtained their one positive result with a quantity measure.

Earlier, Noble (1955) used the Two-Hand Coordination Test and 400 men of the Air Force. The task presents a small moving target that the subject is required to track by moving two lathe-like hand controls. During the early, middle, or late stages of practice, the experimenter stopped the subjects and administered incentive instructions. Specifically, they were told that to pass the test they would have to improve by 25 %. This treatment had absolutely no effect on the difference between groups. It also had no effect within the experimental groups, as Noble showed in an examination of the quartile ability curves.

Fleishman (1958) sought the relationship between incentive instructions and ability level in a study of 400 subjects on the Complex Coordination Test. The task here is to match 3 display lights with 3 movable lights controlled by 3 aircraft-like controls. It was believed a self-paced task would be advantageous in bringing out the effects of incentive-motivation instructions. The motivating instructions contained several components, each of which might serve as an incentive. The treatment was severe because the risk of obtaining more null results was realized. Among the stimuli used was the statement that: "The results of this test are very important to you. They have an important bearing on your future assignment in the Air Force. So, you must do your best. Thus far, you have not been doing as well as you should, so you must try harder. . . ." These strong and other drastic instructions were read to airmen who had just entered the Air Force, and whose career assignments were not all clear to them. Not only this, but additional special exhortations to do better were administered from time to time. The special instructions were introduced after the fifth trial of practice and the scores prior to this were used to stratify the subjects into high and low ability groups. Because psychologists have a hand in their career assignments, airmen reporting to the laboratory always appear attentive and obliging. As a matter of fact, when running airmen, the writer has generally tried to establish a calming effect since some of the men have appeared unduly frightened.

The motivating instructions used by Fleishman brought out just a little better performance in individuals of above-average ability, and they had no effect whatever on those of below-average ability as can be seen in Fig. 2. He pointed out, as had Noble and others, that the instructions consisted of "extra motivation" presumably being added to motivation assumed to exist among airmen (even among those airmen of below-average performance). The most interesting aspect of Fleishman's small positive finding was the almost constant difference throughout the practice between the performance of the motivated high-ability subjects and the unmotivated high-ability subjects. Taken at face value, this constant difference means at the very least that the experimental group did not learn more than the control group, but merely outscored them by, for example, moving faster. If they had learned more, a growing separation between groups would have appeared.

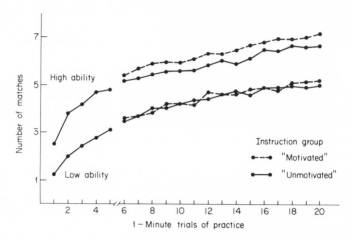

Fig. 2. Acquisition curves for different ability levels and instructions. (After Fleishman, 1958.)

French (1955) has been one of the very few within experimental psychology to say that performance will vary with the typical (preexperimental level) motivation or achievement needs of the individual as well as with the cues in the environment. Motivating instructions may be effective with some people but not with others, and possibly, such a characteristic can be brought out by a selection test. The preexperimental measure of motivation used by French was provided by a questionnaire. A typical item was, "Tom always lets the other fellow win." The subjects explained the behavior of Tom and the explanation was scored for degree of need for achievement. After 90 Officer Candidates for the Air Force had taken this test, they were given a digit-letter substitution task 5 months later under one of the three different conditions of instruction (relaxed, task, extrinsic). The main conclusion was that there was evidence that individuals can be preselected to do better or worse under a particular instruction. French's approach is partly psychometric, of course, and since the mixing of testing and training methods falls between the traditional approaches of tests and measurement on the one hand and learning-experimental on the other, the journals cited in this chapter contain few studies such as French's. This is a pity, of course. (cf. Jones, Chapter 5, Section I, of the present volume.)

One of the more stimulating of the incentive experiments was performed by Walton and Begg (1958). They used imbeciles as subjects, 20 days of practice, and the task emphasized work over learning. In the Leg Persistence Test Walton and Begg used, the subject is instructed to keep a leg above a chair for as long as possible and not to touch the chair with the leg. The score is the number of seconds during which the leg is held in the air. This task had a learning component, but most of all, it had a strong fatigue component. It seems likely that people with high motivation might endure greater fatigue. After all, in cases of emergency, individuals are known to perform all kinds of feats considered impossible under normal conditions. The data show definite, though complicated, differences between four types of treatments: encouragement, competition, goal, and an ignored control group. The control group got worse throughout training. All the groups getting some attention improved at first. The differences between experimental groups are especially marked during the first ten days, but during the last ten days the groups behaved quite alike. It is not clear which of the factors—type of subject, number of days, or work task—produced the positive results. If type of task is important, we are not sure what properties the leg task possesses. Is the task dull and routine or is it exciting and challenging to imbeciles? We simply do not really know, but we can hypothesize the motivations induced by tasks may have to be classified by type of subject. Birch (1964) has measured the speed with which subjects reach for puzzle material and found faster reaching the greater the degree of success at solution.

C. General Shortcomings of Motivational Studies

Many of the studies give an impression of trying to show that, to make up an artificial example, a man blowing 20 smoke rings will learn to execute them better if given a prize for every ring. It has not been fashionable to perform an experiment on the relationship between number of smoke rings blown and amount of money offered—because we already have some idea of that outcome and because of a self-imposed constraint to use a *learning* type of task. Neither performance tasks nor out-and-out performance measures (such as rate, horsepower, time to exhaustion, etc.) are popular in the present-day psychology of learning. This is no surprise since the subject matter is the psychology of learning.

The inquiry has often been limited, unfortunately, to a few learning tasks of the laboratory variety, conventional response measures, and a young-adult subject population as if to determine who can discover the smallest difference between experimental conditions that will produce the largest difference in behavior. It has not seemed fair to use the kind of instructions that would obviously make a difference ("run, don't walk," for example). It has not been considered cricket to investigate situations where the behavior of experimental groups might persist longer than the control and by so doing not only outproduce, but also to go on to outlearn the control comparison. Enough of the more resourceful studies were reviewed above to give a fair representation of how difficult it is to effect an improved response by means of motivating instructions.

Experimental designs should be examined carefully. Even though the results may be different from group to group, the reader should not necessarily infer that the difference is a learning-caused difference even though such a claim is made. The study of Seashore *et al.* with the red filter on the gunnery trainer reviewed earlier made this point. Many studies are old and tired (Hurlock, 1925). The often-cited older studies seem to yield positive results, but these usually have few subjects, no modern small sample statistics, the wrong response measure, and the wrong control group. A common example of woeful design (Bayton & Conley, 1957) is a study with no test for learning masquerading as a learning study. Here, the treatment might be 10 cents delivered per response versus 1 cent per response. If the 10-cent group outproduced the 1-cent group, the odds seem to be that the author reports that the 10-cent group "learned" more and "knows" more. Deese (1962) has written very convincingly of the need to use transfer test designs to separate the learning component from the performance component.

Were the operations of Table I to produce good data, the word "motivation" might be an especially good gathering term. Regrettably, many of the studies we reviewed had procedures in common that might turn out to be faults. Adult college subjects and USAF airmen were used extensively. These subjects may be well motivated even before the investigator begins to offer his treatment. No one has preselected subjects for poor motivation. The experimental procedures seem directed to increase motivation, not to decrease it. The subject worked and trained for only a few minutes and then an impecunious investigator offered a trivial consequence for a trivial performance. No one has offered prized consequences for behaviors which might otherwise lie dormant.

E. A. Bilodeau and Johnson (1963) reported that college men say in a questionnaire that for $10,000 they would abstain from sexual activities for a period of 1 year. For the price of $1000 they would go without food for 5 days. The price was high for 36 rather unusual and inconveniencing assignments, but there usually was a price, the price varying directly with the intensity level contained in the proposition. Individual differences were great, but they were directly related to the magnitude of the mean number of dollars required. The study seems to suggest what has been so difficult to show in the laboratory, but what most investigators implicitly believe to be true: that a theory of verbal and motor performance cannot get along forever without an anchor in motivation. Results from a questionnaire, however, do not bear one way or the other on whether greater motivation per se produces greater learning. Research within the armed forces has been more performance- than learning-oriented, for environmental extremes of food, climate, and clothing (Clark & Dusek, 1967) and stress such as combat, isolation, altitude, and fatigue (Fine, 1967) are routine occurrences in the world at large.

Brown (1961) is friendly to the idea of the necessity for motivation in the psychology of learning. In a portion of a book on the subject, he extends Hull's drive theory from the animal laboratory to perceptual and psychophysical situations. Because "do your best" instructions contain no specific response-directing cues, he prefers to attribute any effect to motivation. Yet, there is a doubt, for "do your best" might bring about response facilitation by arousing superior habits, e.g., sitting more erect, better methods of concentration on the task at hand, etc. Elsewhere in the same chapter, the motivating effects of strong stimuli, especially electric shock, are discussed. Shocks, he notes, can ". . . qualify as associative variables since they provide specific knowledge of results" (p. 232). Even randomized schedules of shock seem to bring about diverse behaviors, and strict motivational interpretations of these data, too, can be criticized. (Feldman, 1961, should be consulted for a discussion of the effects of administering shocks after correct and incorrect choices in a maze problem; Bevan & Adamson, 1960, should be read for a discussion of the problems of scaling electric shock.) Given extensive coverage are motivational differences defined in terms of scores on a scale of manifest anxiety. Several anxiety studies, tracing back to Taylor (1951), have steadily yielded marginal results and were never incorporated into the main body of the motor- and verbal-skills literature (Nance, 1965). But Brown's main point is that most variables alleged to change motivation can just as easily be alleged to change the habit-building environment. The possibility of confounding habit and motivation has certainly frightened away a lot of investigators. Brown's chapter is important in showing that there is room for logical and sensible argument against the view that one procedure is exclusively motivation-related, another exclusively habit-related.

III. Summary

In this chapter we asked if the concept of motivation was really well-established by laboratory data from studies of information feedback. A few studies were found which gave good, strong phenomena. When good data were in hand, a wrangle about the interpretation was always possible.

Among the promising leads were experiments involving work tasks and findings relating to persistence and the conservation of effort. Other leads involved using extra IF, sampling special populations of subjects, and selecting subjects on the basis of preexperimental differences in achievement. The more promising leads were not beyond criticism of classification — a major one contending that experimental designs are not sufficiently advanced to make a separation between the effects of learning and motivation. The variables now used seem inextricably confounded. It was concluded that when and if an unconfounded situation is fashioned, the finding will not help in the classification of the confounded techniques. Of course, we must remain interested in the outcome of certain procedures whether they are confounded or not.

In many null and near-null result studies, the subject was often asked to do his best, was promised something good, was threatened with failure, etc. The null results might be accepted at face value; that is, taken to mean that we now know many circumstances where the needling and cajoling of the subject has no effect upon his behavior. Thus, the search for incentives via laboratory instructions that will succeed according to classic plans is far from accomplished.

The procedures producing null data were carefully examined and a number of common practices were readily observed. The researchers have sampled well from the following populations: *tasks*, the subject is asked to learn to execute better responses; *subjects*, healthy competitive males; *goal*, a higher achievement; *incentive*, praise or a trivial compensation; *method of teaching*, the subject left to employ his own resources for tactics and strategy; *response measure*, crude indices of progress at learning, seldom measures of quantity of output or persistence; *length of observation*, a few minutes is typical; and *experimental design*, often an inadequate test of the stated theoretical issue.

Despite all the evident difficulties with the data, it was clear that psychologists believe in motivation to some extent anyway. It was also clear that most details of such relatively well-developed motivational systems as Hull's take little real part in the design stages of experiments on human beings. None of the experiments in this chapter is especially outstanding for either its design, data, or theory. It should not be taken for granted that a breakthrough is near or that one is possible.

Animal psychologists, conditioning theorists, and laymen are very much concerned with advancing our knowledge of motivation. This is not true of the general run of university psychologists working on motor and verbal skills for they have all but given up, at least for the time being. Not one of them would deny the powerful influence of incentives in general. They all ascribe man's unusual accomplishments, whether approach, avoidance, or escape, to his motives. For example, some individuals will leave home to work for years for incentive or out of curiosity, and so forth. Others will survive extraordinary hardships while others die rather quietly. These strong and complex situations do not yield readily to our standard arsenal of pellets and praise. They cannot readily be studied in the laboratory with simple tasks and college sophomores.

References

Ammons, R. B. Effects of knowledge of performance: A survey and tentative theoretical formulation. *Journal of General Psychology*, 1956, **54**, 279–299.

Annett, J. Learning a pressure under conditions of immediate and delayed knowledge of results. *Quarterly Journal of Experimental Psychology*, 1959, **11**, 3–15.

Archer, E. J., & Namikas, G. A. Pursuit rotor performance as a function of delay of information feedback. *Journal of Experimental Psychology*, 1958, **56**, 325–327.

Bayton, J. A., & Conley, H. W. Duration of success background and the effect of failure upon performance. *Journal of General Psychology*, 1957, **56**, 179–185.

Bell, A. H. Effects of experimentally-induced muscular tension and frequency of motivational instructions on pursuit rotor performance. *Perceptual and Motor Skills*, 1959, **9**, 111–115.

Bevan, W., & Adamson, R. Reinforcers and reinforcement: Their relation to maze performance. *Journal of Experimental Psychology*, 1960, **59**, 226–232.

Bilodeau, E. A. Some effects of various degrees of supplemental information given at two levels of practice upon the acquisition of a complex motor skill. *USAF Human Resources Research Center Research Bulletin*, 1952, No. 52–15.

Bilodeau, E. A. Variations in knowledge of component performance and its effects upon part-part and part-whole relations. *Journal of Experimental Psychology*, 1955, **50**, 215–224.

Bilodeau, E. A. (Ed.) *Acquisition of skill*. New York: Academic Press, 1966.

Bilodeau, E. A., & Johnson, J. W. Tasks, task-intensity, and dollars demanded for performance. *American Journal of Psychology*, 1963, **76**, 293–298.

Bilodeau, I. McD. Performance of an effortful task with variation in duration of prior practice and anticipated duration of present practice. *Journal of Experimental Psychology*, 1953, **46**, 146–153.

Bilodeau, I. McD. Self-paced rest with variation in work loading and duration of practice. *Journal of Experimental Psychology*, 1955, **50**, 245–248.

Bilodeau, I. McD. Information feedback. In E. A. Bilodeau (Ed.), *Acquisition of skill*. New York: Academic Press, 1966.

Bilodeau, I. McD., & Rosenquist, H. S. Supplementary feedback in rotary-pursuit tracking. *Journal of Experimental Psychology*, 1964, **68**, 53–57.

Birch, D. Incentive value of success and instrumental approach behavior. *Journal of Experimental Psychology*, 1964, **68**, 131–139.

Birch, D., & Veroff, J. *Motivation: A study of action*. Belmont, Calif.: Brooks/Cole, 1966.

Brown, J. S. A proposed program of research on psychological feedback (knowledge of results) in the performance of psychomotor tasks. In Research Planning Conference on Perceptual and Motor Skills, *USAF Human Resources Research Center Conference Report*, 1949, No. 49–2, 81–87.

Brown, J. S. *The motivation of behavior*. New York: McGraw-Hill, 1961.

Chapanis, A. Knowledge of performance as an incentive in repetitive, monotonous tasks. *Journal of Applied Psychology*, 1964, **48**, 263–267.

Clark, R. E., & Dusek, E. R. Effects of climate, food, clothing and protective devices on soldier performance. In J. E. Uhlaner (Ed.), *Psychological research in national defense today*. Tech. Rep. S–1. U.S. Army Behavioral Science Research Laboratory, 1967. Pp. 185-198.

Cofer, C. N. (Ed.) *Verbal learning and verbal behavior*. New York: McGraw-Hill, 1961.

Cofer, C. N., & Appley, M. H. *Motivation: Theory and research*. New York: Wiley, 1964.

Deese, J. Skilled performance and conditions of stress. In R. Glaser (Ed.), *Training research and education*. Pittsburgh: Univer. of Pittsburgh Press, 1962. Pp. 199–222.

Feldman, S. M. Differential effects of shock in human maze learning. *Journal of Experimental Psychology*, 1961, **62**, 171–178.

Fine, B. J. Adjustment to military stress. In J. E. Uhlaner (Ed.), *Psychological research in national defense today*. Tech. Rep. S–1. U.S. Army Behavioral Science Research Laboratory, 1967. Pp. 199–206.

Fleishman, E. A. A relationship between incentive motivation and ability level in psychomotor performance. *Journal of Experimental Psychology*, 1958, **56**, 78–81.

French, E. G. Some characteristics of achievement motivation. *Journal of Experimental Psychology*, 1955, **50**, 232–236.

Hauty, G. T., & Payne, R. B. Mitigation of work decrement. *Journal of Experimental Psychology*, 1955, **49**, 60–67.

Hurlock, E. B. An evaluation of certain incentives used in school work. *Journal of Educational Psychology*, 1925, **16**, 145–159.

Locke, E. A. Motivational effects of knowledge of results: Knowledge or goal setting? *Journal of Applied Psychology*, 1967, **51**, 324–329.

McGeoch, J. A., & Irion, A. L. *The psychology of human learning*. (2nd ed.) New York: Longmans, Green, 1952.

Nance, R. D. Pacing and anxiety level on the pursuit rotor. *Perceptual and Motor Skills*, 1965, **20**, 325–326.

Noble, C. E. An attempt to manipulate incentive-motivation in a continuous tracking task. *Perceptual and Motor Skills*, 1955, **5**, 65–69.

Noble, C. E., Fuchs, J. E., Robel, D. P., & Chambers, R. W. Individual vs. social performance on two perceptual-motor tasks. *Perceptual and Motor Skills*, 1958, **8**, 131–134.

Payne, R. B., & Hauty, G. T. Effect of psychological feedback upon work decrement. *Journal of Experimental Psychology*, 1955, **50**, 343–351.

Saufley, W. H., Jr., & Bilodeau, I. McD. Protective self-pacing during learning. *Journal of Experimental Psychology*, 1963, **66**, 596–600.

Smode, A. F. Learning and performance in a tracking task under two levels of achievement information feedback. *Journal of Experimental Psychology*, 1958, **56**, 297–304.

Surwillo, W. W. A new method of motivating human behavior in laboratory investigations. *American Journal of Psychology,* 1958, **71,** 432–436.

Taylor, J. A. The relationship of anxiety to the conditioned eyelid response. *Journal of Experimental Psychology,* 1951, **41,** 81–92.

Underwood, B. J. *Experimental psychology.* New York: Appleton-Century-Crofts, 1949. Pp. 414–416.

Underwood, B. J. *Experimental psychology.* (2nd ed.) New York: Appleton-Century-Crofts, 1966.

Vroom, V. H. *Work and motivation.* New York: Wiley, 1964.

Walton, D., & Begg, T. L. The effects of incentives on the performance of defective imbeciles. *British Journal of Psychology,* 1958, **49,** 49-55.

Williams, D. C. S. Effects of competition between groups in a training situation. *Occupational Psychology,* 1956, **30,** 85–93.

Willis, M. P. Stress effects on skill. *Journal of Experimental Psychology,* 1967, **74,** 460–465.

Zimny, G. H. Effect of various motivational techniques upon learning and performance tasks. *Journal of Experimental Psychology,* 1956, **52,** 251-257.

CHAPTER 9

Information Feedback[1]

INA McD. BILODEAU
Tulane University

I. Introduction

Sensory feedback is both a common and significant event: its significance "... in the organization of behavior arises from the fact that most of the stimulus changes to which the individual reacts are produced by his own motion ..." (Smith, 1962, p. 9). This recent statement and the 2500-year-old empirical dogma that the senses are the gateways to knowledge combine into a strong assertion of sensory feedback's dominant role in ongoing and future behavior. The present chapter deals with a modest portion of sensory feedback, those stimulus consequences of human behavior under the experimenter's control and variously called knowledge of results, reinforcement, and information feedback. Nonetheless, even of this modest topic the immodest claim has been made (E. A. Bilodeau & Bilodeau, 1961, p. 250) without contradiction (Fitts, 1964, p. 280) that "Studies of feedback or knowledge of results . . . show it to be the strongest, most important variable controlling performance and learning. . . ." To demonstrate information feedback's relevance in even a well-established visually guided skill, close your eyes and try to write a few sentences in your best handwriting, or introspect on rhetorical questions

[1]The preparation of this chapter was supported in part by the Air Force Office of Scientific Research, Office of Aerospace Research, United States Air Force, under AFOSR Contract No. F44620-68-C-0072.

such as the fate of a remotely controlled car whose driver gets no indication of where his steering movements put the car.

Such demonstrations can also illustrate the danger to systematic exploration that comes from feedback's obvious importance. Eliminating feedback is neither the only possible manipulation, nor a good one for showing how it controls behavior. Cues can be displaced in time or space as well as omitted, or even varied separately and in any combination (Smith & Sussman, Chapter 4; Gould, 1965) of reactive (from the responding member), instrumental (from the control being moved), and operational feedback (from the environmental item being acted upon). The fact that we can control the kind of feedback signal that behavior produces and how the signal changes as behavior changes is a second reason that information feedback is significant for psychology — outside as well as within the laboratory. Displacements are no more artificial in the laboratory than in the everyday world: equipment designers, parents, and teachers routinely decide how the consequences of behavior will be coded, and examples of feedback transformations are easy to find. Eyeglasses, hearing aids, and mirrors include feedback stimulation in their transformations and so do the magnifying lenses dentists and watch-repairmen use. Radar devices represent an error (off-target, off-course) that is large, three-dimensional, and remote on a small, two-dimensional scope that is present; an airplane's climb, bank, and turn indicators translate position in space to numbers or marker positions on displays a few inches across; a car's speedometer transforms rate to amount of needle deflection. The very presence of an indicator represents a displacement, and there are such additional items of transformation to decide as the indicator's location, size, color, and number of divisions. The advance artillery spotter who relays feedback to the gun station has similar options in the way he codes degree and direction of a miss. These are simple, obvious examples; others, such as the quickened systems and predictor displays discussed in Chapters 7 and 10 involve multidimensional feedback displacements in space and time that are neither simple nor familiar.

A. DEFINITION

Information feedback (IF) refers to stimuli presented during or after the subject's response and contingent on the response according to a function determined by the experimenter.

$$IF_n = f(R_n - R+), \tag{1}$$

where R_n is a quantitative expression of the R made on Trial n, and R+

is the value of the correct (required or goal) R. The f may convert the R difference to "yes" or "no," a deflection on a meter, a number with algebraic sign, or any kind of event: the f represents omission, displacement, or distortion of the error, any temporal or spatial transformation. The essence of IF, then, is in what the f makes of the discrepancy between obtained and required behavior. The object is to find how behavior is related to IF variables, to express

$$R_{n+1} = f(IF_n). \tag{2}$$

For example, a subject on his first trial might flip the third of ten toggle switches when the correct choice is the fifth; $R_1 = 3$, $R+ = 5$, and $IF_1 = f(3\text{-}5)$. If f is the multiplicative constant, -2, $IF_1 = -2(3\text{-}5) = +4$. Should this treatment make picking out the correct switch difficult compared with a multiplicative f of $+1$ (where $IF_1 = -2$ when $R_1 = 3$), then behavior is indeed dependent on the preceding IF.

By this definition IF is a stimulus, an independent variable, and not the subject's cognizance of the consequences of his behavior. The experimenter's making information available [Eq. (1)] is not the same as the subject's taking in, digesting, and using the information [Eq. (2)]. The object of manipulating IF often is just to make inferences about the subject's cognitions or hypotheses and how IF controls them (E. A. Bilodeau, 1953b; Bourne, 1966; Levine, 1966), but these are consequences of IF, classified either as R or as intermediate between IF and an overt R. IF (especially under the name "knowledge of results") is an old topic, and a historical survey would reveal deviations from our definition, including instances in which knowledge of results is defined by the subject's awareness of his behavior's consequences, rather than by the experimenter's manipulations of stimuli. A survey would also show considerable inconsistency in the general class of variable to which IF is assigned; for example, information, making IF a relative of any technique of giving information (instructions, demonstration); reinforcement, where IF is handled as a relative of satisfiers and punishers; motivation, where IF is treated as a member of the class of variables having an energizing function. Though the present treatment has an information bias, the limits of IF and its status in theory have not been clearly and finally established, for reasons elaborated in the chapter on supplementary feedback and instructions (Chapter 8) and in I. McD. Bilodeau (1966, pp. 257–259).

B. Varieties of IF

Holding's (1965) recent survey makes a useful classification of kinds of IF or knowledge of results, summarizing 32 varieties in a branching family tree. Holding makes a first dichotomy into *intrinsic* (present in the standard task) and *artificial* (added to the standard); each of these first order dichotomies is in turn divided into *concurrent* (during R) or *terminal* (after R is completed); the third order of branching distinguishes *immediate* (without gap in time between R and IF) from *delayed* (a gap between R and IF); the fourth order separates *nonverbal* (physical instruments) from *verbal* (words, scores); and the final dichotomy is *separate* (for each R) vs *accumulated* (over several R's). The terms in Holding's classification are necessary vocabulary items for understanding the IF literature.

C. Areas of Research

The present survey, however, follows not kind of IF, but research areas into which present experiments fall. The division into topics is arbitrary, suited to the kind of task stressed here, and not necessarily adequate to the future. Though nearly all research in IF could be considered under the single heading, transformations, as involving some manipulations of *f* in Eq. (1), four separate areas of research are distinguished: frequency and frequency schedules — absolute and relative numbers of IF's in a series of trials; scale transformations — numerical and spatial variations in the function relating the value of IF to R; locus — IF's temporal placement with respect to the R to which it applies and the next R in a series of trials, and also its placement with respect to interpolated activity; and augmented IF — supplementing the standard task with extra IF or, in Holding's schema, adding artificial to the intrinsic IF the standard task provides.

D. Tasks

The following sections include illustrations of variables in a variety of motor tasks — serial, positioning, and tracking — and, though incidentally, in nonmotor tasks, but emphasize positioning. Reducing redundancy is one reason for the imbalance: this volume has no chapter on positioning, while other chapters devoted to a task category, Poulton on tracking and Noble on selective learning (Chapters 10, 11) include feedback contributions, as do Smith and Sussman on cybernetic theory, Briggs on transfer, and E. A. Bilodeau on supplementary feedback (Chapters 4, 7, 8). Another reason is that positioning tasks combine (1) an R that can vary continuously, for versatility in manipulating the R-IF function, with (2) discrete-trial presentation, for relatively uncomplicated demonstrations of the effects of experimental variables. Furthermore, if Fitts (1964, p. 280) is correct about feedback that ". . . from a theoretical standpoint, there appears to be little in this area that is peculiar to skill learning as distinct from other tasks . . . ," the task used in reviewing the topic is mostly, though not always, a matter of convenience. The major sections of the research review treat positioning; other tasks are treated under comment subsections.

Positioning R's are motor R's that can vary in extent or degree along some continuum and can be scored along the continuum for the experimenter's record. They are used with certain procedural restrictions in most contemporary investigations of IF. Figure 1 represents the standard sequence of events in positioning studies of IF: the subject sets a control (which can be the same wheel, lever, or rudder met in tracking); a single setting is made in a trial; there is a break after an R before the next R is called for; and IF comes in the break between R's. IF is reported in arbitrary scale units to reduce unwanted transfer of training from past experience with familiar scale units — a 5° error in turning a wheel might be represented by a 2-inch deflection of a marker on a dial, a 4-inch line by the number 64 (written or oral), a 16-ounce pressure by the tenth lamp in a column, etc. Two procedures are common. When R amplitude is reported, the instructions include the value of the required R, and some function of the value of the obtained R follows R (both in arbitrary units); for example, if R+ is a 67.5° displacement of a lever, subjects might be instructed to try for a score of 45 (or 45 units) and an R or 75° would be reported as 50 units. When error is reported, the IF for a 75° R would be "5 long" in the arbitrary units above and a 61.5° R would be "4 short"; instructions for the error procedure sometimes include the value of R+ (as 45 units, not 67.5°) and sometimes advise the subject to "try to make an R of the correct amplitude."

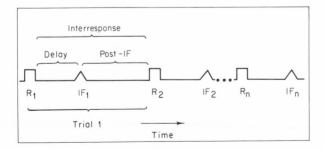

Fig. 1. Typical sequence of events in a positioning task. (From I. McD. Bilodeau, 1966.)

Figure 1 shows IF as terminal, and unless concurrent cues are deliberately introduced, the subject is kept (by blindfold, screens, fixation-point) from watching any effect of his R during its execution; extraneous auditory, tactile, and other cues the apparatus might contribute are also controlled. Experimenter, control, and IF display are all concealed from the responding subject in the standard terminal IF treatment, so that, in effect, the experimenter manipulates what can be considered either instrumental or operational IF with minimal reactive cues (Smith & Sussman, Chapter 4). The usual mean R indices, amplitude and absolute error (preferred when Trial 1 has little constant error), show regular trends over a series of IF's.

II. Frequency

Both absolute (total number of IF's) and relative frequency (IF for some, but not all R's) have been manipulated. Frequency takes precedence of the other topics because it shows that learning, or at least the learning curve, depends upon the presence of IF and its absolute frequency. This appears very clearly in the need for IF in improving and sustaining performance, or in three repeatedly demonstrated empirical effects: performance fails to improve unless IF is introduced; performance improves with IF; and performance either deteriorates if IF is withdrawn, or shows no further improvement. Figure 2 plots representative data showing these phenomena in a positioning task.

There are some limitations and restrictions on these assertions. (1) They are not meant to claim that IF is responsible for all modification of behavior, or even all improvement. (2) They presume the general kind of situation and definition of IF described earlier.

1. Adaptation changes behavior, and can reduce error. There is even a rare example of improvement in performance taking place with practice when there is neither obvious IF nor a ready adaptation explanation (Pearson & Hauty, 1960). In some highly overlearned tasks previous learning rather than present IF may control R, and warm-up might be mistaken for learning. Pretraining instructions and demonstrations can also benefit performance by providing useful information that precedes R and is not, strictly, IF (E. A. Bilodeau & Bilodeau, 1961). It would be inconsistent to rate the information in IF as the important aspect and then maintain that only IF can change behavior. The order in which information and R occur may sometimes be trivial, but as the usual order is R-IF, IF is ordinarily necessary.

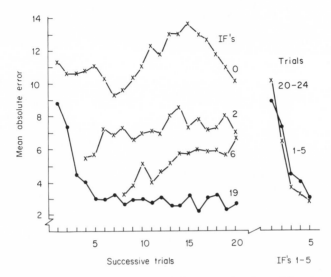

Fig. 2. The effects of introducing and withdrawing IF early and late in a series of trials. On the left, mean error against trials with no IF, IF withdrawn after two or six trials, and IF on every trial; on the right, the first five trials with IF for Groups 19 (Trials 1-5) and O (Trials 20-24), showing no latent learning in Group O. (After E. A. Bilodeau, Bilodeau, & Schumsky, 1959.)

2. We are taking for granted a task in which external R-contingent cues have been eliminated except the ones the experimenter deliberately provides. Some devices have IF built in; adding another signal does not introduce IF, nor does withdrawing the addition bring IF to zero. Extra signals are matters of supplementary (artificial or augmented) IF (Chapters 7 and 8), not of frequency. (If a person can see whether he has drawn a 3-inch line, telling him whether he has would make little difference unless the seen and heard IF's are markedly different functions of R value.)

Eliminating R-contingent external cues does not mean removing R-produced internal stimulation, such as kinesthetic feedback, but not all R-produced cues are IF. By our definition, IF means either a stimulus whose value is determined by the difference between obtained and required R's or separate stimuli coding obtained and required R's. Only if kinesthetic standard or kinesthetic error stimuli are offered (Lincoln, 1956) do we label kinesthetic stimulation IF. When we ask if R-produced stimulation that does not satisfy our definition of IF is sufficient for learning, the answer seems to be quite generally that it is not. In positioning, as Fig. 2 illustrates, neither a learning curve nor evidence of latent learning shows up when there is kinesthetic feedback but not IF. Kinesthetic feedback is important, of course

(Holding, 1965), and one way to look at learning is as the building of a scale relation between feedback and IF—as Bahrick, Fitts, and Schneider (1955) refer to using knowledge of results to sharpen the use of kinesthetic feedback (see also Kay, Chapter 2). But unless happy chance fits an old scale to a new situation (where we explain with transfer of training, not present learning), IF is necessary to a proper present translation.

The final item of digression is the distinction between frequency and R-contingent procedures in which R's of one class are followed by an external signal and R's of another class are not. R-contingent treatments, as when the experimenter says "right" after correct R's but nothing after incorrect, fall under scale transformations and are treated there. On early trials, the absence of right or wrong may be equivalent to omitting IF—the data certainly support this view—but the subject can deduce its meaning; more important, of course, is that saying nothing is an R-contingent cue when its occurrence depends on behavior; whether it is a good cue is another question. Relative frequency is involved only when a blank can follow an R of any value, i.e., when blanks are prescheduled and the absence of right, wrong, or any score is ambiguous (Bourne, Guy, & Wadsworth, 1967).

The data in Fig. 2 present one kind of evidence of the role of IF's absolute frequency in performance and learning: (1) with succeeding IF's performance improves—error falls toward a minimum; and (2) residual benefits are greater when IF is withdrawn after the larger number of IF's. Figure 2 also verifies that a first series of R's without IF does not lead to latent learning. Other evidence of the influence of absolute frequency (total number of R's followed by IF) and relative frequency (ratio of IF's to R's) have been obtained by giving occasional IF's in a series of R's, as in the fixed-ratio treatments in Fig. 3. Subjects turned a knob once (R_1) and received IF_1; thereafter, however, depending on treatment group, IF followed every R̄ (100%), every third (33%), every fourth, or every tenth R. The total number of R's was adjusted so that all subjects received 10 IF's.

Absolute frequency's effect is presented in the left half of Fig. 3, where only R's immediately after an IF are plotted; absolute number of IF's is the same for the four groups and relative frequency differs. With absolute frequency constant, no differences are left to attribute to relative frequency, and the experimenters concluded that absolute frequency was the learning variable, relative frequency irrelevant, at least up to a 10% ratio. Performance, plotted in the right half of Fig. 3 against ordinal number of R, rather than IF, supports this view. The 100% treatment yields a continuous curve while the other curves are discontinuous, step-functions. Blank trials without IF make little

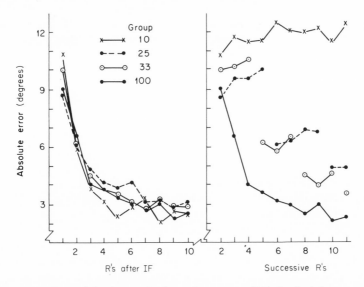

Fig. 3. The effects of absolute and relative frequency of IF. On the left, mean error on trials immediately after IF, with absolute frequency constant and relative frequency variable); on the right, mean error on Trials 2–11, breaks in the discontinuous curves indicating IF's, with absolute and relative frequencies variable. (After E. A. Bilodeau & Bilodeau, 1958a.)

change in R (error, overall, increases a little), change occurring between an R for which IF is given and the next R in the sequence. A later study (Larré, 1961, discussed in Section IV, B) verified the finding that R improvement (the learning curve) depends upon IF and its absolute frequency.

A. FREQUENCY COMMENT

Roughly analogous techniques in the more complex tasks treated in Chapters 7 and 10 also produce losses when IF is removed or given intermittently (Battig, Voss, & Brogden, 1955; Poulton, 1957). Frequency's role seems clear across a wide variety of tasks, motor or not. Psychophysical judgments and watchkeeping behavior are modified when IF is introduced (Chinn & Alluisi, 1964). In four-dimensional discrimination problems for which he could infer the subject's hypothesis from choices on blank trials, Levine (1966) gave an arbitrarily prescheduled "right" or "wrong" after every fifth choice and found blank-trial effects quite like those in Fig. 3: response-patterns gave no evidence that blank trials led to any change in the subject's hypothesis. Estes discusses comparable findings in reviewing probability learning (1964, pp. 104–106). Bourne and Pendleton (1958) and Taylor and Noble (1962) varied relative frequency of IF and found greater R-error over a block or series of choices the fewer the IF's within a block; and Bourne *et al.* (1967) report absolute frequency the controlling variable for "correct" and/or "wrong" IF's.

III. Scale Transformations

This section covers numerical and spatial displacements, for example, variations in the number reported to the subject as his score and in the location of a target follower on a display. Transformations are significant because they make IF independent of the value of R, separating IF's effect on R-change from the value of R itself: different IF's can follow the same R in different treatments and the same IF can follow different R's. At the extreme, the IF's can be decided in advance and chance allowed to determine which R's will be paired with which IF's (E.A. Bilodeau, Sulzer, & Levy, 1962; Levine, 1966). Varying the kind and degree of relationship between behavior and its feedback [manipulating f in Eq. (1)] yields the most direct evidence of IF's most important property: that R-change depends upon the direction and magnitude of error signaled in IF. Rate of acquisition or limit of accuracy varies with the function converting R-error to IF, and if one R-IF relation can establish an R, another can as readily steer one away from the R (Fig. 7). *Frequency* manipulations show that R-change is contingent upon IF and *scale transformations* show how. Frequency stresses the cumulative residuals of IF experience and scale transformations the importance of the most recent IF.

A point to note about displaced IF, or the definition IF = $f(R)$, is that IF (score reported to the subject) is not R, nor the experimenter's proper R-measure. The experimenter measures R on the same scale for all groups in an experiment. While he rounds in entering R in his records (reads 3.127 inches and records 3.13, 3.1, or 3 inches), he rounds all groups to the same tolerance, measuring R before, not after transforming. The IF may be "a hit," but the R recorded is the same −13° that would be taken for the same R in a treatment where IF = −13°; or the R measure is taken from the subject's pencil track through a maze or his joystick position, not from the TV screen that provides displaced IF or the CRT display that presents some function of stick position. Otherwise subjects may differ in score because they act alike but get different scores for the same behavior, or because their behaviors differ (I. McD. Bilodeau, 1966, p. 279). It is also advisable to record the R-measure more accurately than to two or three categories: the difference between a hit and a miss can be less than the difference between two hits or two misses; and the kind of error can be as significant as frequency of hits.

IF, then, as a function of the difference between the R executed and the R required, can be any function, simple or complex, arbitrarily determined by the experimenter; and how behavior (scored on a common scale for all treatments) is affected by the function relating IF_n to R_n is the primary question in IF research.

To begin with, an equipment designer is free to specify sensory modality and stimulus values: the error for pushing, pulling, or turning a knob can be tied to dial and pointer, words, or tones through earphones; the particular dial, word code, etc., are as optional. Further, deciding, say, that R is drawing a line, limited to the range 0–12 inches, and IF is pointer position on a 4-inch dial does not fix what pointer position will correspond to what length of line. In line-drawing and other positioning tasks what remains to be decided provides the topics of the areas surveyed below: *scale grain*, rounding error in converting R's to discrete IF's on a discontinuous IF scale; *continuous transformations*, kind and degree of distortion from simple proportionality between R and IF scales; and *goal shifts*, varying the value of R+ between trials. Though numerical displacements are more frequent than spatial in positioning, there are examples of the spatial displacements typical of tracking displays, and the distinction has not so far proved important in terminal IF treatments.

A. Scale Grain

Rounding error is most easily summarized: rounding (for example, to the nearest tenth, whole number, multiple of 10, etc.) reduces R accuracy, but positioning behavior is not sensitive to coarseness of IF scale grain. Obvious scale-grain variables are the tolerance allowed in signaling a hit (target size) and the number of other IF values—the coarser the grain, the fewer the different scores possible. The relation of IF to R is stepwise and discrete, in either case, and the size of the step may vary with the value of R. Figure 4 presents illustrative scale-grain transformations in which tolerance about R+ is constant for all treatments; though they were used in tracking, they represent positioning possibilities nicely. The steps may be few and large (A); intermediate and with a smaller step about R+ (B); uniform and small (C); essentially continuous, (D); or any other size and arrangement. The R-scale, or R-error measure, is, of course, unaffected by the error displayed to the subject. The R-IF function is:

$$IF_n = (R_n - R+_n) - (R_n - R'_n), \tag{3}$$

where R'_n is the midpoint of the step interval in which R_n falls and $(R_n - R'_n) \leq 1/2$ (i), the size of the interval.

Trowbridge and Cason (1932) early demonstrated that terminal feedback for amount and direction of error was more effective than right and wrong. Rounding to the nearest unit, multiple of 5, 10, . . . 50 units in reporting error to the subject (for turning a knob without visual cues, R+ = 8 full turns or 200 units), E. A. Bilodeau and Rosenbach (1953) found only the severest rounding (steps of 40 and 50 units) detrimental to performance, and only early in practice. The writer used the same task in an unpublished study that illustrates both rounding's effectiveness and its limitations. One group received information about magnitude and direction of error (MD), another direction (D) alone, and the third magnitude (M) only. All groups improved with IF, and in this case D (with only three possible IF's, "low," "hit," and "high") was as good as MD, but M was inferior. Optimal positioning accuracy does not demand carefully refined IF; and though there is no present clear example, it may be that overrefinement can be detrimental.

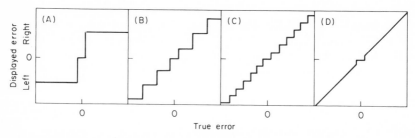

Fig. 4. Discontinuous transformation: scale grain. Displayed error (IF) against R error. (After Hunt, 1961.)

B. Continuous Transformations

Rounding introduces unsystematic distortion into the R-IF conversion, on one trial shrinking, on another inflating the R error in translating to IF, and positioning behavior is not susceptible to this noise. Increased-(IE) and reduced-error (RE) treatments are continuous transformations, related to rounding error, that have a systematic bias in displacing IF-from R-scale. With scale grain they cover the topic, target size or the range of values about R+ for which IF is "a hit" (E. A. Bilodeau, 1955a). The insert in Fig. 5 gives an example of an RE transformation and its IE opposite. Comparing the functions in the insert in

Fig. 5 with those in parts C and D of Fig. 4 brings out both their joint coverage of target size and the differences between the discrete and continuous displacements.

In an RE condition IF is expressed as

$$IF_n = (R_n - R+) - k \qquad (4)$$

when $(R_n - R+) \geqq k$,

$$IF_n = (R_n - R+) + k \qquad (5)$$

when $(R_n - R+) \leqq k$, and

$$IF_n = 0 \qquad (6)$$

when $/(R_n - R+)/ \leqq /k/$,
and in an IE treatment as

$$IF_n = (R_n - R+) + k \qquad (7)$$

when $R_n \geqq R+$, and

$$IF_n = (R_n - R+) - k \qquad (8)$$

when $R_n \leqq R+$.

In RE any R within the range $R + \pm k$ will yield "a hit" as IF, and any error is reduced by up to k units. In IE no R can produce "a hit," and IF exaggerates any R error.

The data plots in Fig. 5 show the effects of systematic distortion on turning a knob hidden from view. Direction of displacement is represented by RE and IE parameters, magnitude, the independent variable in Fig. 5, by different values of k for different groups in both RE

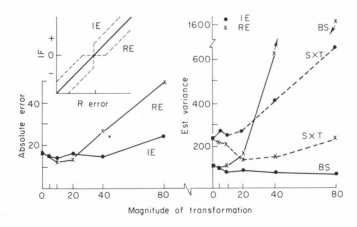

Fig. 5. Continuous transformation: increased and reduced error. In the insert, an example of the R–IF displacements; on the left, the effects of kind and amount of displacement on mean error at the end of practice; on the right, the effects on between- and within-subject variability. (After E. A. Bilodeau, 1955a.)

and IE. The left half of Fig. 5 shows that systematic increases and decreases in reported score produce the same kind of R trend as rounding: subjects are not easily affected, but very severe displacements do have adverse effects on performance, especially in RE.

The estimated variances in the right half of Fig. 5 use the data of the last three trials and suggest how R-repetition and R-change depend upon the direction and amplitude of reported error, and they account for the interaction of IE and RE R-error trends. A point on a between-subject (BS) curve reflects the variability of the individual's mean for the three trials from the general mean of his group; the subject × trials (S × T) component reflects the magnitude of trial-to-trial swings within a subject's R-profile. The more the subjects of a group differ from each other in average R-amplitude, the larger the between-subject estimate; the more a subject differs from himself from R_n to R_{n+1}, the larger the subjects × trials.

All four variance trends in Fig. 5 are consistent with magnitude and direction of error as the key variables in getting human beings to repeat or vary their behavior. Under the experimental conditions (everyone free to choose his amplitude of R_1), Trial 1 showed wide between-subject differences. The IF in severe RE distortions should serve to continue these differences: everyone's IF_1 is "correct" or "close," cuing the subject to repeat R_1 or modify its amplitude only slightly in his second try. The IF_2's, in turn, are "hits" or numbers indicating near-hits, etc. Subjects whose IF_n cues little or no change from R_n to R_{n+1} are encouraged to continue making their initial constant errors. They should differ widely from each other and be consistent from trial to trial, in keeping with the steeply rising between-subjects (X's, solid curve on the right in Fig. 5) and the flat subjects × trials (X's dashed curve) trends for RE. This constant error in R amplitude accounts for the positive acceleration of absolute error with increasing RE (X's, left side of Fig. 5). Quite the opposite is true of IF and behavior under IE. There is no "correct" to cue R repetition. If R_1 has a small undershoot, IF reports a large undershoot, a cue to an overshoot in R_2; IF_2 inflates the degree of R_2's overshoot, cuing a small R_3, etc. The IF, always an error signal, encourages alternate ups and downs, and wider swings the larger the IE distortion (closed circles, dashed lines on the right in Fig. 5), and discourages constant errors -- the overshoot on one trial balancing the undershoot on the next (closed circles, solid lines).

One hypothesis on the ineffectiveness of fair-sized RE distortions is that there is a limit to R-accuracy (note the 20-unit asymptote in Fig. 5 at RE = 0) and that IF accuracy under this limit is wasted. A more specific hypothesis is that generalized R-tendencies about R+ summate to produce a dominant R+ for a fair range of RE values. Summation effects, however, should be less when R+ varies from trial to trial, and an unpublished lever study by the writer showed no interaction of two RE values and constant (C) vs variable (V) goals. A V subject had a different goal (R+) on each of 13 trials and was told what value of R+ to try for on every trial, sequence of goals different for different subjects. A C subject had the same goal on every trial, different subgroups representing the V group's various goals, so that every goal entered both V and C on every trial. Average R error was about twice as large for V as C at the end of training, but RE had no more effect on V than on C.

Other continuous transformations vary the R–IF function to change the size or direction of reported error with curvilinear transformations and linear transformations that vary size and sign of slope and IF intercept. The data in Fig. 6 (from an unpublished study by E. A. Bilodeau) show the effect of positive linear transformations of IF for two different goals: rate of approach to the limit, but not limit of accuracy, is affected by magnitude of transformation. Magnitude of reported error shows its effect in the r of .70 between IF_1 and R_2 (with r = .10 between R_1 and R_2) in a reworking of data from a similar study (E. A. Bilodeau, 1953b); the importance of direction of reported error appears in the drop from R_1 to R_2 produced by giving smaller scores for larger R's (Schumsky, 1959).

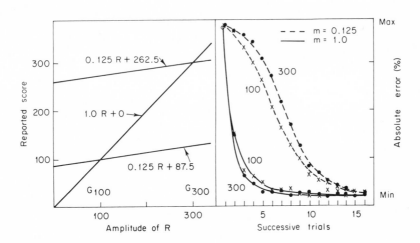

Fig. 6. Continuous transformation: linear transformations. On the left, the R-IF transformations; on the right, the effects of linear transformation and amplitude of goal R. Mean error is plotted as a percentage of the obtained range of error for each goal. (From an unpublished experiment by E. A. Bilodeau.)

C. GOAL SHIFTS

The purpose of changing goals between trials or trial blocks — using different R–IF relations on different trials — is to relate R and R-change to an error signal that cues an R different from R's cued by earlier IF's — to determine the weight of IF_n in controlling R_{n+1} against the weight of recent R-IF history, and with such variables as size and number of shifts. The data show that magnitude and direction of error reported in the immediately preceding IF have major influence on R change.

The transformations, $f_1, f_2, \ldots f_n$, in this section can be expressed as goal changes, i.e.,

$$f_1 = (R - R+_1) \tag{9a}$$
$$f_2 = (R - R+_2) \tag{9b}$$

$$\cdot$$
$$\cdot$$
$$\cdot$$

$$f_n = (R - R+_n) \tag{9c}$$

or, as accurately, as changes in the IF intercept (b) in the linear function, $IF = m (R - R+) + b$, m and R+ constant,

$$f_1 = (R - R+) + b_1 \tag{10a}$$
$$f_2 = (R - R+) + b_2 \tag{10b}$$

$$\cdot$$
$$\cdot$$
$$\cdot$$

$$f_n = (R - R+) + b_n \tag{10c}$$

The more general heading, *R–IF Shifts*, would be misleading, as positioning has ignored other parameters of the R-IF function in shifting from one continuous function to another. This has not been the case of other kinds of tasks.

Positioning studies have also confounded instructions and variety of goal alternation though this is not necessary, and behavior depends on both IF and instructions, which are sufficiently related to be considered together in the preceding chapter.

Positioning work on goal shifts falls into three groups. (1) Countertraining, in which subjects first acquire an R of given amplitude and then, without instruction, receive $IF_n = (R_n - R+) + nb$ on successive trials. Figure 7 summarizes a countertraining treatment, the "Goal"

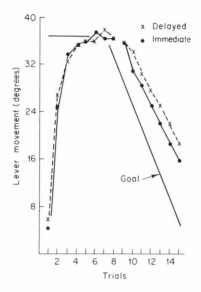

Fig. 7. Goal shifts: countertraining. R–IF transformation (Goal) and its effects on R amplitude in countertraining trials given at 1-week intervals with IF immediate or delayed (1 week). Training trials to the constant goal were given in one closely-spaced block and with immediate IF. (After Ryan & Bilodeau, 1962.)

line, and its outcome. (The immediate-delayed distinction can be ignored). After eight lever training trials, 20 units (4°) were added to the obtained discrepancy (from R+ = 180 units) on the first countertraining trial, 40 units on the second, etc. The first modified IF shortened R (R_9 in Fig. 7) and further countertraining continued to reduce R amplitude. However, the subjects did not anticipate the next modification in IF, but corrected for the last error signal, and undercorrected, even when scored for following, rather than anticipating. While R+ = 180-20n on the nth trial of countertraining, R_n approximated 180-15(n-1), rather than either the 180-20n of perfect anticipatory correction or the 180-20(n-1) of perfect following. (2) Unsystematic goal changes from trial to trial, the subject told to guess each trial's goal, usually test the properties of specific feedback models, but make the point of other transformations: that the reported difference between R and R+ controls R change. Rosenberg (1963), for example, found good agreement between the distributions of goals and R's with a knob-turning task. In one of Rosenberg's treatments, the standard deviation of the distribution of goals was 3 times that of another, a difference comparable to a difference in magnitude of two IE treatments, and with like effects. The within-subject variance under the large error-signal exceeded variance under the smaller through 15 10-trial blocks. (3) Systematic cyclical, goal-alternation over blocks of trials, the subject not told that his goal will change, as in a lever study by E. A. Bilodeau (1952) that varied magnitude and direction of goal shift between alternate 5-trial blocks and found both effective. All groups had $f_1 = R$ in block 1, shifted to different f_2's, $R + b$, in block 2, returned to f_1 in block 3, etc. In the unmodified blocks (f_1), all groups approached the common R+, and in modified (f_2) blocks they diverged. Undershoot IF's (negative values of b) increased R in proportion to their absolute value; overshoots produced proportional decreases in R, as in counter-training. There was no learning-to-learn transfer over cycles; amplitude change from R_n to R_{n+1} with a shift in goal was more related to R_n and IF_n than to ordinal number of the cycle. A second experiment (E. A. Bilodeau, 1953a) varied the number of trials in a cycle. Again R changed with every goal shift, but not enough for a hit; as trials in the new block continued, obtained R's more closely approximated the new R+. When R+ changed in single-trial cycles, obtained R tended toward a compromise halfway between the two goals, with decreasing between-trial variability from the first to the last shift. Less obvious, but apparent, damping trends appeared in the behavior of groups with 2-, 4-, 6-, and 8-trial cycles, where the final R in successive cycles was slightly closer to an R intermediate between the alternate goals. In two-choice situations the relative probabilities of the two choices being correct influences the subjects toward a probability-matching solution (Estes, 1964). But when a compromise in R amplitude is possible, some compromise is taken, minimizing the frequency of very large reported discrepancies between required and obtained R's. While change from R_n to R_{n+1} at points of shift was clearly related to IF_n, the damping is an example of residuals of prior experience acting to control behavior.

D. Transformation Comment

Both scale-grain and full-scale transformations have been studied in tracking (see Hunt, 1964, for good examples) and the transfer of training literature provides evidence of the effects of many ways of shifting the R-IF relation (see Chapter 7). Some obviously comparable manipulations, scale grain, for example (Hunt, 1961), affect tracking much as positioning. Others fit one of our major classes — for example, the choice of compensatory or following display (Hartman & Fitts, 1955; Poulton, Chapter 10) is a continuous transformation — but have meaningful subclass labels already assigned them in the tracking literature. *Goal-shifts* makes little sense where the required R varies throughout a trial, though display noise, changing the tracking pattern, and shifting control-display relations all have some analogy to varying R+; the reader should refer to Chapters 7 and 10 for tracking transformations and to Chapter 4 for a cybernetic treatment of displacements in general.

For nonmotor tasks, again, there are likenesses and differences, but certainly transformation treatments (Bourne, 1966, pp. 310–311). A very common transformation is *infirming* and *confirming* IF in choice or discrimination tasks. These are R-contingent treatments, closely related to, and sometimes crossed with, frequency (Levine, 1966; Bourne *et al.*, 1967), that demonstrate that an error signal is critical for R-change and improvement. Bourne (1966, pp. 308–309) and Bourne *et al.* (1967) have excellent, brief, critical summaries of the variety of interpretations of the characteristic result. The usual procedure is for the subject to choose one of two or more discrete alternatives — select a word from each pair in a list, or sort a deck of cards into 2, 3, or 4 categories; R's are scored as correct or incorrect; in the standard r (confirming) condition "right" follows correct R's and the experimenter is silent after wrong choices; in the standard w (infirming) condition, "wrong" follows incorrect choices, nothing correct choices.

The *wn* combination characteristically scores as well as the control ("right" for correct and "wrong" for incorrect R's) and the *nr* combination scores worse. The earlier emphasis on differential reinforcing values for "right" and "wrong" has been yielding to information processing and absolute frequency accounts (Bourne *et al.*, 1967) as experimental design and data analysis have become more sophisticated.

The primary factor in the typical outcome by the usual scoring methods seems, however, to be the contingency of R-change on IF's signaling that R is in error. Transformation studies show that (1) a person changes what he is doing when he gets a signal that what he is doing is wrong (whether it is or not), and (2) continues what he is doing (within task-dependent limits) when he gets a signal that his behavior is not in error. The frequency studies add to this that (3) behavior does not change (again within limits) when there is no signal at all; though n is an R-contingent cue and can acquire directive properties, it has none at first and in early trials can be considered equivalent to omitting IF. Table I spells out the implications of these three generalizations for the differences in scores to be expected in the usual three combinations of r, w, and n when the subject chooses one of two

Table I

ILLUSTRATION OF CHANGE IN PROBABILITY OF R's SCORED CORRECT
AND INCORRECT WITH RIGHT (r), WRONG (w), AND NOTHING (n) IF.[a,b]
ENTRIES ARE HYPOTHETICAL PROBABILITIES OF R+ AND R−.

IF	Trial	R-contingency					
		wn		*nr*		*wr*	
		R+	R−	R+	R−	R+	R−
w → change	1		.50				.50
	2	.50				.50	
r → repeat	1			.50		.50	
	2				.50		.50
n → no change	1	.50		.50			
	2	.50			.50		
	Trial 1	.50	.50	.50	.50	.50	.50
	Trial 2	.00	1.00	.50	.50	1.00	.00

[a]Entries are hypothetical probabilities of R+ and R−.
[b]Arrows in the body of the table indicate into which R_2 scoring category a given class
of R_1's is expected to fall.

items and several pairs of items define a trial. Table I assumes that the
probabilities of correct and incorrect R's are equal on Trial 1 and (less
reasonably) that the rules work perfectly. In this oversimplified hypothetical example, both the infirming and the control groups are 100%
correct in their choices on the second trial, while the confirming
treatment remains at the 50% level. Clearly, this effect is a scoring artifact for any interpretation of score differences in terms of "wrong" as
more potent as a punisher than "correct" as a satisfier; for such an interpretation, scores for choices followed by nothing are irrelevant,
whereas in Table I it is the difference in the scores for "nothing"
choices that makes the difference between infirming and confirming conditions. The effectiveness of "wrong" vs "correct" is at
issue but choices are equally correct on Trial 2 regardless of whether
they were wrong on Trial 1 and followed by "wrong" or correct and
followed by "correct." Moreover, we can predict the rank orders of
confirming, infirming, and control treatments without recourse to differential strengths of reinforcement for "right" and "wrong."

Though the kind of situation Table I presumes seems unlikely to
provide a critical test, Spence (1964) using just such a situation did
find evidence in accord with the present account. Plotting percent
correct over trials, and breaking down not only by treatment group,
but according to whether items were correct or incorrect on the last

trial, showed little or no treatment differences for items correct on the preceding trial, and a large treatment difference for items scored incorrect on the preceding trial, i.e., if the choice was correct it was just as likely to be correct next time when the experimenter said nothing after the choice as when he said "right"; but if the choice was wrong, the choice on the next trial was much more likely to be correct after "wrong" than after nothing. Spence concluded that these and earlier data can be explained by nothing's acquiring information value more rapidly with w than r feedback; if so, the rate of information gain is likely a function of the error signal's getting the subject to change his R. Certainly giving meaning from the start by telling the subjects that right (wrong) R's will not be followed by "correct" ("wrong") wipes out the difference between wn and nr (Spence, Lair, & Goodstein, 1963).

Levine (1966), has a neat illustration of the $w \rightarrow$ change, $r \rightarrow$ repeat, $n \rightarrow$ no change expectation under conditions where n cannot acquire r- or w-meaning. That Bourne *et al.* (1967) were able to relate performance to total number of IF's w's and/or r's, by varying the proportion of both r and w signals, suggests that we may need to combine R-change and frequency accounts.

IV. Locus

Locus means IF's position in the trial cycle and includes three intervals (see Fig. 1): delay—time from R_n to IF_n; post-IF—time from IF_n to R_{n+1}; and interresponse—the sum of delay and post-IF intervals, time from R_n to R_{n+1}.

Delay of IF is the only interval with a lengthy history, a history of dispute, attributable to enthusiastic misapplication of gradients of food delay from instrumental conditioning. Though conditioning sought variables that controlled slope and extent of *gradients*, human learning looked for one gradient of IF delay corresponding to one food-delay gradient. Champion and McBride (1962) point out also that R-error measures are used with human, latency with animal subjects; their latency measure, though delay and interpolated activity were confounded, did yield delay of IF effects. For both feedback and food, moreover, systematic thinkers have doubted the effectiveness of (empty) delay alone. Human positioning studies reinforce their doubts. Less of the controversy can be blamed on conflicting data despite the fact that only the delay interval was considered until recently, while adequately designed studies of positioning and other simple tasks find only the other two intervals of consequence.

A. EMPTY INTERVALS

Lorge and Thorndike (1935) used a simple task, discrete trials, and IF_n before R_{n+1} ". . . to discover the effect of sheer empty delay . . . ," and intervals without deliberately introduced activity are the standard here for much the same reason. Later parts of this section cover intervals filled with other than our minimum standard, the subject's normal activities.

Though there are three intervals to consider, they are confounded in Fig. 1 and their effects cannot be separated without careful experimental design. Fixing two determines the third; if one is held constant, varying one of the others varies both. If the interresponse interval stays constant, for example, the post-IF period shortens as delay lengthens, and behavioral effects can as reasonably be assigned to the post-IF as the delay variable. Current designs control the three intervals in several ways. For example, a subject can get IF and later a reminder of IF to hold post-IF interval constant (from the reminder) as interresponse or delay interval varies; a single experiment can have three sets of treatments, a different one of the three intervals constant from set to set; if one of the intervals has an expected optimal value, it can be held at its presumed optimum as the other two are covaried to see if either is effective. Positioning studies using these techniques report that lengthening the interresponse interval (E. A. Bilodeau & Bilodeau, 1958b; Denny, Allard, Hall, & Rokeach, 1960) or shortening the post-IF interval has adverse effects on performance (Weinberg, Guy, & Tupper, 1964).

Neither recent nor older studies give much empirical support to a gradient of delay in positioning, or in other tasks where the subject learns a single R and gets IF before he has to use it. The outcome in Fig. 8 is typical, the difference between delayed and immediate treatments in Fig. 7 is not, and the experimenters attributed their .05 level difference to chance. Very crudely, the fading-trace notion considered only delay and presumed that the hypothetical trace of R_n decayed over time; if R_n was correct, immediate IF stamped in a connection at a trace level similar to the trace at the time R+ was made, and delayed IF stamped in at a very different trace level. If IF was wrong, stamping out happened with traces like and unlike the wrong-R trace for immediate and delayed IF, respectively. But R_n is not the only event that can decay or be interfered with; IF, alternative R's, and the new

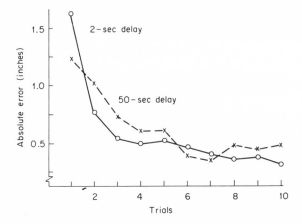

Fig. 8. The ineffectiveness of empty delay of IF in positioning. Mean error against trials, with short and long delay. (Based on data in Larré, 1961.)

dominant tendency are all at least potentially susceptible to forgetting (E. A. Bilodeau *et al.*, 1962; E. A. Bilodeau & Levy, 1964). Time after as well as before must be considered: it takes time to take in IF_n and plan R_{n+1}; and the interresponse interval is always taken into account when there are at least two trials.

B. INTERPOLATED ACTIVITY

Delaying IF can reduce positioning accuracy when the delay interval exceeds the interresponse interval, displacing IF by one or more R's (trials-delay). For example, with a 1-trial delay the sequence is R_1, $R_2 - IF_1$, $R_3 - IF_2$, ... $R_n - IF_{n-1}$; with a 3-trial delay the sequence is R_1, R_2, R_3, $R_4 - IF_1$, ... $R_n - IF_{n-3}$. Accuracy improves over successive IF's even with 5-trial delays, but is better the less the trials-delay, though the subjects know about the displacements (I. McD. Bilodeau, 1956). The writer suggested that making other R's between R_n and IF_n increases the opportunity for interference and confusion, analogous to the demands on the subject in tracking with lag. Larré (1961), however, showed that merely making R's did not matter, at least when subjects were told in advance which R's would have IF. Even 6 R's without IF, made either before IF_n (with 50-seconds delay in IF), or after IF_n (with 2-seconds delay), did not influence the accuracy of R_{n+1}. There was no effect at all, much less a differential effect for locus (delay or post-IF interval) of interpolated activity. Larré's subjects held R amplitude constant over R's without IF, changing R only immediately after IF (as in other relative frequency treatments) so that confusing the R to which IF belonged could not have serious consequences. R-change cued by IF seems to be critical for the combined effect of delay and interpolated R's under trials-delay treatment.

Less has been done with interpolated activity in the post-IF interval. Larré (above) varied number of R's without IF interpolated between IF_n and R_{n+1} and Blick and E. A. Bilodeau (1963) varied the amplitude of a forced interpolated R, both without effect, but Boswell and E. A. Bilodeau (1964) introduced set-breaking activity into the post-IF interval and found it effective. The best present guess is that it will not be easy to find successful manipulations, but that there are some. Goal-shift studies (interpolated R-IF pairs between trial-blocks) also offer reason for optimism.

C. Locus Comment

Whenever the experimenter uses the sequence of within-trial events schematized in Fig. 1, the delay aspect of locus is irrelevant and the post-IF interval can be important. Recent attempts to replicate the rare positive delay outcomes of the past have not been successful (Bourne, 1966, pp. 304–305), nor, except in positioning, does the interresponse interval seem to have important effects separable from the problem-solving activity of the post-IF interval (Bourne, Dodd, Guy, & Justesen, 1968).

The first thorough investigation of the post-IF interval and good demonstration of its significance were in concept identification where delay of IF yielded null results (Bourne & Bunderson, 1963). Later research in concept and verbal tasks has borne out and extended the original work to show important interactions with task complexity, feedback mode, and interpolated activity (Bourne, 1966, pp. 302–308; Jones, 1968). Simple, uncomplicated delay of IF does not work; lengthening the post-IF period (which subjects presumably fill with their own thinking activity) improves performance, though there is an optimum length, varying with task complexity, beyond which performance falls off.

The picture for delay is very different in tracking, handwriting, or speech. When the subject responds continuously to a continuously changing display, or waits until the end of a series of R's for his IF, lag in the R-IF sequence is disruptive (Chapter 10; Section VI, B). Even in positioning, concurrent IF is superior to terminal. Figure 9 shows how trial-and-error learning profits from (serial) IF after each choice compared with (terminal) IF at the end of a series of choices.

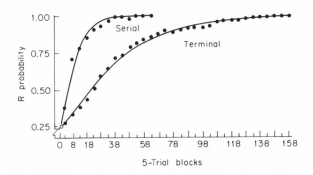

Fig. 9. An effect of delay and interpolated R's. Probability of a correct R in trial-and-error practice with serial and terminal IF. (After Noble & Noble, 1958.)

Continuous-R tasks, however, do not test the effects of empty time (of which few psychologists expect much), though they do point to significant variables that can fill the time between R and its IF. To correct a present tracking error on the basis of a displayed error partly determined by present preprogrammed input, partly by past R output, would require separating the two, remembering both past program- and R-input, and estimating the effects of intervening R's for which there has not yet been feedback. Any variable that reduces the accuracy of short-term prediction is detrimental to tracking performance (Conklin, 1957), and human beings are imperfect at keeping account of past events (Pollack & Johnson, 1964) or extrapolating target courses (Battig *et al.*, 1955).

V. Augmented IF

Here augmented IF has the same meaning as artificial, extra, or supplementary IF and implies no distinction between (1) extrinsic and intrinsic R-consequences that are natural or necessary to responding or (2) IF's that enhance learning and those that benefit performance (see Holding, 1965). Supplementary IF is any R-contingent stimulus added to a standard task, the standard task defined either arbitrarily or by its usual form. If a click and the words "a hit" accompany R+ in the standard task, adding a flashing light after R+ (or after errors of larger than 20 units) augments IF. If standard IF is "a hit" and a new version of the apparatus adds a click for R+, the click version has extra IF. Because studies of augmented IF test for residual effects of augmented training in standard test, they can be treated in transfer of training (Chapter 7) or under shifting the R-IF transformation.

A. Terminal versus Concurrent IF

Training and transfer effects in positioning can be very briefly summarized at the present stage because of the uniformity of treatment from experiment to experiment. The standard task offers terminal IF; for example, after the subject turns a knob his display lights up and he can see the position of his R marker relative to the target. Augmented IF is concurrent; for example, the subject can watch his R marker move toward the target throughout R's course — and score hits on every trial. Experimental groups, trained with augmented IF, are tested for transfer to the standard task, or augmented- and standard-trained groups are compared in tests without IF. Procedural variations concern mapping or patterning various combinations of augmented, standard, forced, and non-IF trials. While it is present, the augmented IF increases accuracy, but standard training yields superior accuracy in either a standard test or one without IF. Transfer of training from augmented to standard IF in positioning is positive, however, and increases with the number of preshift trials.

B. Augmented Comment

Most of the augmented-IF effort in positioning asks how training cues bear on how well subjects manage later on with minimal R-contingent cues. This question's similarity to the heavy skills question about kinds of manipulations that bear on the later effectiveness of standard IF justifies lumping together two quite different sets of IF transformations. Augmented tracking tasks include the standard IF (for example, distance between target and follower on a display screen — not always "a hit") and an additional transformation of the R-error (say, a tone when the R is within certain limits of R+). A standard-trained control group is compared with augmented-trained groups in a standard test for transfer of training, but experimental designs frequently shift from standard to augmented IF as well. The augmented cues have been continuous and discrete, delayed and immediate, on-target and off-target, mapped in various proportions (relative frequency of augmented IF) with standard-only IF, etc. Outcomes are correspondingly more diverse in continuous-R tasks, but are briefly summarized here because two other chapters (Chapters 7 and 8) consider them. The variety of results likely depends on variables in the augmented IF (Williams & Briggs, 1962) and variables that could be controlled in the standard task (I. McD. Bilodeau, 1966, p. 277).

During training, augmented IF for continuous performance is not always superior to standard; for example, novices at the piano or typewriter make fewer errors when they watch their hands (augmented, visual, reactive IF), but the final ceiling of performance is much higher under standard (touch) than augmented (sight) IF. Laboratory comparisons often find adding extra IF beneficial to scores in training, perhaps because so many use the Pedestal Sight Manipulation Test with its notoriously poor standard IF. Extra IF has less effect on devices in which standard IF is not so obviously poor; there are cases of no difference, better, and even worse performance. The between-experiment differences during training (while the supplementary signal is present) suggest the standard task's importance. Obviously, if standard performance is good, if attention is not divided over several displays, if the standard R-IF function is near optimal, etc., there is little room for profit from extra IF. Some start has been made toward identifying relevant variables in standard IF (Kinkade, 1963) and relating over all and component performance to extra IF for single components of multicomponent tasks (E. A. Bilodeau, 1955b), but most of what can be done awaits exploration.

Residual effects of training treatments appear in the large amounts of positive transfer from augmented to standard and standard to augmented IF. When the extra IF has an advantage in training, much of the advantage is, usually, lost with a shift to standard IF and the residual continues to shrink as the standard test continues. (See I. McD. Bilodeau, 1966, pp. 276–278.)

Predicting how standard tests will rank augmented- and standard-trained groups requires a combination of what we need to know about the standard task to predict training, and about variables in the augmented IF itself. Chapter 8 gives an idea of the conflicting positions possible. Even an information view of adding another IF transformation that works must take into account at least three possibilities. (1) The extra IF might add a second set of independent R's cued only when the extra IF is present and therefore irrelevant to the test. (2) Extra IF might help in interpreting the standard (also given), and benefit training- and later standard-performance. (Extra and standard IF could, of course, be conflicting cues to the direction and amplitude of R-change required to correct an error, to the detriment of training and test.) (3) Augmented IF might provide the dominant cues to error correction, leaving the subject in the standard test with cues that he has not learned to respond to in training. There are hints of all three in continuous R studies, but further discussion is not profitable without evidence from deliberately manipulated standard and augmented variables.

VI. Summary

Information feedback (IF) is defined as an independent variable and as any function of the discrepancy between the R made and the R required. The function relates IF to R by some transformation in space, time, degree, number of different functions presented together, etc. The four research areas reviewed support the conclusion that IF determines whether subjects will continue with or change their behavior.

1. Frequency treatments show that behavior changes and improves only when IF is present. Positioning findings also show residual effects of past IF's.

2. Scale transformations relate direction and amplitude of behavior change to direction and magnitude of reported error, emphasizing the importance of the present IF. Even a single large reported error can shift subjects away from a well-established positioning R; and it is a common conclusion in tracking that skill is more a matter of reacting quickly to displayed error than of acquiring fixed sequences of R's.

3. Locus includes more than delay of IF. Unfilled (and sometimes filled) delay from R to IF is ineffective. Accuracy does decline when the subject must make his next R before he has IF for the last R as a cue to the required modification in behavior, and temporal lag in continuous-R tasks is damaging to performance. The wait from one IF to the next R is an effective variable in many tasks and the total time between adjacent R's affects the accuracy of simple motor R's.

4. Augmented IF has different effects from task to task, both while the extra IF is present and in tests after it is removed. These inconsistencies should become predictable effects of IF when the R-IF transformations of both augmented IF and IF in the standard task are controlled.

References

Bahrick, H. P., Fitts, P. M., & Schneider, R. Reproduction of simple movements as a function of factors influencing proprioceptive feedback. *Journal of Experimental Psychology*, 1955, 49, 445–454.

Battig, W. F., Voss, J. F., & Brogden, W. J. Effect of frequency of target intermittence upon tracking. *Journal of Experimental Psychology*, 1955, **49**, 244–248.

Bilodeau, E. A. Some effects of modification of information about a previous response upon the acquisition of two lever positioning habits. *USAF Human Resources Research Center Research Bulletin*, 1952, No. 52–1.

Bilodeau, E. A. Acquisition of two lever-positioning responses practiced over several periods of alternation. *Journal of Experimental Psychology*, 1953, **46**, 43–49. (a)

Bilodeau, E. A. Speed of acquiring a simple motor response as a function of the systematic transformation of knowledge of results. *American Journal of Psychology*, 1953, **66**, 409–420. (b)

Bilodeau, E. A. Motor performance as affected by magnitude and direction of error contained in knowledge of results. *Journal of Psychology*, 1955, **40**, 103–113. (a)

Bilodeau, E. A. Variations in knowledge of component performance and its effects upon part-part and part-whole relations. *Journal of Experimental Psychology*, 1955, **50**, 215–224. (b)

Bilodeau, E. A., & Bilodeau, I. McD. Variable frequency of knowledge of results and the learning of a simple skill. *Journal of Experimental Psychology*, 1958, **55**, 379–383. (a)

Bilodeau, E. A., & Bilodeau, I. McD. Variation of temporal intervals among critical events in five studies of knowledge of results. *Journal of Experimental Psychology*, 1958, **55**, 603–612. (b)

Bilodeau, E. A., & Bilodeau, I. McD. Motor-skills learning. *Annual Review of Psychology*, 1961, **12**, 243–280.

Bilodeau, E. A., Bilodeau, I. McD., & Schumsky, D. A. Some effects of introducing and withdrawing knowledge of results early and late in practice. *Journal of Experimental Psychology*, 1959, **58**, 142–144.

Bilodeau, E. A., & Levy, C. M. Long-term memory as a function of retention time and other conditions of training and recall. *Psychological Review*, 1964, **71**, 27–41.

Bilodeau, E. A., & Rosenbach, J. H. Acquisition of response proficiency as a function of rounding error in informative feedback. *USAF Human Resources Research Center Research Bulletin*, 1953, No. 53–21.

Bilodeau, E. A., Sulzer, J. L., & Levy, C. M. Theory and data on the interrelationships of three factors of memory. *Psychological Monographs*, 1962, **76**, No. 20 (Whole No. 539).

Bilodeau, I. McD. Accuracy of a simple positioning response with variation in the number of trials by which knowledge of results is delayed. *American Journal of Psychology*, 1956, **69**, 434–437.

Bilodeau, I. McD. Information feedback. In E. A. Bilodeau (Ed.), *Acquisition of skill.* New York: Academic Press, 1966. Pp. 255–296.

Blick, K. A., & Bilodeau, E. A. Interpolated activity and the learning of a simple skill. *Journal of Experimental Psychology*, 1963, **65**, 515–519.

Boswell, J. J., & Bilodeau, E. A. Short-term retention of a simple motor task as a function of interpolated activity. *Perceptual and Motor Skills*, 1964, **18**, 227–230.

Bourne, L. E., Jr. Comments on Professor I. McD. Bilodeau's paper, Information feedback. In E. A. Bilodeau (Ed.), *Acquisition of skill.* New York: Academic Press, 1966, Pp. 297–313.

Bourne, L. E., Jr., & Bunderson, C. V. Effects of delay of informative feedback and length of postfeedback interval on concept identification. *Journal of Experimental Psychology*, 1963, **65**, 1–5.

Bourne, L. E., Jr., Dodd, D. H., Guy, D. E., & Justesen, D. R. Response-contingent intertrial intervals in concept identification. *Journal of Experimental Psychology,* 1968, **76**, 601–608.

Bourne, L. E., Jr., Guy, D. E., & Wadsworth, N. Verbal-reinforcement combinations and the relative frequency of informative feedback in a card-sorting task. *Journal of Experimental Psychology,* 1967, **73**, 220–226.

Bourne, L. E., Jr., & Pendleton, R. B. Concept identification as a function of completeness and probability of information feedback. *Journal of Experimental Psychology,* 1958, **56**, 413–420.

Champion, R. A., & McBride, D. A. Activity during delay of reinforcement in human learning. *Journal of Experimental Psychology,* 1962, **63**, 589–592.

Chinn, R. McC., & Alluisi, E. A. Effect of three kinds of knowledge-of-results information on three measures of vigilance performance. *Perceptual and Motor Skills,* 1964, **18**, 901–912.

Conklin, J. E. Effect of control lag on performance in a tracking task. *Journal of Experimental Psychology,* 1957, **53**, 261–268.

Denny, M. R., Allard, M., Hall, E., & Rokeach, M. Supplementary report: Delay of knowledge of results, knowledge of task, and intertrial interval. *Journal of Experimental Psychology,* 1960, **60**, 327.

Estes, W. K. Probability learning. In A. W. Melton (Ed.), *Categories of human learning.* New York: Academic Press, 1964. Pp. 90–128.

Fitts, P. M. Perceptual-motor skill learning. In A. W. Melton (Ed.), *Categories of human learning.* New York: Academic Press, 1964. Pp. 244–285.

Gould, J. D. Differential visual feedback of component motions. *Journal of Experimental Psychology,* 1965, **69**, 263–268.

Hartman, B. O., & Fitts, P. M. Relation of stimulus and response amplitude to tracking performance. *Journal of Experimental Psychology,* 1955, **49**, 82–92.

Holding, D. H. *Principles of training.* New York: Macmillan (Pergamon), 1965.

Hunt, D. P. The effect of the precision of informational feedback on human tracking performance. *Human Factors,* 1961, **3**, 77–85.

Hunt, D. P. Effects of nonlinear and discrete transformations of feedback information on human tracking performance. *Journal of Experimental Psychology,* 1964, **67**, 486–494.

Jones, R. E., Jr. Effects of delay of informative feedback, postfeedback interval, and feedback presentation mode on verbal paired-associates learning. *Journal of Experimental Psychology,* 1968, **77**, 87–93.

Kinkade, R. G. A differential influence of augmented feedback on learning and on performance. *USAF WADC Technical Report,* 1963, No. 63–12.

Larré, E. E. Interpolated activity before and after knowledge of results. Unpublished doctoral dissertation, Tulane Univer., 1961.

Levine, M. Hypothesis behavior by humans during discrimination learning. *Journal of Experimental Psychology,* 1966, **71**, 331–338.

Lincoln, R. S. Learning and retaining a rate of movement with the aid of kinesthetic and verbal cues. *Journal of Experimental Psychology,* 1956, **51**, 199–204.

Lorge, I., & Thorndike, E. L. The influence of delay in the after-effect of a connection. *Journal of Experimental Psychology,* 1935, **18**, 186–194.

Noble, C. E., & Noble, J. L. Human trial-and-error learning under joint variation of locus of reward and type of pacing. *Journal of Experimental Psychology,* 1958, **56**, 103–109.

Pearson, R. G., & Hauty, G. T. Role of postural experiences in proprioceptive perception of verticality. *Journal of Experimental Psychology,* 1960, **59**, 425–428.

Pollack, I., & Johnson, L. Keeping track of the immediately past states of variables. *Perceptual and Motor Skills*, 1964, **18**, 55–58.

Poulton, E. C. On the stimulus and response in pursuit tracking. *Journal of Experimental Psychology*, 1957, **53**, 189–194.

Rosenberg, S. Behavior in a continuous-response task with noncontingent reinforcement. *Journal of Experimental Psychology*, 1963, **66**, 168–176.

Ryan, F. J., & Bilodeau, E. A. Countertraining of a simple skill with immediate and 1-week delays of informative feedback. *Journal of Experimental Psychology*, 1962, **63**, 19–22.

Schumsky, D. A. The use of transformations of knowledge of results with negative slope on a simple motor response. Unpublished master's thesis, Tulane Univer., 1959.

Smith, K. U. *Delayed sensory feedback and behavior*. Philadelphia: Saunders, 1962.

Spence, J. T. Verbal discrimination performance under different verbal reinforcement combinations. *Journal of Experimental Psychology*, 1964, **67**, 195–197.

Spence, J. T., Lair, C. V., & Goodstein, L. D. Effects of different feedback conditions on verbal discrimination learning in schizophrenic and nonpsychiatric subjects. *Journal of Verbal Learning and Verbal Behavior*, 1963, **2**, 339–345.

Taylor, A., & Noble, C. E. Acquisition and extinction phenomena in human trial-and-error learning under different schedules of reinforcing feedback. *Perceptual and Motor Skills*, 1962, **15**, 31–44.

Trowbridge, M. H., & Cason, H. An experimental study of Thorndike's theory of learning. *Journal of General Psychology*, 1932, **7**, 245–260.

Weinberg, D. R., Guy, D. E., & Tupper, R. W. Variation of postfeedback interval in simple motor learning. *Journal of Experimental Psychology*, 1964, **67**, 98–99.

Williams, A. C., & Briggs, G. E. On-target versus off-target information and the acquisition of tracking skill. *Journal of Experimental Psychology*, 1962, **64**, 519–525.

CHAPTER 10 _____

Tracking

E. C. POULTON
Medical Research Council,
Applied Psychology Research Unit
Cambridge

I. Introduction

In *pursuit* tracking the man has to keep a response marker in line with a moving target. The display on the left of Fig. 1(A) contains a spot labeled "track," which moves up and down. The man tries to keep the short horizontal line superimposed upon it, so that both move up and down together. In the psychological laboratory the pursuit rotor presents a simplified version of pursuit tracking. The student holds one end of a loosely hinged stylus. The other end rests by gravity on a horizontal platform, and has to be kept in contact with a small rotating target (Ammons, 1955).

In *compensatory* tracking there is only one moving element. This has to be held stationary over a fixed reference mark, from which it tends to move away. The display on the left of Fig. 1(B) contains a spot labeled "error," which moves up and down. The man tries to keep it on the fixed horizontal line. Imagine holding the needle of the speedometer of a car stationary at a given point on the scale. This is done by driving at a fixed speed, and is an example of compensatory tracking. In both pursuit and compensatory tracking a continuous disturbance is normally fed into the display. Here it will be called the "track" or "input," but engineers usually call it the "forcing function."

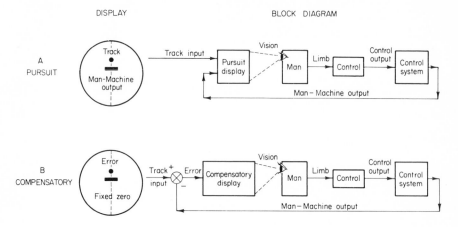

Fig. 1. Displays and block diagrams for (A) pursuit and (B) compensatory tracking. In pursuit tracking the track and the man have separate markers. The man has to keep his marker (the short horizontal line in the display above on the left) superimposed upon the track marker (the round spot). In compensatory tracking there is only one moving display marker (the round spot). This shows the difference between the movements produced by the track and by the man. The moving marker has to be held stationary on the fixed line.

In *acquisition* tracking the target and response marker usually start stationary and superimposed. One of them suddenly steps to a new position, and the man has to superimpose the marker on the target again. Acquisition tracking can be regarded as a special case of pursuit or compensatory tracking in which the track consists of steps separated by periods of no movement.

Two other kinds of tracking have received less attention in the laboratory. Both involve a track extended in space like a wiggly line or road. The commonest in everyday life can be called "self-paced contour" tracking. Here the man moves along the track at his own speed. Examples are tracing the contour of a map with a pencil, and driving a car along a narrow wiggly road.

In *paced contour* tracking the man moves along the track at a predetermined speed. For example he may steer a car which has been engineered to travel at a fixed speed. Figure 2 shows a laboratory example. Here the track is drawn on a paper tape which approaches at a fixed speed. The man controls a stylus or marker which moves across the paper tape at right angles to its direction of approach. He has to keep the marker superimposed upon the wiggly track as it passes. In both kinds of contour tracking the man can normally see the track some distance ahead. When this preview is taken away the task resembles pursuit tracking.

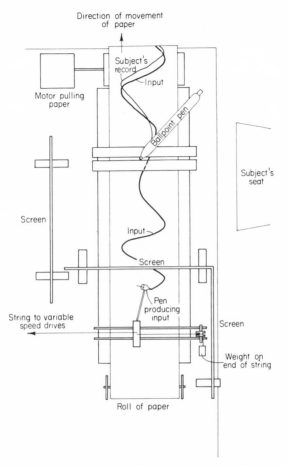

Fig. 2. An experimental arrangement used in paced contour tracking, seen from above. The paper tape moves up the figure at a fixed speed. At the bottom of the figure a pen draws a wiggly track on the paper. This comes into view from behind a screen. The experimental subject holds a ball-point pen in the groove formed by two bars of transparent Plexiglass. He attempts to keep the tip of the pen on the wiggly track as it passes. (After Poulton, 1964.)

II. Characteristics of tracking Tasks

A. Precision of Movement

All behavior can be said to involve decision and action. The study of selective motor learning is concerned mainly with decision. The man may have to decide which one of four buttons to press, or in which of four directions to move a lever. His error is determined by whether the response selected is the correct one or not. The button or lever has simply to be moved sufficiently far to make an electrical contact. The exact distance it moves and the exact force exerted on it by the man are not considered.

In contrast the study of tracking is concerned more with the execution of the response. Here error is assessed in terms of the precision of the movement, the exact distance moved or the exact force exerted. The man is usually supplied with only one control; he does not have to choose between controls as he often does in selective motor learning. Thus studies in selective motor learning and in tracking emphasize different aspects of motor behavior.

B. TIMING

In selective motor learning the man is usually required to respond as quickly as possible, and his response time is measured. The same applies to acquisition tracking. But in all other kinds of tracking the response required depends upon the time taken to make it. At any instant the man has to make a movement of a required size, but the required size changes all the time (see Fig. 2). Making the correct size of movement either too early or too late is equivalent to making the wrong size of movement, and is penalized accordingly.

C. THE INDEPENDENT VARIABLES

In an experiment on tracking the experimenter has to decide what kind of track he is going to use, what kind of display, what kind of control, and what kind of control-system dynamics. These independent variables are represented by the block diagrams of Fig. 1. In each case the experimenter has to select from a number of possible alternatives, and his experimental results will be determined by his choices. In this chapter it will be assumed that independent variables other than the one under discussion have values which complicate the picture as little as possible. The independent variables do interact, but the effects of the isolated variables must be understood before looking at the interactions.

III. The Track

A. ISOLATED STEPS AND BALLISTIC RESPONSES

Acquisition tracking has the advantage that the visual stimulus to which the man responds can be defined precisely. One of the display markers suddenly steps to a new position, and he has to restore alignment as quickly as possible. When the man cannot anticipate the stimulus, his reaction time is almost independent of the size of the step. But with a simple lever control his rate of movement and acceleration vary with the amplitude of the step, being greater for larger steps (Searle & Taylor, 1948; Taylor & Birmingham, 1948). The man's first shot at restoring alignment tends to be accurate to within about ± 10%. If an appreciable error remains and he has plenty of time, he may have another shot. This also will be accurate to within about ± 10% of the misalignment it is correcting (Craik, 1947).

It seems clear from the consistent pattern of acceleration of the movement, and from the short time of about .2 second which it normally takes, that the movement is carried out without voluntary monitoring. The display can be covered up while the movement is being made without affecting its accuracy (Craik, 1947). Thus the movement must be prepared in advance and triggered off as a unit. Craik described it as a ballistic movement. The right portion of Fig. 3 illustrates what happens if the experimenter unexpectedly alters the apparatus and thereby tricks the man into making the wrong movement. It takes him almost .3 second after he notices that something is wrong

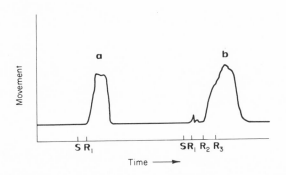

Fig. 3. Oscillographic chart illustrating the reaction time for the amendment of a response. The man heard a click, the time of which is marked S on the chart. He had then to pull a lever, which required a force of about 3 ounces, to move a pen over to a marked position. A typical response labeled *a* is shown on the left. On rather less than a quarter of the trials a solenoid unexpectedly operated as soon as the lever started to move. This increased the load on the lever to about 20 ounces, and required a more powerful response labeled *b* on the right. For three experimental subjects the mean reaction time to the click (the time between S and R_1 on the chart) was .21 second. The mean reaction time to the increased load on the lever (the time between R_1 and R_2) was .30 second. The response in the figure at time R_2 was not powerful enough to move the pen as far as the marked position, and a third response had to be made at a time R_3 which is difficult to specify. (After Hick, 1949.)

before he can correct it. By this time the initial movement will normally have been completed (Hick, 1949).

B. Pairs of Steps and the Psychological Refractory Period

When the stimulus of a second step is presented within about .5 second after a previous stimulus, the second response is likely to be delayed. The man may not expect a second stimulus so soon, and may not be ready for it (Poulton, 1950). But if the interval between the two stimuli is less than about .2 second, the response to the second stimulus will be delayed by about .1 second even when the man is expecting to have to make a second response at this time. This has led to the concept of a psychological refractory period comparable to the refractory period of an isolated nerve, but of longer duration (see Welford, 1967).

The psychological refractory period can be investigated by presenting the man with one of two possible stimuli, to which he has to make the appropriate response perhaps with his left hand. Soon afterward the man is presented with one of two more possible stimuli, to which he has to make the appropriate response with the other hand. When the interval between the two presented stimuli is .3 second or longer, the second response need not be delayed if the man has had sufficient practice. Instead the response to the first stimulus may be delayed, though only by about .05 second on average (Gottsdanker, Broadbent, & Van Sant, 1963). The man apparently reserves some of his computing capacity in readiness for the second stimulus, and so does not have the necessary capacity available to deal at maximum rate with the first stimulus. When the interstimulus interval is variable and can be as short as .05 second, the second stimulus may occasionally arrive before the man has started to respond to the first stimulus. He can then make a single combined response to the two stimuli (Craik, 1948).

Acquisition tracking has not proved a very successful method of studying the psychological refractory period. The two responses tend to run into each other when the interval between the stimuli is short. If this happens it is not always possible to tell where the first response ends and the second response begins. The difficulty is illustrated at *b* in Fig. 3. The response at time R_2 was not powerful enough to move the pen all the way over to the required position. An additional response was therefore superimposed upon it. The time at which the additional response started, shown on the abscissa as at R_3, is not easy to identify with any degree of confidence. This difficulty of interpretation has been overcome by using responses which are recorded separately.

C. SERIES OF STEPS AND THE RANGE EFFECT

When the man is presented with a random series of steps, he learns their average size, and his responses are partly determined by it. With the larger steps the man's rate of movement tends to be slower than it was before learning, and he tends to undershoot them. With the smaller steps his rate of movement tends to be faster than it was before learning, and he tends to overshoot. This range effect is shown in more marked form when the steps follow each other in rapid succession (Slack, 1953a, b).

If the man is presented with a repeating series of steps, he soon learns the sequence, and the amplitude of his responses becomes more accurate (Poulton, 1956). He may initiate a movement a little too soon, like a premature reaction in the classic reaction-time experiment. Even if he always waits for the stimulus before responding, he can sometimes be caught out by a surprise step which calls for a movement of unexpected direction or size. The man may make the response appropriate to the expected step, instead of to the surprise step (Slack, 1953a).

D. RAMPS AND RATE MATCHING

A ramp track produces a constant disturbance. The ramp used most frequently in tracking has a constant velocity. Constant acceleration and constant rate of change of acceleration ("jerk") tracks have also been used. At the start of practice with a constant-velocity track and a simple lever control the man tends to lag behind the track. He corrects his error on average about once every .5 second. But once he becomes aware of the nature of the track, these intermittent corrections have superimposed upon them a constant rate of movement. The man responds at a rate which more or less matches the rate of the track, and intermittently corrects the error between the two. The rate element in the man's response is clearly apparent at the end of the ramp. He continues to respond at the same rate for rather more than a reaction time. Eventually he notices that the ramp has ceased, and stops responding (Craik, 1947).

E. SINGLE SINE WAVES AND PROGRAMMED RESPONSES

The task set in tracking a single sine wave depends upon its frequency. When the frequency is only 1 or 2 cycles per minute or less,

the task is not unlike that of tracking a constant-velocity ramp. At
higher frequencies the practiced man may attempt to match the rate of
the track by including an acceleration term in his response, corresponding to the learned acceleration or deceleration of the track. Often
the intermittent corrections of misalignment involve changes in rate
rather than discrete movements altering position, and are difficult to
detect.

When the frequency of a single sine-wave track is 60 cycles per
minute or above, the man attempts to generate a function something
approaching a sine wave of the correct frequency and amplitude. He
adjusts its phase, amplitude, and position on the display, from time to
time to match those of the track. This is illustrated in Fig. 4. It is very
much easier to do in pursuit tracking than in compensatory, since the
man can see the movements of the track which he is trying to copy,
and the nature of any error he makes. With practice he may not need to
correct his performance for periods of a second or two (see Fig. 4). He
may be able to track during this time as accurately with his eyes shut
as with his eyes on the display (Poulton, 1957).

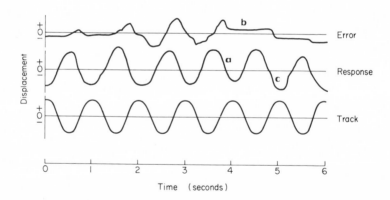

Fig. 4. Oscillographic chart illustrating the performance of a man tracking a sine wave
of 60 cycles per minute. He used a pursuit display and a simple lever control. The error
function at the top was derived automatically by adding the response function below it
to the track function at the bottom, paying attention to the sign. As time passed the
man's cyclical response function tended to lag further and further behind the track. This
is reflected by the increasing amplitude of the error function shown at the top. After 4
seconds the man introduced a correction by reducing the amplitude of the downward
response labeled a. This eliminated the time lag, but left a constant position error on the
display, labeled b on the error function. A second later he overcorrected it by making a
downward response of unduly large amplitude labeled c. (From an unpublished research report circulated in 1950.)

F. Multiple Sine Waves and Their Learnable Charac-
teristics

A combination of two sine waves can produce a track which appears fairly random for short periods, provided the frequencies and amplitudes are carefully selected. However, to avoid the possibility of the man learning the sequential nature of the track, it is safer to use three or more sine waves of different frequencies with phase relationships which vary in a nonrepetitive fashion. A still more irregular track is provided by white noise with the higher frequencies attenuated by a filter. Some of the learnable characteristics of these quasirandom tracks are the mean position on the display, the mean and approximate maximum amplitude, the mean frequency, and the approximate maximum rate of movement. It must be emphasized that no irregular track can be really random if a man is to track it successfully. High frequencies of large amplitude make tracking virtually impossible, and have to be excluded.

White noise presents a far greater problem to the man than a track with a learnable sequence. Difficulty can be increased by increasing either its frequency or its amplitude. Doubling either doubles the average velocity. But whereas doubling the amplitude practically doubles the average size of the tracking error, doubling the frequency may have more or less effect than this, depending upon the characteristics of the other independent variables.

IV. The Display

A. Pursuit and Compensatory Displays

The difference between a pursuit and a compensatory display was described in Section I and is illustrated in Fig. 1. A pursuit or true-motion display has two moving markers. On the left of Fig. 1(A) the round spot shows the track movements, or the required state of the system at the present time. The horizontal line shows the actual state of the system which results from the man's response movements.

A compensatory or relative-motion display has one moving and one stationary marker. On the left of Fig. 1(B) the horizontal line is fixed. It shows the required state of zero error. The moving spot shows the nature of the error. This is the difference between the track movements and the outcome of the man's response movements.

From the point of view of the man a pursuit display has four distinct advantages over a compensatory display (Poulton, 1952a, b).

1. The man can see the movements of the track marker independently of his response movements. Thus he can learn the sequential and statistical characteristics of the track relatively quickly.

2. From the visible rate of the track marker, he can predict where it will be, and the rate at which it will be moving, a short time ahead. With irregular tracks of high frequency, the visible rate of the track marker alone is not enough for accurate prediction. The man needs to know also the sequential and statistical characteristics of the track (see Section III,F). Once he has learned these (as he can relatively quickly with a pursuit display) he can make better predictions based upon both the present visible rate and the known characteristics of the track.

Successful prediction is essential if the man is to compensate for his reaction-time lag. In order to keep up with the track, he needs to know what it will be doing during his reaction time. Prediction is particularly important when the control system has a time lag built into it which is much larger than the man's own reaction time. It is necessary to aim well in front of a flying bird in order to shoot it. If the target is moving really fast, like a racing car or a low-flying airplane, it is necessary to predict still further ahead.

3. A third advantage of a pursuit display is that the man can see the results of his response movements independently of the track movements. If the output of his control is transformed by the dynamics of a control system before it affects the display, he can learn what effect a particular control movement or pattern of movements has. And since he receives immediate knowledge of results of the effects of his control movements, he can discover what movement or pattern of movements is required to produce a particular effect.

4. A final advantage is the status information available in a pursuit display. If an error develops, the man can see whether it was caused by an unexpected movement of the track, or by an error in his control movements.

A compensatory display has the four corresponding disadvantages. The man cannot see the track movements uncomplicated by the output of his control system. And he cannot see the outcome of his control movements uncomplicated by the track movements. Thus it takes him a good deal longer to learn the track and to learn his control system.

In predicting the future course of the track, the man can use only any knowledge he has of its statistical characteristics; he cannot see its present rate. If he succeeds in tracking really accurately, all he can see is a stationary error pointer. This gives him no visible indication of what response to make next. Finally, he can never be sure whether an error which arises is due to his failure to appreciate the track movements, or to his failure to make the correct pattern of control movements. Many so-called "radar-assisted" collisions between ships in fog used to be due to errors of navigation caused by this lack of status information in the then standard compensatory radar display (Calvert, 1960).

The only advantage of a single compensatory display over a pursuit display is when the tracking task is so easy that the error is small even with the compensatory display. It is then possible to increase the gain of the compensatory display, until the error marker moves over most of the face of the display without disappearing off the edge. This magnifies the error, and so improves the man's performance somewhat if it is being held back by the size of the smallest error which he can see or is willing to tolerate. It is not possible to increase the gain of a pursuit display beyond the point where the track marker covers most of the face of the display, however well the man tracks; for he cannot tell what to do if the track marker disappears.

But when the tracking task with a compensatory display is difficult, the effect of the man's control movements may at times add to the error produced by the track movements. It is then necessary to reduce the gain of the display beyond the point where the error marker would never disappear off the edge of the display by itself, to the point where a track movement combined with an inappropriate control movement would not make the error marker disappear off the edge. With a pursuit display the man's responses do not affect the movement of the track marker, which determines the optimal display magnification. Thus with a difficult task the display magnification may have to be smaller for a compensatory display than for a pursuit display.

Unfortunately, most of the experiments in which the two types of display have been compared have used factorial designs, in which the same men have performed a number of different tasks in close succession. Such designs often produce asymmetrical transfer effects between conditions, and are quite unsuitable for this kind of research (Poulton & Freeman, 1966). Using a simple design in which the transfer effects could be evaluated, Andreas, Green, and Spragg (1954) found reliable positive transfer when a pursuit display was followed by a compensatory display, but no transfer in the reverse direction. This favored the compensatory display. Asymmetrical transfer effects of this kind may account for the results of the odd experiments in which pursuit and compensatory displays have been compared, and the compensatory display has been found to be the better (see Poulton, 1966, p. 372).

B. Quickened and Predictor Displays

When the dynamics of the control system are complex, it is possible to relieve the man of the necessity of learning them. This is done by presenting him with a display which takes them into account. A quickened display shows the man how to move his control in order to achieve and maintain the required output of the system (Birmingham & Taylor, 1961). He has simply to make control movements proportional to the size of the displayed error. He does not have to learn to understand the control system. Quickening the display changes the task performed by the man from tracking low frequencies with a complex control system, to tracking higher frequencies with what appears to him to be a simple control system without lag. By easing the man's task it can greatly reduce the error put out by the system (Taylor & Birmingham, 1956).

A prototype predictor display for tracking in one dimension is shown in Fig. 5. This display also relieves the man of the necessity of learning the dynamics of the control system. The ordinate shows him the difference between the required output of the system and the predicted output, while the abscissa extends this information from the present time into the future. The man can see what future results his present control movements will have, and can adopt control movements which will bring about the required output of the system. This again reduces the difficulty of tracking with a complex control system (Kelley, 1962).

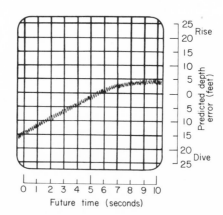

Fig. 5. A prototype predictor display for controlling the depth of a submarine. It shows the predicted error in depth over the next 10 seconds on the assumption that the man gradually returns his control to the neutral position. (After Kelley, 1962.)

The predictor display allows more flexibility than the quickened display, in that it offers the man a choice. He can select any one of a number of paths to his goal, depending upon how quickly he wishes to achieve it. With the quickened display only one path is offered. But both display systems suffer a disadvantage of automatic systems. The systems work well only under conditions similar to those for which they were designed. If conditions become too different, the offered path or the predicted outcome may cease to be correct. Using the display system may then lead to disaster.

C. LINEAR AND NONLINEAR DISPLAY MAGNIFICATION

There is an optimal size of linear magnification of a display (see Section IV,A). When the magnification is too low, the man cannot see the misalignment and rate of movement sufficiently well. When the magnification is too high, a moving marker is liable to disappear from the face of the display every time the amplitude of the track is too large or the man makes a large error (Battig, Nagel, & Brogden, 1955; Hartman & Fitts, 1955).

Markers can be prevented from disappearing from the face of a display by the use of nonlinear display magnification. The central part of the display, where the moving markers spend most of their time, is magnified. The magnification of the peripheral part of the display, where the markers do not go so often, is correspondingly reduced. By a skillful selection of the kind and degree of nonlinearity, it might in principle be possible to obtain the benefit of magnification without the disadvantage of losing the markers. However what results there are have been disappointing. People are not accustomed to displays where the center is magnified and the magnification falls off symmetrically toward the edges. They have come to assume that displays are linear. With the nonlinear display an error does not look as large as it in fact is when the markers happen to be near the edge. So the man is likely to make too small a correction.

D. ALTERNATIVE SENSORY DIMENSIONS

Tracking displays almost invariably use the sensory dimension of visual direction and length. This is clearly so much better than other sensory dimensions that few experimental studies have been reported comparing them. Ever since early childhood people have been reaching for objects in different directions at different distances, and they have got pretty good at it. Other sensory dimensions have not received anything like so much practice.

The best alternative visual display so far discovered is probably a pair of flashing lights, one on each side of the man's field of view. The direction of the error is shown by which of the two lights is on and flashing. Size of error is indicated by rate of flash; the larger the error, the faster the rate of flash. This display has been found to be as good as a rather small and poorly designed conventional compensatory display. Its disadvantage is the usual one of displays using a sensory dimension other than visual length: it is not easy to tell from the rate of flash how large the error is. Its advantage is the very clear indication which it gives the man of the direction of the error (Brown, Holmqvist, & Woodhouse, 1961).

Changes in brightness also have been used to indicate the size of the error, but they are not as good as changes in visual length (Moss, 1964). The same holds for changes in rates of movement. It is easier to try to hold a display marker on a fixed reference line than it is to try to hold it stationary anywhere on the display (Poulton, 1967). This is because when there is an error of a certain size, it is easier to assess its size from the distance away of a reference mark than from a rate of movement.

Presenting a sound to one ear or the other gives an excellent indication of the direction of the error. As always, the problem is how to signal the size of the error. The rate of interruption of the sound has been used. This corresponds to the rate of flash of a visual signal. But tracking is nowhere near so accurate with this auditory display as with a conventional visual compensatory display like that in Fig. 1(B) (Mowbray & Gebhard, 1961). Vibratory displays placed against the skin have also been tried, but the results appear no more promising (Hahn, 1965).

V. The Control

A. STYLUS AND JOYSTICK

The most precise tracking is achieved by using the muscles of the hand and wrist as they are used in writing and drawing. Thus a stylus, held like a pencil and moved over the surface of the display, is about twice as quick for locating targets as is a joystick operated by the hand (Baker, 1960, p. 157). An additional advantage of the stylus is that its tip is actually the controlled display marker. This is the most compatible control-display relationship (see Section V, B).

If a joystick has to be used, there may not be much to choose between one operated by the thumb, the hand, or the forearm when the task is easy. But when the task is difficult the hand joystick is the best, and the joystick operated by the forearm is the worst (Hammerton & Tickner, 1966). This is because the anatomy of the hand is designed to enable it to make quick precise movements, and the hand practices them all the time. The thumb also is designed for quick precise movements, but it does not normally have to make movements of the kind used in operating a thumb joystick. The forearm is designed as much for strength as for speed and precision. Foot pedals permit the use of still greater force, but with still less speed and precision.

B. COMPATIBILITY OF CONTROL WITH DISPLAY

The perfectly compatible control is the display marker itself. When the man wants to move the marker, he simply takes hold of it and moves it directly. The nearer a control can approach to this ideal, the simpler the coding problem becomes for the man. In order to minimize the coding problem the control should be mounted as close as possible to the display, should move in the same direction as the display marker, and should have the minimum of control-system dynamics upsetting the direct relationship between control and display movements.

A single joystick is more compatible with a two-dimensional display on a cathode ray oscilloscope than are two levers for movements in the x- and y-planes, respectively. Thus where the dynamics of the control system are the same in both dimensions, tracking is more accurate with the single joystick. But where the dynamics are different for the two dimensions and do not interact, the man has in effect two separate tasks to perform. In this case two levers are best, because a response intended for one control system does not accidentally operate the other one (Chernikoff & LeMay, 1963).

C. CONTROL RESISTANCE

A joystick or lever gives the best tracking performance when it is spring centered. The distance it moves, which determines the effect it has, is then proportional to the force used to operate it. And it returns to its central position of zero output when the man lets go. If an accurate output is required, a simple lever control should be allowed to move through its fullest extent (see Section VI, C). But if speed of reaction is what matters, and the exact size of the output is of only secondary importance, a pressure stick is better. This is a stick which virtually does not move at all, and which gives an output proportional to the pressure exerted on it. In operating a pressure stick time is taken only in exerting pressure on it. No time is taken in having to move the stick to the required position, as is the case with a free-moving control. And as soon as the pressure is released, its output returns instantly to zero.

The advantage of spring centering is that the spring resistance gives the man a sensory indication or "feel" of the amplitude of his control movement. It is particularly useful to him where he cannot obtain the information directly from the display. This is the case when he has a compensatory display, or when the relationship between a control movement and its effect upon the display is complicated by the dynamics of the intervening control system.

Performance with a spring-centered control is not improved by adding other forms of control resistance. But performance with a control without resistance, which falls when the man lets go of it, can be improved by adding a small amount of almost any form of resistance. The resistance helps to prevent accidental operation. It also helps to filter out unintentional tremor and jerks.

When a control has friction, a constant force has to be exerted in order to move it. Once this threshold has been exceeded, a little extra force moves the control rapidly, since the only remaining restraints are those built into the man's responding limb. Thus a control with a good deal of friction as the only form of resistance cannot easily be moved at a constant slow speed. The attempt tends to result in alternate rapid movements and stops, as the force exerted by the man rises above and falls below the threshold required to move the control. This does not produce very accurate tracking (Helson, 1949). (Lay a rubber pencil eraser on a flat horizontal surface, and press it firmly against the surface with one hand to produce friction. Then try sliding the eraser slowly by pushing it horizontally with the other hand.)

Viscous friction feels like moving a spoon through thick syrup, or like running through water deep enough to cover the thighs. Rate of movement is directly proportional to the force exerted. Inertia is met in starting a heavy flywheel. The force exerted has little immediate effect, since it produces only an acceleration in the flywheel, which has to operate for an appreciable time before the flywheel begins to move reasonably fast. Both viscous friction and inertia oppose quick control movements, and are therefore disadvantageous in most tracking tasks (Howland & Noble, 1953). The arm has enough viscous friction and inertia of its own; it does not need any extra.

In a tracking task like pointing a long telescope, some viscous friction and inertia necessarily result from the physical characteristics of the telescope and its mount. Where the forces involved are not too great, the man tracks more accurately if he can feel the viscous friction and inertia, as when he himself moves the telescope. This is preferable to giving him a power-operated control system. For here he cannot feel the viscous friction and inertia which he has to deal with (Notterman & Page, 1962).

VI. The Control-System Dynamics

A. ORDER OF CONTROL

The order of control system most suited to human capabilities is position or zero order, for there is an immediate and obvious relationship between control and display movements. In order to acquire a target it is only necessary to move the control the corresponding distance in the correct direction. This is illustrated in Fig. 6. With a rate-control or first-order system two movements are necessary: one to put on the rate of movement, and another to take it off again when the target has been reached.

The right side of Fig. 6 shows that with an acceleration-control or second-order system three movements are required to acquire a target: one to put on the acceleration which in time produces the rate of movement; one which gradually takes off the rate of movement again;

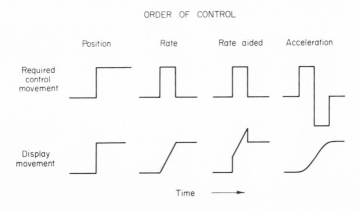

Fig. 6. Control movements required in acquisition tracking with different orders of control system. To move the display indicator upward with a position control system, a single upward movement is required; with rate and rate-aided control systems two movements are required, upward followed by downward; with an acceleration control system three movements are required, upward, twice as far downward, and then upward again. The lower part of the figure shows the resulting display movements as a function of time.

and then a final movement to return the control to the central position. Movements after the first have to be correctly timed. It is necessary to start to remove the rate before the target is reached, or the display indicator will overshoot. And the control has to be returned to the central position as the display indicator comes to rest, or it will be left with a residual velocity.

An aided control system combines two or more orders of control. In the rate-aided system illustrated in Fig. 6, a control movement moves the display indicator directly, and also gives it a rate of movement in the same direction. If a control system has to have components of higher order, it should also have a position component if at all possible; thus it should be aided rather than pure rate. Whenever the man moves his control, he then sees an immediate movement of the controlled indicator in the display. This improves the control-display compatibility (see Section V, B).

Unfortunately experiments in which position-control systems have been compared with rate-control and aided-control systems, have generally used factorial designs in which the same people have performed the various tasks one after the other. These designs may discriminate against the position-control system, and should therefore not be used in making the comparisons. Lincoln (1953) found that there was positive transfer when changing from a position-control system to either of the other two, and also when changing between aided- and rate-control systems. But there was negative transfer when changing from either of these two to the position-control system (see Poulton & Freeman, 1966).

B. Control Time Lags

With a simple transmission lag the control system does not respond when the man first moves his control. After a fixed time interval the normal effect of the control movement appears in the display. This is illustrated in Fig. 7. It is not possible for the man to compensate for a transmission time lag unless he knows what the track will be doing at the corresponding time ahead. If the man does have this information, he can advance his control movements in time so that they match the track movements after the transmission time lag.

The effects of a transmission lag of constant duration become more damaging as the frequencies in the track are increased. This is illustrated in Fig. 8. The sine wave of 15 cycles per minute, represented by the thick line at the top of the figure, does not move very far during a transmission lag of .25 second. Thus the displacement error between it and the response function with the transmission lag is not very

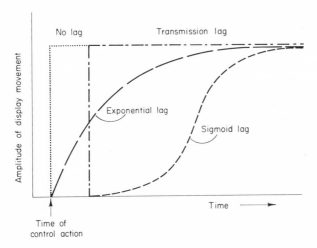

Fig. 7. Amplitude of display movement as a function of time with various control time lags. Without a time lag the effect of the control movement (dotted line) has been assumed to be an instantaneous step, such as might be produced by closing a switch. With an exponential time lag the display indicator starts to move as soon as the man responds, but only gradually reaches its final position. With transmission and sigmoid time lags the display indicator does not move until some time after the man responds. When the display movement does take place after a transmission time lag, it corresponds to the control action. With a sigmoid time lag the display movement first accelerates and then decelerates.

large. The two functions in the middle of the figure show that when the track frequency is doubled while the transmission lag remains constant and small, the mean size of the displacement error is almost doubled.

The functions at the bottom of Fig. 8 are 90° out of phase, because the transmission lag of .25 second is one quarter the duration of the track cycle time of 1.0 second. When the response function starts rising from the midline, it is correcting a displacement error produced by the track which is already being corrected by the track. And when the response function starts to return from its highest point, it is producing a displacement error which adds to the error being produced by the track. Thus the amplitude of the displacement error is larger than it would have been if there had been no response.

An exponential lag is the commonest kind of time lag in electronic equipment. Something happens almost as soon as the man moves his control. But the full effect of the control movement appears only gradually, following an exponential time function like that in Fig. 7. In

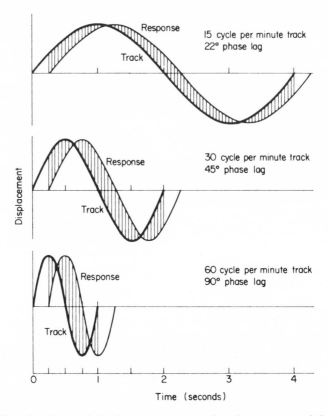

Fig. 8. The phase lags and displacement errors produced at various track frequencies by a transmission time lag of .25 second. The sine-wave track at the top, represented by the thick line, repeats every 4 seconds. In .25 second it has spent one quarter of the time which it takes to move from the midline to its highest point. The response after the transmission lag of .25 second is represented by the thin line. The vertical lines between the two functions show the sizes of the displacement errors at various times. The track halfway down the figure moves twice as quickly. In .25 second it has spent half the time which it takes to move from the midline to its highest point. The displacement errors between it and the response after the .25 second transmission lag are therefore larger. The track at the bottom reaches its highest point in .25 second. At this time the response with its transmission lag has not left the midline. By the time the response reaches its highest point, the track is crossing the midline traveling in the reverse direction. This leads to displacement errors larger than those produced by the track alone.

order to acquire a target reasonably quickly using a control system with an exponential time lag, the man has to move his control further than he does when tracking without a lag. An exponential time lag is thus somewhat similar to a reduction in control gain (see Section VI, C).

Having produced a relatively quick movement of the display indicator by a large control movement, the man then has to avoid the overshooting which will gradually occur as a result of the remainder of the exponential time function. This means moving the control back to the near side of its final position, in order to cancel the remainder of the initial exponential time function. Gradually the control has then to be moved out again to its final position. Thus there are three successive movements: far out, back a good way, and finally out a bit further. The two reversals in the direction of movement correspond to the two reversals required in acquiring a target with an acceleration-control system (see Fig. 6).

A sigmoid lag behaves rather like a combination of a transmission lag and an exponential lag. Figure 7 shows that nothing much happens when a control movement is first made, and then the effect appears and disappears gradually. With all three kinds of time lag the longer the lag is, the worse the man's tracking becomes. Performance is improved by any condition which assists prediction (Conklin, 1957). For if the man can predict what the track and the output of his control system will be doing a little time ahead, he can make the appropriate response early, and thus help to compensate for the time lag.

Referring back to the block diagrams of Fig. 1, control time lags are located between the box labeled control and the box labeled control system. They need to be distinguished from display time lags, which are located between the box labeled control system and the box labeled display. Both kinds of lag are present when controlling from the earth a manipulator located in a spacecraft on the moon. There is the transmission control time lag while a message from the man is traveling to the spacecraft. There may be an additional control time lag, perhaps exponential, while the manipulator is responding to the message. And there is the transmission display time lag before the man on earth receives the message from the spacecraft which enables him to see what the manipulator is doing.

From the point of view of the man on earth, the control and display transmission time lags can be lumped together. When summed they represent the time between his response movements and the appearance of the changes in his display which they produce. They have been called delayed feedback by Smith (see Chapter 4). They greatly increase the difficulty of the man's task.

Exponential or sigmoid control and display time lags cannot be lumped together in this way because they alter the signal; they do not merely delay it (see Fig. 7). An exponential control time lag alters the dynamics of the control system. As long as the display time lags are only of the transmission type, the man will eventually see what the

control system has done. He can therefore modify his response movements to make the control system do what he wants. An exponential
display time lag distorts what the man sees. The higher frequencies in
the output of the control system are attenuated when they reach the
display. The man is not aware of their true amplitude, and so does not
make adequate attempts to correct them (Garvey, Sweeny, & Birmingham, 1958).

C. Control Gain and Control-System Output

Control gain has been studied most thoroughly in acquisition
tracking. Figure 9 illustrates how the gain of a position control
affected the two components of acquisition time. The function sloping
up to the left shows the average time it took to bring the display
indicator within .1 inch of the target. In their classic experiment
Jenkins and Connor (1949) used a rotary knob as their position control. On the extreme left the control gain was so low that a number of
rotations of the knob were required, and this took several seconds.

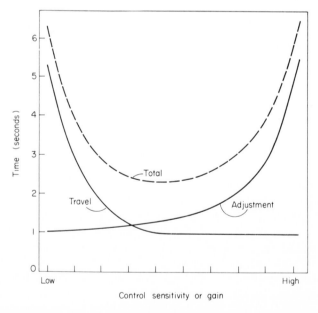

Fig. 9. The relationship between control sensitivity and the two components of acquisition time. Travel time is defined as the time taken to bring the display pointer from
3.1 inch to within .1 inch of the target. Adjustment time is the remaining time taken by
the man to line the pointer up with the target. Summing the two components gives the
total time indicated by the broken line. (After Jenkins & Connor, 1949.)

The function sloping up to the right of the figure shows the average time it took to make the final fine adjustment which aligned the display indicator with the target. On the extreme right the control gain was so high that only a very small control movement was required. This rather difficult task was accomplished by trial and error, and took several seconds on average.

Adding together the two components of acquisition time produces the **U**-shaped function in the figure. Over the middle third at the bottom of the **U** the height of the function does not alter very much. There are a number of different control sensitivities which are all about equally good.

This **U**-shaped model has to be modified when a joystick or lever position control is used. A control stick does not normally move as far as 90° on either side of its central position. It is almost as quick to move a stick through 90° as through a smaller distance. The function in Fig. 9 for travel time is thus practically horizontal. There is nothing to correspond to the numerous full rotations of the control knob which were required in Jenkins and Connor's experiment. Hence with a stick position control the relationship between acquisition time and control gain is **J**-shaped like the function for adjustment time on the right of Fig. 9 (Jenkins & Olson, 1952). The optimal gain is obtained by equating maximum stick movement with the maximum required movement of the display marker.

When a control stick is used with a rate- or acceleration-control system, either model may be found to apply, depending upon the experimental procedure. If the gain of the control is changed by changing the output of the control system, a **U**-shaped function is found. This is because the output of the control system can be reduced to such an extent that it takes several seconds to approach the target even with full stick deflection. At the other extreme, with a very large control-system output the final alignment with the target takes several seconds on average because even a small control movement may produce gross overshooting. Thus the target is acquired most rapidly with a control-system output of intermediate size, and the relationship between control gain (or system output) and acquisition time is **U**-shaped.

However, in most practical control systems the maximum output is fixed by the design. An automobile has a limited power of acceleration. The only method of increasing the gain of the accelerator pedal is to let full power be obtained with the pedal partly depressed, instead of fully depressed. This only very slightly reduces the time taken by the foot to move the pedal from its zero position to the position of full power. Its main effect is to reduce the foot's ability to select just the required amount of power. If the gain of the control is changed in this way, the relationship between acquisition time and control gain is **J**-shaped like the function for adjustment time in Fig. 9. The optimal gain is achieved by equating full power with the full range of movement of the control (Hammerton, 1962).

These models apply only to acquisition tracking. Where a continuous disturbance has to be tracked, travel time is far more important than adjustment time. The man is mostly engaged in chasing after the target; he does not often get near enough to do any fine adjustments. As the frequencies in the track are increased, the importance of minimizing travel time also increases. Figure 8 shows that a short time delay causes much larger displacement errors when tracking high frequencies. Differences in travel time which are negligible when acquiring a stationary target become all important. Thus continuous tracking calls for a higher control gain than acquisition tracking. The higher the frequencies in the track, the higher the control gain needs to be. With tracks of high frequency a pressure stick is the control of choice. This is a stick which has an almost infinite gain, since it barely moves when pressed. Its output is proportional to the pressure exerted on it, and can be changed without spending time altering the position of the control (see Section V, C).

VII. Human Limitations

A. Limited Human Decision Rate

A man may be able to tap for a short period at a rate of between 7 and 9 taps per second. But each tap is not preceded by a decision to tap. If the man is unexpectedly told to stop, or the piece of paper which his pencil is tapping on is removed, he will make one or two more taps before he can stop. His tapping is preprogrammed. He made an initial decision to tap rapidly, and from then on he makes decisions to go on tapping. These subsequent decisions occur at a rate of perhaps once or twice per second, almost certainly not faster than about 3 times per second. For where each response is preceded by a decision, it is not possible to achieve rates above about 3 responses per second. To ensure that each response is preceded by a decision, it is necessary to change the required response upon a proportion of occasions. Thus a single response may be called for on 68 out of a sequence of 100 consecutive occasions, and 4 other responses may each be called for on 8 of the remaining 32 occasions. After 2 weeks of practice on this task, a group of 6 young men averaged only about 2.5 responses per second, the individual rates ranging from 2.3 to 2.8 per second. Their learning curves gave little expectation of much further increase in the rate of responding with additional practice (Leonard & Newman, 1965).

An average response rate of about twice per second is often clearly visible in the oscillographic records of people when they first start to use a position control with a slow-moving track. No doubt the mean rate of these discrete responses correcting the visible error could be increased until it approached the maximum tapping rate. But instead the man begins to respond to the rate of the track. He adopts a program which seems to him to match the track, and simply corrects for the error between the program and the track (see Section III, D).

With further practice the discrete corrections often blend with the program and become obscured. Instead of correcting a misalignment by a quick displacement of the control, the man simply changes the rate at which he moves the control, so that the error is nulled gradually as the program carries on. If the track is a single sine wave which can be learnt, the man may insert acceleration and deceleration terms in his program. And in so far as the program is successful in matching the track, he may not correct it for a second or two until a fairly large error is apparent (see Section III, E). During this time the man can be assumed to be making decisions now and again not to interfere with the program.

B. HUMAN REACTION TIME

A man takes about .2 second to react to a visual stimulus, a little longer if he has just responded to a previous stimulus (see Section III, B). If he always copied the track movements as he saw them, his responses would lag in time well behind. Time lags become more serious as the speed of the track increases, since a greater distance is covered during the lag time. Time lags also become more serious as the track frequencies increase. The bottom of Fig. 8 shows what happens if a man tracks a sine wave of 60 cycles per minute with a time lag of .25 second. Half the time his response function actually increases the size of the displacement error caused by the track (see Section VI, B). Clearly some strategy is called for to reduce the man's reaction-time lag.

In contour tracking the man can normally see the track some way ahead. In order to eliminate his reaction-time lag he has simply to copy the track he sees at a distance ahead corresponding to his reaction time, instead of reacting to the track as it reaches his stylus or display marker. By the time he has responded, his output will then synchronize with the track movements.

In pursuit and compensatory tracking the man has no preview of the track ahead. All he can do is to predict the track one reaction time ahead, and respond according to this prediction. With single sine waves and constant-velocity ramps he can predict reasonably well with practice. Thus his responses can be accurate in both timing and size. But with multiple sine waves of high frequency accurate predictions cannot be made .2 seconds ahead. The most the practiced man can do is to predict rather better than chance. In these circumstances he tends to adopt a strategy which is a compromise between making the correct sizes of response movements a reaction time too late, and making correctly timed responses of sizes based upon his rather inaccurate predictions. He accepts a degree of error in the sizes of his response excursions in order to reduce his time lag (Poulton, 1962). The higher the frequencies in the track, the more damaging his time lag becomes. Hence the more likely he is to attempt to time his responses accurately regardless of their correct size.

C. Spare Human Channel Capacity and the Challenge Effect

In tracking in one dimension the typical display consists simply of two markers, one or both of which move over and back. Right at the start the task appears to the man to be interesting and challenging. But with easy tracks and simple control systems he soon discovers what he can and cannot achieve, and settles down to give what he considers to be an adequate performance. A small error comes to be tolerated, and effort is directed only at preventing or correcting large errors (Helson, 1949, p. 495). The task becomes analogous to a vigilance task, and fails to occupy the man's full channel capacity or attention. In the case of the pursuit rotor, the suboptimal performance has been likened to conditioned inhibition (Kimble, 1949).

At this stage the level of performance can be improved by presenting the man with a challenge. With a compensatory display the size of the error can be magnified. This appears to the man to indicate poorer performance, and he tracks more accurately as a result (Helson, 1949). Another method is to draw the man's attention to this performance by presenting him automatically with an auditory signal whenever his error is below a critical value (Reynolds & Adams, 1953). Or he can be told his integrated error score after each trial (Karlin & Mortimer, 1963). Both these forms of knowledge of results can reduce the size of the error which the man will tolerate, and so raise the standard of his performance.

Unfortunately, a change in experimental conditions that makes the task harder may also present a challenge to the man. This means that the poorer performance which is to be expected as a result of the increased difficulty of the task may be partly offset by the challenge effect. Tracking in one dimension is thus not as sensitive to changes in experimental conditions as are tasks which occupy the man's channel capacity more fully; an example is a task which combines tracking with some other function such as monitoring (Poulton, 1965).

D. HUMAN TIME SHARING

Flying an airplane by manual control can be regarded as a multiple tracking task combined with various additional monitoring functions. The pilot usually checks one instrument at a time, and responds to each in turn. While he is attending to one of them, the remaining instruments have to go unattended. They may be registering quite large errors before he gets around to correcting them.

In the laboratory blacking out a single display for periods as short as .25 second every 1.25 second has been found to reduce the accuracy of tracking. Here the man did not have to attend to another display during the blackouts (Poulton & Gregory, 1952). Increasing the number of independent tracking tasks which have to be carried out simultaneously from 1 to 4 lowers the standard of performance on them all (Bilodeau, 1957; Hoffeld, Seidenstein, & Brogden, 1961). If success is scored in terms of the time the man is on target on all the tasks combined, adding an extra task also provides an extra dimension in which he may be off target.

Where two simultaneous tracking tasks are presented on separate displays, performance is more accurate when the displays are close together, because it reduces the sizes of head and eye movements. If the tasks are both in one dimension, the two displays can be integrated by using the x- and y-coordinates of a single cathode ray oscilloscope. Tracking then becomes rather more accurate still, because the two displays can be seen simultaneously. If the dynamics of the control systems are the same in the two dimensions and do not interact, an additional advantage may be gained by halving the number of display markers, and making them move in both dimensions (Chernikoff & LeMay, 1963). The man does still better if the two controls are changed to the more compatible arrangement of a single joystick (see Section V, B). He then no longer has to look at two displays in turn, and each time make the appropriate response. He has only to note the oblique error on a single display, and make a single oblique control movement to correct it.

However, tracking in two dimensions can never be done quite as accurately as tracking in one dimension. For when tracking in two dimensions the man has to respond in precisely the correct direction. Whereas when tracking in one dimension, as with the displays of Fig. 1, he need choose only between responding upward or downward. Simply swapping a lever which will move the display marker only in one dimension for a joystick which will move it in two dimensions makes compensatory tracking in one dimension less accurate (Garvey & Taylor, 1959). When the extra dimension is present, errors are almost bound to occur in it from time to time. And when they do, correcting them presents the man with a more complex task than correcting errors in a single dimension.

VIII. Summary

Five rather different kinds of tracking have been studied: pursuit and compensatory (Fig. 1A and B), acquisition or step tracking, and selfpaced and paced contour tracking (Fig. 2). Tracking differs from selective motor learning in that it demands precise movements which have to be timed correctly.

In acquisition tracking the man typically makes ballistic movements which are prepared in advance and triggered off as a unit. When the time interval between 2 steps is less than about .2 second, the response to the second step will be delayed. The brain becomes refractory during the reaction time to the first stimulus. The man can learn the statistical properties of a series of steps. His responses to the individual steps are then influenced by the range and sequential characteristics of the series.

Ramps of constant velocity and single sine wave tracks are soon learned. Instead of making ballistic movements about twice per second, the man tends to copy the track. He corrects his copy when necessary to make it a better match (Fig. 4). The statistical properties of multiple sine waves and white noise tracks can also be learned.

Pursuit or true motion displays (Fig. 1A) are easier to use than compensatory or relative motion displays (Fig. 1B) because they present status information on the track and on the output of the control system. Quickened and predictor displays (Fig. 5) are developments respectively of the compensatory and pursuit display concepts. They can help the man when the dynamics of his control system are complex. Nonlinear display magnification is not compatible with the common assumption that displays are linear. The sensory dimension of visual direction and length (Fig. 1) gives better performance than any other sensory dimension.

A control operated by the muscles used in writing gives the greatest precision. The movements of the control should be compatible with the display movements they produce. Joysticks and levers should be spring centered, with as little friction, viscous friction, and inertia as possible. However, if the control system has to have viscous friction or inertia, the man tracks better when he can feel it.

A position or zero order control system is the most compatible with display movements. It is also the easiest to use in acquiring a target (Fig. 6). An acceleration or second order control system should have a component of lower order if possible, preferably position.

Control time lags (Fig. 7) degrade performance. A transmission time lag simply delays the signal. The higher the frequencies in the track, the more damaging the delay becomes (Fig. 8). An exponential time lag alters the time characteristics of the signal, and attenuates the high frequencies. In acquisition tracking a control system with an exponential time lag behaves somewhat like an acceleration control system. In tracking sine waves it behaves somewhat like a control system with a reduced gain. A sigmoid time lag is rather like a combination of a transmission and an exponential time lag.

Figure 9 shows how the 2 components of acquisition time vary with the gain of the control. Both components are important if a rotary position control is used which allows a number of rotations. Both components are also important if the gain of a rate or acceleration control is altered by changing the output of the system. Adjustment time is the important component if a joystick position control is used, or if the gain of a rate or acceleration control is altered without changing the system output. In continuous tracking, travel time is the important component. When the track contains high frequencies, a pressure stick is the best control because it minimizes travel time.

A man cannot make decisions about his responses more rapidly than about 3 times per second. A decision may change the position, rate, or acceleration of the control. With practice the man copies the track, and his corrections are hard to pick out.

With high frequency tracks the man's reaction time lag produces a large error (Fig. 8). In contour tracking with a preview of the track ahead (Fig. 2), the man can compensate for his reaction time lag by copying the track an equivalent time ahead. In tracking without preview the man has to copy his prediction of the future track. He risks increasing the error in the amplitude of his responses in order to reduce the error in their timing.

After tracking for a while the man tends to tolerate larger errors than he need. His performance can then be improved by presenting him with a challenge. When he has 2 tracking tasks to perform simultaneously, he responds to each in turn. This normally lowers the standard of his performance on both. He does somewhat better if the 2 tasks are compatible, and can be combined as a single two-dimensional task.

References

Ammons, R. B. Rotary pursuit apparatus: I. Survey of variables. *Psychological Bulletin*, 1955, **52**, 69–76.

Andreas, B. G., Green, R. F., & Spragg, S. D. S. Transfer effects between performance on a following tracking task (modified SAM two-hand co-ordination test) and a compensatory tracking task (modified SAM two-hand pursuit test). *Journal of Psychology*, 1954, **37**, 173–183.

Baker, C. H. Factors affecting radar operator efficiency. *Journal of the Institute of Navigation*, 1960, **13**, 148-163.

Battig, W. F., Nagel, E. H., & Brogden, W. J. The effects of error-magnification and marker-size on bidimensional compensatory tracking. *American Journal of Psychology*, 1955, **68**, 585–594.

Bilodeau, E. A. Patterns of internal consistency in multipart skilled performances. *American Journal of Psychology*, 1957, **70**, 550–559.

Birmingham, H. P., & Taylor, F. V. A design philosophy for man-machine control systems. In H. W. Sinaiko (Ed.), *Selected papers on human factors in the design and use of control systems*. New York: Dover, 1961. Pp. 67 – 87.

Brown, I. D., Holmqvist, S. D., & Woodhouse, M. C. A laboratory comparison of tracking with four flight-director displays. *Ergonomics*, 1961, **4**, 229–251.

Calvert, E. S. Manoeuvres to ensure the avoidance of collision. *Journal of the Institute of Navigation*, 1960, **13**, 127-137.

Chernikoff, R., & LeMay, M. Effect of various display-control configurations on tracking with identical and different coordinate dynamics. *Journal of Experimental Psychology*, 1963, **66**, 95–99.

Conklin, J. E. Effect of control lag on performance in a tracking task. *Journal of Experimental Psychology*, 1957, **53**, 261–268.

Craik, K. J. W. Theory of the human operator in control systems: I. The operator as an engineering system. *British Journal of Psychology*, 1947, **38**, 56-61.

Craik, K. J. W. Theory of the human operator in control systems: II. Man as an element in a control system. *British Journal of Psychology*, 1948, **38**, 142-148.

Garvey, W. D., Sweeny, J. S., & Birmingham, H. P. Differential effects of "display lags" and "control lags" on the performance of manual tracking systems. *Journal of Experimental Psychology*, 1958, **56**, 8–10.

Garvey, W. D., & Taylor, F. V. Interactions among operator variables, system dynamics, and task-induced stress. *Journal of Applied Psychology*, 1959, **43**, 79–85.

Gottsdanker, R., Broadbent, L., & Van Sant, C. Reaction time to single and to first signals. *Journal of Experimental Psychology*, 1963, **66**, 163–167.

Hahn, J. F. Unidimensional compensatory tracking with a vibrotactile display. *Perceptual and Motor Skills*, 1965, **21**, 699–702.

Hammerton, M. An investigation into the optimal gain of a velocity control system. *Ergonomics*, 1962, **5**, 539–543.

Hammerton, M., & Tickner, A. H. An investigation into the comparative suitability of forearm, hand and thumb controls in acquisition tasks. *Ergonomics,* 1966, **9,** 125–130.

Hartman, B. O., & Fitts, P. M. Relation of stimulus and response amplitude to tracking performance. *Journal of Experimental Psychology,* 1955, **49,** 82–92.

Helson, H. Design of equipment and optimal human operation. *American Journal of Psychology,* 1949, **62,** 473–497.

Hick, W. E. Reaction time for the amendment of a response. *Quarterly Journal of Experimental Psychology,* 1949, **1,** 175–179.

Hoffeld, D. R., Seidenstein, S., & Brogden, W. J. Proficiency in finger-tracking as a function of number of fingers. *American Journal of Psychology,* 1961, **74,** 36–44.

Howland, D., & Noble, M. E. The effect of physical constants of a control on tracking performance. *Journal of Experimental Psychology,* 1953, **46,** 353–360.

Jenkins, W. L., & Connor, M. B. Some design factors in making settings on a linear scale. *Journal of Applied Psychology,* 1949, **33,** 395–409.

Jenkins, W. L., & Olson, M. W. The use of levers in making settings on a linear scale. *Journal of Applied Psychology,* 1952, **36,** 269–271.

Karlin, L., & Mortimer, R. G. Effect of verbal, visual, and auditory augmenting cues on learning a complex motor skill. *Journal of Experimental Psychology,* 1963, **65,** 75–79.

Kelley, C. R. Predictor instruments look into the future. *Control Engineering,* 1962, **9,** 86–90.

Kimble, G. A. An experimental test of a two-factor theory of inhibition. *Journal of Experimental Psychology,* 1949, **39,** 15–23.

Leonard, J. A., & Newman, R. C. On the acquisition and maintenance of high speed and high accuracy in a keyboard task. *Ergonomics,* 1965, **8,** 281–304.

Lincoln, R. S. Visual tracking: III. The instrumental dimension of motion in relation to tracking accuracy. *Journal of Applied Psychology,* 1953, **37,** 489–493.

Moss, S. M. Tracking with a differential brightness display: I. Acquisition and transfer. *Journal of Applied Psychology,* 1964, **48,** 115-122.

Mowbray, G. H., & Gebhard, J. W. Man's senses as information channels. In H. W. Sinaiko (Ed.), *Selected papers on human factors in the design and use of control systems.* New York: Dover, 1961. Pp. 115–149.

Notterman, J. M., & Page, D. E. Evaluation of mathematically equivalent tracking systems. *Perceptual and Motor Skills,* 1962, **15,** 683–716.

Poulton, E. C. Perceptual anticipation and reaction time. *Quarterly Journal of Experimental Psychology,* 1950, **2,** 99–112.

Poulton, E. C. Perceptual anticipation in tracking with two-pointer and one-pointer displays. *British Journal of Psychology,* 1952, **43,** 222–229. (a)

Poulton, E. C. The basis of perceptual anticipation in tracking. *British Journal of Psychology,* 1952, **43,** 295–302. (b)

Poulton, E. C. The precision of choice reactions. *Journal of Experimental Psychology,* 1956, **51,** 98–102.

Poulton, E. C. On the stimulus and response in pursuit tracking. *Journal of Experimental Psychology,* 1957, **53,** 189–194.

Poulton, E. C. On simple methods of scoring tracking error. *Psychological Bulletin,* 1962, **59,** 320–328.

Poulton, E. C. Postview and preview in tracking with complex and simple inputs. *Ergonomics,* 1964, **7,** 257–266.

Poulton, E. C. On increasing the sensitivity of measures of performance. *Ergonomics,* 1965, **8,** 69–76.

Poulton, E. C. Tracking behavior. In E. A. Bilodeau (Ed.), *Acquisition of skill.* New York: Academic Press, 1966. Pp. 361–410.

Poulton, E. C. Tracking a variable rate of movement. *Journal of Experimental Psychology*, 1967, **73**, 135–144.

Poulton, E. C., & Freeman, P. R. Unwanted asymmetrical transfer effects with balanced experimental designs. *Psychological Bulletin*, 1966, **66**, 1–8.

Poulton, E. C., & Gregory, R. L. Blinking during visual tracking. *Quarterly Journal of Experimental Psychology*, 1952, **4**, 57–65.

Reynolds, B., & Adams, J. A. Motor performance as a function of click reinforcement. *Journal of Experimental Psychology*, 1953, **45**, 315–320.

Searle, L. V., & Taylor, F. V. Studies of tracking behavior: I. Rate and time characteristics of simple corrective movements. *Journal of Experimental Psychology*, 1948, **38**, 615–631.

Slack, C. W. Learning in simple one-dimensional tracking. *American Journal of Psychology*, 1953, **66**, 33–44. (a)

Slack, C. W. Some characteristics of the "range effect." *Journal of Experimental Psychology*, 1953, **46**, 76–80. (b)

Taylor, F. V., & Birmingham, H. P. Studies of tracking behavior: II. The acceleration pattern of quick manual corrective responses. *Journal of Experimental Psychology*, 1948, **38**, 783–795.

Taylor, F. V., & Birmingham, H. P. Simplifying the pilot's task through display quickening. *Journal of Aviation Medicine*, 1956, **27**, 27–31.

Welford, A. T. Single-channel operation in the brain. *Acta Psychologica*, 1967, **27**, 5–22.

CHAPTER 11

Outline of Human Selective Learning[1]

CLYDE E. NOBLE
The University of Georgia

The topic of this chapter is nonverbal selective learning: how man acquires the ability to produce available, discrete responses on cue as distinct from learning how to make new responses. Attention is focused on the simpler associative processes with emphasis on the three R's of learning: response, repetition, and reinforcement.

I. Multiple-Choice Situations

A. THORNDIKE'S CONTRIBUTIONS

The nineteenth-century origins of contemporary interest in multiple-choice learning are found among the behavior-oriented zoologists of the post-Darwinian era. Romanes, Morgan, Loeb, and Jennings were the leaders. Their mission was to undertake a comparative analysis of the intellectual and problem-solving abilities of infrahuman organisms. Hobbled by the limitations of naturalistic observation and the anecdotal method, however, early comparative psychology failed

[1]The present essay is an abridged and updated revision of the chapter entitled "Selective Learning" in an earlier text (Noble, 1966a). For financial assistance I am indebted to the U.S. Air Force Office of Scientific Research (Grant AFOSR-1099-68), the University of Georgia's Research and Development Center in Educational Stimulation (Contract OE-6-10-061), and the University's Office of General Research.

to accomplish much of scientific value until the advent of Thorndike (1898). He applied the experimental method to animal trial-and-error learning via the puzzle box. Thorndike's influential formulations of the empirical law of effect and the theory of connectionism (selecting and connecting) contributed significantly toward transforming classic association psychology into a genuine laboratory science. He observed that his hungry cats' behavior on the initial trials was characterized by errorful groping and extended latencies until they chanced to trip the release mechanism that provided access to the lure. With successive reinforcements the subjects' errors and latencies gradually diminished. Eventually they came to restrict their movements to the critical area of the apparatus and thereby selected the correct or adaptive responses more efficiently.

Thorndike saw no necessity for assuming any ideational processes to explain his cats' behavior—nor did Guthrie (1952) with more elaborate instrumentation—but those of a Gestalt turn of mind set about to design simpler problems which would permit animals to produce sudden ("insightful") solutions (Hilgard & Bower, 1966). Subsequent investigators explored a variety of string-pulling, bar-pressing, key-pecking, stick-pushing, and latch-opening tasks, with rewards running the gamut from food to shock-avoidance to poker chips. Although the trial-and-error versus insight issue (a subdivision of the continuity-noncontinuity issue) has still not been resolved to everyone's satisfaction, the work of Harlow (1959) on learning-set formation in primates has convincingly demonstrated that either gradual or sudden acquisition curves can be produced through the manipulation of transfer-of-training variables.

B. Yerkes' Multiple-Choice Method

Thorndikean apparatus was designed only to reflect gross R_t (time) measures. No provision was made to record R_f (frequency) scores or to isolate the varied behaviors of the subjects in puzzle boxes. It remained for Yerkes (1914) to contribute a more analytic technique by elaborating the animal quadruple-choice method of Hamilton (1911) into a generalized, multiple-choice method for man. Originally developed for studying different species' stereotyped reactions to insoluble problems, the Hamilton technique was modified by Yerkes to provide five new emphases: (1)R_f scores in addition to R_t scores, (2) acquisition of correct responses rather than extinction of erroneous responses, (3) variations in complexity, (4) soluble problems instead of insoluble problems, (5) wider interspecies applicability. For human subjects Yerkes' (1921) apparatus contained 12 retractable keys, two or more of which would be presented on a given trial (key setting). The subject's task was to avoid the incorrect keys (R−) and press the correct key (R+). Reinforcing feedback was provided by a buzzer following each R+, and practice was continued until either mastery or some arbitrary proficiency criterion was reached. Yerkes favored relational problems (e.g., middle key of five) whose elements were changed from trial to trial. He believed that their solutions entailed ideational or reasoning abilities based upon the "perception of a certain constant relation among a series of objects" (Yerkes, 1916, p. 10).

A psychologist who called himself a behaviorist (Yerkes, 1914) yet espoused many Gestalt principles, Yerkes is perhaps best considered a functionalist. He was clearly less interested in the multiple-choice method as a reference task for discovering the laws of selective learning than in its utility for testing animal intelligence and developing human norms. Thus, he avoided studies of serial learning, retention, and transfer of training. Had he not been so reluctant to employ the Yerkes Box as a learning device, he might have found that it is a reliable piece of apparatus when used in a deliberately unconventional manner. This was achieved in our laboratory (Noble, 1957a) by defining settings as choice points instead of trials. We gave his most difficult problem (Yerkes, 1921, No. 10) to 100 college subjects using a commercial Yerkes Box. The solution was to alternate left and right of any middle key. Presenting just four trials of 10 choices each, an odd-even-trials reliability coefficient (corrected) of .85 was obtained for R_f scores.

Unfortunately, as compared with the fruitfulness of classical-conditioning, maze-learning, operant-response, and discrimination-learning techniques, little data of any systematic importance had emerged from this method by the 1930's when learning theories came into vogue. The Yerkes Box was generally bypassed in favor of Köhler's tool-using situations, Hunter's spatial and temporal mazes, Maier's reasoning tasks, the Lashley jumping stand, Tolman's T mazes, the Skinner Box, Spence's discrimination problems, the Mowrer-Miller Box, and Harlow's Wisconsin General Test Apparatus. To the end of his life, however, Yerkes remained optimistic about the untapped resources of the multiple-choice method; he encouraged younger psychologists to exploit its potentialities (personal communication, 1954). My own emphasis upon measuring relative frequency of R+, i.e., empirical response probability (R_p) scores, on the Selective Mathometer (cf. Fig. 1), may be regarded as a further development of the Thorndike-Yerkes tradition, coupled with contemporary experimental and statistical methodology.

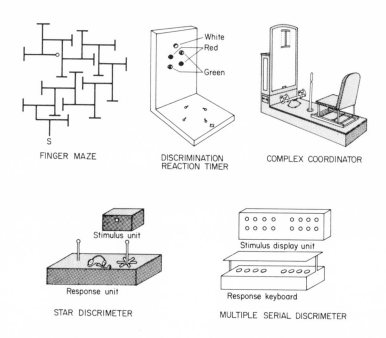

FINGER MAZE

DISCRIMINATION
REACTION TIMER

White
Red
Green

COMPLEX COORDINATOR

Stimulus unit

Response unit

STAR DISCRIMETER

Stimulus display unit

Response keyboard

MULTIPLE SERIAL DISCRIMETER

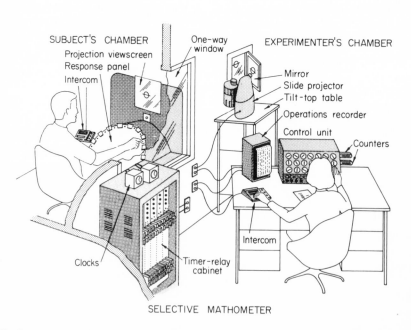

SUBJECT'S CHAMBER
Projection viewscreen
Response panel
Intercom

One-way
window

EXPERIMENTER'S CHAMBER

Mirror
Slide projector
Tilt-top table

Operations recorder

Control unit

Counters

Intercom

Clocks

Timer-relay
cabinet

SELECTIVE MATHOMETER

Fig. 1. Apparatus for research in human selective learning. (After Noble, 1966a.)

322

C. CONTEMPORARY HUMAN APPARATUS

In Fig. 1 are line drawings of the selective-learning devices most frequently cited in research reports of recent vintage. The paragraphs below contain brief summaries of the functions and reliabilities of each apparatus. More detailed descriptions, wiring diagrams, etc., may be found in the original sources.

Oldest of all apparatus for trial-and-error learning is probably the human maze. The great hedge-maze of Henry VIII's Hampton Court Palace in England served as the prototype for the first rat maze of 1899. After several simplifications, the high-relief Finger Maze, designed by Walter R. Miles in 1928, became the most popular human laboratory version (Woodworth & Schlosberg, 1954). The blindfolded subject's task is to trace the pattern with his forefinger from start to goal as quickly as possible and with a minimum of errors. Proficiency is typically measured by R_t and R_f scores, employing the correction procedure. Three different forms (T, U, Y) and many lengths (10 to 40 choice points) have been used, cognate varieties being "mental" (verbal), stylus, punchboard, and bolthead mazes. Since the latter two devices possess the virtue of allowing either the correction or the noncorrection procedure,[2] extra feedback stimuli (usually auditory signals) have to be added to the tactile and kinesthetic cues normally present for reinforcement. Reliability coefficients of .927 and .955 have been reported for stylus and punchboard error scores, respectively (Hilgard, 1951); coefficients varying from .600 to .975 for different methods and groups on Miles' Finger Maze (Spence, 1932); and coefficients of .772 for errors and .967 for speed scores on a semilinear multiple-T Finger Maze of the Warden type (Noble, Noble, & Alcock, 1958c).

Next in seniority is the USAF Complex Coordinator, a World War II modification of a cockpit-simulating apparatus designed by Neely C. Mashburn in 1934 (Melton, 1947). The subject's task is to learn to align a pattern of red lights presented in three dimensions with a matching pattern of green lights. This is done by appropriate movements of the handstick (aileron, elevator) and footbar (rudder) controls. When the lights have been correctly matched for .5 second a new pattern appears automatically, conferring reinforcing feedback. A modified-correction method is the only one available. Proficiency is typically measured by cumulating the subject's R_f scores over a block of 8-minute trials, although time per match has been used also. Reli-

---

[2]Definitions of the correction, modified-correction, and noncorrection procedures are provided in Section II,C.

ability coefficients range from .710 to .917 depending upon the correlation method, sample size, and stimulus patterns chosen (Melton,
1947; Noble, 1966a).

Another World War II product of the USAF is the Discrimination
Reaction Timer, designed by John T. Finan in 1942 (Melton, 1947).
The subject's task is to learn to snap one of four toggle switches in response to the simultaneous onset of a pair of red and green signal
lamps. The relative position of the red lamp with respect to the green
determines which of the four switches is correct. A modified-correction procedure is the only one available. Reinforcing feedback is provided by the offset of a white light. Proficiency is typically measured
by cumulating a subject's R_t scores over a trial block of twenty 3-sec-
ond stimulus presentations, with an interblock interval of 40 seconds.
Reliability coefficients vary from .870 to .930 (Melton, 1947).

The Star Discrimeter was designed by Carl P. Duncan and Benton
J. Underwood in 1950 under a contract with the USAF. The subject's
task is to learn to respond to each of six colored lights emanating from
the stimulus unit by moving the right-hand lever into one of six corresponding slots. The slots are arranged radially in the shape of an aster-
isk on the response unit, while the colors appear automatically in a
continuous random sequence of red, orange, and yellow hues. The
task is usually performed while executing a hand-steadiness action
with the left hand, error information being delivered by earphones.
The correction method is the only one available, reinforcing feedback
occurring when a new light comes on. Proficiency is typically measured by computing a subject's R_f scores during a 20-second trial.
Fixed intertrial intervals of 10 seconds are conventional, but interblock intervals have varied from 1 to 3 minutes. Reliability coefficients range from .883 to .965 (Duncan, 1953). The Iowa model
(McAllister, 1953) omits the steadiness test.

The Multiple Serial Discrimeter was designed by David A. Grant in
1951 under a contract with the USAF. The subject's task is to learn to
respond to two of eight red stimulus lights on a horizontal display by
pressing the correct two of eight reaction keys on the control panel
below. This matches up a pair of green lamps to provide reinforcing
feedback. Two hands are employed by the subject, the left operating
keys 1–4, the right operating keys 5–8. Any number of lights can be
presented, and the light-key relationships may be scrambled. Either
apparatus pacing or self pacing is possible, but the latter (correction)
method is most common. A trial consists of a presentation of two
stimulus lights, which are grouped randomly in blocks of 25 with a 1-
minute rest between blocks. Proficiency is typically measured by

computing R_t scores per trial, but R– scores are also used. Reliability coefficients have not been reported (Morin & Grant, 1955).

The Selective Mathometer, designed by Clyde E. Noble in 1952, is the fifth legacy of the USAF psychology program to the field of selective learning (Noble & Farese, 1955), and it is now fully automatic (Noble, Fuchs, & Thompson, 1963). Figure 1 shows the present layout in the Georgia laboratory. The subject's task is to discover which one of 19 microswitch keys (numbered left to right) is to be pressed in response to each of a series of distinctive slides (e.g., circuit symbols, dot patterns) presented on the screen. The keys are arranged in a semicircle on the reaction panel. Correction, modified-correction, and noncorrection methods are available, and there is separate control of stimulus duration, interstimulus interval, intertrial interval, and stimulus sequence. The reinforcing stimulus (S_g) is the onset of a green light centered above the keyboard. Either serial or terminal S_g is delivered automatically, together with independent variation of delay, duration, and periodicity. All events are recorded by counters and by a continuous, print-out recorder. Proficiency is typically measured by computing a subject's R_p scores over a trial of 10 different 2-second stimulus presentations, although R_t scores have been used also. The interstimulus and intertrial intervals are usually 2 seconds and 8 seconds, respectively. Reliability coefficients range from .938 to .989, varying with type of score, training method, and task complexity (Noble, 1957a; Noble *et al.*, 1958c; Noble, 1966a).[3]

D. DESCRIPTIVE ANALYSIS OF SELECTIVE LEARNING

By a selective-learning task I refer to any multiple-choice situation in which an organism acquires the threefold ability to (1) make a joint selection from the relevant stimuli present and from its own repertoire of available discrete responses, (2) form the necessary associative connections between the stimuli and responses required by the task, and (3) link these S-R pairs together in a coordinated behavior sequence. The emphasis is upon cuing, pairing, and chaining rather than upon the development of fine perceptual discriminations or precision motor skills. Selective-learning tasks, in short, deemphasize stimulus learning as well as response learning. Rarely does selective

---

[3]Apparatus used in symmetrical-choice experiments on verbal-expectation or probability-discrimination problems have been excluded. For reasons given elsewhere (Noble, 1966a, pp. 53–54), these tasks are not regarded as instances of selective learning. Verbal-expectation research seems to deal more with concept formation than with the kinds of associative learning required by the devices listed above.

learning require gradations in amplitude, force, or timing of action as do the classic psychomotor skill devices employed for research in tracking, dexterity, and compensatory pursuit (Noble, 1968).

Of course, not all selective-learning tasks are factorially pure in this respect, but the devices pictured in Fig. 1 are representative of my present emphasis. Fitting the criteria best, I believe, are the Multiple Serial Discrimeter (MSD) and the Selective Mathometer (SM). The Discrimination Reaction Timer (DRT) is weighted somewhat heavily on the perceptual side, just as the Complex Coordinator (CC) leans toward the motor side. The Finger Maze (FM) and the Star Discrimeter (SD) fall somewhere in between, to the left and right, respectively. Thus, the perceptual-motor continuum of my mind's eye has the approximate order sketched below:

DRT	FM	MSD	SM	SD	CC
Perceptual emphasis		Selective-learning emphasis		Motor emphasis	

There are four basic elements in selective-learning situations (Spence, 1956): (1) a motivated organism, (2) a multiple-choice stimulus situation in the external environment, (3) the organism's initial repertoire of discrete responses, and (4) the subsequent physical events together with their aftereffects which are relevant to the organism's motivational state. In Fig. 2 is a diagram of a simple selective-learning problem in which all of the dominant responses (R_1, R_2, R_3) are irrelevant or incorrect ($R-$). The percentage values above the arrows denote hypothetical reaction tendencies of different relative initial strengths. Arbitrarily I have designated the last response (R_n) as the correct one ($R+$); i.e., the first-to-be-learned pair is $S_n \longrightarrow R_n$. This paradigm illustrates the fact that organisms do not enter upon multiple-choice situations behaving in a blind or random fashion, but rather they begin with a hierarchy of systematic response tendencies which, on the basis of hereditary or acquired factors, are more likely to be uncorrelated with the task designed by the experimenter than to be correlated positively or negatively (Hull, 1952). Thus it comes about that the subject's initial habit hierarchy must be reorganized if he is to solve the problem. Selective learning *is* this reorganization.

By the law of effect and the S-R reinforcement theory, the probability, speed, and amplitude of R+ will be strengthened because the goal event (G) that follows it reinforces the habit connection. In the case of human subjects pressing buttons for green lights (cf. Fig. 1) the rein-

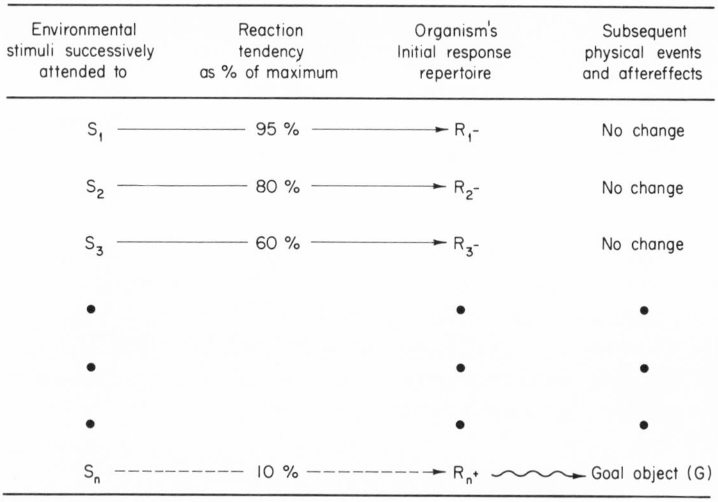

Environmental stimuli successively attended to	Reaction tendency as % of maximum	Organism's Initial response repertoire	Subsequent physical events and aftereffects
S_1 ——————— 95 % ———————➤ R_1-			No change
S_2 ——————— 80 % ———————➤ R_2-			No change
S_3 ——————— 60 % ———————➤ R_3-			No change
•		•	•
•		•	•
•		•	•
S_n ————————— 10 % ——————— ➤ R_n+ 〰〰➤ Goal object (G)			

Fig. 2. A simple (nonserial) selective-learning situation. (After Noble, 1966a.)

forcers are secondary; or, if you prefer, the feedback signals are informative. At any rate, learning is complete when errors (R—) are eliminated and correct responses (R+) occur promptly on every trial. For convenience we shall continue to refer to the class of goal events (mostly green lights) by the symbol S_g.

After description, explanation. In the next section we undertake a theoretical analysis of multiple-choice phenomena.

II. Theory of Selective Learning

A. ROLE OF THEORY

It is sometimes necessary to remind ourselves that a psychological theory is not intended to describe the structure of any particular living being. Rather, it is designed to provide a model—a schematic, hypothetical organism—whose functions are analogous to those of real organisms. A theory's chief aim is thus to explain and predict a large number of phenomena with a small number of assumptions. Obviously, then, theoretical models are not supposed to be mere collections of empirical facts. They are broad conceptual paradigms which permit scientists to arrange facts into meaningful patterns. The principal criteria of a valid theory are two in number: it must provide the basis of interpreting or understanding inductively known facts, and it should aid deductively in the discovery of new facts. Whether a theory is statistical, topological, mechanical, chemical, or neural is beside the point. What matters is that it have the capability of explanation and prediction (Noble, 1966a, b).

Selective learning presents formidable theoretical obstacles because of the multiplicity of events occurring, the inadequacy of experimental control over the relevant variables, and some unfortunate mathematical quirks (Noble, 1966a). When R+, R−, and R_t scores are recorded concurrently in analytic multiple-choice tasks like the Selective Mathometer (cf. Fig. 1), it is clear that several different processes are going on at about the same time: (1) strengthening of R+ through reinforcement, (2) weakening of R− through nonreinforcement, (3) occasional recovery of an extinguished R− with time, (4) generalization of approach from R+ to R−, and (5) generalization of avoidance from R− to R+. The isolation and explanation of these processes require clever experimental design combined with ingenious quantitative theorizing. A number of different theories and models for selective learning have been employed, notable among which have been the formulations of Hull (1943, 1952) and Spence (1956, 1960). Reviews of these and other approaches may be found in Hilgard and Bower (1966) and in Noble (1966a, b). Our own strategy has been to choose a descriptive equation whose form and parameters can be rationalized and thereby coordinated with the general theory of Hull and Spence. To be satisfactory the formula selected should conform to most of the following desiderata: it should (1) bear close similarity to the numerical approximations developed by them for R_p data, (2) provide an excellent statistical fit to empirical R_p data from conditioning and selective-learning experiments, (3) exist in closed form, (4) have fewer total parameters than the Hull-Spence equations, (5) be capable of at least some parameter-free (preexperimental) predictions consistent with the theory, and (6) be amenable to rapid curve-fitting techniques.

An equation satisfying all six criteria is the complex growth curve originated by Gompertz (1825) and elaborated by Courtis (1932), which I have adopted (Noble, 1954, 1957a,b, 1966a) with the following psychological rationale:

$$R_p = a(i)^{r^N} \tag{1}$$

where R_p = probability of correct choice based on the pooled responses of a group of subjects, varying from .00 to 1.00; a = asymptote or limit of R_p, theoretically dependent on feedback (S_g) factors and possibly age (O_y), sex (O_s), and capacity (O_c); i = initial probability of R+ at outset of learning, given empirically by the reciprocal of the number of available independent and mutually exclusive responses, and theoretically related to complexity (S_c) and transfer (S_t) factors; r = rate parameter calculated by curve-fitting methods, theoretically governed by feedback factors (S_g), complexity (S_c), transfer (S_t), work distribution (S_w), aptitude (O_h), and possibly age (O_y), sex (O_s), and motivation (O_d); N = number of practice trials providing differential reinforcement by correction, noncorrection, or modified-correction procedures.

Equation (1) specifies the dependent variable (R_p) as a double-exponential function of the major independent variable (N); its three parameters govern the asymptote (a), origin (i), and rate of change (r). With respect to a, if a given problem is soluble then R_p will approach 1.00 as a function of successive reinforced trials. With respect to i, when no practice has been given, $N = 0$. Therefore, since $r^N = r^0 = 1.00$, the R_p value at Trial $0 = a(i) = i$, which is the probability of an R+ occurring before the first choice point of Trial 1. For simplicity, I have disregarded the effects of transfer and position preferences. The former are expected to affect r, while the influence of the latter on i is minimized by statistical counterbalancing of the possible response permutations (Noble, 1955, 1957a). By systematic variation of four stimulus variables (S_c, S_g, S_t, S_w) and five organismic parameters $(O_c, O_d, O_h, O_s, O_y)$, holding constant the values of a and i, it should be possible to rationalize r by thus anchoring it to selected S and O factors (Noble, 1966b).

In general, the curve of Eq. (1) exhibits a positive slope, is asymmetrical and sigmoidal, and has an inflection point (for soluble problems) at the ordinate $1/e = 1/(2.718) = .368$. So if $i < .368$, and if i and r vary between 0 and 1, it can be shown that the curve inflects at an abscissa value of $N > 0$ (Noble, 1966a). Courtis (1932, p. 89) pointed out that a log-log transformation of the dependent variable is rectilinear over time (N in our case), implying that the percentage of "growth" (R_p in our case) increases to equal powers of itself in equal time periods ("isochrons"). He also worked out a molar theory which is remarkably similar to Hull's, even to the extent of incorporating postulates for variance and threshold.

There is a convenient estimation formula for obtaining r (Noble, 1957c, 1966a), but we shall merely sketch it here. Consider a typical experiment in which subjects are practicing on the Selective Mathometer with three or more keys available. Normally they are either trained to a mastery criterion (five successive perfect trials), or a constant-trials design is used in which there are rational grounds for assuming $a = 1.00$. A free-hand curve is first drawn among the resulting data points from i up to about $R_p = .50$. Next, from the intersection of the fitted segment with an extended ordinate line at $R_p = .368$, a perpendicular is dropped to the abscissa. This trial value is substituted in the estimation formula which is then solved for a likely value of r. Successive solutions of Eq. (1) will generate a set of theoretical (expected) response probabilities $(\tilde{R}_p)$ which may then be compared with the empirical (observed) probabilities (R_p) for goodness of fit. The above procedure is repeated for selected values of r, each time calculating the variance of the residuals or vertical deviations:

$$\sigma^2_{res} = \Sigma (R_p - \tilde{R}_p)^2/n. \tag{2}$$

A least-squares solution is obtained by minimizing σ^2_{res}. This method avoids the linear reduction procedure (Courtis, 1932; Lewis, 1960), which requires the calculation of double logarithms, is more laborious, and gives a best fit only to the transformed data. In selective mathometry we are fundamentally interested in predicting R_p values rather than in the logarithms of the logarithms of R_p values.

Finally, a goodness-of-fit index (F), expressed in percentage terms, is computed directly from the minimum σ^2_{res} value and the observed variance of the R_p scores (σ^2_{obs}) by the formula:

$$F = 100 \left(1 - \frac{\sigma^2_{res}}{\sigma^2_{obs}} \right). \tag{3}$$

With Eq. (3), which is analogous to the coefficient of determination in linear regression, we may specify the percentage of variance in the dependent variable (R_p) accounted for by Eq. (1); i.e., F measures the precision with which R_p can be predicted from N when a, i, and r are constant.

In the case of experiments involving less than three choices or, more generally, when $i \geqslant 1/e$, the curve is negatively accelerated throughout. The fact that data from two-choice situations (e.g., most discrimination-learning tasks) rarely manifest an inflection point can, therefore, be nicely represented by Eq. (1). Another exception occurs when i cannot be calculated in advance of the experiment, as in certain transfer-of-training designs, or where R_p might be expected to begin at zero, as in conditioning studies. Since i must have a nonzero value in order to generate a series of R_p scores, the stimulus events producing the first observed R_p measurement are simply redefined as Trial 0, whereupon former Trial 2 becomes Trial 1, etc. Shortly the author will have occasion to use this artifice (Fig. 3).

B. ADEQUACY OF THE MODEL

The pragmatic worth of Eq. (1) may be evaluated with respect to its similarity either to theory or to data, or its joint similarity to both. The latter approach devotes equal attention to the two domains, and is the one employed here. A set of theoretical R_p scores for a simple conditioning task was derived by Lewis (1960, pp. 511–516) from the Hull-Spence theory. Lewis calculated 32 values of R_p, but the present analysis will deal only with his Trials 7 to 32, which are redesignated Trials 0 to 25 inclusive. Letting $a = 1.00$ and $i = .017$, the best-fitting r parameter computed for Eq. (1) by the residual minimization method described above is .756. As shown in the upper left quadrant of Fig. 3 the agreement is very close; by Eq. (3) the index $F = 99.93\%$. The error variance is less than 0.1 %.

For the next test we shall consider some animal-learning data. A set of empirical R_p scores from 30 dogs trained to make a conditioned avoidance response (foreleg flexion) to a bell was reported by Brogden (1949). He administered daily 20-trial blocks of bell plus shock until a criterion of 100 % conditioning was achieved. By redefining his first 13 trial blocks as Blocks 0 to 12 inclusive, letting $a = 1.00$ and $i = .058$, we find that the best-fitting r parameter for Eq. (1) is .697. As can be seen in the upper right quadrant of Fig. 3 the fit is excellent; by Eq. (3) $F = 99.98\%$. Instead of using Vincentized scores (Hilgard, 1951) as Brogden (and also Lewis, 1960, pp. 84–88) did, we calculated the data points in Fig. 3 from the original R_f scores tabulated in Brogden's article (1949, p. 297).

Turning now to the lower left quadrant of Fig. 3, we find two sets of theoretical R_p scores derived for a two-choice selective-learning task by Hull (1952, pp. 21–33) which will also be fitted by Eq. (1). In Case I the competing reaction tendencies are initially both equal and weak, hence the R_p value on Trial 1, redesignated as Trial 0, is $i = .50$. The curve is negatively accelerated, with $a = 1.00$, $r = .660$, and $F = 99.70\%$. In Case IV, which is the classic trial-and-error situation, the two competing reaction tendencies are initially unequal with the erroneous tendency considerably stronger. Hull's derived R_p value on Trial 1, redefined to be Trial 0, is taken as $i = .017$. This curve is clearly sigmoidal, with $a = 1.00$, $r = .707$, and $F = 99.60\%$. Although different in appearance, both curves are in good agreement with Eq. (1).

Finally, the lower right quadrant of Fig. 3 presents a set of empirical R_p scores from two groups of 48 subjects each who practiced four-unit problems on the Selective Mathometer (Noble, 1955). There were

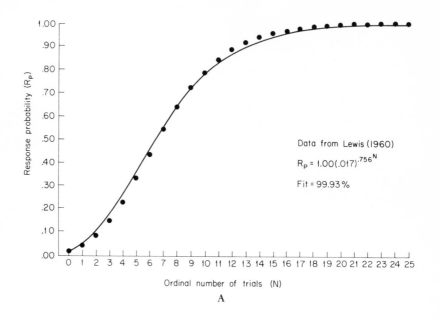

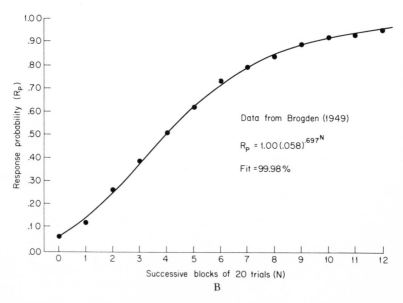

Fig. 3.   Theoretical and empirical curves of response probability (R_p) as a function of number of trials (N), all fitted by Eq. (1). Graphs A and B are for conditioned-response learning. (After Lewis, 1960; Brogden, 1949.)

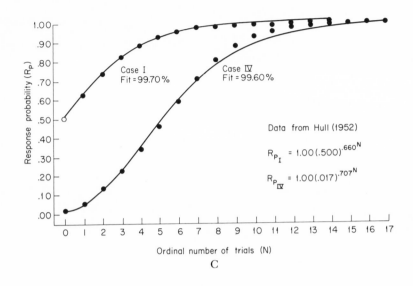

C

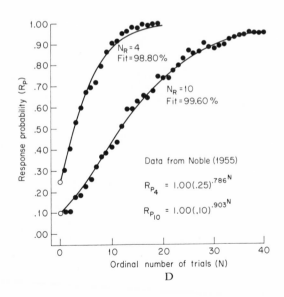

D

Fig. 3 *(cont.)*. The graphs C and D are for selective learning. (After Hull, 1952; Noble, 1955.) Open circles denote rational origins. (After Noble, 1966a.)

333

different numbers of responses (N_R) available to the two groups, denoted by $N_R = 4$ and $N_R = 10$ for the upper and lower curve, respectively. Letting $a = 1.00$ and $i = .25$, the r parameter for the $N_R = 4$ curve is .786 whereupon $F = 98.80\%$. For the $N_R = 10$ curve, where $a = 1.00$ and $i = .10$, the r parameter is .903 with $F = 99.60\%$.

To summarize, the evidence from three theoretical curves and three empirical curves, varying widely in parametric values and task complexity, is that Eq. (1) provides a close approximation to hypothetical data as well as an excellent fit to experimental data. Predictability indices range from 99.60 to 99.98% with a mean of 99.77%. That the fits to the derived curves are not perfect suggests that some systematic discrepancy exists either in the postulates of the Hull-Spence theory or in the characteristics of my formula. Which one of these requires revision is not yet known, although the order of magnitude of the error variance ($<1\%$) is tolerable at this stage of theoretical development. The general batting average of Eq. (1), based on evidence from several dozen experiments in our laboratory, runs in excess of 98%.

A final topic to be included in this section concerns the validity of rival hypotheses in accounting for selective-learning performance. Consequently, we shall discuss next some evidence bearing on the contiguity-reinforcement and continuity-noncontinuity issues (Guthrie, 1959; Kimble, 1961; Spence, 1960).

C. Frequency, Postremity, and Reinforcement

One of the first psychologists to evaluate experimentally the classic associationistic concepts of recency and frequency in human selective learning was Peterson (1922). He compared predictions and outcomes of the individual responses of 16 subjects run to mastery (three perfect trials) on a two-choice 10-unit verbal maze. Peterson's results led him to conclude that recency was uncorrelated with R+ and that frequency tended to strengthen R− rather than R+. He mentioned the possible relevance of Thorndike's law of effect but did not elaborate.

Disagreeing with Peterson's interpretation, especially with its implications for Guthrie's (1952) recency principle, Voeks (1948) reanalyzed his data to find (1) that 68.4% of his 4518 recency predictions were correct, and (2) that when the last response of a trial was an R+ it was repeated on 73.0% of the next trials, as opposed to 63.9% repetitions of R− choices. Voeks proceeded to perform three experiments as a more adequate test of the Guthrian hypothesis (now renamed postremity). For her first experiment (Experiment I) Voeks used a two-choice 18-unit Finger Maze of the type shown in Fig. 1. College students were run to mastery (three perfect trials) by the correction procedure. She reported 88.74 % correct predictions via postremity. In Experiment II a two-choice 30-unit punchboard stylus maze and the noncorrection method were employed, resulting in 82.30 % correct postremity predictions. This procedure was repeated in Experiment III with a threaded stylus, the postremity outcome being 83.05 %. Since all three experiments involved two-choice tasks, the mean prediction index for 57 subjects of 84.69 % is 34.69 % better than chance. Voeks presented no separate analysis of frequency predictions, but she said that about 71 % of her predictions were correct by postremity even when opposed by frequency, although this conflict reduced postremity's accuracy. Curiously, there was no analysis of the reinforcement factor. With respect to R+ vs R— scores she asserted: "by the present hypothesis, postremity is neutral, having no differential effect on the correct and incorrect responses" (Voeks, 1948, p. 497).

A third investigation of this problem (Waters & Reitz, 1950) used a two-choice 15-unit Finger Maze on which 20 subjects were each given 15 trials by the noncorrection procedure. Half of the group received a changing stimulus situation from Trials 11 through 15 to see whether postremity predictions would be adversely affected. Waters and Reitz reported an average postremity score of 70 % correct predictions based on 4200 responses. This figure, 20 % over chance, is doubtless smaller than Voeks' margin because the subjects were not carried to mastery. A more interesting aspect of the Waters-Reitz experiment, however, is their trial-by-trial analysis. Since the constant and variable groups were not significantly different on the last five trials (an embarrassing result for the Guthrie-Voeks viewpoint), they may be combined. Doing this we found that the percentage of correct predictions increased with stage of practice, rising from 53 % on Trial 2 to 80 % on Trial 15. Extrapolating to the Peterson-Voeks criterion of three perfect trials in a row, it is obvious that postremity would eventually predict with 100 % accuracy if practice were carried far enough. Like Voeks, and Peterson earlier, Waters and Reitz made no analysis of reinforcement predictions. Clearly, more extensive comparative data of a detailed nature are needed.

In an effort to contribute information toward this objective, the author reported two theoretical studies on the Selective Mathometer (Noble, 1966a) that evaluate the relative efficacy of the postremity, frequency, and reinforcement principles under correction, noncorrection, and modified-correction procedures. The first study used data collected from 100 subjects performing on standard 10-choice 10-unit Mathometer problems for 20 trials (Noble, Alcock, & Noble, 1958b). Half the subjects practiced by the modified-correction method (permitting alternative corrective responses, but only for the 2-second duration of a slide): the remaining 50 practiced by the noncorrection method (requiring one and only one response per slide). Both groups were experimenter paced. From the graphic records of 20,000 choice points, individual pushbutton behavior was analyzed under the two S_c conditions. Extending and improving the scoring method developed by Voeks, we made three independent predictions for each subject's first response (R) at each choice point beginning with Trial 2. The three predictions were based on the following specific hypotheses derived from classic association theory.

1. *Postremity*: the last nominal (numbered) R occurring at a given choice point (whether R+ or R−) on the immediately preceding trial is predicted, regardless of consequences (aftereffects, feedback, etc.), a prediction being made at every choice point.

2. *Frequency*: the nominal R occurring most often at a given choice point (whether R+ or R−) on all preceding trials is predicted provided $R_p > .50$, no predictions being made if the frequencies are equal.

3. *Reinforcement*: the nominal R most frequently reinforced by the green light (S_g) at a given choice point on all preceding trials is predicted provided $R_p > .50$, no predictions being made if the frequencies of reinforcement are equal.

To be as fair as possible to the three contenders, a few ground rules were adopted in advance of scoring. For reinforcement predictions, late errors were counted but late (unreinforced) corrects were ignored; in frequency and postremity predictions, both late R+ and late R− choices were counted. All double R's were scored as singles, but no intertrial R's were scored. Omissions were counted as disagreements only if the hypothesis predicted an overt R.

The percentage of agreement between prediction and fact was then computed for each hypothesis by subjects and by trials, with the results shown in Fig. 4. Note that the ordinate scales display the performance not of subjects but of hypotheses. Looking first at the modified-correction method (upper left graph), we see that reinforcement predictions are generally far superior to predictions by frequency or postremity, the latter being definitely inferior to frequency. Looking next at the noncorrection method (upper right graph), an even greater superiority of the reinforcement hypothesis is evident. Although frequency is still ahead of postremity, its margin of superiority is less.

Our second study used data collected from 192 subjects performing on the same kinds of 10-choice Mathometer problems as in the first report. In this experiment half the subjects practiced for 20 trials by the correction method (requiring corrective responses until reinforcing feedback was received); the remaining 96 practiced by the noncorrection method as defined earlier. In other words, the correction group was subject-paced whereas the noncorrection group was experimenter-paced. From the graphic records of 38,400 choice points, individual responses were analyzed under the two S_c conditions, as described above.

Returning now to Fig. 4 and looking first at the correction method (lower left graph), we see that there is little difference in the predictive efficacy of the three hypotheses. Reinforcement still leads frequency (albeit by a tiny margin), and both are superior to postremity until the last quarter of practice when they merge above the 80% ordinate. Looking next at the noncorrection method (lower right graph), we find essentially a replication of the earlier investigation. In general, Fig. 4 shows that reinforcement predictions are consistently and decisively more accurate than all others, with frequency winning out over postremity in a close race. All three hypotheses improve in validity as practice continues, and would probably converge if mastery were approached.

The overall results of these four independent comparisons, pooling the observations of 292 subjects responding one or more times at 58,400 choice points, are summarized in Fig. 5 as mean percentages (rounded) of correct predictions during Trials 2 to 20. With the random accuracy level at 10%, the reinforcement principle predicts 70.9% better than chance when the two noncorrection groups are averaged. Frequency and postremity exceed chance by only 36.0 and 33.8%, respectively. We may conclude that in the noncorrection situation, reinforcement's accuracy for a 10-choice task is about twice that of its rivals. After five trials we can predict around 75% of the time what the initial R at the next choice point will be merely by keeping a record of the subject's reinforcement history. By Trial 18 the predictability is close to 90%. Using frequency or postremity, our predictions on those same trials would average only 33 and 60%, respectively. For analytic purposes, in consequence, maximum differentiation among the three hypotheses is provided by the noncorrection procedure, followed by the modified-correction and correction procedures in that order. In the correction method, since a reinforced response must always be last, no one will be surprised to find postremity predicting almost as well as reinforcement. Similarly, since the reinforced response tends with extended practice to become the most frequent response in the correction procedure, frequency also is able to predict at about the same level as reinforcement. Regardless of practice method, however, the validity of the reinforcement hypothesis for selective learning is strikingly demonstrated in these analyses. At the same

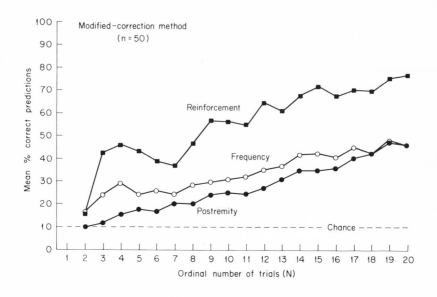

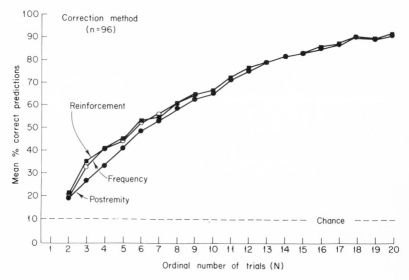

Fig. 4. Comparative predictabilities of the reinforcement, frequency, and postremity hypotheses under three methods of practice as functions of stage of practice. (After Noble, 1966a.)

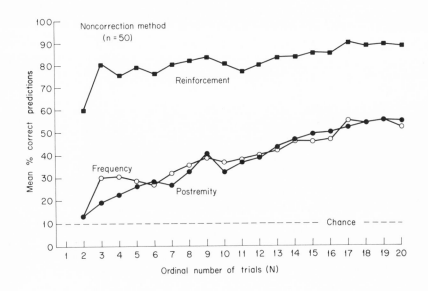

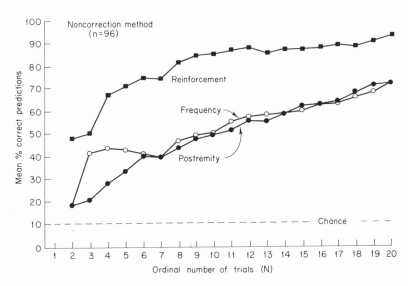

Fig. 4 *(continued).*

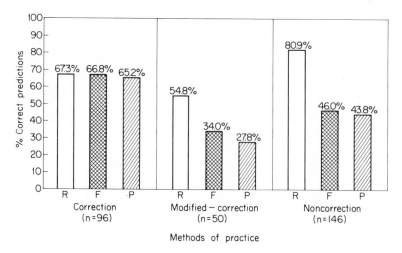

Fig. 5. Histograms of the mean percentage of correct predictions by the reinforcement (R), frequency (F), and postremity (P) hypotheses under three methods of practice during Trials 2–20 on the Selective Mathometer. Numbers of subjects (*n*) are shown in parentheses. (After Noble, 1966a.)

time they appear to present a formidable challenge to nonreinforcement theories (Guthrie, 1952; Harlow, 1959; Voeks, 1948) and to theories which construe learning as a random event (cf. Hilgard and Bower, 1966).

With respect to the contiguity-reinforcement issue, it is instructive to observe that while all three hypotheses assume S-R contiguity, two of them are distinctive in exploiting R-R components (e.g., correlating the last or the modal response with the next response). The power of the S-R-contiguity-frequency-reinforcement hypothesis, to enumerate all of its elements, is that it includes an extra experimental component: the operation of reinforcing S→R+ connections. As Seward, Dill, and Holland (1944) found in a straightforward S-R-contiguity-recency pushbutton experiment of the type Guthrie's (1952) theory would propose, the paradigm S→R$_1$ followed by S → R$_2$ failed to produce R$_{p2}$ > R$_{p1}$. Unlike Voeks' postremity, then, reinforcement is not neutral; it does exert differential influences on R+ and R− choices. This is what accounts for the massive increments in going from the frequency to the reinforcement curves in Fig. 4 (for all but the correction procedure). Additional factors, which are mentioned later in the chapter, are the significant effects of generalization and nonreinforcement. By combining all these elements, as we are attempting to do in the Georgia laboratory, we believe that the average predictability of individual behavior (for carefully selected initial and boundary conditions) can be extended well into the 90 % range.

With respect to the continuity-noncontinuity issue, there are few relevant human-learning investigations, apart from a spate of recent verbal-behavior experiments on the role of item selection and other artifacts in producing ostensible "one-trial-learning" results. The methodological defects of the early paired-associate substitution designs have been exposed by Underwood and Keppel (1962). To the discomfiture of most S-S as well as some S-R noncontinuity theorists, those star-crossed studies turned out to be exercises in the control of performance factors rather than proofs that habit strength is saltatory. While no dogmatic assertion is possible yet on the question of all-or-none versus incremental principles of habit formation, it is manifest that advocates of the noncontinuity viewpoint have not exactly improved their defensive posture vis-à-vis those of the continuity persuasion. The incrementalists are deployed in positions of strength for several reasons: (1) most empirical group acquisition curves measured in terms of R_p, R_a, or $R_{1/t}$ can be described as continuous positive functions of N (Hall, 1966; Woodworth & Schlosberg, 1954); (2) the results of animal discrimination studies have generally favored the continuity view (Kimble, 1961); (3) the rapidity of changes in learning-set scores among infrahuman and human subjects is a cumulative function of the amount of interproblem training (Harlow, 1959); (4) human overlearning-retention experiments are consistent across memory drums and finger mazes in showing positive correlations and a diminishing-returns principle (McGeoch & Irion, 1952); (5) the occasional appearance of discontinuous R_p scores can be handled within continuity theory by attenuating the oscillation function, as in cases of increased experimental control (Spence, 1956).

For a sampler of human selective-learning experiments supporting the incremental principle, I shall mention three. Prentice (1949) adapted the classic two-choice cue-reversal discrimination-learning paradigm for college students, finding the reversal group's performance inferior to that of the nonreversal group. This is as it should be if erstwhile reinforced choices must be extinguished and former avoidance responses replaced by approach when the cues are altered for the reversal subjects. In a similar investigation Walk (1952) also got continuity results from a pair of discrimination-learning experiments, although the negative transfer effects were brief. Finally, there is a demonstration by Paul and Noble (1964) of the positive transfer effect of successive habit reversals on the Mathometer which turned up some evidence inconsistent with the ahistorical postulate of Gestalt theory. We noticed that the number of subjects attaining perfect scores on the second postreversal trial of each block increased steadily with amount of reversal training. These data were reanalyzed and suggest that although insight may be a within-subject phenomenon, it can be manipulated like any dependent variable, then assessed as a between-subject effect. In sharp refutation of the noncontinuity credo that insight is independent of repetitive training, Fig. 6 shows that the probability of one-trial reversals occurring is a continuous positive function of N.

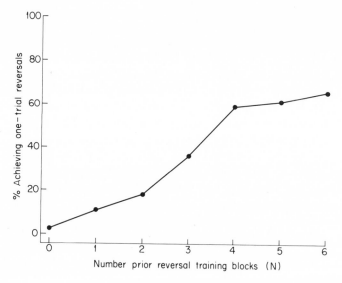

Fig. 6. Percentage of subjects achieving perfect one-trial reversals as a function of the number of previous 10-trial blocks of reversal training (N). Each point is based on the data of 44 subjects. (After Paul & Noble, 1964.)

To recapitulate, the odds-on favorite in the learning lottery is an S-R reinforcement theory that assumes an underlying continuity for the growth of associative (habit) strength. Now, in the final section, I turn to a brief review of the laws of selective learning, prefacing the discussion of each group of phenomena by a tentative coordination with the Gompertz-Courtis equation.

III. Laws of Selective Learning

The empirical laws of selective learning are observed regularities or consistencies that connect three major classes of operationally-defined objects or events in multiple-choice situations. These groups of conditions are denoted by the traditional symbols S, O, and R: (1) S-variables include antecedent (input) events of an independent, manipulable, "causal" type, (2) O-variables include organismic, human-factor parameters of a modulating and mediating (i.e., anatomic, physiological) type, and (3) R-variables include consequent (output) events of a dependent, correlated, "effect" type. Our major interest is in $R_p = f(S_n)$, as specified in Eq. (1). The frame of reference that one speaks of as S-O-R, therefore, is not a theory but a general functional orientation within which experimental and differential psychologists meet on common ground (Noble, 1966b).

The laws of selective learning [$R = f(S_n)$] may be codified under the following five rubrics: (1) Task Complexity (S_c), (2) Feedback Contingencies (S_g), (3) Work Distribution (S_w), (4) Transfer of Training (S_t), and (5) Individual and Group Differences (O_c, O_d, O_h, O_s, O_y). The R-variables may be measured in terms of frequency (R_f), amplitude (R_a), or time (R_t). Our descriptive schema, in abstract form, is:

$$R = f[S_n(S_c, S_g, S_w, S_t, O_c, O_d, O_h, O_s, O_y)]. \qquad (4)$$

This means that the empirical task in *mathometrology*[4] is to discover inductively the laws and interactions among these three classes of events. Here now are the five categories, with capsule reviews attached.

A. COMPLEXITY OF TASK: $R = f(S_c)$

The S_c factors are hypothesized to affect the parameters *i* and *r* of Eq. (1) in addition to the variance of R_p, and they are believed to be nonassociational performance variables.

Evidence supporting this principle comes from experiments that manipulated the number of available responses (N_R) and/or the number of choice points (N_P). As shown in the lower right portion of Fig. 3, significant differences due to N_R result (Noble, 1955) and the fits are good (Noble, 1957a). Other studies of N_R have produced comparable results (Noble, 1957b; Kaess & Zeaman, 1960; Seibel, 1963), as have investigations of N_P (Noble, 1953; Brogden & Schmidt, 1954a,b; Noble, 1957c, 1966a). Uniformity of the S-R sequence is a complexity

[4]The term mathometrology is derived from Greek: *manthano* (to learn) + *metron* (measure) + *logos* (field of study). It refers to the quantitative science of learned behavior. A mathometrologist (equal accents on second and fourth syllables) is, therefore, a psychologist who specializes in observation, experimentation, measurement, and theory pertaining to the phenomena occurring within the field of learning and performance.

Clyde E. Noble

variable that influences difficulty as well as variability (Barch, 1960; Farese & Noble, 1960). Some error curves from the Selective Mathometer are presented in Fig. 7. Other operations included under the S_c label are simultaneous vs successive presentation, stimulus patterning, and cue similarity in two-choice discrimination tasks (Loess & Duncan, 1952; Perkins, Banks, & Calvin, 1954; White & Spiker, 1960); display-control relationships (Adams, 1954a; Morin & Grant, 1955; Nystrom & Grant, 1955; Fitts, 1964); and correction vs noncorrection practice methods (Noble, 1966a).

B. FEEDBACK CONTINGENCIES: $R = f(S_g)$

The S_g factors are hypothesized to affect the parameters a and r of Eq. (1) in addition to the extinction of R_p, and they are believed to be both learning and performance variables.

Evidence supporting this principle comes from experiments that manipulated serial vs terminal feedback (Noble & Noble, 1958), delayed serial feedback (Noble & Alcock, 1958), and delayed terminal feedback together with different types and combinations of feedback

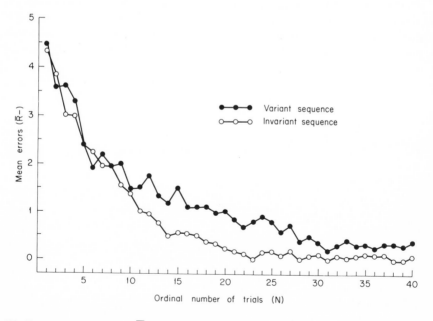

Fig. 7. Mean error curves ($\overline{R}-$) in selective learning as functions of the number of practice trials (N), with uniformity of the S-R sequence (S_c) as the parameter. Each curve is based on the data of 48 subjects. (After Farese & Noble, 1960, p. 118.)

(Noble, 1966a). Birch (1964) used a two-choice puzzle task to explore the relationship between difficulty and incentives; Morin and Grant (1955) employed the Multiple Serial Discrimeter to study the interaction of S_g with corresponding vs noncorresponding S-R matches; and Terrell and Kennedy (1957) compared the effects of candy reward with praise or reproof in two-choice discrimination learning by children. On the motivating properties of feedback, there are significant experiments on noxious stimulation in maze learning by Jones (1945), Freeburne and Schneider (1955), Bevan and Adamson (1960), and by Feldman (1961). In the area of stress and motivating instructions a number of papers are relevant (Castaneda, 1956; Palermo, 1957; Birch, 1958; Fleishman, 1958; Lipsitt & LoLordo, 1963). The effects of nonreinforcement were investigated by Cantor and Spiker (1954) with a two-choice task, Hubbard (1951) with a three-choice task, and by Taylor and Noble (1962) with a four-choice task. An extension of the latter study (Noble, 1966a) produced the extinction curves shown in Fig. 8. Then there is the role of asymptotic restrictions in Eq. (1). When the a parameter was experimentally reduced from 1.00 to .40 in different groups (Chambers & Noble, 1961), initial R_p scores dropped correspondingly from .10 to .04 because a and i are multiplied in Eq. (1). The acquisition curves growing toward appropriate final levels are presented in Fig. 9. It may be noted that the inflection points in this experiment occurred not at $1/e$ on the ordinate but at a/e, as predicted.

C. WORK DISTRIBUTION: $R = f(S_w)$

The S_w factors are hypothesized to affect only the r parameter of Eq. (1), and they are believed to influence learning by way of performance.

Evidence supporting this principle comes from experiments that manipulated the number of response evocations in two-choice tasks (Siegel, 1950; Thompson, 1952) and the intertrial interval in ten-choice tasks (Noble & Taylor, 1959). Recent work with the Selective Mathometer using correction vs noncorrection practice methods and several intertrial intervals indicates that decrements in R_p curves due to massed practice occur independently of reminiscence, even when habit strength is equated (Noble, 1968). The effects of different rates of pacing were compared with self-paced performance on the Complex Coordinator (Adams, 1954b) and on the Multiple Serial Discrimeter (Nystrom, Morin, & Grant, 1955). Briggs and Brogden (1954) examined part vs whole practice conditions, and Neumann and

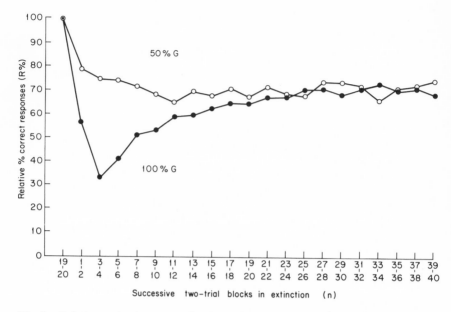

Fig. 8. Relative extinction curves (R%) in selective learning as functions of the number of nonreinforced trials (*n*), with original reinforcement schedule (S_g) as the parameter. Each curve is based on the data of 96 subjects. (After Noble, 1966a.)

Ammons (1957) evaluated retention over intervals ranging from 1 minute to 1 year.

D. Transfer of Training: $R = f(S_t)$

The S_t factors are hypothesized to affect the parameters *i* and *r* of Eq. (1); depending on various conditions they may produce either learning or performance changes.

Evidence supporting this principle comes from experiments that manipulated specificity of instructions (Noble, Alcock, & Farese, 1958a; Noble, Alcock, & Frye, 1959) and habit reversal (Paul & Noble, 1964) on the Selective Mathometer, as illustrated in Fig. 6. Some excellent papers on the role of facilitation and interference in complex coordination were reviewed by Bilodeau and Bilodeau (1961). Significant research on amount and variety of pretraining and/or intertask similarity employing the Star Discrimeter was performed by Duncan (1953), Duncan and Underwood (1953), McAllister (1953), McFann (1953), J. H. Cantor (1955), and by Lewis and Miles (1956). Null results for verbal stimulus familiarization and pronunciation during learning were reported for the Selective Mathometer by Noble, Allison, and Jones (1966). There are numerous other learning-transfer experiments cited by Noble (1966a) which have employed a variety of lamp, key, and switch devices, two-choice discrimination apparatus, transposition problems, and spatial generalization tasks with children as well as adults (e.g., Brown, Clarke, & Stein, 1958; Jeffrey & Cohen, 1964; Zeiler, 1964).

E. INDIVIDUAL AND GROUP DIFFERENCES: $R = f(O_c, O_d, O_h, O_s, O_y)$

The organismic or O factors [capacity (O_c), drive (O_d), habit aptitude (O_h), sex (O_s), and age in years (O_y)] are hypothesized to affect the parameters a and r of Eq. (1), and they are believed to be performance variables.

Evidence supporting this principle comes from experiments that employed batteries of printed and apparatus tests in conjunction with the Selective Mathometer wherein it was found that O_h is relevant but neither O_s nor O_d (Noble et $al.$, 1958c). Examples of R_p acquisition curves varying only in the r parameter are shown in Fig. 10. Similar results have been seen for O_h by Jones (1945) on the Finger Maze and by Adams (1957) on the Discrimination Reaction Timer (cf. Fig. 1). The latter apparatus also reveals significant differences and interac-

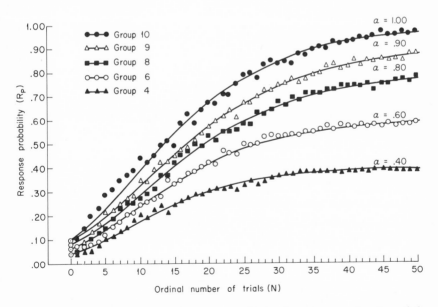

Fig. 9. Response probability (R_p) curves in selective learning as a function of the number of practice trials (N), with different asymptotes (a) as the parameter. For computations of the rational origins, see text. Each curve is based on the data of 30 subjects. (After Chambers & Noble, 1961, p. 419.)

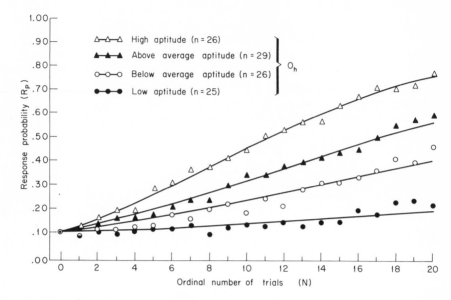

Fig. 10. Response probability curves (R_p) in selective learning as a function of the number of practice trials (N), with individual differences in aptitude (O_h) as the parameter. All curves have been fitted by Eq. (1), with only the r parameter varying. (After Noble *et al.*, 1958c, p. 164.)

tions due to O_c, O_d, O_s, and O_y (Grice, 1955; Noble, Baker, & Jones, 1964; Noble, 1966a; Noble & Hays, 1966), but an exponential equation is more appropriate than Eq. (1) when speed scores ($R_{1/t}$) are employed (Noble, 1968).[5] The variables O_c and O_y have not yet been examined with the Selective Mathometer. Some investigators have gotten main effects of O_d and $S_n \times O_d$ interactions on the Finger Maze, but others have not (Noble, 1966a). Finally, Patel and Grant (1964) observed a three-factor $S_n \times O_s \times S_w$ interaction among subjects performing on the Multiple Serial Discrimeter.

IV. Summary

This chapter has provided an outline of the variables, theories, and laws of human nonverbal selective learning. Multiple-choice situ-

---

[5]Evidence of racial differences affecting the O_c and O_h parameters on the Discrimination Reaction Timer is presented in a recent monograph (Noble, C. E., *Perspectives in Biology and Medicine*, 1969, **12**, No. 4).

ations were presented in historical perspective together with a survey and classification of six contemporary selective-learning apparatus. Some theoretical aspects of selective learning were examined next, and a quantitative formulation of response probability (R_p) scores was described.

The adequacy of the equation $R_p = a(i)^{r^N}$ was evaluated by curve-fitting techniques and its parameters were rationalized. The average predictability of group curves on the Selective Mathometer was greater than 98%. A comparative analysis of 58,400 individual response predictions under three methods of practice indicated that an S-R reinforcement theory is more tenable than a simple frequency or postremity viewpoint. For intermediate stages of practice on ten-choice noncorrection tasks, the average predictability for single subjects was about 81%.

Finally, the laws of selective learning $[R_p = f(S_n)]$ were classified under five headings: Task Complexity (S_c), Feedback Contingencies (S_g), Work Distribution (S_w), Transfer of Training (S_t), Individual and Group Differences (O_c, O_d, O_h, O_s, O_y). Data generated from representative experimental variables are in close agreement with the equation, and its parameters vary according to theoretical expectation.

References

Adams, J. A. Psychomotor response acquisition and transfer as a function of control-indicator relationships. *Journal of Experimental Psychology*, 1954, 48, 10–14. (a)

Adams, J. A. The effect of pacing on the learning of a psychomotor response. *Journal of Experimental Psychology*, 1954, 47, 101–105. (b)

Adams, J. A. The relationship between certain measures of ability and the acquisition of a psychomotor criterion response. *Journal of General Psychology*, 1957, 56, 121–134.

Barch, A. M. Serial paired-associate performance: I. Effect of sequence complexity and irrelevant cues. *Perceptual and Motor Skills*, 1960, 10, 175–178.

Bevan, W., & Adamson, R. Reinforcers and reinforcement: Their relation to maze performance. *Journal of Experimental Psychology*, 1960, 59, 226–232.

Bilodeau, E. A., & Bilodeau, I. McD. Motor-skills learning. *Annual Review of Psychology*, 1961, 12, 243–280.

Birch, D. Motivation shift in a complex learning task. *Journal of Experimental Psychology*, 1958, 56, 507–515.

Birch, D. Incentive value of success and instrumental approach behavior. *Journal of Experimental Psychology*, 1964, 68, 131–139.

Briggs, G. E., & Brogden, W. J. The effect of component practice on performance of a lever-positioning skill. *Journal of Experimental Psychology*, 1954, 48, 375–380.

Brogden, W. J. Acquisition and extinction of a conditioned avoidance response in dogs. *Journal of Comparative and Physiological Psychology*, 1949, 42, 296–302.

Brogden, W. J., & Schmidt, R. E. Acquisition of a 24-unit verbal maze as a function of number of alternate choices per unit. *Journal of Experimental Psychology*, 1954, **48**, 335–338. (a)

Brogden, W. J., & Schmidt, R. E. Effect of number of choices per unit of a verbal maze on learning and serial position errors. *Journal of Experimental Psychology*, 1954, **47**, 235–240. (b)

Brown, J. S., Clarke, F. R., & Stein, L. A new technique for studying spatial generalization with voluntary responses. *Journal of Experimental Psychology*, 1958, **55**, 359–362.

Cantor, G. N., & Spiker, C. C. Effects of nonreinforced trials on discrimination learning in preschool children. *Journal of Experimental Psychology*, 1954, **47**, 256–258.

Cantor, J. H. Amount of pretraining as a factor in stimulus predifferentiation and performance set. *Journal of Experimental Psychology*, 1955, **50**, 180–184.

Castaneda, A. Effects of stress on complex learning and performance. *Journal of Experimental Psychology*, 1956, **52**, 9–12.

Chambers, R. W., & Noble, C. E. Effects of various asymptotic restrictions on human trial-and-error learning. *Journal of Experimental Psychology*, 1961, **61**, 417–421.

Courtis, S. A. *The measurement of growth.* Ann Arbor, Mich.: Brumfield & Brumfield, 1932.

Duncan, C. P. Transfer in motor learning as a function of degree of first-task learning and inter-task similarity. *Journal of Experimental Psychology*, 1953, **45**, 1–11.

Duncan, C. P., & Underwood, B. J. Retention of transfer in motor learning after twenty four hours and after fourteen months. *Journal of Experimental Psychology*, 1953, **46**, 445–452.

Farese, F. J., & Noble, C. E. Trial-and-error vs. mixed-selective learning in man. *Perceptual and Motor Skills*, 1960, **10**, 115–122.

Feldman, S. M. Differential effects of shock in human maze learning. *Journal of Experimental Psychology*, 1961, **62**, 171–178.

Fitts, P. M. Perceptual-motor skill learning. In A. W. Melton (Ed.), *Categories of human learning*. New York: Academic Press, 1964. Pp. 243–285.

Fleishman, E. A. A relationship between incentive motivation and ability level in psychomotor performance. *Journal of Experimental Psychology*, 1958, **56**, 78–81.

Freeburne, C. M., & Schneider, M. Shock for right and wrong responses during learning and extinction in human subjects. *Journal of Experimental Psychology*, 1955, **49**, 181–186.

Gompertz, B. On the nature of the function expressive of the law of human mortality, and on a new mode of determining the value of live contingencies. *Philosophical Transactions*, 1825, **115**, Pt. 1, 513–585.

Grice, G. R. Discrimination reaction time as a function of anxiety and intelligence. *Journal of Abnormal and Social Psychology*, 1955, **50**, 71–74.

Guthrie, E. R. *The psychology of learning.* (Rev. ed.) New York: Harper, 1952.

Guthrie, E. R. Association by contiguity. In S. Koch (Ed.), *Psychology: A study of a science*. Vol. 2. New York: McGraw-Hill, 1959, Pp. 158–195.

Hall, J. F. *The psychology of learning.* Philadelphia: Lippincott, 1966.

Hamilton, G. B. A study of trial and error reactions in mammals. *Journal of Animal Behavior*, 1911, **1**, 33–66.

Harlow, H. F. Learning set and error factor theory. In S. Koch (Ed.), *Psychology: A study of a science*. Vol 2. New York: McGraw-Hill, 1959. Pp. 492–537.

Hilgard, E. R. Methods and procedures in the study of learning. In S. S. Stevens (Ed.), *Handbook of experimental psychology.* New York: Wiley, 1951. Pp. 517–567.

Hilgard, E. R., & Bower, G. H. *Theories of learning.* (3rd ed.) New York: Appleton, 1966.

Hubbard, W. R. Secondary reinforcement of a simple discrimination in human beings. *Journal of Experimental Psychology,* 1951, **41,** 233–241.

Hull, C. L. *Principles of behavior.* New York: Appleton, 1943.

Hull, C. L. *A behavior system.* New Haven, Conn.: Yale Univer. Press, 1952.

Jeffrey, W. E., & Cohen, L. B. Effect of spatial separation of stimulus, response, and reinforcement on selective learning in children. *Journal of Experimental Psychology,* 1964, **67,** 577–580.

Jones, H. E. Trial and error learning with differential cues. *Journal of Experimental Psychology,* 1945, **35,** 31–45.

Kaess, W., & Zeaman, D. Positive and negative knowledge of results on a Pressey-type punchboard. *Journal of Experimental Psychology,* 1960, **60,** 12–17.

Kimble, G.A. *Hilgard and Marquis' conditioning and learning.* (Rev. ed.) New York: Appleton, 1961.

Lewis, D. *Quantitative methods in psychology.* New York: McGraw-Hill, 1960.

Lewis, D., & Miles, G. H. Retroactive interference in performance on the Star Discrimeter as a function of amount of interpolated learning. *Perceptual and Motor Skills,* 1956, **6,** 295–298.

Lipsitt, L. P., & LoLordo, V. M. Interactive effect of stress and stimulus generalization on children's oddity learning. *Journal of Experimental Psychology,* 1963, **66,** 210–214.

Loess, H. B., & Duncan, C. P. Human discrimination learning with simultaneous and successive presentation of stimuli. *Journal of Experimental Psychology,* 1952, **44,** 215–221.

McAllister, D. E. The effects of various kinds of relevant verbal pretraining on subsequent motor performance. *Journal of Experimental Psychology,* 1953, **46,** 329–336.

McFann, H. H. Effects of response alteration and different instructions on proactive and retroactive facilitation and interference. *Journal of Experimental Psychology,* 1953, **46,** 405–410.

McGeoch, J. A., & Irion, A. L. *The psychology of human learning.* (2nd ed.) New York: Longmans, 1952.

Melton, A. W. (Ed.) *Apparatus tests.* Washington, D.C.: U.S. Govt. Printing Office, 1947. (AAF Aviation Psychology Program Research Report No. 4.)

Morin, R. E., & Grant, D. A. Learning and performance on a key-pressing task as function of the degree of spatial stimulus-response correspondence. *Journal of Experimental Psychology,* 1955, **49,** 39–47.

Neumann, E., & Ammons, R. B. Acquisition and long-term retention of a simple serial perceptual-motor skill. *Journal of Experimental Psychology,* 1957, **53,** 159–161.

Noble, C. E. Amount set and the length-difficulty function for a self-paced perceptual-motor skill. *Journal of Experimental Psychology,* 1953, **46,** 435–439.

Noble, C. E. The difficulty-complexity relationship in compound trial-and-error learning. *American Psychologist,* 1954, **9,** 443.

Noble, C. E. Compound trial-and-error learning as a function of response availability (N_R). *Journal of Experimental Psychology,* 1955, **49,** 93–96.

Noble, C. E. Human trial-and-error learning. *Psychological Reports,* 1957, **3,** 377–398 (Monograph Suppl. 8). (a)

Noble, C. E. Supplementary report: Response availability in human trial-and-error learning. *Journal of Experimental Psychology,* 1957, **53,** 359–360. (b)

Noble, C. E. The length-difficulty relationship in compound trial-and-error learning. *Journal of Experimental Psychology,* 1957, **54,** 246–252. (c)

Noble, C. E. Selective learning. In E. A. Bilodeau (Ed.), *Acquisition of skill.* New York: Academic Press, 1966. Pp. 47–97. (a)

Noble, C. E. S-O-R and the psychology of human learning. *Psychological Reports,* 1966, **18,** 923–943 (Monograph Suppl. 4–V18). (b)

Noble, C. E. The learning of psychomotor skills. *Annual Review of Psychology,* 1968, **19,** 203–250.

Noble, C. E., & Alcock, W. T. Human delayed-reward learning with different lengths of task. *Journal of Experimental Psychology,* 1958, **56,** 407–412.

Noble, C. E., Alcock, W. T., & Farese, F. J. Habit reversal under differential instructions in compound trial-and-error learning. *Journal of Psychology,* 1958, **46,** 253–264. (a)

Noble, C. E., Alcock, W. T., & Frye, R. L., Jr. The joint influence of practice and instructions on discrimination reaction time. *Journal of Psychology,* 1959, **48,** 125–130.

Noble, C. E., Alcock, W. T., & Noble, J. L. The interaction of type of choice procedure with amount of practice in trial-and-error learning under two reward conditions. *Journal of Psychology,* 1958, **46,** 295–301. (b)

Noble, C. E., Allison, J. P., & Jones, T. A. Stimulus familiarization (*n*) in nonverbal selective learning. *Psychonomic Science,* 1966, **5,** 453–454.

Noble, C. E., Baker, B. L., & Jones, T. A. Age and sex parameters in psychomotor learning. *Perceptual and Motor Skills,* 1964, **19,** 935–945.

Noble, C. E., & Farese, F. J. An apparatus for research in human selective learning. *Journal of Psychology,* 1955, **39,** 475–484.

Noble, C. E., Fuchs, J. E., & Thompson, J. D. A new automatic circuit for the Selective Mathometer (MK II). *Journal of Psychology,* 1963, **55,** 241–257.

Noble, C. E., & Hays, J. R. Discrimination reaction performance as a function of anxiety and sex parameters. *Perceptual and Motor Skills,* 1966, **23,** 1267–1268.

Noble, C. E., & Noble, J. L. Human trial-and-error learning under joint variation of locus of reward and type of pacing. *Journal of Experimental Psychology,* 1958, **56,** 103–109.

Noble, C. E., Noble, J. L., & Alcock, W. T. Prediction of individual differences in human trial-and-error learning. *Perceptual and Motor Skills,* 1958, **8,** 151–172 (Monograph Suppl. 2). (c)

Noble, C. E., & Taylor, A. Influence of work distribution upon complex learning by the noncorrection and modified-correction methods. *Journal of Experimental Psychology,* 1959, **58,** 352–356.

Nystrom, C. O., & Grant, D. A. Performance on a key pressing task as a function of the angular correspondence between stimulus and response elements. *Perceptual and Motor Skills,* 1955, **5,** 113–125 (Monograph Suppl. 1).

Nystrom, C. O., Morin, R. E., & Grant, D. A. Effects of amount, rate, and stage of automatically-paced training on self-paced performance. *Journal of Experimental Psychology,* 1955, **49,** 225–230.

Palermo, D. S. Proactive interference and facilitation as a function of amount of training and stress. *Journal of Experimental Psychology,* 1957, **53,** 293–296.

Patel, A. S., & Grant, D. A. Decrement and recovery effects in a perceptual-motor learning task as a function of effort, distribution of practice, and sex of subject. *Journal of General Psychology,* 1964, **71,** 217–231.

Paul, N. T., & Noble, C. E. Influence of successive habit reversals on human learning and transfer. *Journal of Experimental Psychology,* 1964, **68,** 37–43.

Perkins, M. J., Banks, H. P., & Calvin, A. D. The effect of delay on simultaneous and successive discrimination in children. *Journal of Experimental Psychology,* 1954, **48,** 416–417.

Peterson, J. Learning when frequency and recency factors are negative. *Journal of Experimental Psychology,* 1922, **5,** 270–300.

Prentice, W. C. H. Continuity in human learning. *Journal of Experimental Psychology*, 1949, **39**, 187–194.

Seibel, R. Discrimination reaction time for a 1,023-alternative task. *Journal of Experimental Psychology*, 1963, **66**, 215–226.

Seward, J. P., Dill, J. B., & Holland, M. A. Guthrie's theory of learning: A second experiment. *Journal of Experimental Psychology*, 1944, **34**, 227–238.

Siegel, P. S. Reactive inhibition as a function of number of response evocations. *Journal of Experimental Psychology*, 1950, **40**, 604–608.

Spence, K. W. The reliability of the maze and methods of its determination. *Comparative Psychology Monographs*, 1932, **8**, 1–45.

Spence, K. W. *Behavior theory and conditioning*. New Haven, Conn.: Yale Univer. Press, 1956.

Spence, K. W. *Behavior theory and learning*. Englewood Cliffs, N.J.: Prentice-Hall, 1960.

Taylor, A., & Noble, C. E. Acquisition and extinction phenomena in human trial-and-error learning under different schedules of reinforcing feedback. *Perceptual and Motor Skills*, 1962, **15**, 31–44.

Terrell, G., Jr., & Kennedy, W. A. Discrimination learning and transposition in children as a function of the nature of the reward. *Journal of Experimental Psychology*, 1957, **53**, 257–260.

Thompson, M. E. Reactive inhibition as a factor in maze learning: III. Effects in the human stylus maze. *Journal of Experimental Psychology*, 1952, **43**, 130–133.

Thorndike, E. L. Animal intelligence. An experimental study of the associative processes in animals. *Psychological Monographs*, 1898, **2**, No. 8.

Underwood, B. J., & Keppel, G. One-trial learning? *Journal of Verbal Learning and Verbal Behavior*, 1962, **1**, 1–13.

Voeks, V. W. Postremity, recency, and frequency as bases for prediction in the maze situation. *Journal of Experimental Psychology*, 1948, **38**, 495–510.

Walk, R. D. Effect of discrimination reversal on human discrimination learning. *Journal of Experimental Psychology*, 1952, **44**, 410–419.

Waters, R. H., & Reitz, J. G. The role of recency in learning. *Journal of Experimental Psychology*, 1950, **40**, 254–259.

White, B. N., & Spiker, C. C. The effect of stimulus similarity on amount of cue-position patterning in discrimination problems. *Journal of Experimental Psychology*, 1960, **59**, 131–136.

Woodworth, R. S., & Schlosberg, H. *Experimental psychology*. (Rev. ed.) New York: Holt, 1954.

Yerkes, R. M. The study of human behavior. *Science*, 1914, **39**, 625–633.

Yerkes, R. M. The mental life of monkeys and apes: A study of ideational behavior. *Behavior Monographs*, 1916, **3**, 1–145.

Yerkes, R. M. A new method of studying the ideational behavior of mentally defective and deranged as compared with normal individuals. *Journal of Comparative Psychology*, 1921, **1**, 369–394.

Zeiler, M. D. Component and configurational learning in children. *Journal of Experimental Psychology*, 1964, **68**, 292–296.

Author Index

Numbers in italics refer to the pages on which the complete references are listed.

Subject Index

A

Abilities, aptitudes, 10–11, 41, 44–47, 49, 143, 150, 154, 155, 166, *see also* Individual differences, Operator functions

Acquisition tracking, 288–293, 307–308

Analysis, *see also* Components
  correlational, 141–168, 182–186, 190
  cybernetic, 103–138
  factor, 164–166
  performance, 53
  task of, 142–144

Apparatus and tasks
  continuous response, *see* Apparatus and tasks, tracking, work
  in cybernetic analysis, 109, 112, 115, 117, 121, 126, 129, 131
  free recall, 194
  multiple choice, *see* Apparatus and tasks, selective learning
  multiple task performance battery, 66–76
  positioning, 176–177, 258–259
  selective learning, 319–327
  serial, *see* Apparatus and tasks, selective learning
  stimulated recall, 193–194, 196
  tracking, 287–290
  trial-and-error, *see* Apparatus and tasks, selective learning
  work, 59–60

Aptitude, *see* Abilities, aptitudes, Individual differences, Operator functions

Arbitrary IF, *see* Prescheduled feedback

Artificial IF, 258, 261, *see also* Augmented feedback, Supplementary feedback

Association(s)
  hierarchies, 196–197
  pre-experimental, 198
  among training events, 194–195

Associative clustering, 197

Associative strength, 198–200

Associative structure, 195–200

Augmented feedback, 228–230, 237–247, 258, 261, 279–282

C

Compatibility
  control-display, 300–301, 303–304, 313
  S-R, 223–225

Compensatory tracking, 287, 294–297, 300, 311–312

Component(s), *see also* Analysis, Within-trial events
  of acquisition time, 307–310
  combination rules, 21–22
  control system, 303–304
  forgetting, 178
  intercorrelations in retention, 180
  of motor tasks, 178
  of skill, 232
  of training and retention, 178–187
  verbal components in motor tasks, 178

Concurrent feedback, 259, *see also* Displaced feedback, Terminal feedback

Contiguity, 337–341

Contour tracking, 288, 311

Control
  compatibility with display, 223–225, 300–301, 303–304, 313
  control device variables in transfer, 217–223
  system in tracking
    acceleration, 303, 307, 309
    aided, 303–304
    automatic, 298
    dynamics, 296, 302–310, 313
    learning, 296, 297–298
    maximum output, 309
    order, 302–303
    position, 303, 308–309

Time lags in tracking
  control, 298, 304–308
  display, 307–308
Time sharing, 83–90, 220–221, 313–314
Tool using, 106–108, 130–133
Track, 287, 288, 290–295
  high frequency, 305, 310–312
  learning, 295–296
  ramps, 293, 294
  sine waves, 293–295
  steps, 288, 290–293
  white noise, 295
Tracking, 287–315
  adjustment time, 309–310
  challenge effect, 312–313
  decision rate, 310–311
  factorial designs in, 297, 304
  independent variables, 290
  isolated steps, 290
  knowledge of results, 312
  multiple, 313
  two dimensional, 289–290
Training, *see* Learning, Practice
Transfer of training, 19–22, 157–158,
    205–232, 239, 280–282, 297, 304,
    346
  asymmetrical, 217–223, 297, 304
  control device variables, 218–223
    control-display ratio, 221–223
    elasticity, 218–221
    friction, 218–219
  definition, 205–206
  design, 206–207, 248
  display variables
    compensatory vs. pursuit, 214–215
    visual noise, 215–217
  feedback, 225–230
  input variables, 212–214
  learning to learn, 272
  measures, *see* Transfer of training,
    transfer indices
  paradigms, 206
  S-R compatibility, 223–225
  transfer hypotheses, 230–232
    relative difficulty, 230–231

  similarity, 231–232
  skill components, 232
  transfer indices, 206–208
Transformations of feedback
  continuous, 266–269
  discrete, 265–266
  numerical, 264–272
  spatial, 107–113, 120–124, 265
  temporal, 111, 124–132, 275–279
Travel time in tracking, 307–310
Tuition, 239–240
Twin studies, 163–164

V

Validity, 61–65, 72–75, 93–95
Verbal reinforcement combinations in IF,
    262, 263–264
Verbal tasks, *see also* Motor skills
  information feedback and, 262–264,
    273–275, 278
  learning, 193–196
  retention, 171–176
  stimulated recall in, 196–199
  transfer, 231–232
Vigilance, 69, *see also* Monitoring, Watch-
    keeping

W

Warm-up, *see* History of skill
Watchkeeping, 65–66, 70–73, 83, 86–87,
    90, *see also* Monitoring, Vigilance
Whole-part, 12–13, 21–22, 232, *see also*
    Analysis, Component(s), History of
    skill, Transfer of training
Within-trial events, 178–187
Work, *see* Distribution of practice, Sus-
    tained performance, Work-rest sched-
    ules
Work loading, 152–155
Work-rest schedules, 75–87
  diurnal cycles, 78–85
  of long duration, 79–85
  of short duration, 77–79
  sleep loss, 78, 85